# Black Skin, Blue Books

## African Americans and Wales, 1845–1945

### Writing Wales in English

DANIEL G. WILLIAMS

UNIVERSITY OF WALES PRESS
CARDIFF
2012

*British Library Cataloguing-in-Publication Data*
A catalogue record for this book is available form the British Library.

ISBN 978-0-7083-1987-1
e-ISBN 978-0-7083-2532-2

THE *A*SSOCIATION FOR
*W*ELSH *W*RITING IN *E*NGLISH
*C*YMDEITHAS *L*LÊN *S*AESNEG *C*YMRU

Typeset by Mark Heslington Ltd, Scarborough, North Yorkshire
Printed by CPI Antony Rowe, Chippenham, Wiltshire.

# Black Skin, Blue Books

*Writing Wales in English*

CREW

**CREW series of Critical and Scholarly Studies**
**General Editor: Professor M. Wynn Thomas (CREW, Swansea University)**

This *CREW* series is dedicated to Emyr Humphreys, a major figure in the literary culture of modern Wales, a founding patron of the *Centre for Research into the English Literature and Language of Wales* and, along with Gillian Clarke and Seamus Heaney, one of *CREW*'s Honorary Associates. Grateful thanks are due to the late Richard Dynevor for making this series possible.

**Other titles in the series**
Stephen Knight, *A Hundred Years of Fiction* (978-0-7083-1846-1)
Barbara Prys-Williams, *Twentieth-Century Autobiography* (978-0-7083-1891-1)
Kirsti Bohata, *Postcolonialism Revisited* (978-0-7083-1892-8)
Chris Wigginton, *Modernism from the Margins* (978-0-7083-1927-7)
Linden Peach, *Contemporary Irish and Welsh Women's Fiction* (978-0-7083-1998-7)
Sarah Prescott, *Eighteenth-Century Writing from Wales: Bards and Britons* (978-0-7083-2053-2)
Hywel Dix, *After Raymond Williams: Cultural Materialism and the Break-Up of Britain* (978-0-7083-2153-9)
Matthew Jarvis, *Welsh Environments in Contemporary Welsh Poetry* (978-0-7083-2152-2)
Diane Green, *Emyr Humphreys: A Postcolonial Novelist?* (978-0-7083-2217-8)
Harri Garrod Roberts, *Embodying Identity: Representations of the Body in Welsh Literature* (978-0-7083-2169-0)
M. Wynn Thomas, *In the Shadow of the Pulpit: Literature and Nonconformist Wales* (978-0-7083-2225-3)
Linden Peach, *The Fiction of Emyr Humphreys: Contemporary Critical Perspectives* (978-0-7083-2216-1)
Daniel Westover, *R. S. Thomas: A Stylistic Biography* (978-0-7083-2413-4)
Jasmine Donahaye, *Whose People? Wales, Israel, Palestine* (978-0-7083-2483-7)
Judy Kendall, *Edward Thomas: The Origins of his Poetry* (978-0-7083-2403-5)
Damian Walford Davies, *Cartographies of Culture: New Geographies of Welsh Writing in English* (978-0-7083-2476-9)

*I Sioned a Lowri (unwaith eto) ac i Dewi (am y tro cyntaf)*

# CONTENTS

# General Editor's Preface

The aim of this series is to produce a body of scholarly and critical work that reflects the richness and variety of the English-language literature of modern Wales. Drawing upon the expertise both of established specialists and of younger scholars, it will seek to take advantage of the concepts, models and discourses current in the best contemporary studies to promote a better understanding of the literature's significance, viewed not only as an expression of Welsh culture but also as an instance of modern literatures in English worldwide. In addition, it will seek to make available the scholarly materials (such as bibliographies) necessary for this kind of advanced, informed study.

M. Wynn Thomas
*CREW* (*Centre for Research into the English Literature and Language of Wales*)
Swansea University

# Acknowledgements

I have incurred such a range of scholarly, practical and personal debts while writing this book, that it is virtually impossible to account for them all in one consolidated list. Academic debts of a general nature are covered in the footnotes. I would like to give particular thanks to Eirug Davies for drawing my attention, during my first visit to Cambridge, Massachusetts, almost twenty years ago, to some of the sources (such as the Welsh translation of Moses Roper's narrative at Harvard's Widener Library) that would make this project possible. Keith Hughes kindly shared his research on Frederick Douglass with me in 2003, and has been a source of advice ever since. I am grateful to my colleagues Kirsti Bohata and Dai Smith for discussing some key ideas with me as they were being formulated. Jerry Hunter, Rachel Farebrother, and Werner Sollors, read chapters 1, 2 and 3 respectively, and I am immensely grateful to them for making very useful suggestions, for correcting some of my errors, and more generally for their enthusiastic support for my work. I am indebted to Stefan Collini for reading and commenting on parts of this book in the erratic order in which they were completed. My greatest scholarly debt is to my colleague M. Wynn Thomas who has not only read the whole book, but has also been a continual source of encouragement and friendship throughout the period of its writing and preparation for publication.

I am grateful to everyone who has discussed, debated, or corresponded about, this material with me over the last decade. These have included: Jane Aaron, David Anderson, the late Ian Bell, Adam Bradley, Simon Brooks, Tony Brown, Grahame Davies, Jasmine Donahaye, Justin Edwards, Richard Ellis, Gwenno Ffrancon, Joyce Flynn, Adam Frost,

Henry Louis Gates Jr, Kate Gibbs, the late Victor Golightly, Katie
Gramich, Melinda Gray, Tudur Hallam, Wendy Hayes-Jones, Macartan
Humphries, E. Wyn James, Matthew Jarvis, Nigel Jenkins, Dave Jones,
Richard Wyn Jones, Glenn Jordan, Mel Kohlke, Catherine McKenna,
Susan Manning, Ceri Rhys Matthews, Scott Newstock, Michael Newton,
Chris O'Connor, Mark O'Connor, Alistair Pettinger, Alan Rice, Richard
Robinson, Steve Sarson, Marc Shell, J. Beverley Smith, Jeffrey C.
Stewart, Ned Thomas, Sid Thomas, Theresa Vara-Dannen, Chris
Williams, Sian Williams and Jen Wilson. I've received valued assistance
from librarians and archivists in charge of the collections listed in the
bibliography, and the efficient team at the inter-library loan office at
Swansea University Library made the writing of this book possible.
    The volume was written with the aid of an Arts and Humanities
Research Council grant which gave me a respite from teaching and
administrative duties, matched by sabbatical relief from Swansea
University. The English Department at Swansea University has proved a
congenial place to work during the past ten years, and staff and postgraduate students at the Centre for Research into the Literature and Language
of Wales, in particular, have allowed me to develop ideas and interests
that may have been regarded as marginal and unconnected elsewhere. I
am grateful to Lisa Scholey for compiling the index, and to everyone at
the University of Wales Press who worked on this book, especially Sarah
Lewis and Siân Chapman for their patience and support, and Dafydd
Jones for guiding me around the last lap.
    Every effort has been made to trace the owners of copyright material,
and the publishers will be pleased to correct any omissions brought to
their notice at the earliest convenience. Acquiring rights is a time
consuming and often prohibitively costly process. I am grateful to:
Penguin Books UK who granted permission to quote from the works of
W. E. B. Du Bois; The David Higham Agency, and Random House, who
allowed me to quote from the works of Langston Hughes; HarperCollins
Publishers and Virago Press, an imprint of Little, Brown Book Group,
for the right to quote from Zora Neale Hurston (copyright for *Their Eyes
Were Watching God* © renewed 1965 by John C. Hurston and Joel
Hurston); Parthian Press for the right to quote from Margiad Evans and
Gomer Press for the right to quote from the poems of Idris Davies. *Letter
to Cicely Tyson* (copright © Emlyn Williams 1983), held at the National
Library of Wales, is quoted by permission of Alan Brodie Representation
Ltd. The rights for the images are noted on page xv. The assistance of
Jeff Childs and Andre Scoville in locating the original images of the

Pontardawe Carnival and the Red Cross at Libanus Chapel, Morriston, was greatly appreciated.

I am particularly grateful to Professor John Callahan, literary executor of the Estate of Ralph Ellison, who granted me access to and permission to use citations from Ellison's unpublished short stories set in Wales. Michael Harper, a poet whom I have admired for over twenty years, kindly granted permission to quote his poem 'A Visit to Abercanaid'. I would also like to thank Susan Robeson for her interest in, and support for, my work – even when not always agreeing with my interpretations – and for continuing her family's connections with Wales.

Sections of some of the chapters were published in preparatory or shorter form elsewhere: in *Comparative American Studies*, *Slavery and Abolition* and *New Welsh Review*; in *Wales and its Boxers* (ed. Peter Stead and Gareth Williams); in the Welsh language publications *Y Traethodydd, Gweld Sêr: Cymru a Chanrif America* (ed. M. Wynn Thomas) and *Canu Caeth: Y Cymry a'r Affro-Americaniaid* (ed. Daniel G. Williams). I am grateful to the publishers and editors for allowing me to draw on these pieces. Some of the material was also tried out in the form of public lectures, and I would like to thank the following institutions and individuals for invitations, hospitality and inspiration: The Rhys Davies Annual Lecture, University of Glamorgan (Meic Stephens and Sam Adams); The Annual Lecture of The Cardiff Centre For Welsh American Studies, Cardiff University (E. Wyn James and Bill Jones); The American Studies Research Seminar, University of East Anglia (Christopher Bigsby and Richard Crockatt); The Wales–Ireland Research Network, Cardiff University (Claire Connolly and Katie Gramich); the AHRC Diasporas Network on the Welsh in North and South America, Bangor University (Jerry Hunter); Afro-Amerikaner in Berlin: Geschichte einer intellektuellen Begegnung, John F. Kennedy Institute, Freie Universität Berlin (Winfried Fluck); Liberating Sojourn 2: Transatlantic Abolitionism 1845–1860, University of Liverpool and the University of Central Lancashire (Alan Rice and Fionnghuala Sweeney); Symbiosis / STAR Conference, University of Edinburgh (Keith Hughes and Susan Manning); Margiad Evans Centenary Conference, CREW, Swansea University (Kirsti Bohata); Celts in the Americas Conference, St Francis Xavier University, Nova Scotia (Michael Newton). I would also like to record my thanks to all those who participated in the conference on 'African Americans and the Celtic Nations' that I organized at Swansea University in 2007.

Closer to home, my father Gareth read the whole book and made his usual range of astute observations. Thanks also, as always, to my mother

Mary for her support in this and all endeavours. My parents-in-law, Eirwen and Philip, helped with childcare thus giving me some crucial time to write. Some of the reasons for writing this book can no doubt be traced to an early passion for jazz, shared with my trumpet-playing brother Tomos, and I have explored some of the connections analysed here in a different medium with him and the many musicians who have been kind enough to play with us over the years, from Deian Hopkin to Jean-Paul Bourelly.

In an unpublished short story that I discuss later in this book, the African American novelist Ralph Ellison notes that 'although American Negro and Welsh historical backgrounds were different, there were also certain cultural and temperamental similarities; both Welshmen and Negroes loved to sing, to dance, to talk long over drinks, to laugh and to enjoy a good argument'. While it is probably best to take a somewhat sceptical attitude towards such romantic notions as 'temperamental similarities', I shall indulge them here, for *Black Skin, Blue Books* was written to the accompaniment of the singing and dancing of my children, Lowri and Dewi, and the laughter, long talks over drinks, and occasional good argument, with my wife Sioned. It is dedicated, *gyda chariad*, to them.

Daniel G. Williams
Alltwen
July 2011

# ILLUSTRATIONS

# Introduction

I

In the summer of 1911 – three years before the outbreak of the First World War, and eight years before the race riots sweeping through Britain and the United States reached their respective peaks in Cardiff and Chicago – the British Empire was celebrated in all its gaudy splendour at the investiture of the prince of Wales at Caernarfon Castle, and at the coronation of George V in London.[1] That summer also saw a remarkable array of the world's leading politicians and intellectuals gathered in imperial London for the Universal Races Congress. The congress took place from 26 to 29 July, and boasted an international Honorary General Committee that ran into hundreds of names including leading intellectuals such as Emile Durkheim, Georg Simmel, Ferdinand Tonnies, Franz Boas and H. G. Wells. While comparatively few of these men were actually at the congress, more than twenty governments provided official representation and each session was attended by over a thousand participants.[2] The congress had been conceived by many activists involved in the transatlantic humanitarian, pacifist and ethical movement, most notably the congress's chairman, Professor Felix Adler of Columbia University, and the secretary of its General Committee, Gustav Spiller, who went on to edit a record of the proceedings. The congress is primarily connected today, however, with the African American sociologist, philosopher, author and activist W. E. B. Du Bois, who dedicated a great deal of effort to ensuring that delegates from Africa, Asia, North and South America and Europe would attend the event, and who believed that this gathering of intellectuals would lead to an 'international committee' that would achieve world peace through interracial coopera-tion.[3] The liberal universalism which underpinned the desire to unite the races, religions and languages of the world in a mutual striving for peace, was expressed eloquently by Du Bois in his 'A Hymn to the Peoples', one of several 'Odes of Salutation' delivered at the congress's opening ceremony.

> Save us, World-Spirit, from our lesser selves!
> Grant us that war and hatred cease,
> Reveal our souls in every race and hue!
> Help us, O Human God, in this Thy Truce
> To make Humanity divine![4]

The congress, as Paul Rich argues, can be seen as a late expression of a Victorian liberalism that was to be undermined by the First World War, and whose belief that the power of reason could ensure a growing unity amongst the world's peoples was challenged by internal racial tensions within the imperial nations in the post-war years, and a growing anti-colonial nationalism outside their borders.[5] In the summer of 1911, however, the dominant view seemed to be that of Cambridge don Oscar Browning, who believed that the 'racial amity' promoted by the congress was 'the only sure basis for the formation of empires'.[6]

The way in which a defence of imperial relations could coexist with a liberal desire to ameliorate the suffering of the 'Negro' masses in the United States and Africa was illustrated in the paper delivered by the educational reformer and practising medical doctor, Frances Hoggan. Hoggan presented her paper 'The Negro problem in relation to white women' in the sixth session, immediately following W. E. B. Du Bois's detailed, sociological account of 'The Negro race in the United States of America'.[7] She established at the outset that 'the danger to white women from black men' was seen to be at the root of much racism, and wondered why 'so little feeling comparatively is shown when the white man is the aggressor and the victim has a coloured skin'. This progressive anti-racism was reinforced later where she addressed the gross injustice of denying the 'natives' an 'outlet for their energies in the land that was theirs long before the settlement of whites in Africa', and noted that 'outrages on women' were more common 'in civilised countries' than 'in those at the outskirts of civilisation'. Her paper addressed attacks on white women within colonial societies, which she ascribed to the waning of tribal communal structures and the rise of a 'race consciousness' among the 'Natives' that was no longer 'controlled by the brotherhood of sentiment'. More revealingly, she suggested that the practice in South Africa of having 'boys' attend on 'ladies' who are 'either in bed or very slightly clothed' is a 'contributory factor'. Her suggestion was that the

> more extended employment by ladies of Native women in immediate attendance on their own persons would not only lead to the more rapid spread of civilisation among Native women, but it would also tend to remove an obvious though perhaps remote source of danger ...[8]

The terms of Hoggan's analysis are here made clear. While there is much that is unjust and unequal about colonial societies, there is nothing inherently wrong with imperial practices. The desired 'rapid spread of civilisation' is the product of white colonizers' intermingling with black 'Natives', and far from challenging the colonial system the liberal's desire is to alleviate the more unpalatable aspects of the system, thus making the colony a less threatening space for 'ladies'. Drawing on her knowledge of South Africa, Hoggan concluded that a policy of racial uplift, overseen by whites, offered 'our only chance of escaping from a colour conflict of unparalleled magnitude' and argued that

> no greed of wealth or power, nor unworthy jealousy of a rising and developing race whose destinies we control, should be allowed to intervene, and to choke the good intention of the governing whites towards the black millions who look to them for guidance and light in matters spiritual and in matters temporal, as well as for the ideal towards which to strive.[9]

While embracing Congress organizer Gustav Spiller's view that the peoples of the world were 'to all intents and purposes essentially equals in intellect, enterprise, morality and physique', there was no question in Hoggan's mind as to who set the parameters of 'culture' and 'controlled' the process of human striving.[10]

In this respect it was fitting that Hoggan followed W. E. B. Du Bois, for the African American man of letters concluded his paper with an attack on Booker T. Washington's 'business-based' solution to the 'race problem', and advocated in its place the 'supply of well-educated, intellectual leaders and professional men for a group so largely deprived of contact with the cultural leaders of the whites'.[11] Despite the fact that Du Bois located the catalysts for social advancement among the 'talented tenth' of African Americans while Hoggan saw white colonialists as the vehicles for 'elevating' the natives, both shared a middle-class ideology of racial uplift that measured race progress in terms of an allegedly 'universal' civilization.[12]

This shared belief was reiterated in, and formed the basis for, the long correspondence between Du Bois and Hoggan which lasted from her arrangements for his 1906 sojourn in Europe, through her support for Du Bois's wife and daughter to be domiciled in England in 1914, to her death in 1927.[13] Remembered as 'an English friend' in Du Bois's autobiography *Dusk of Dawn*, and appearing as 'Frances Hoggan, England' in the list of 'distinguished scholars' on the 'advisory board' of Du Bois's *Encyclopaedia Africana* in 1909, Hoggan was in fact born on 20 December 1843 as Frances Morgan in a vicarage in Brecon in mid Wales.[14] She is primarily remembered as the first British woman, and the second in Europe, to achieve the degree of Doctor of Medicine, which was awarded to her at Zurich University as women were not allowed to become university-trained doctors in Britain. After postgraduate work in Vienna, Prague and Paris, she married George Hoggan, himself an eminent doctor, in 1874, and they established the first husband-and-wife medical practice in Britain. She first visited Du Bois at Atlanta University in 1907, a year in which, at the age of 65, she also set sail for South Africa. Her studies of health conditions there formed the basis for her paper at the 1911 congress.[15]

To reveal that Hoggan was Welsh does not take us beyond the somewhat anodyne lists of national achievers which are perhaps particularly prevalent in minority cultures. What is significant, and helps to illustrate the benefits that may accrue from the comparative approach adopted throughout this study, is that Hoggan's Welshness influences and complicates her location as a benevolent but ultimately patronizing European contributor to the proceedings of the Universal Races Congress. For Hoggan's embrace and promotion of 'uplift' for the wretched of the earth was a cultural and political strategy which she developed while campaigning for female education in Wales. During the 1870s and 1880s Hoggan embarked on a campaign to increase the educational provision for women in Wales, 'setting foot' as she noted revealingly 'on what might be called educational virgin soil'.[16] In Wales, the Victorian ideal of domestic womanhood was connected to a desire for national vindication following claims of moral laxity and social degradation amongst the principality's women in the Report on the State of Education in Wales (the 'Blue Books' of this volume's title, which will be discussed further in chapter 1). Gender became attached to a civilizationist mission in which women were the disseminators of the morality, sobriety, temperance that the bourgeoisie wished to foster. As Jane Aaron and W. Gareth Evans have documented, the keynotes of this construction of the Welsh mother echo throughout the periodicals of nineteenth-century Wales.[17] While seeking to take advantage of the image of the woman as the disseminator of 'culture' in society, Hoggan also challenged the cult of domesticity. In her paper on 'The past and future of the education of girls in Wales', delivered at the Cardiff National Eisteddfod of 1883, her focus was on the middle classes as she argued that '[w]hat we have to do now is what we have not done in the past – to educate our middle-class girls'.[18] Culture would trickle downward from an enlightened middle class, and Hoggan's thought, especially her gender consciousness, both reflected and challenged the middle-class ideology of uplift that characterized Victorian Wales. Her radical calls for female education were fused with the period's language of national reinstatement.

> Patriots, republicans, friends of the people and all who deeply care for the welfare of the Principality, all admit that it is only by making the foundations of education strong and deep – so strong and deep that it will reach not one sex only, but both – that the full measure of national prosperity, of national happiness and usefulness, and of national growth can be attained.[19]

'Other nations have to re-model, we have to model and to make', argued Hoggan in the 1880s, 'other nations have to cast away from them the outgrown clothes of former systems of teaching; we have little but rags to throw away'.[20] Having taken her place 'in the vanguard of the quest for female education in the Principality', she seems never again to have played a political role in the cultural and political life of her motherland.[21] Moving primarily to London, but also spending time in India, South Africa and the United States, Hoggan dedicated the next forty years of her life to the educational advancement of other peoples who had 'little but rags to throw away': Indian, South African and, most significantly for the purposes of this volume, African American.

While never making a direct connection between her struggles on behalf of women in Wales and her educational campaigns in other parts of the world, Hoggan was consistent in her belief that the creation of an educated middle class of women was the surest method of raising the social, ethical and cultural standards of the ignorant majority. Despite being written for a white audience – 'I am sure that you will feel with me that Negro women have well filled their first fifty years of freedom' – and making no reference to her African American female contemporaries such as Ida B. Wells and Anna Julia Cooper, Hoggan's article of 1913 on 'American Negro women during their first fifty years of freedom' attempts to insert the black female experience into the middle-class ideology of racial uplift that, in Kevin Gaines's words, 'measured race progress in terms of civilization, manhood and patriarchal authority'.[22] It is worth quoting from Hoggan's little known piece at some length.

> Fifty years ago Negro women were uneducated, poor, downtrodden, the easy prey of white libertines, whom they had been taught they must not resist, on peril of their lives. They were what slavery had made them – lax in morals, shiftless, improvident – with many notable exceptions even then, or we could never have known a Margaret Gardener, a Harriet Tubman, or a Sojourner Truth. They are now rapidly emerging into a state of civilized and cultured prosperity. True, the uneducated, ignorant and weaklings are still dragging at their skirts, but instead of shaking them off, the stronger women are doing their utmost to lift them up, realizing, as they aptly put it, that a chain can be no stronger than its weakest link. Race consciousness is growing year by year, and the race is becoming daily more self-sufficing. Negro women speak easily and well; they are learning by practice the rules of debate and how to conduct business in a businesslike manner; their music and their rich and in many cases well trained voices are a never failing source of delight; their social aptitudes are also undergoing marked development. Altogether coloured women are on what Americans call 'the up grade'. They are rising in an orderly and well balanced manner, and their progress is in many respects unprecedented. Negro women share in the loyalty felt towards the country by its dark citizens, notwithstanding the slights and indignities they suffer, and they proudly point to the fact that no Negro has ever yet been found to betray his country or to assassinate its chosen ruler. Negro women who have been called by one of their own pastors 'the ladder by which the race is climbing', have every reason to rejoice in the immense strides their sex has made during their first fifty years of freedom.[23]

With its metaphor of the 'ladder' and emphasis on 'lifting' and 'rising' the passage offers a distilled expression of the ideology of racial uplift that connects the ethnic and gender struggles of Wales and African America in the second half of the nineteenth century, and which will be discussed in detail in chapter 1. Hoggan's piece can also be read as a distinctively feminist rewriting of her friend Du Bois's notion of the 'talented tenth' of race leaders, for here it is explicitly the women who function as the vehicles for racial vindication following the debasing effects of slavery. Hoggan emphasizes that 'women are moving on steadily towards intellectual leadership' and notes that those, like herself,

> who are looking on as the problem evolves, can but marvel at the respectful consideration our coloured sisters have won for themselves from their men folk in the first half-century of emancipation from the grossest and most

demoralizing thraldom ever known, that of slavery, with no protection whatever against the violence and lust of men, black or white.[24]

The consistent defence of African American women is a characteristic of
Hoggan's piece as she aims to counter both the anti-suffragist rhetoric
which warned ominously that 'suffrage, employment, women's education, and other forms of public activity ... produced unwomanly
shrews', and the similar white-supremacist argument that votes for
African Americans had not led to equality but to domination.[25] She thus
embraces the era's rhetoric of domesticity, but in such a way that it reinforces the case for female enfranchisement. Thus, Hoggan notes that
African American women 'place home duties first unquestioningly', and
argues that 'those extensions of mother duties – the care of children, the
poor, the weak, the sick, and the erring' are all 'comprised in their
conception of civic duties, for the due accomplishment of which they
claim the vote'.[26] African American female participation in 'suffrage
societies' is celebrated, as are the 'sacrifices self-imposed, and willingly
borne, to secure better schools and longer school terms for their children', and, having 'seen a great deal of the Negro women in their homes,
their churches and their clubs' in the state of California where African
American women are able to vote, Hoggan 'has no hesitation in saying
that they are a serious and useful addition to the electorate' for, crucially,
they bring 'the mother's point of view in all matters of public interest'.[27]
This emphasis on motherhood was a characteristic of African
American women reformers of the *fin de siècle* whose rhetoric of
domestic service was perhaps necessary to ensure support in a context
where black education in even its most conservative forms might
provoke violent opposition from racist whites. Even domestic training,
as Evelyn Brooks Higginbotham has noted, could be accused of
'educating the nigger up to think they are the equals of the white folks'.[28]
Hoggan thus argues that the contemporary African American woman is a
fusion of two types of woman, 'the heroic and the maternal', resulting in
a citizenry marked by their 'consecration' to their race, and 'a loyalty' to
their country.[29] If, in Hoggan's native Wales, the growing anglicization
attendant upon industrialization drove a culturally defined Welshness
back into the domestic and religious spheres of 'hearth', home and
chapel, then, in the immeasurably more inhospitable context of America,
racist Jim Crow practices and disenfranchisement contaminated the
public sphere to the extent that reformers focused on those areas
perceived to be within their control: the domestic and religious realms.

The patriarchal family was a symbol of the race's triumph over slavery, and Du Bois spoke for many reformers when he noted that 'we look most anxiously to the establishment and strengthening of the home among members of the race, because it is the surest combination of real progress'.[30] While Hoggan's distance from the group being described is underlined by her description of the struggle of African American women as a 'an object lesson' worthy of 'study in all its phases', her article is a striking expression of the rhetoric of uplift developed, in very different contexts, by African American and Welsh female reformers in the 1890s and 1900s.[31]

## II

With the notable exception of Gareth Evans's studies, little attention has been given to Frances Hoggan in Wales or elsewhere. My intention in opening this analysis of African American and Welsh literature and culture by discussing her connections with W. E. B. Du Bois is to indicate the ways in which new areas for study and exploration may be opened up by the comparative approach pursued throughout this book. *Black Skin, Blue Books* discusses African American culture in relation to Welsh culture in the belief that a comparative approach to the respective experiences of these peoples might help to identify features that could pass undetected, or be misinterpreted, if they were studied separately by other means. There is always a danger that a work of comparative minority studies becomes predicated on a binary model in which virtuous peripheries are seen to resist the dominating and homogenizing centre. I hope to have avoided such simplistic binaries in this book, but to analyse the transnational exchanges between minority traditions, as represented by the correspondence between Frances Hoggan and W. E. B. Du Bois, is to reinforce Irish critic Luke Gibbons's contention that not all 'roads to modernity' need to go through 'the main thoroughfares of capitalism'.[32]

For Paul Gilroy, the history of 'transnational linkages' manifested in the 1911 United Races Congress is 'one that we would do well to reassess today when the overriding appeal of "ethnic" sameness has become an obstacle to living with difference'.[33] The transnational turn in American studies emerged with the questioning of exceptionalist readings of the history and literature of the United States, and resulted in the rejection of a 'model of complicity' whereby 'literary texts are deployed to shore up and enforce a national self-image'.[34] Paul Gilroy's *The Black*

*Atlantic* (1993) has been seen as a significant contributor to this shift in emphasis and, while that book has been criticized for its exclusions of Canada and Latin America and its anti-materialist emphasis on literary texts, it has also been widely celebrated as a study that embodies the contemporary 'undermining or transcendence of the nation state'.[35] Gilroy believed that the 'idea that identity and culture are exclusively national phenomena, and the related notion that unchanging essences of ethnic or national distinctiveness are automatically, though mysteriously produced from their own guts' constituted 'a major political problem'.[36] He therefore sought to reject the narratives of ethnic nationalism in favour of 'forms of identity and struggle developed – of necessity – by dispersed people for whom nationality, ethnicity and the nation state are perhaps not so tightly associated'.[37] While the 'dispersed people' of whom Gilroy spoke were primarily the variously hyphenated peoples of African and Asian descent in western Europe and North America, his problematization of the relationships between nationality, ethnicity and the state had also been reflected – also of necessity – by the peripheral, stateless peoples and minority language communities within the established nation-states of Europe.

Writing in 1983, Raymond Williams noted that opposition to the ways in which national identity was mobilized by states 'for wars or to embellish and disguise forms of social and political control and obedience' came from 'hostile minority peoples who have been incorporated within the nation-state' who develop their own 'form of an alternative (Irish or Scots or Welsh or Breton or Basque) nationalism'.

> The complex interactions between such nationalisms and more general radicalisms have been evident and remarkable, though in general it is true that unique forms of national-radical bonding, unavailable by definition in the larger nation-state, come through and have powerful effects. It is sadly also true that not only the majority people, with 'their own' nation-state, but also many among the minority peoples, regard this kind of nationalism as disruptive or backward-looking, and are even confident enough to urge 'internationalism' against it, as a superior political ideal. It is as if a really secure nationalism, already in possession of its nation-state, can fail to see itself as 'nationalist' at all. Its own distinctive bonding is perceived as natural and obvious by contrast with the mere projections of any nationalism which is still in active progress and thus incomplete.[38]

Much transatlantic criticism as practised in Britain can be criticized in these terms, for the critique of American exceptionalism and emphasis on American diversity is often mounted from a seemingly

uncomplicated and unscrutinized 'British' or 'English' (these terms are
still often conflated) position.[39] Houston A. Baker offers an insight into
the biases informing Gilroy's work when he observes that, from an
African American perspective, the 'peculiar form of Gilroy's work – its
privileging of "the Atlantic" – ultimately rings ... a surprisingly
"changing same" on the old popular imperialist anthem "Rule Britannia!
Britannia rules the Waves"'.[40] Thus to insert 'Wales' into narratives of
the black Atlantic may be a means of resisting the embrace of an 'universalism' which is oblivious to its own biases and occlusions, and of
problematizing the equation of 'Britishness' with 'Englishness' in transatlantic studies.

While I conceive of this book as a contribution to this 'transnational'
emphasis in cultural studies, the reference to 'Wales' and to 'African
Americans' in its subtitle may be seen to endorse a return to those very
categories – 'nation' and 'ethnicity' – that a transatlantic approach is
meant to reject. One of the paradoxes of writing on Welsh culture today
is that a measure of self-government has occurred at a time when to
speak of 'the nation' or of 'the Welsh' in academic circles is to be accused
of, at best, a romantic nostalgia, or, at worst a reactionary politics. While
the tendency to talk of national and ethnic identities as if they simply
existed became outmoded as cultural critics and historians began to
discuss nations as 'invented traditions' or 'imagined communities', there
is now a tendency to discuss cultural identities as if they have no specificity or content: the nation is regarded by many post-colonial critics as a
vessel in which any plurality of cultural voices may coexist with equal
validity.[41] This is certainly generously accommodating in theory, but
such a view has fairly obvious limitations in practice, for any attempts at
forming distinctive policies for Wales, perhaps especially in the field of
education, entails some notion of a distinctive Welsh culture. Henry
Louis Gates Jr describes a similar problem for African American critics
when he asks us to 'consider the irony' of the fact that, just as black
critics 'obtain the wherewithal to define our black subjectivity in the
republic of Western letters, our theoretical colleagues declare that there
ain't such a thing as a subject, so why should we be bothered with that?'[42]
At the very moment where a more inclusive and varied American literary
canon was being formed and taught, Gates noted that attempts by critics
to define and articulate a distinctive African American canon, characterized by its own 'themes, topoi, and tropes', were 'decried as racist,
separatist, nationalist or "essentialist"'.[43] Most minority literary traditions, having had to define themselves against the hegemony of a more

dominant tradition, will have witnessed a version of this tension between cultural universalism and particularism. The issue is addressed at several points in this volume, not least in relation to Ralph Ellison, whose essay 'The world and the jug' offered a powerful critique of attempts at placing his work within a 'black' tradition. In responding to a review by Irving Howe, which discussed his novel *Invisible Man* exclusively in relation to other African American texts, Ellison noted that '[w]hatever the efficiency of segregation as a socio-political arrangement, it has been far from absolute on the level of culture' and, rather than being primarily influenced by Frederick Douglass and Richard Wright, Ellison described his attraction to 'books which seldom, if ever, mentioned Negroes' by 'T. S. Eliot, Pound, Gertrude Stein and Hemingway'. Such works, he noted, were 'to release me from whatever "segregated" idea I might have had of my human possibilities'.[44] In the less charged context of Wales, the modernist Welsh-language short-story writer Kate Roberts responded similarly to the attempts made by the political and cultural nationalist Saunders Lewis to place her work within a specifically Welsh literary tradition. Roberts resisted Lewis's attempts at canon building by noting that her influences were not Glasynys and other nineteenth-century Welsh-language predecessors, but Chekhov and Katherine Mansfield.[45]

Canon formation, of any kind, entails selection, and no literary canon will encompass the range of influences impacting upon its selected authors. In this respect attempts at defining 'the canon', 'the people' or, indeed, 'the nation' are homologous, with each inevitably resulting in a selectivity which fails to acknowledge the full range of difference and variety within a given group, or within a geographical space. Ralph Ellison wondered with some exasperation 'why is it that so many of those who would tell us the meaning of Negro life never bother to learn how varied it really is?' and, in drawing attention to the celebrated connection between Paul Robeson and Wales (discussed at length in chapter 3), Charlotte Williams asks, if we are to think romantically that 'the Welshman' is 'a black man at heart', where does that place 'the black man who is Welsh or the Welshman who is black'?[46]

Barbara Foley's description of all nationalisms as being 'metonymic' may be useful in this connection. Foley describes 'metonymic nationalism' as 'a representational practice that treats a social group within a nation as empowered to signify the larger totality that is the nation'.[47] The common claim made in the Victorian era that 'the Nonconformists of Wales are the people of Wales' can be seen to be an example of this process whereby the connection between religious denominationalism and national sentiment was made explicit, at a time when less than 50 per cent of the Welsh people actually attended a place of worship.[48] Such was the success of Nonconformist propaganda that, according to one of Wales's leading contemporary historians, 'the irreligious are a lost element in Welsh historiography'.[49] Minorities are often particularly sensitive to the metonymic logic of identity politics, where the behaviour of some is seen by the dominant society to represent the whole. This lay at the heart of the furore caused by Caradoc Evans's debasing depictions of rural Welsh speakers in *My People* (1915), and was at the root of W. E. B. Du Bois's concern that the Jamaican Claude McKay had used 'every art and emphasis to paint drunkenness, fighting, lasciviousness, sexual promiscuity' in Harlem, thus satisfying the white society's desire for 'fierce and unrestrained passions'.[50] 'The average colored man in Harlem', noted Du Bois, 'is an everyday laborer, attending church, lodge and movie and as conservative and as conventional as ordinary working folk everywhere'.[51] Debates about ethnic representation often revolve around the issue of which part should be regarded as being representative of the whole.

For some, such as Paul Gilroy, the inevitable selectivity involved in the process of canon formation and imagining nationhood are grounds for abandoning all canon- and nation-building projects. Retracing the history of an event such as the Universal Races Congress of 1911 is, for Gilroy, an attack on those 'critics who resent the intrusion of global concerns into their ethnically cleansed canon-building operations'.[52] For Henry Louis Gates Jr, however, the pursuit of literary interpretation from within the black American canon is not to 'refute the soundness' of an integrated American or Western canon or, by extrapolation, transatlantic or transnational approaches. It is no more or less essentialist to claim the existence of an African American canon, notes Gates, than it is 'to claim the existence of French, English, German, Russian or American literature' and '[f]or anyone to deny us the right to engage in attempts to constitute ourselves as discursive subjects is for them to engage in the double privileging of categories that happen to be preconstituted'.[53]

While accepting the metonymic nature of any reference to 'the people', it seems to me that without some conception of 'the Welsh' and 'the African Americans' this comparative project could not proceed. The designations 'Welsh' and 'African American' are invoked as the terms of comparison in this study with an awareness of the variety of experiences which they can never wholly encompass, a realization that the content of the groups constituted by the signifiers 'Welsh' and 'African American' change over time, and an acknowledgment that markers of 'Welshness' or 'Blackness' are historically contingent. I do think that it is legitimate to maintain these designations as the basis for comparative study, for to do away with them would ultimately reinforce the assimilationism of the dominant 'American' and 'British' contexts in which the 'African Americans' and the 'Welsh' have always had to define themselves. In the Welsh context, Jane Aaron is surely right to accept that the construction of 'human communities capable of cooperation and of maintaining a wealth of cultural diversity while eschewing nationhood may be an ideal worth working for', while noting that it is difficult to see how the abandonment of 'Welshness' would contribute to this process. Having rejected the notion of national distinctiveness the people of Wales would not 'float in limbo', notes Aaron, but 'in a world otherwise inhabited by nationals' would inevitably be 'rebranded' as unproblematic members of 'the British nation state, still very heavily English-dominated'.[54] Cornel West makes a similar point, but with a different emphasis, when he notes that, 'whatever name we come up with', African Americans would 'never disappear' because 'we're still going to have the blues and John Coltrane and Sarah Vaughan and all those who come out of this particular history'.[55] Throughout this study I aim to situate my use of 'Welsh' and 'African American' within specific historical contexts in order to explore how socio-historical forces converge to shape particular notions of identity in different periods, and how they influence the formal and aesthetic representations of those identities in written texts. My opening discussion of Frances Hoggan is an indicative example of the method adopted. Hoggan was a woman who pursued her educational and medical careers outside the borders of her beloved 'Principality'. Generally ignored in accounts of nineteenth-century Welsh history and culture, she is brought into dramatic view by the comparative perspective adopted here which sees her correspondence with Du Bois as a key moment of transatlantic exchange. It is, as Gates suggests, 'a question of perspective, a question of emphasis'.[56]

If the terms used to describe the peoples, literatures and cultures compared in this book are problematic enough, further problems arise from the attempt at placing Welsh culture within a comparative context. For some, the comparative approach of the type adopted in this volume will amount to little more than an attempt at placing Wales 'in a glamorously international context'.[57] It is, of course, rare to hear that transatlantic approaches to English or American cultures result in 'glamorization', for the barely hidden assumption, where Wales is concerned, is that an attractive veneer is being painted on the disablingly drab world of the periphery. This resistance to comparison is intensified in cases where the making of connections between Wales and other minority and post-colonial contexts is seen to be little more than an act of 'self-aggrandising self victimisation'.[58] When asked to elaborate on his reservations regarding 'recent historical fashions', Britain's leading Marxist historian Eric Hobsbawm drew attention to the rise of 'fanzine history, which groups write in order to feel better about themselves': 'Just the other day I noticed a new labour history journal which has an article on blacks in Wales in the eighteenth century. Whatever the importance of this to blacks in Wales, it is not in itself a particularly central subject.'[59]

Such analyses are perhaps not 'central' in relation to global politics, but the historical presence of 'blacks' in Wales plays a key role in undermining notions of cultural homogeneity while also offering case studies of the experiences of cultural interaction, of acculturation, and of racialization, within a particular culture. I have no intention in this volume of making anyone feel 'better about themselves'. While studies of the nature and pattern of slaveholding among the Welsh in America, and of the ways in which the industrialization of Wales was funded by slavery, would call for an economic and historical analysis of a kind not found in the primarily literary and cultural analyses of this book, *Black Skin, Blue Books* does explore, among other things, forms of racism in the nineteenth century (chapter 1), the role of race in the making of a Welsh working-class identity in the 1930s (chapter 3) and the racial tensions of the Second World War era (chapter 4 and the Conclusion).[60] Hobsbawm's comments reflect a wider resistance to historical and cultural analyses that aim to construct comparative methods calibrated to the conditions of European minorities. The fear is that a reactionary, atavistic, nationalism hides itself behind the 'trendy' desire to compare a minority European experience with that of 'oppressed' or 'colonial' peoples. Francis Mulhern and Chris Williams have been dismissive of those who have tried to understand the Irish and Welsh experiences respectively in comparative, post-colonial terms (although they do accept that some of the theoretical approaches developed within post-colonial studies may be useful). Williams emphasizes that 'Wales's colonial status ended in the sixteenth century, and from that time forward it has to be seen as part of what was, until the late nineteenth century, the most advanced imperial and commercial state in the world' and views comparisons of Wales with colonial situations as 'self-indulgent and potentially offensive illusions'.[61] Mulhern accepts that 'Ireland is different', but proceeds to ask 'in relation to what putatively normal society? There is none. Ireland is different, and in that perspective the same as everywhere else.'[62] While I can see his point, it is surely also true that, as Declan Kiberd notes, the Irish were 'brought up to regard English culture and society as some kind of human norm, against which they were the errata, the oddities'.[63] This is also the case in Wales where the world continues to be largely seen through the lens of a London-centric press and media. Thus, from Emrys ap Iwan in the nineteenth century through to Raymond Williams in the twentieth, many of those who have tried to conceptualize and discuss Welsh culture have attempted to break out of the perceptual confines of 'Britishness' to make a wider set of comparisons, in which 'England' itself becomes defamiliarized – which may explain why Raymond Williams was able to write a series of ground-breaking studies on English culture and thought.

If this process of comparative analysis has been pursued under the problematic banner of post-colonialism in recent years, Joe Cleary's approach to Ireland may prove more useful for the purposes of this study where neither of the subjects of comparison is unambiguously 'colonial'. Cleary notes that, while questions relating to 'geo-cultural location and constitutional statute' are important in the post-colonial debate, they are not the decisive issues.[64] For if

> colonialism is conceived as an historical process in which societies of various kinds and locations are differentially integrated into a world capitalist system, then it is on the basis of the comparative conjunctural analysis of such processes that debate must ultimately be developed.[65]

The point then is not to adduce whether Ireland or Wales is 'just like' any other more unambiguously 'colonial' situation, but to 'think of the ways in which specific national configurations are always the product' of the 'dislocating intersections between local and global processes' that characterize the workings of capitalism.[66] Today an increasingly wider set of comparative materials are brought to bear on Welsh culture and society, and this book is a contribution to that process. The example of Francis Hoggan, with which I began, is useful here again, for her essentially imperial belief that the benighted natives would be lifted by their benevolent white superiors, coexisted with her 'subaltern' sympathy for women and the disenfranchised and her call for the expansion of educational provision.[67] In this respect she may be seen to embody the complexities of the Welsh situation, lying 'at the intersection of both metropolitan and subaltern histories'.[68]

The key question that arises is that asked by Charlotte Williams in her response to a special edition of the journal *Comparative American Studies* on the 'Celtic nations and the African Americas'. 'What are the points of comparison being sought and why?', she asks before arguing that

> there is little mileage in pursuing parallels with the experiential dimensions of the subjugated positioning of the African American or the dynamic of racism, unless, that is, they are deployed for the purpose of interrogating the dominant national imagining within the regional peripheries and the way in which these regions are implicated in these processes.[69]

The interrogation of dominant national imaginings (whether 'Welsh' or 'British', 'American' or 'African American') is a running thread through this volume and, as already noted, there is always a danger, when comparing two very different experiences, of callous appropriation or of buttressing potentially offensive illusions. It is worth stating in the bluntest terms that the experiences of racism and subjugation do not cross from the African American to the Welsh context, and they mark a fundamental difference (there are of course many others) between the two experiences. But I would also argue that the 'regional peripheries' are not only 'implicated' in the processes of imperialism and racism, but have also developed forms of thought and action that are themselves resistant to the 'dominant forms' of 'national imagining'. The political and cultural forms of acculturation and resistance that were developed by the Welsh and by the African Americans are certainly not identical, but they are analogous. James Baldwin thought as much in the 1970s when an argument for the recognition of 'Black English' led him to note that 'much of the tension in the Basque country and in Wales is due to the Basques and Welsh determination not to allow their languages to be destroyed'.[70] This comparison took a more substantive form in American sociologist Michael Hechter's controversial study *Internal Colonialism: The Celtic Fringe in British National Development* (1975). While Hechter noted that he 'had no particular emotional commitment to the [Celts], and in fact had never set foot in the British Isles', his book grew from the fact that

> Oppressed groups [in the US], particularly Blacks, had recently become politically mobilised. Initially, Black political organisations . . . were committed to the implementation and extension of Federal civil rights statutes, especially in the South. Their ultimate goal was the integration and assimilation of Blacks

in American society . . . By the middle of [the 1960s] a deep split had emerged
in the Black community between those traditionalists clinging to assimilation
as their ultimate goal, and a younger, more militant group who, instead, argued
for a radical separation of Blacks from white society and culture . . . In exam-
ining the interaction of Anglo-Saxon and Celtic peoples over the long run,
these alternative strategies for the liberation of oppressed minorities – assimilationism versus nationalism – can be elaborated and analyzed in some
detail.[71]

While I do not adopt rigid 'internal colonial' or 'post-colonial' models
in this book, my comparative approach to African American and Welsh
cultures is based on the fact that, located within the imperial states of the
United Kingdom and the United States, these peoples – in all their
internal variety and despite their myriad historical differences – produced
movements for integration as well as for autonomy. Hechter seems to
suggest that there is a developmental narrative in which an initial assimilationism gives way to nationalism. The problem in designating
'nationalism' or 'assimilationism' as elements within a sequential historical narrative is that it can lead to an unquestioning complacency
regarding the existence of one or the other during one historical period,
and an impatience at their continued existence at another stage when
they are assumed to be outmoded. Comparative literary study can offer a
corrective in this respect, for, unlike the didacticism of political
pamphlets and chronological development of national histories, literature often embodies the multiple possibilities, the residual and emergent
social forces, and the diverse range of possible social identities that characterize ideas of nationhood and ethnicity in any period. Cultural and
literary analysis has an important role to play here, for no historical event
or relationship – as the historians of *mentalité* have long argued – is
finally separable from the way in which it is symbolized in social
consciousness.

In discussing the nature of historical research, Alberto Toscano notes
that 'analogy is an inextricable component of any cognition which seeks
to understand and judge phenomena that are not the objects of direct
perception'. Analogies, he suggests, function 'as bridges between the
known and unknown'. [72] These observations may be equally true of
comparative cultural studies. If, for Toscano, historical analogies involve
a calibration of 'the degree of identity and difference between now and
then', cultural analogies call for a similarly fraught calibration of the
degree of identity and difference between 'us' and 'them'.[73] This process
of 'calibration' is 'fraught' because any analogy's capacity for

illumination cannot be separated from its ideological effects. In reviewing my recent collection of Welsh-language essays on Wales and African America, T. Robin Chapman argues that the volume's authors select aspects of African American history and culture for their 'usefulness'. He acutely notes that at its worst this gesture amounts to a kind of colonial appropriation, and suggests that the only refuge from charges of voyeurism is an old fashioned, and perhaps discredited, humanist belief that in relating one culture to another we somehow expand our cultural, emotional and empathetic horizons.[74] If *Black Skin, Blue Books* does indeed draw on the liberal humanism of W. E. B. Du Bois or Frances Hoggan – a universalism which, as Ross Posnock and others have noted, 'has been held under suspicion during the reign of postmodernism' – this book also has a more materialist grounding in a realization that the process of constructing and symbolizing 'Welshness' from the nineteenth century onwards often involved comparative references to other minorities, and that the African American example appeared with a teasing regularity.[75] Drawing on Stuart Hall's work on the composite nature of identity and his, by now widely embraced, suggestion that identities 'come from outside, they are the way in which we are recognized and then come to step into the place of the recognitions which others give us', it seemed to me that it should be possible to trace the ways in which the Welsh (in their always changing linguistic, class and ethnic diversity) constructed their sense of a national identity in the mirror of the African American experience (or at least in their own distorted understating of it) in a variety of cultural places, many of them unexpected and most not yet examined.[76] What was more surprising as the project developed was the discovery that the process worked in both directions, with Wales occasionally appearing as a point of comparison in African American writing.[77] To read Paul Robeson tracing the roots of his internationalism to his experiences in south Wales, or Ralph Ellison recounting that his seminal examination of black identity in *Invisible Man* grew out of his experiences as a GI in wartime Swansea, reinforced the sense that I was exploring the mutual constructions of African American and Welsh identities.

This book has grown into an extended analysis of such moments of contact and comparison. The volume's chronological scope was partly dictated by this approach, and partly by questions of length. For reasons explored in chapter 1, the 1840s is seen as a decisive decade in the emergence of Welsh national consciousness, and is also a decade that sees the publication of the most influential slave narratives which are often regarded by literary critics as the beginning of an identifiable African American literary tradition in the United States. That Fredrick Douglass – the author of the most famous slave narrative – was in Wales in 1846 seemed to bring these moments together and formed the basis for the analysis in chapter 1 of aspects of Welsh and African American literary and intellectual history in the nineteenth century. Chapter 2 is more comparative in approach, and looks at the forms taken by early twentieth-century literary modernism in Wales and African America. Chapter 3 explores Paul Robeson's connections with Wales and seeks to identify the cultural and political circumstances that made 1930s Wales so receptive to Robeson's persona and performances. Chapter 4 discusses African American novelist Ralph Ellison's depictions of Wales in one published and two unpublished short stories based on his experiences during the Second World War as a GI in Swansea and neighbouring Morriston.

My approach is historical and analytical, but focuses primarily on literary sources and draws on a range of approaches – from translation to ethnic studies, from feminism to anthropology – that are varied and possibly discrepant. Different similarities and distinctions will come to the fore as the analysis develops, and according to the terms of comparison and models adopted. The comparison of Welsh and African American sources has allowed me in places to look at some of the intellectual strains within both traditions in what I hope is a new and illuminating light (which is what I aimed to achieve in challenging the common distinction between 'assimilationism' and 'nationalism' in chapter 1). It has led to discussions of some canonical figures (such as Saunders Lewis, Margiad Evans, Ralph Ellison and Zora Neale Hurston) in new contexts, and has brought some figures who are less widely discussed in from the margins of their respective traditions (for example, Samuel Ringgold Ward, Samuel Roberts and Jack Jones). Frances Hoggan is one such figure, and to chose to begin by considering her connections with W. E. B. Du Bois is to foreground this volume's consistent emphasis on actual examples of cultural correspondence and exchange. I hope that, as the discussion proceeds, some of the approaches adopted here will be useful to others working in the field of transatlantic studies, and, as the examples multiply, that even the most sceptical of readers will begin to see the validity, value and interest of the comparisons being made.

# 1

# Black Skin, Blue Books: Frederick Douglass, Abolitionism and Victorian Wales

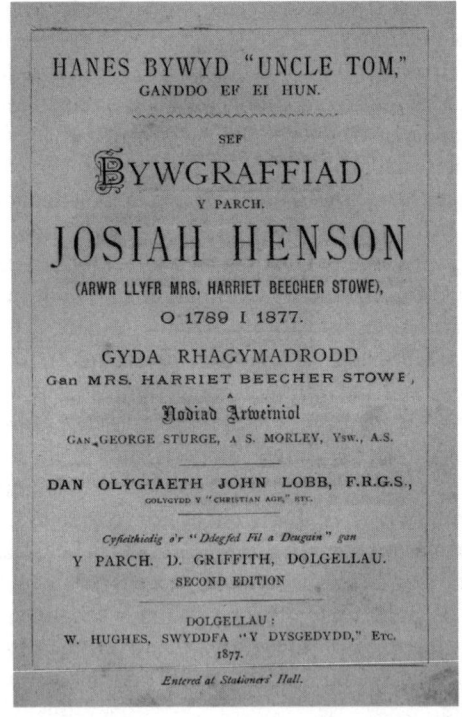

1. The Welsh translation of *Uncle Tom's Story of His Life:
An Autobiography of the Rev. Josiah Henson* (1876).

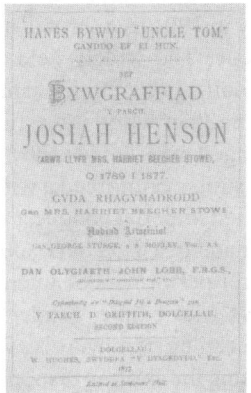

Having briefly visited his father's birthplace, Hay-on-Wye, in 1883, the celebrated American novelist William Dean Howells returned to Wales in 1904 to travel widely among a people whom he described as his 'co-racials'.[1] He found some elements of Welsh culture surprising, from the 'more than mid-Asian remoteness' of the place names, to the popularity of the blackface minstrels that he encountered in Aberystwyth and Llandudno.

> They dote upon Niggers, as they call them, with a brutality unknown among us except to the vulgarest white men and boys, and the negroes themselves in moments of exasperation. Negro minstrelsy is almost extinct in the land of its birth, but in the land of its adoption it flourishes in the vigor of undying youth; no watering-place is genuine without it . . . The decay of their gay science began among us with the fall of slavery, and the passing of the old plantation life; but as these never existed in Great Britain the English [*sic*] version of negro minstrelsy is not affected by their disappearance . . . At Llandudno the blackness of the Niggers was absolute, so that it almost darkened the day as they passed our lodging, along the crescent beach on their way to the open air theatre beyond it . . . There they cracked their jokes, and there they sang their songs; the songs were newer than the jokes, but they were both kinds delivered with a strong Cockney accent, and without an aspirate in its place. But it was all richly acceptable to the audience, who laughed and cheered and joined in the chorus when asked.[2]

While there is good reason to question the claim that the 'gay science' of minstrelsy had 'decayed' by the early twentieth century in the United States, Howells, who would participate in the founding of the NAACP

(National Association for the Advancement of Colored People) in 1909, clearly views minstrelsy in 1904 as a 'brutal' and 'vulgar' element of the British cultural landscape. The widely held view that minstrelsy was wholly based on the trivialization of black aspirations to full citizenship, and offered nothing more than white travesties and imitations of black culture, has been challenged in recent years by cultural historians.[3] While fully accepting that minstrelsy reinforced a widespread belief in the hierarchy of races that justified imperial conquest and racist practices, critics such as W. T. Lhamon Jr and Eric Lott have sought to explore the ways in which particular minstrel performances interacted in complex and not always predictable ways with ethnic, gender and class identities.[4] The current notion that the meaning of minstrelsy was historically contingent can be illustrated by tracing the shifting responses of Frederick Douglass, who was the pre-eminent African American abolitionist of his time and is the most widely canonized nineteenth-century African American author today. He is a figure to whom I shall return as a point of reference throughout this chapter.[5]

During his last visit to Europe in 1887, Douglass perceived a change in racial attitudes since his previous visits in the 1840s and 1850s. While most of the British and French remained 'sound in their convictions and feelings concerning the colored race', American prejudices were being adopted increasingly, reinforced by blackface minstrels 'who disfigure and distort the features of the Negro and burlesque his language and manners in a way that make him appear to thousands more akin to apes than to men'.[6] In discussing Douglass's 1845–7 visit to the British Isles, Sarah Meer suggests that the existence of eloquent African Americans such as Douglass at antislavery meetings in Britain provided 'a crucial counter-representation to the blackface entertainments already patronized by British audiences in the 1840s'.[7] While Douglass did express concerns at the tendency of minstrel troupes to 'exaggerate the exaggerations of our enemies' during his first tour of Britain, he tended to view minstrelsy as a part of the abolitionist struggle at this time.[8] He believed, for example, that the spectacle of an African American group, Gerritt's Original Ethiopian Serenaders, performing to white audiences was a sign of progress, and argued that some of the songs associated with minstrelsy, such as 'Lucy Neil', expressed the 'finest feelings of the human nature . . . [and] awaken the sympathies for the slave, in which Antislavery principles take root, grow up, and flourish'.[9] Speaking to an American audience at Cincinnati in 1852 he used the popularity of 'Nigger songs' among whites as a basis for arguing that 'I don't believe you want to get rid of us after all', and argued on another occasion that minstrel songs 'constitute our national music, and without which we have no national music'.[10] Douglass's ambivalent feelings were expressed in his awareness that the popularity of minstrelsy was partly to account for the success of his anti-slavery speeches in Britain: 'It is quite an advantage to be a nigger here. I find I am hardly black enough for British taste, but by keeping my hair as woolly as possible I make out to pass for at least half Negro at any rate.'[11] The complex connections between minstrelsy and anti-slavery in the mid-nineteenth century is illustrated further by the fact that by 1854 Harriet Beecher Stowe's 'Uncle Tom' had supplanted 'Jim Crow' as the leading minstrel figure. Uncle Tom was the last great role of the white performer Thomas Dartmouth Rice who had first brought the song and dance act called 'Jim Crow' to Britain in 1836. W. T. Lhamon argues that Rice's Uncle Tom was 'a revolutionary statement' that lived up to what the *New York Tribune* had described as 'the deep sentiment of human brotherhood' that his Jim Crow performances had evoked.[12]

The connection between a form of entertainment that offered a grotesquely comic view of black humanity and a commitment to the struggle against slavery is embedded within the text of Stowe's *Uncle Tom's Cabin*.[13] Stowe included two minstrel scenes in her novel, both associated with black children. The first occurs in the opening chapter where Harry, the son of mulatto slaves George and Eliza Harris, performs a show for his master, Shelby, who evokes minstrel conventions by referring to the boy as 'Jim Crow'. Harry performs 'one of those wild, grotesque songs common among the negroes, in a rich, clear voice, accompanying his singing with many comic evolutions of the hands, feet, and the whole body, all in perfect time to the music', before being asked to 'walk like Uncle Cudjoe, when he has rheumatism', and to lead a psalm like 'old Elder Robbins'.[14] The way in which the scene is framed makes it clear that Stowe wishes to expose the ways in which the child's performance is exploited in the context of a slave transaction between two masters, but the effect is to reinforce the grotesque childishness of black slaves, an impression reinforced later in the novel when Augustine St Clair buys Topsy – 'a funny specimen in the Jim Crow line' – for his cousin Ophelia. Topsy is told to 'give us a song, now, and show us some of your dancing':

> The black, glassy eyes glittered with a kind of wicked drollery, and the thing struck up, in a clear shrill voice, an odd negro melody, to which she kept time with her hands and feet, spinning round, clapping her hands, knocking her

knees together, in a wild, fantastic sort of time, and producing in her throat all
those odd guttural sounds which distinguish the native music of her race; and
finally, turning a summerset or two, and giving a prolonged closing note, as
odd and unearthly as that of a steam-whistle, she came suddenly down on the
carpet, and stood with her hands folded, and a most sanctimonious expression
of meekness and solemnity over her face, only broken by the cunning glances
which she shot askance from the corners of her eyes.

   Miss Ophelia stood silent, perfectly paralyzed with amazement.[15]

While spoken by a third-person omniscient voice, words such as
'unearthly', and the reference to Topsy as 'the thing', suggests that we
are seeing things from Miss Ophelia's point of view. Stowe seems to be
suggesting that both the grotesque performance and the way in which it
is being viewed result from the inhumanity of slavery, but by the
post-Civil War period this message had been lost as 'Topsy' came second
only to 'Uncle Tom' as the most popular character in minstrel shows.[16]
Gerald Early argues that Stowe's association of the 'darky stage antics'
of minstrelsy with the black child was damaging in two ways:

> It strongly reinforced in the minds of whites, who already in the 1850s were
> waxing sentimental about 'the old plantation', sentimentality and nostalgia
> for 'darky' antics, by connecting them with children and childhood. It also,
> contrarily, distinguished black children as being apart from white children,
> and thus separated the idea of black childhood from white childhood, linking
> black children to deviltry, mischief, silliness, and an intensely exhibitionist
> nature.[17]

Early concludes his analysis by noting that it is 'one of the curious paradoxes of American culture' that *Uncle Tom's Cabin*, 'so sincerely and
powerfully antislavery, should have so successfully trapped blacks in a
series of images that so thoroughly discounted their humanity while so
fervently pleading for their character'.[18]

   Early offers a convincing account of a widely held view of Stowe's
novel. This was not the view at the time of its publication, however, for it
was welcomed by abolitionists as 'a godsend destined to mobilize white
sentiment against slavery just when resistance to the southern forces was
urgently needed'.[19] If William Dean Howells was perturbed by the presence of minstrels in Llandudno, he believed that Stowe's *Uncle Tom's
Cabin* was 'one of the great novels of the world, and of all time'. Writing
in 1897 he argued that America had no real novels until after the Civil
War, 'except *Uncle Tom's Cabin*', a book that transcended its time and
place: 'The fact that slavery was done away with does not matter; the

interest in *Uncle Tom's Cabin* will never pass, because the book is really
. . . true to human nature.'[20] In his third and final autobiography of 1893,
Frederick Douglass described Stowe's novel as 'a work of marvellous
depth and power', noting that 'nothing could have better suited the moral
and humane requirements of the hour'.[21] This view was consistent with
the laudatory reviews and references to the novel that appeared in
Douglass's abolitionist journal *The Frederick Douglass Paper* when
*Uncle Tom's Cabin* first appeared in 1852. Robert Levine notes that
Douglass consistently championed the unprecedented impact that the
novel was having on readers not only in the Northern states, but in the
South and across the Atlantic as well.[22] In drawing attention to its success
in places such as Paris and Moscow, Douglass was reinforcing his argu-
ment that 'Uncle Tom has his mission in Europe, and most conscientiously
is he fulfilling it'.[23] Further evidence for the novel's transatlantic impact
was offered in the 'Literary Notices' section of the *Frederick Douglass
Paper* of 31 December 1852, where readers were told that 'Uncle Tom's
Cabin has been translated into Welsh, and bears the title of "Caban
F'Ewythr Tum"' (*sic*).[24]

The first full-length Welsh version of *Uncle Tom's Cabin* was
published by John Cassell in London in 1853, in a translation by Hugh
Williams with illustrations by George Cruikshank. Chapters had already
appeared in the Liverpool based Welsh newspaper *Yr Amserau* (The
Times) in 1852, and in March 1853 the journal *Y Cyfaill o'r Hen Wlad*
(The Friend from the Old Country) could report that there were three
different Welsh versions of Stowe's novel in circulation, translated
respectively by Hugh Williams, Williams Rees ('Gwilym Hiraethog')
and Thomas Lefi ('Y Lefiad').[25] In addition to *Y Cyfaill o'r Hen Wlad,*
the Welsh-American journal *Y Cenhadwr Americanaidd* (The American
Missionary) also serialized the novel, and its editor Robert Everett
produced an amended version of Hugh Williams's translation for an
American audience in 1854.[26] Welsh-language translations of English
and European texts were widespread in nineteenth-century Wales, but
even in the context of a thriving translation industry the sheer number of
versions of *Uncle Tom's Cabin* produced within a two-year period is
remarkable.[27] It is clear that Stowe's novel resonated with Welsh audiences. While many no doubt read the story as a tale of exotic 'others',
William Rees's transposition of the story into a Welsh context in his
*Aelwyd F'Ewythr Robert* ('Uncle Robert's Hearth', to which I shall
return) suggests that some sought to make connections and correspondences between New England anti-slavery, the African American

experience and nineteenth-century Wales.[28] If, as Gerald Early suggests, the success of Stowe's novel derived partly from the fact that it 'came along at a time when American popular culture was developing a consensus view about a number of American types', then, in translating 'old Elder Robbins' in the passage from chapter 1 quoted above as 'hen Robin y blaenor' ('old Robin the [chapel] deacon'), African American types became familiar Welsh types, a process perhaps reinforced by the fact that the story's central African American family have a familiar Welsh surname – Harris.[29] I shall return to discuss the meaning and significance of translating the experience of slavery later in this chapter, but it is worth noting here that if the Welsh response broadly mirrored the enthusiasm for *Uncle Tom's Cabin* across Britain, the process of translation meant that the novel was being made to speak to a specific audience and to a distinct linguistic culture.

The translations of *Uncle Tom's Cabin* appeared within the context of a thriving print culture in the Welsh language, and first impressions would suggest that the nineteenth was, both materially and culturally, a prosperous century for Wales. Industrialization led to a quadrupling of the population. In rural Wales, the stranglehold of the gentry class was broken, and the Nonconformist chapels attracted vast congregations across the nation, with the Sunday schools ensuring a high degree of literacy. Educational institutions multiplied, Welsh speakers increased in numbers decade by decade (although decreasing as a percentage of the population) and the reinvented 'Eisteddfod' (a cultural festival) proved an unmitigated success. Circumstances seemed right for a confident assertion of national consciousness, for the creation of firm political and cultural foundations for the nation and for the emergence of an innovative Welsh literature. But, as several cultural historians have lamented, this did not happen. There is a broad historical consensus that one of the key events of the century was the publication of the 'Blue Books' of this chapter's title: the 1847 Royal Commission into the State of Education in Wales. The commission responsible for the report was established following a proposal by a Welshman, William Williams, MP for Coventry. In light of the concern for the growing hold of Dissent and Nonconformity over the common people, the lack of provision for education in Wales and the growth of political unrest over the previous decades, culminating in the working-class Merthyr Rising of 1831, the Chartist risings of 1839 and the agrarian anti-tollgate movement known as 'Rebecca' from 1839–43, Williams urged the government to inquire into the state of education in Wales and 'especially into the means afforded to the labouring classes of acquiring knowledge of the English language'.[30] While the material poverty of Wales meant that there was some justification for the three English commissioners' views on educational provision, they reported on much besides that in their blue books, suggesting that the Welsh lived a life of moral laxity, dishonesty, perjury and drunkenness. This behaviour had linguistic roots:

> The Welsh language is a vast drawback to Wales and a manifold barrier to the moral progress and commercial prosperity of the people. Because of their language the mass of the Welsh people are inferior to the English in every branch of practical knowledge and skill . . . Whether in the country or among the furnaces the Welsh element is never found at the top of the social scale, nor in its own body does it exhibit very much variety of graduation. In the works, the Welsh workman never finds his way into the office . . . Equally in his new or old hole his language keeps him under the hatches being one in which he can neither acquire nor communicate the necessary information. It is the language of old fashioned agriculture, of theology and of simple rustic life, while all the world about him is English . . . [H]e is left to live in an under-world of his own and the march of society goes completely over his head.[31]

The promise of a commission of inquiry into the state of education had raised great hopes amongst the Welsh for far-reaching reforms in the nation's education. The commissioners' attacks on the principality's culture and the people's morals resulted in uproar and the report came to be known as 'Brad y Llyfrau Gleision', 'The Treachery of the Blue Books' – an epithet that drew on a tradition of oral storytelling and on Victorian medievalism in referring back to the 'Treachery of the Long Knives', a plot that had furthered Anglo-Saxon interests in the age of Vortigern.

Socio-linguists, historians and literary critics have, in their various ways, traced the paradoxical and contradictory responses that followed the publication of the Blue Books.[32] On the one hand, it made the Welsh more nationalistic than they had been; on the other, it implanted in the leaders of the official Welsh way of life a terror of further exposés, leading them to engage in a committed effort to answer the criticism of the commissioners by encouraging the people to become more like the dominant model of Englishness – practical, hard-headed and business-like. These responses are not necessarily contradictory, however, for, as Dale Patterson has noted in a suggestive comparative analysis of African American and Russian literatures, the creation of what he terms a 'missionary nationalism', which encourages a 'backward' people to 'sacrifice its native culture' in the making of an universal global order, 'is

particularly attractive . . . among ethnic groups that feel themselves positioned on the margins of an expanding cultural system'.[33] Described by
the Blue Books' commissioners as a people living in an 'underworld'
oblivious to the 'march of society', the Welsh embraced a nationalism
that, like that of their African American and Russian counterparts, 'first
arose in the guise of a missionary nationalism advanced by . . . Christian
Westernizers determined to reconstruct a "backward" native culture'.[34]
The Welsh manifestation of this process of reconstruction resulted in the
idea of the 'gwerin' ('folk'), described precisely and colourfully by the
historian Gwyn A. Williams:

> A whole people did indeed form along this line [of religious Nonconformism];
> like the Czechs, they came to think of themselves as classless, a *gwerin*, to use
> the popular term. Everything outside them came to seem only half-Welsh,
> they were the real Welsh. As they became more radical in their politics they
> came to feel that they, as a Nonconformist people, were the Welsh nation.
> Henry Richard, one of their leading spokesmen, put it in so many words,
> echoed by Gladstone himself, 'The Nonconformists of Wales are the people of
> Wales'.[35]

Thus an ethnic conception of Welshness developed in the nineteenth
century, rooted in Nonconformity and temperance, with abolitionism
also appearing as a fundamental political belief. Indeed, the leaders of
Welsh Nonconformity, in Wales and America, were as fervent in their
anti-slavery as they were in their animosity towards the Irish who were
coming to settle in their midst.[36] 'Welshness' became associated with a
moral struggle for the hearts and minds of the people, and was based on
a curious combination of a belief in social equality and an intolerance of
anyone who embraced a different religion and embraced a different
culture. Even on census day 1851 nearly half of the Welsh adult population went neither to church or chapel, yet Welshness became increasingly
defined along the lines of chapel morality; its 'sweeping spiritual vision'
and 'opening to talent, particularly in verse and music', but also its
'crabbed narrowness' and 'mean-spirited tyranny'.[37]

These forces are reflected in the period's vibrant print culture, with a
useful example for my purposes occurring in Ieuan Gwyllt's journal *Y
Cerddor Cymraeg* ('The Welsh Musician'). During the 1860s Gwyllt
used the pages of his journal as a pulpit for cultivating his nation's
musical tastes. While opening his readership's eyes to developments in
Europe, he feared that 'sensation music' imported from overseas would
subvert the religious morality and respectability of Wales's musical
culture, and warned against popular music's ability to 'borthi y nwydau

mwyaf llygredig' ('feed the most debased instincts').[38] The kind of music that he had in mind was made explicit in a review of March 1871:

> Nid gwlad y Negroaid ydyw Cymru; ac anghyfiawnder mawr a'n cenedl ydyw ceisio ei darostwng i sefyllfa gerddorol yr hanner anwariaid hyny. Ymgodwch ati o ddifrif, feirdd a chantorion Cymru, i ddeall, i deimlo, ac i gyweirio eich tanau wrth deimladau ac egnion gorau eich gwlad.

> (Wales is not the land of Negroes; and the debasement of our nation to the musical standards of those semi-barbarians is a great travesty. Arise, Welsh bards and singers, to understand and to feel, and to tune your strings to the finest feelings and energies of your nation.)[39]

Ieuan Gwyllt makes no distinction between music performed by African Americans (such as the spirituals – described by a Swansea newspaper as 'weird slave songs' – performed by the Fisk Jubilee Singers who toured Britain for the first time in the 1870s) and the music performed by blackface minstrels.[40] In making his protest Gwyllt clearly believes that there is a danger that Victorian Wales may, indeed, become 'the land of Negroes', and the presence of African Americans was not limited to the musical sphere. In her concluding remarks to *Uncle Tom's Cabin*, Stowe drew attention to individuals who 'but yesterday burst from the shackles of slavery, who, by a self-educating force, which cannot be too much admired, have risen to highly respectable stations in society', and mentioned 'Douglas [*sic*] and Ward' in particular.[41] The ex-slaves Frederick Douglass and Samuel Ringgold Ward were amongst the African Americans who visited Wales in the nineteenth century, and encountered a people who, during the period of the Blue Books, were also desperate to prove themselves worthy of occupying the most 'highly respectable stations in society'.

In his second autobiography *My Bondage and My Freedom* (1855) Douglass described his 'times and labours, while abroad' in 1845–7 as having been divided 'between England, Ireland, Scotland and Wales', yet with the exception of references to the name of the Cunard liner on which Douglass was forced to travel in steerage to Britain and back – *The Cambria* – the Welsh dimension of his tour has been wholly ignored by critics and biographers.[42] Perhaps this is not a major omission for Douglass did not share a platform with any major Welsh political figures, as he had with the Irish 'liberator' Daniel O'Connell in Dublin, nor had he engaged in a major national dispute as he had in calling on the Free Church in Scotland to 'send back the money' that it had received from American slaveholders.[43] Nevertheless, while Douglass was travelling

through Wales in 1846, so were the three English commissioners who
would publish their Blue Books a year later. Douglass's presence in what
may be one of the most significant years in the history of nineteenth-
century Wales offers a valuable comparative perspective on the making
of Welsh identity, and presents a suitable beginning for a study that I
hope will contribute to the opening up of new perspectives in the emergent field of transatlantic studies.

## WALES AND TRANSATLANTIC ABOLITIONISM

Among the major events of Douglass's first visit to Britain was a meeting
held on 9 October 1846 at Wrexham Town Hall, where he was accompanied on stage by the leading white abolitionists William Lloyd Garrison
and George Thompson. The lengthy and detailed account that appeared
under the heading 'Great meeting at Wrexham to review the proceedings
of the Evangelical Alliance' in the *Carnarvon and Denbigh Herald*
suggested that the inhabitants of north-east Wales were already familiar
with, and eagerly anticipating, their esteemed guests.

> On Friday evening last a highly important meeting, in connexion with the
> above society, was held at the Town-hall, Wrexham, being the first of a series
> of meetings intended to be held in the Principality, similar to those which are
> now in the course of being held throughout the kingdom. The excitement in
> the town occasioned by the visit of the three celebrated anti-slavery mission-
> aries, Messrs. Thompson, Garrison and Douglass, is admitted never to have
> been equalled, except upon one occasion, when the first of the above-named
> gentlemen delivered a lecture upon the subject of free-trade . . . Upon the
> present occasion the capacious room itself, as well as the stairs and avenues
> approaching, was crowded with highly respectable auditory. The intensive
> interest felt in the proceedings is proved by the fact that the meeting was
> protracted to a later period than any that had been previously known in the
> town.[44]

The Liverpool-published Welsh-language paper *Yr Amserau* offers
further light on the nature of the meeting:

> Prydnawn dydd Gwener, wythnos i'r diwethaf, cynhaliwyd cyfarfod pwysig-
> fawr yng Ngwrexham gan aelodau y Gymdeithas Wrth-gaethwasiol, y cyntaf
> o gyfres o gyfarfodydd cyffelyb a fwriedir gynnal yn y Dywysogaeth, a thrwy
> yr holl Deyrnas Gyfunol gyda golwg ar brofi teimladau pobl y wlad hon, ac yn
> neillduol y dosparth crefyddol, gyda golwg ar weithrediadau hynodol y
> Cyngrair Efengylaidd, a chondemnio y goddefiad mewn effaith yr heurir

ddarfod i'r Gymdeithasfa hono, yn gystal ag Eglwys Rydd Scotland ei roddi i'r Gaethwasiaeth Americanaidd, drwy eu cydgyfathrach broffesedig a chennadau neillduol o'r wlad hono. Yr oedd Llysdy y Dref, yn yr hwn y cynhelid y cyfarfod, wedi ei orlenwi. A llaweroedd yn methu dyfod mewn. Allan o 5,000, nifer poblogaeth y dref, yr oedd yn agos i fil yn bresenol yn y cyfarfod.

(On Friday afternoon last week a highly important meeting was held in Wrexham by members of the Anti-Slavery League, the first of a series of similar meetings that are planned for the principality and for the United Kingdom as a whole, designed to test the feelings of the people, and especially religious people, as to the actions of the Evangelical Alliance, and to condemn that Alliance's, and the Free Church of Scotland's, alleged support for American Slavery, through their reported connections with particular co-religionists from that country. The town's Court House, in which the meeting was held, was overflowing, with many unable to enter. Out of the 5,000 inhabitants of the town, nearly 1,000 were present at the meeting.)[45]

The accounts in the *Carnarvon and Denbigh Herald* and *Yr Amserau* suggest that the Wrexham meeting took the form of an initial sequence of attacks on slavery by Douglass, Garrison and Thompson (in that order), followed by a debate between these guest speakers and local clergy on the issues of the day – primarily the Free Church of Scotland's links with Southern American slaveholders, and the Evangelical Alliance's connections with Southern clergy who supported slavery.[46] The call on the Free Church to 'send back the money' was not successful, but by the end of 1846 the Evangelical Alliance had refused membership to slaveholders.[47] The letters of William Lloyd Garrison suggest that the Wrexham meeting was particularly memorable:

I left Dublin with much regret, on Thursday eve – the 9th inst., and arrived in the steamer at Liverpool the next morning, where I found Geo. Thompson and Frederick waiting for me at Brown's hotel, Clayton square. From thence, we went immediately to Wrexham, in Wales, to our warm-hearted friends Sarah and Blanche Hilditch, (the latter deaf and dumb) who gave us a sisterly welcome. In the evening, we held a public meeting in the town hall, which was densely packed until near midnight – and the expression of enthusiasm, on the part of those present was overwhelming.[48]

*Yr Amserau* reported that the meeting ended at half past ten, while the *Carnarvon and Denbigh Herald* reported that the meeting ended 'about half past eleven' and, according to an 1889 biography of Garrison, the Town Hall in Wrexham was 'packed till midnight'.[49] We can fairly confidently conclude that the meeting, packed with an enthusiastic audience, went on for longer than was usual. Garrison wrote to Sarah Hilditch, a Wrexham-based abolitionist and primary organizer of the event, to express his gratitude:

> I want to tell you how much I feel indebted to you for your sisterly reception, your ardent co-operation, your self-sacrificing spirit, your words of encouragement and love, your unmerited devotion to the cause of poor bleeding, fettered, crushed humanity. I shall ever feel grateful to Heaven for having been permitted to become acquainted with you and dear Blanche, whose case excites my utmost sympathy, my warmest admiration, my brotherly regard. Tell her, that though I was compelled to be mute in her presence, not knowing what signs to make to hold intelligent converse with her, I felt that our spirits needed no vocal utterance.[50]

Little is known about the fascinating sisters Sarah and Blanche Hilditch, who lived together at 25 King Street, Wrexham.[51] Garrison referred to them in letters, and also drew on Blanche Hilditch's deafness in his Wrexham address to develop an argument that reflected the fundamental tenets of his brand of abolitionism. In admiring those individuals who had dedicated their lives to the struggle for abolitionism he noted that:

> There is before me a lady who has also given her mind to that course, year after year, and yet was deaf and dumb (cheers). She is known on the other side of the Atlantic for her benevolence, and with much eloquence her heart is there pleading for the poor slaves. She knows that there are also in America three million of the human family who are also deaf and dumb, not by birth, or the providence of God . . . and she says 'I will do what I can to enable them to speak'.[52]

The image of a woman who could not speak, yet whose influence could span the Atlantic divide and give a voice to the voiceless slave is a powerful manifestation of the philosophy of 'moral suasion' that informed Garrisonian abolitionism.[53] Moral suasionists believed that amoral or immoral beliefs could be changed through the example of the morally correct actions of others. The expression of moral truth could thus transcend verbal communication, a position embraced by Douglass at the time of his visit to Britain, where he noted in Belfast that 'truth needs but little argument, and no long drawn metaphysical detail to establish a position. There is something in the heart which instantly responds to its voice.'[54] Garrison used the example of Blanche Hilditch as an embodiment of this argument: despite her muteness her 'heart' could be heard 'pleading for the poor slaves'. Suasionists, therefore, emphasized the transformative potential of morally righteous communication and behaviour, and generally argued against insurrection or rebellion as a means of ending slavery.[55] Accounts in the press suggest that the arguments of the moral suasionists were widely embraced by Welsh abolitionists.[56]

The edition of *Yr Amserau* in which the report of the Wrexham meeting appeared included a lengthy article on the debate regarding the admission of American slaveholders into the Evangelical Alliance, and a letter from an inhabitant from Montgomeryshire who reported that he had heard Douglass, Garrison and Thompson at Liverpool's 'Concert Hall' and wished to express his view that

> Y mae argoelion fod teimladau dwysion yn ffynnu drwy ymerodraeth Brydain yn erbyn gorthrymderau y gaeth-fasnach, a bod y teimladau hyn yn cryfhau ac yn ymledu o hyd. Y mae yn eithaf cyfreithlawn i'r teimladau hyny gael eu hamlygu drwy yr argraffwasg, ac mewn cyfarfodydd cyhoeddus; ac yr ydym yn hyderus obeithio y bydd i hyny ddylanwadu mor rymus ar grefyddwyr America, nes eu cynhurfu i gydymorchestu ar unwaith i symud ymaith o'r ffordd yr anfad ysgylerder ag sydd . . . yn andwyo eu taleithiau ardderchog.

> (There are signs that profound feelings are growing in the British Empire against the oppressions of the slave trade, and that these feelings are continually strengthening and spreading. It is perfectly lawful that these feelings should be expressed in print and in public meetings; and we confidently hope that this will have such an influence on the religious leaders of America, that they are stimulated to act with us in removing this heinous blot which mars their excellent States.)[57]

It is, therefore, hoped that the legal expression of anti-slavery sentiment in Britain will carry sufficient moral weight to transform the activities of pro-slavery co-religionists in the United States. While the letter quoted above emphasizes the potentially transformative role of the 'British Empire', such a view also allowed the inhabitants of a small nation such as Wales to imagine that they could have an exemplary role to play on the world stage. Audrey Fisch has documented the ways in which the embrace of anti-slavery reinforced a sense of English superiority over the 'barbaric' Americans following the abolition of slavery in the British Empire in 1833, and a similar case can be made in relation to Wales where, by the mid-nineteenth century, opposition to slavery, aligned with temperance, became a fundamental belief of religious Nonconformity.[58] Speaking at Wrexham in 1846, William Lloyd Garrison described a disturbing change that he felt was taking place in Britain. The *Carnarvon and Denbigh Herald* reconstructed his words as follows:

The evangelical alliance also had since resolved, like the priest and the Levite of old, to pass by on the other side, and give no hear to those who had fallen among thieves (hear). At first they had something like a condemnation of slavery upon their records; but the pro slavery delegates from America caused them to blot everything out, and leave nothing to be found upon their proceedings respecting the system. Is it not astounding that, while pro-slavery America is fast becoming anti-slavery, anti-slavery England, Scotland, Ireland and Wales are becoming pro-slavery. (hear)

Mr C. Sabine: No, no, not Wales.

Mr. Garrison: 'No, not Wales' says a friend. Well, we will make the exception (loud cheers).[59]

Having made that exception, Garrison proceeded to say that while

The present was his first visit to Wales . . . he hoped it would not be his last (cheers), for he believed that they everywhere abhorred slavery in their souls, and had no desire to connive at the enslavement of any portion of the human race. If they would not tolerate slavery amongst themselves, they could not but deeply sympathise with those who were deprived of all rights, whatever might be the distance at which they resided from this land.[60]

This view of the Welsh as a nation of ardent abolitionists who would 'not tolerate slavery amongst themselves' is also in evidence in American periodicals of the period. In noting the appearance of *Uncle Tom's Cabin* in Welsh the *New York Independent* evoked Welsh national history in celebrating the fact that 'Uncle Tom in his Welsh dress, strong and beautiful, will make a fine appearance and gain thousands of friends among the descendants of Prince Llywelyn and Owain Glyndwr'.[61] Having received a letter of support from Robert Everett, who, as noted above, was editor of *Y Cenhadwr Americanaidd* and *Y Dyngarwr* (The Philanthropist), the *Frederick Douglass Paper* printed the following passage:

We have made more than one resolution, (somewhat in vain, we must confess) not to increase out list of Exchanges; but we cannot deny ourselves the gratification of sending our Paper (as requested) to the Editor of The American Messenger, and, at the same time, of expressing our satisfaction at learning that there is, at least, one 'purely Anti-Slavery Paper' published by the Welsh people of this country. This is as it should be. It is consistent that a people who have loved Freedom so much, for themselves, should lend their efforts towards obtaining it for others. It is, at once, the pride and the boast of the Welsh people that they were never conquered. From their earliest hours, their stern and hardy ancestors inhaled the breath of Freedom in their mountain homes; dearly they loved, and highly they prized this Heavenly boon; and when the invader sought (and vainly sought) to wrest it from them, they knew how to struggle how to suffer and how to die but, never how to surrender. They were ever an indomitable race as unyielding as their native storms and as free as the winds of Heaven. Time was when the now vaunting Anglo-Saxon bent his neck before the conquering Norman, and wore the badge of serfdom but time never was when a Welshman wore chains, or called any man his master.[62]

Flattery proved a useful strategy for drawing a wide range of ethnic groups into the rainbow coalition that constituted the transatlantic abolitionist movement, and the positive comparison of the free Welshman and conquered Saxon is clearly designed to appeal to Welsh-American readers. This passage would probably have been written by Julia Griffiths, who was born in London (though her surname suggests Welsh ancestry), and had met Douglass during his 1845–7 tour. From 1848 to 1852 she lived in Rochester, New York, and wrote most of the 'Literary Notices' in Douglass's paper where she would often draw attention to *Y Cenhadwr Americanaidd*, noting that 'our Welsh friend reaches us regularly', but regretting 'that it needs an interpreter before we can understand it'.[63]

Despite Griffiths's concern at the language barrier (to which I shall return), the anti-slavery movement can be seen to have offered the leaders of Welsh opinion a context in which they could imagine themselves to be at the heart of a global political struggle. This was particularly significant at a time when the Blue Books of 1847 had given the impression that education in Wales was in an appallingly underdeveloped state, leading to a fear that the nation was being left behind by Western 'progress'. Abolitionism thus played a role in the construction of an image of the Welsh as a highly moral, devout and essentially peaceful people who could play a valuable role in the cultural and political life of Victorian Britain.

In this context, the most striking account of the Welsh by an African American in the nineteenth century occurs in the penultimate chapter of Samuel Ringgold Ward's *Autobiography of a Fugitive Negro: His Anti-Slavery Labours in the United States, Canada and England*, published in 1855. Ward, a leading abolitionist who had fled to what is now Ontario, Canada, to avoid arrest in 1851, was in Wales in August 1854 as part of a fundraising trip to the British Isles that he undertook on behalf of the Anti-Slavery Society of Canada. In recalling his visit in his *Autobiography* Ward noted that with the exception of 'black people', 'no country, no people, ever pleased me so much' as the Welsh.[64] I shall make several references to Ward's autobiography as my discussion proceeds, but wish to note here that his account of Wales serves to reinforce the image of respectability, sobriety, thrift and peacefulness that the Welsh bourgeoisie were desperate to convey following the Blue Books. Ward notes that there are 'few cases of scandalous crimes' in Wales, which emphasizes the 'immense' difference 'betwixt Wales and Ireland'.[65] He emphasizes how 'quiet and moral' Welsh towns are when compared with towns in 'England, Ireland or Scotland'. He celebrates the fact that 'a drunken peasant is, indeed, a rare sight in Wales', for the 'temperance case has done more for Wales than for any other part of the kingdom', and that the 'cleanliness of the peasantry is most striking'. Ward deems the 'industry of the poorer classes' to be 'commendable' and is struck by the way in which Nonconformist ministers 'take special care and pains in looking after their flocks'; their influence is having 'the very best effects upon a remarkably straightforward, simpleminded people'.[66] With the possible exception of his reference to 'simplemindedness', Ward's chapter on Wales amounted to a powerful expression of the very characteristics that the respectable leaders of Welsh public opinion desperately wished their compatriots to embrace. While Ward accepts that his 'stay was so short that I can say but little of Wales', it seems that Richard Griffiths Esq., whom Ward thanks for arranging his visit, managed to give the desired impression of his country.[67] What is perhaps most interesting, however, is that Ward is aware that his views of Wales are somewhat unorthodox.

I know what will be said, in other countries than Wales, in reply to what I say of the chastity of the Welsh female peasantry. Reference will be made to the stupid system of courtship called 'bundling' – a practice for which there is no defence: most certainly, I have no word to utter in its behalf. That it has not been attended with far worse consequences, is to me a marvel. But I have the great happiness to know, that the pulpit, which is more powerful in Wales than in any Protestant country elsewhere, has turned its whole power and influence against this barbarous practice, so that not even it, to any extent, forms a draw-back to the remarks I have made upon the morality of the Welsh peasantry. It is to be hoped that a custom which has nothing better than its antiquity for its apology, but is liable to the very gravest objections on the score of morality and decency, will soon be known merely as a matter of history. Surely, when a custom so pernicious shall once be put away, all will rejoice, and all will wonder that a people of such sterling sense should have suffered it to continue so long. It certainly has outlived the former bad taste of the people; and there-fore, if for no higher reason, it ought to live no longer. Most earnestly is it to be hoped that this abominable relic of ancient British barbarism will soon be so completely banished, as no longer to mar the otherwise good and exemplary character of the honest youths and maidens of that delightful Principality.[68]

While the Blue Books are not named in this passage they are clearly hovering behind the text. The commissioners had noted in 1847 that 'the want of chastity' among Welsh women resulted from 'the practice of "bundling", or courtship on beds during the night – a practice still widely prevailing'.[69] In a country with a cold, wet climate and in an era when houses had few rooms, the practice of 'bundling' – where a couple would get to know each other in bed 'bundled' in a pillow case, or with a bolster placed between them, to keep a decorous distance – evolved as a practical ritual. According to the Blue Books the practice was 'much increased' by the mixed 'night prayer-meetings' of the Nonconformists and 'the intercourse which ensues in returning home'.[70] Ward shares the Blue Books commissioners' outrage at the 'barbarous practice', but, as an African American Nonconformist minister himself, is keen to note that 'the pulpit, which is more powerful in Wales than in any Protestant country elsewhere, has turned its whole power and influence' against it.[71] For Ward, 'bundling' is the one blot on the landscape of 'the most moral and religious country . . . that I know'.[72]

When Ward notes that 'Negroes are in feeling the most religious people in the world . . . with perhaps the exception of the Welsh', he is suggesting a correspondence between two peoples who, in very different contexts, were particularly concerned with issues of ethnic 'representation' in the nineteenth century.[73] Hywel Teifi Edwards has traced in detail the ways in which the Welsh sought to prove to the world – or more especially to the English – that they were superior to every other nation in respectability and moral purity, and African Americans placed particular emphasis on the ways in which they 'represented' themselves, hoping that their very presence would be seen to embody the best of what the slaves could become.[74] This was particularly the case for those who embraced the Garrisonian gospel of moral suasion, for they believed that in demonstrating 'enviable character traits' their example would help convince the government and civil authorities of the humanity, or potential humanity, of the slave community.[75] In his Wrexham speech Garrison prefaces his references to Blanche Hilditch by recalling a meeting in Bristol where 'some blind children . . . were desirous of seeing his dear friend Fredrick Douglass, not having the power of bodily vision, they felt him over, and found that he felt like a brother man'.[76] Garrison thus suggested that if Blanche Hilditch's actions as an abolitionist could transcend the limits placed upon her by her deafness, then Douglass's very presence could communicate across the limits of blindness. Indeed, those who had seen Douglass at abolitionist meetings in Britain tended to comment more on his presence and mode of speech, rather than on what he actually said. For Sarah Hilditch, for example, Douglass was 'a living example of the capabilities of the slave, and though we do not expect all to be equally gifted, he proves that they are not what they have been mis-represented, mere chattels – with bodies formed for herculean labour but without minds, without souls'.[77]

During the course of his time in Britain, Douglass became increasingly resistant to being the object of other people's speeches, and became increasingly aware of the limitations of moral suasion and of the 'politics of representation'.[78] In describing his first speech at a Nantucket abolitionist meeting Douglass recalled the way in which William Lloyd Garrison 'followed me, taking me as his text'.[79] To be taken as the 'text' of others' oratory became Douglass's primary role in his early career. His body functioned as a text that was open, like the Bible, for the minister or white abolitionist's interpretation. Douglass's first *Narrative* was introduced with two letters from the leading white abolitionists who had accompanied him to Wrexham, William Lloyd Garrison and Wendell Phillips. Phillips welcomed the fact that Douglass did not make 'wholesale complaints' that would detract from the 'truth, candor and sincerity' of his narrative. Garrison, drawing on the last tragic speech that Othello delivers in Shakespeare's play, drew attention to the fact that 'nothing has been set down in malice, nothing exaggerated, nothing drawn from the imagination', seemingly suggesting that the reflection of Douglass's own subjectivity in the text would detract from the desired representation of the slave's life as that experienced by a 'fair specimen' and a 'case' (and perhaps also a 'noble Moor').[80] Douglass omitted Garrison's and Philips's introductions when he came to write his second autobiography, *My Bondage and My Freedom*, in which he recalled that

> I was generally introduced as a '*chattel*' – a '*thing*' – a piece of southern '*property*' – the chairman assuring the audience that *it* could speak. Fugitive slaves, at that time, were not so plentiful as now; and as a fugitive slave lecturer, I had the advantage of being a '*brand new fact*' – the first one out.[81]

Douglass was advised by his fellow abolitionists to keep 'a little of the plantation manner of speech' and to 'give us the facts . . . we'll take care of the philosophy'.[82] It seems that this was largely the role that Douglass continued to play on his tour of the British Isles in 1845–7. In reporting on the Wrexham meeting, *Yr Amserau* drew attention to the fact that

Frederick Douglass spoke first, but offered the briefest synopsis of what he said:

> Mr Frederick Douglass a roddai hanes y Gaethwasiaeth yn Nhalaethau Deheuol America, ac a wnai apeilad grymus at Gristnogion Prydain am eu cynhorthwy i ddymchwelyd y trefniant dieflig.

> (Mr Frederick Douglass offered a history of slavery in the Southern States of America, and made a powerful appeal for the assistance of British Christians in bringing an end to the devilish institution.)[83]

The remainder of the report is taken up with accounts of what was said by the various white abolitionist speakers, with considerable space given to the words of William Lloyd Garrison. Thus in the report, as on the stage, it is Douglass's presence, rather than what he actually said, that is deemed most significant. The balance is somewhat restored in the lengthy English-language report of the *Carnarvon and Denbigh Herald*. Here Douglass's words are quoted at length, to be followed by a detailed account of Garrison's speech which illustrates the use that Garrison made of Douglass's presence:

> You have (said Mr. Garrison) just listened to the words of an American slave; and what do you think of him? (cheers). Does he look like a man? He has spoken with the voice of a man. Does he not 'give the world assurance of a man'? You will all answer 'yes'. (loud cheers). What if his complexion be somewhat darker than ours?
>
> 'A man's a man for a' that.'
>
> (cheers). We do not all of us look alike: we are not all of us of the same height, bulk or complexion. And what is he, but a tyrant in God's creation, who shall dare to stand up, and say to his brother man 'Because thou art not like myself in height, bulk, or complexion, I will make thee my slave, and thou shalt be my property' . . . People of Wales, what must be the character of the religion of a government, where a man like my brother Frederick Douglass is not and may not be, treated as a human being? Broad as is our country, there is not a single inch of ground upon which he can stand constitutionally, under the law of the country, and be safe from the slave hunters who may wish to seize him, and hurry him back again into slavery.[84]

Garrison does not ask for his audience's views of Douglass's testimony but, rather, their response to his physical presence. Terry Baxter suggests that the audience at such an event would feel as though they had witnessed a beast becoming a man before their very eyes, and while the visible proof of the slave's humanity could undoubtedly have a strong influence on popular opinion, there was also an element of the circus or theatre in such proceedings.[85] Douglass's increasing frustration at the attempts to limit his lectures to facts and not analysis led him, following his tours of England, Ireland, Scotland and Wales, to use funds from British supporters to found *The North Star* – an anti-slavery newspaper perceived by Garrison to be in direct competition with his own *Liberator*. The *North Star* soon became *The Frederick Douglass Paper* and, in creating a vehicle for the expression of his own voice and his own ideas, Douglass moved away from the tenets of Garrisonian moral suasionism and became a champion of direct political action. The infamous vituperative response that followed Douglass's split with the Garrisonians reflected not only a disappointment and regret at a further division within the anti-slavery movement, but also an unwillingness on the part of Garrison and his followers to allow the leading African American abolitionist to speak his own mind.[86] Henry Louis Gates Jr argues that Douglass's auto-biographies narrate, and embody, a shift from being viewed as an object, to being able to speak as a subject.[87] 'It did not entirely satisfy me to narrate wrongs', recalled Douglass, 'I felt like denouncing them'.[88]

In nineteenth-century America, Douglass's denunciations were not limited to the English language. The 15 June 1843 edition of the short-lived Welsh-American temperance and abolitionist journal *Y Dyngarwr* (The Philanthropist), for example, contained an article enti-tled 'Y Gymdeithas Wrthgaethiwol Americanaidd' (The American Anti-Slavery Society) which included the following quotation:[89]

Dywedir nad yw y caethion yn y Deau yn gwybod dim am yr ymdrechiadau a wneir drostynt a thros ryddid dynol ym mhob man trwy y taleithiau gogleddol a gorllewinol. Nid yw hyn yn wir. Y maent yn ei wybod. Gwyddant hyn er y pryd y cyneuwyd y wreichionen leiaf yn ein tir. Gwyddant ef mor fuan ag y gwyddech chwithau, Syr, yn eich Lloegr Newydd . . . Cyn y symudiad hwn, Syr, nid oedd i'r caethwas yn ei gadwynau un gobaith am waredigaeth – un gobaith o dangnefedd a dedwyddwch yn y dyffryn galar hwn. Tywyllwch ac anobaith a orphwysai yn bruddaidd dros ei ragddisgwyliadau, ac nid oedd un pelydr o oleuni yn tywynu. Ond pan glywodd am yr ymdrech gwrthgaethiwol gobaith a darddodd i fyny yn ei fynwes, ac ym mynwesau llawer ereill. Mi ddyallais, mi deimlais innau, fod y gwir uwchlaw anwir, fod iawnder uwchlaw camwri, fod egwyddor yn rhagori ar fydol ddoethineb; a than weithrediad heddychol a daionus gwrthgaethiwaeth teimlais y byddwn ryw ddydd yn wr rhydd. (Cymeradwyaeth uchel a pharhaol).

(It has been imagined that the slaves of the South are not aware of the move-ments made on their behalf, and in behalf of human freedom, everywhere throughout the northern and western States. This is not true. They do know it. They knew it from the moment that the spark was first kindled in the land. They know it as soon as you know it, sir, in your own New England . . . Prior to this moment [the Welsh version has 'movement'], sir, the slave in chains had no hope of deliverance – no hope of any peace or happiness within this vale of tears. Darkness and despair rested gloomily upon his prospect, and not a ray of light was thrown across. But when he heard of this movement, hope sprang in my mind, and in the minds of many more. I knew, I felt, that truth was above error, that right was above wrong, that principle was superior to policy; and under the peaceful and beneficent operation of abolitionism, I felt that I should one day be free. (Loud and protracted applause).])[90]

These words were spoken by Frederick Douglass at the tenth anniversary meeting of the American Anti-Slavery Society held in New York City on 9 May 1843. Douglass recalled that 1843 was a year 'of remarkable antislavery activity', and his 'The Anti-Slavery Movement, the Slave's Only Earthly Hope' was one of that year's keynote speeches.[91] It was first published in the *National Anti-Slavery Standard* on 18 May and in William Lloyd Garrison's *Liberator* a day later.[92] That Douglass's speech had appeared in Welsh within a few weeks of its delivery is a minor but indicative example of a much wider phenomenon. While Douglass was later to draw attention to the differences between America where 'they speak of me in connexion with sheep, horses and cattle', and Britain, where 'the very dogs ... know that I am a man', his eighteen-month visit to the United Kingdom may be seen not only to have provided him with an opportunity to make new contacts with English, Irish, Scottish and Welsh abolitionists, but also to reinforce and develop alliances and associations across ethnic and linguistic lines that had already been forged in multi-ethnic and multilingual America.[93] Indeed, Douglass's own formation as part of an evolving abolitionist movement partly accounts for what Maria Diedrich describes as his interest in 'spreading his political message beyond the English-speaking world'.[94]

The existence of Welsh-language accounts of Douglass's appearances suggests that if the abolitionist movement was transnational in scope, it was multilingual in practice – a fact that has hardly been registered by cultural historians. In discussing recent attempts at re-examining American literature and history in the light of multilingualism, Paul Giles resists 'the assumption sometimes made concomitantly, that the cultures of Britain and the United States should be symbiotically conflated into one hegemonic discourse which languages from other

parts of the globe strive to decenter'.[95] Giles argues that this is too
simplistic for 'the literatures of England (*sic*) and the United States have
enjoyed mutually antagonistic as well as a mutually constitutive relationship'.[96] The more substantial basis for resisting the model of an
Anglo-American 'centre' and marginalized 'peripheral' languages
derives from the fact that the literatures of Britain and the United States
were already multilingual; the English critic need not go to 'other parts
of the globe' to find languages other than English. As I have noted elsewhere, the multilingual turn in American studies aims not to 'deceneter',
but to redefine the centre itself.[97] The translation of Frederick Douglass's
speeches in Welsh journals raises questions relating to the broader
process of translating the texts of the anti-slavery movement: What was
the effect of translating slavery into Welsh? What displacements and
shifts in meaning took place in translating the experience of slavery? Do
these acts of translation suggest that nineteenth-century Wales was
particularly receptive to the abolitionist message, or did translation ultimately unmoor these texts from the pressured contexts and discourses
(of slavery, race and gender) from which they emerged, transforming
them into exotic documents offering insights into the lives of 'dark
skinned men in a faraway land'?[98]


TRANSLATING SLAVERY

Douglass's desire to begin 'denouncing' rather than merely 'narrating'
wrongs entailed a command of English oratory, and several critics have
drawn attention to the rhetorical strategies that he employed in his
speeches.[99] If Eric Sundquist describes Douglass's *Narrative* as a
'memorised lecture', Robert Stepto believes it to be an 'act of taking
authorial control', and it is by now commonplace to draw attention to the
particular importance that Douglass gives to the acquirement of literacy
in his narratives.[100] It is Mr Auld's warning to his wife when she begins
to teach the young slave to read – 'if you teach that nigger . . . how to
read . . . [h]e would at once become unmanageable, and of no value to
his master' – that offers Douglass an insight into 'what had been to me a
most perplexing difficulty – to wit, the white man's power to enslave the
black man'.[101] In remembering the acquisition of his 'ABCs' Douglass is
not merely invoking the tutelage of his master's wife, but is also enacting
his access to 'the word', linking the ability to read with an ability to
reconceptualize reality and to redefine the self (a redefinition that is

reflected literally in his adopting the name 'Douglass' from Scott's *The Lady of the Lake*).[102] This process of gaining an illegally won literacy is echoed in many slave narratives, both preceding and following the famous examples in Douglass's works.

William A. Andrews regards the *Narrative of the Adventures and Escape of Moses Roper, from American Slavery* (1837) as the text that set the template for future slave narratives.[103] Roper makes an explicit connection between liberation and literacy when describing the acquiring of a forged pass, a document that he hopes will enable him to escape from North Carolina:

> [H]aving heard several freed coloured men read theirs [free passes], I thought I could tell the lad what to write. The lad sat down and wrote what I told him, nearly filling a large sheet of paper for the passport, and another sheet with recommendations.[104]

Helen Thomas reads this scene as indicating that 'the written word functioned metaphorically as the slave's passport to freedom', and that the slave's 'literary' entrance 'into the dominant order was . . . dependent upon his/her appropriation of the established linguistic order'.[105] This kind of argument is common in accounts of slave narratives, but if we read on beyond the passage quoted by Thomas, Roper's scene carries a slightly different meaning:

> Going along I took my papers out of my pocket, and looking at them, although I could not read a word, I perceived that the boy's writing was very unlike other writing that I had seen, and was greatly blotted besides; consequently I was afraid that these documents would not answer my purpose, and began to consider what other plans I could pursue to obtain another pass.[106]

Rather than illustrating the connection between liberty and literacy, Roper is in fact revealing the dangers of limited or incomplete literacy, and is drawing attention to the arbitrary nature of the sign, the uneasy relationship between the spoken ('what I told him') and the written ('the boy's writing'). The 'boy' is clearly more literate than the 'slave', but the slave is shrewd enough to know that 'the boy's writing was very unlike other writing that I had seen'. While Henry Louis Gates's argument that literacy 'stood as the ultimate parameter by which to measure the humanity of authors struggling to define an African self in Western letters' has been widely accepted, Roper's inaccurately forged passport may usefully lead us to consider what we mean by 'literacy' in this context.[107]

Roper toured Britain in the late 1830s, promoting the sale of his *Narrative of the Adventures and Escape of Moses Roper, from American*

*Slavery* (1837), and reported that he had 'addressed meetings in upwards of two thousand towns and villages' including many 'remote places' where many 'did not know there was such a curse as slavery in America'.[108] Roper's tour reflected a shift in the abolitionist movement following the votes to abolish the Atlantic slave trade in 1807, and to outlaw non-indigenous slavery in the British Empire in 1833. By the late 1830s the abolitionist battleground had shifted to the United States where it was becoming increasingly clear that the South would resist liberalization and would seek to preserve the 'peculiar institution' of slavery. The sphere of publication was affected by this development with an increasing number of abolitionist periodicals emerging in American cities from the 1820s onwards, and an increasing market for the autobiographical testimonies of African American slaves. Published in London in 1837, Roper's narrative crossed the Atlantic a year later and crossed the language barrier into Welsh in 1841.[109] In the introduction to the 1841 Welsh translation of the *Narrative* Roper notes that

> Yr wyf yn wybodus fod yr hanes ganlynol yn fwy cyffrous nag a feddyliodd y Cymro gael, gan fod y rhan fwyaf yn hollol anwybodus o gaethiwed yn America – GWLAD RHYDDID!


> [I am aware that the following narrative is more eventful than the Welshman might expect, as the majority are wholly ignorant of slavery in America – THE LAND OF THE FREE!][110]

The widely observed didactic impulse informing the writing of slave narratives is here made explicit, as Roper seeks to rectify Welsh ignorance of the slave trade. By 1844 Roper was claiming that 25,000 English-language copies and 5,000 Welsh-language copies of his narratives had been purchased.[111] If Roper's *Narrative* set the template for future slave narratives, his travels throughout Britain could also be seen to have formed a template for future abolitionist speakers. The 1848 English-language reprint of the *Narrative* included an appendix listing the churches and chapels in which he had lectured in Britain. All Welsh counties are represented, and the range of places visited is staggering from Nefyn in the north-west to Caerleon in the south-east. Some congregations in Wales are defined linguistically, such as in Rhymney where it is listed that Roper spoke at 'Rymney, Eng.' and 'Rymney, Welsh', and many of the audiences at Roper's talks would have been made up of monolingual Welsh speakers.[112] Indeed, given that the number of Welsh speakers remained consistently around 67 per cent between 1841 and 1871, this would have been the case for the majority of anti-slavery meetings that took place in Wales in the mid-nineteenth century.[113] When 'preaching three times' on a 'Sabbath at Bangor, north Wales' in 1854, Samuel Ringgold Ward was surprised to encounter

> audiences of whom some could not understand sufficient English to follow a discourse. They came, however, because they wished to encourage the cause I represented, and to show their interest in the gospel, though preached in a language of which they could understand but few words. In one instance, however, there was a sermon in Welsh from one of the native ministers. This gave those who could not understand me an opportunity to receive benefit in their own tongue.[114]

The 'native minister' would probably have offered a synopsis of what the African American abolitionist had said, and then used the slave's experience as a basis for the ensuing sermon. Ward used his experiences in Wales to argue that in order for the 'brave little Principality' that he so admired to be 'more visited and considered' its people needed to 'cling with less tenacity to their mother tongue'.[115]

In this respect Ward was reflecting the views of many of the leaders of Welsh opinion in the years following the publication of the education commissioners' Blue Books. If (as noted earlier) the practices of religious Nonconformity were seen to be one of the sources for Welsh 'immoralities' in the Blue Books, the continuing use of the Welsh language was another. Indeed, William Williams's call in 1846 for the setting up of an enquiry into the state of education in Wales was motivated by his belief that the Welsh language was proving a hindrance to the development of his native country. English was 'the only road to knowledge' and 'the road to improvement and civilisation', he noted reiterating a view that was repeated in Welsh and English periodicals throughout the nineteenth century.[116] The teaching of English would ensure 'a knowledge of the arts and comforts of civilised life among the poor Welshmen, which while it improves the face of their beautiful country, will make them a more happy, a less servile – a superior people'.[117] A case for making the Welsh a happier and less servile people was unlikely to carry much weight in the House of Commons and Williams also emphasized the social cohesion that would result from the wider dissemination of English:

> If the [Welsh] people had been acquainted with the English language, had had proper instruction provided, instead of being, as they now are, a prey to designing hypocrites with religion on their lips and wickedness in their hearts

. . . they [the Welsh] would be at this moment . . . the happiest as well as the most peaceful and prosperous population in the world.[118]

The three Anglican, English, monolingual young barristers who prepared the bulky Blue Books reinforced these views in their reports, and drew on appropriate evidence to buttress their prejudices. They quoted the barrister E. C. Hall, for instance, who argued not only that ignorance of English was 'a decided drawback in a Court of justice', but also that there were fundamental defects in the Welsh language itself:

> Their [the Welsh people's] mode of numeration produces great errors; they have almost to do an Addition sum in their heads before they can express some numbers. The Welsh language is peculiarly evasive, which originates from its having been the language of slavery.[119]

While historians and cultural critics have explored the paradoxical response to the Blue Books, what I wish to note here is the way in which language was perceived to be a barrier to social advancement. If literacy for the ex-slave 'stood as the ultimate parameter by which to measure the humanity of authors struggling to define an African self in Western letters', to be literate in Welsh did not offer an entrance into Western letters as the language was perceived increasingly to be inferior and outmoded.[120] The use of a discourse of slavery and incarceration is in evidence in the descriptions of linguistic difference in the Blue Books: Welsh is the language of a 'servile' people, it is the 'language of slavery' keeping the Welshman in an 'underworld of his own'.[121]

The status of the translated slave narrative assumes a rather ambiguous position within this linguistic context. On the one hand, the very act of translation gives the language of the translated text (Welsh, in this instance) a certain prestige, and, indeed, a remarkable amount of translation into Welsh took place in the nineteenth century.[122] While the effect of reading Moses Roper's slave narrative in any language is to witness the slave's development from illiteracy to a mastery of language, 'literacy' in the translated Welsh text is experienced by the reader as literacy in Welsh. Indeed, the frontispiece makes no reference to the fact that the text is a translation, the translator is never named nor referred to, and in referring specifically to 'y Cymro' ('the Welshman) in his introduction Roper gives the impression that the book has been composed in Welsh with a Welsh audience in mind.[123] Welsh is thus the language of 'literacy' in the translated text, if not in reality. Just as the English-language slave narratives were designed to appeal to a white, literate audience, the Welsh narrative assumes a Welsh reader who, when reading the narrative in translation, shares the privileged position of the white English-speaking reader. On the other hand, the slave narrator's struggle to gain literacy in English may have been seen to mirror the Welsh reader's own attempts at gaining literacy in English. If the translated text placed the Welsh speaker in the privileged position of the reader on whom the slave is pleading for sympathy, is it not also possible that Welsh readers of Roper's narrative may have empathized with aspects of the slave's experience, especially his depictions of the debilitating effects of a limited literacy in the increasingly dominant English language?[124]

The question of how the reader is positioned, of whether she is meant to adopt a position of distanced sympathy or engaged empathy, is raised by the four Welsh translations of *Uncle Tom's Cabin* that appeared between 1852 and 1854.[125] The problem for any Welsh translator of *Uncle Tom's Cabin* was that it might be read as exotic entertainment. Hugh Williams's translation *Caban F'Ewyrth Twm* is the most accurate of the Welsh translations, and he makes little attempt to alter the text for a Welsh audience. Florine Thayer McCray, an early biographer, described the range of translations in Harriet Beecher Stowe's possession, drawing attention to Hugh Williams's Welsh translation with illustrations by George Cruikshank, and expressing surprise at another translation 'from Abertawy, India, in the provincial dialect'.[126] The translation from 'Abertawy' did not come from India, for 'Abertawy' was a common nineteenth-century form of Abertawe (Swansea in English), and it is interesting that Thomas Levi's *Caban Newyrth Tom* (published, according to the frontispiece, by 'Rosser of Abertawy') does indeed rely considerably on the use of dialect registers, conveying the language of Tom and Topsy in a pidgin-Welsh that may have been drawn from the dialects used in the increasingly industrial villages of the Swansea valley. Levi – who was born near Ystradgynlais and worked initially in the local steel works – thus makes an implicit connection between the slave in America and the industrial worker in Wales.[127] A more striking attempt to make Stowe's novel speak directly to a Welsh-speaking audience occurs in Robert Everett's first version, serialized from January 1853 in *Y Cenhadwr Americanaidd*. Everett used the translation that had appeared in the Liverpool based Welsh newspaper *Yr Amserau* as a basis for his version, but changed the title from *Caban F'Ewyrth Twm* to *Bwthyn F'Ewythr Tom*. Melinda Gray suggests that *bwthyn* (cottage) must have seemed to Everett 'a more accurate translation for the humble dwelling where Uncle Tom resides at the beginning of Stowe's novel'.[128] There were likely to have been reasons other than accuracy in Everett's amendment, for *bwthyn* was to become one of the keywords in the making of the *gwerin* (folk) – the myth of a morally upright, honest, Welsh-speaking and God-fearing Nonconformist people. The *bwthyn* was the idealized dwelling of the *gwerin*, the sacred space in which the assumed characteristics of the Welsh – particularly their religion and the language – were preserved and transmitted. 'Y Bwthyn Bach To Gwellt' (The Little Thatched-Roofed Cottage) became one of the most popular folk songs of the nineteenth century, and spoke particularly to the nostalgic yearnings of the increasing numbers of Welshmen and women who had left their rural areas to find work in English cities or in the rapidly industrializing valleys of south Wales. E. G. Millward notes that in the industrial valleys of the south-east, and in the majestic chapels of Liverpool, Birmingham and London, it was a balm to the soul to hear nostalgic songs celebrating the values and traditions of the fields and hills that had been left behind in the search for material wealth.[129] This would also be true of the chapels and streets of Utica, Milwaukee and New York. By the time the man of letters O. M. Edwards and the poet Crwys nostalgically celebrated the values of 'Gwerin Cymru', the Welsh *bwthyn* of the humble peasant was seen to have outlasted the ruined Norman castles, just as the humble meeting house had triumphed over the ruined papist priory.[130] In Stowe's novel the values and aspirations of the slaves in their cabins are seen as superior to the hypocrisy and cruelty of the slave owners in their mansions, and to make Uncle Tom's 'Cabin' a 'Bwthyn' was to suggest a possible (if questionable) correspondence between the experiences of African American slaves and those of the Welsh *gwerin*.[131]

While the translations by Hugh Williams, Thomas Levi and Robert Everett remain fairly faithful to Stowe's original novel, *Aelwyd F'Ewythr Robert* (Uncle Robert's Hearth), the version by William Rees (popularly known as Gwilym Hiraethog) is a more ambitious experiment in which the original American novel is placed in a charged relationship to the experiences and stories of a group of Welsh peasants. *Aelwyd F'Ewythr Robert* is a record of a series of readings of Stowe's *Uncle Tom's Cabin* at a farmhouse, 'Hafod y Ceiliogwydd' (Gander Farmhouse), and the narrative moves back and forth from Stowe's novel to discussions amongst the Welsh listeners. In noting that Hiraethog's novel appeared at a time when prose fiction was beginning to establish itself in the Welsh language, E. G. Millward suggests that *Aelwyd F'Ewythr Robert* was a crucial text in the development of the Welsh novel in the nineteenth century.[132] The context of its appearance is apparent in the novel's structure. Ioan Williams, who has usefully traced the ways in which Hiraethog amended and reorganized Stowe's novel in the retelling of it, suggests that much of the novel's substance arises from the characters' consciousness of 'the complex process in which they are involved', and much of the interest of the novel from a contemporary perspective derives from the suggested relationships between its narrative levels.[133] *Uncle Tom's Cabin*, the most successful novel of its time, is read to a group of Welsh peasants by one James Harris, the son of a neighbouring family and thus a representative of a new generation, and the evening's events are being recorded by a somewhat mysterious 'man from Liverpool'. Hiraethog's initial attempt at translating Stowe's novel had appeared in the pages of the Liverpool-based paper which he edited, *Yr Amserau*, and his novel is predicated on the assumption that the 'man from Liverpool' has accurately described the events at 'Hafod y Ceiliogwydd'. The novel's structure thus mirrors the process by which a new generation who are literate in English communicate the most successful product of an emergent print culture to a group of monolingual Welsh peasants who still embrace the traditions of an older oral culture. Francis Mulhern describes the essential modernity of the novel in ways that illuminate the shift from the oral peasant culture of the 'tale', to the urban print culture of the 'novel':

> Two general historical conditions detach the novel irrevocably from the world of the tale. The first is institutional, involving a change in the social relations of narration. Storytelling as a form presupposes a basic community of values binding teller and audience: shared intuitions of what is interesting, intelligible, pleasing or repugnant, fitting or not. Indeed, being oral, it depends on the actual co-presence of the two: the moral affinity is confirmed in time and space. Novelistic narrative, in contrast, is mediated as a printed text for the market. Both the physical and the cultural supports of the tale fall away. Writing is temporally prior to reading, which, like writing, is now privatized, and practically variable in a way listening is not. The audience is not only privatized; unknowable to the writer at work, it is also, in principle, unknown in its cultural disposition. Thus, the social relationship that grounds and is fertilized by the tale is cancelled.[134]

In having Stowe's novel read aloud by James Harris, and in offering an account of the Welsh listeners' responses, Hiraethog takes the new novel form and attempts to root it back in the oral culture of the Welsh peasantry. In this respect he is engaging in an attempt at limiting the 'variability' of responses to the novel; a printed text, mediated by the market, also speaks to a 'community' where a set of shared values 'bind teller and audience' together. Hiraethog's text may be read, on the one hand, as an attempt to ground the Welsh novel in the very same social world that fertilized the oral tales of old while, on the other, it could be interpreted as part of the post-Blue Books attempt at uplifting the culture of the Welsh peasantry, making a case for the simultaneous modernity and respectability of both the emergent novel form and the residual oral tradition.[135] The latter reading is supported by the fact that the group of people gathered at 'Hafod y Ceiliogwydd' approximate a Methodist *seiat* – a late night religious meeting which was represented as a source of immorality by the Blue Book commissioners who railed against

> the bad habit of holding meetings at dissenting chapels or farmhouses after night, where the youth of both sexes attend from a distance for the purpose of walking home together . . . The investigation of numerous cases of bastardy I have found most of them to be referred to the opportunities of meeting above mentioned.[136]

Far from being a breeding ground for immorality, the late-night gathering in Hiraethog's novel is a forum for communicating the Calvinist teachings offered by Modryb Elin throughout the novel, and for the dissemination of the tenets of Christian anti-slavery informing Stowe's novel. What is perhaps interesting in this respect is that Hiraethog bases his Welsh adaptation on elements present in Stowe's original text. Wilson J. Moses notes that the thesis of *Uncle Tom's Cabin* was that slavery was an assault on the values of the Victorian 'hearthside', and in naming his novel *Uncle Robert's Hearth* Hiraethog was self-consciously aligning the values of the *seiat* with the ideals informing Stowe's Christian commitment to antislavery.[137] If the values of the Welsh *seiat* seemed to reflect those of the New England hearthside, in naming his central character 'Uncle Robert', Hiraethog also seemed to be constructing a correspondence between the Welsh peasant and the American slave. This correspondence is underlined by the fact that the words of Uncle Robert and Uncle Tom are rendered in a dialect that differs from both the standard Welsh and English used by the narrative voice in *Aelwyd F'Ewythr Robert* and *Uncle Tom's Cabin* respectively, and from the standard Welsh used by James Harris in Hiraethog's text when he introduces his readings to the assembled group.

The most significant moment of correspondence occurs, however, at the death of Stowe's Eva. When St Clare views his daughter for the last time in Stowe's novel, the narrator addresses the reader:

Why was no word spoken between the two? Thou canst say, who hast seen that same expression on the face dearest to thee; – that look indescribable, hopeless, unmistakable, that says to thee that thy beloved is no longer thyne.[138]

The ideal reader of this scene, it would seem, is one who has experienced the loss of a child, a loss that Stowe had experienced herself and one that was common in nineteenth-century America and Britain. Ewythr Robert and Modryb Elin are such readers (or in this case, listeners), for Eva's death leads them to recall the death of their 'Joni bach' (little Johnny) who had died some years before. If this is an explicit connection between the novels of Hiraethog and Stowe, there are also other implicit connections between the read novel and the listeners' experiences during this scene. Before dying Eva calls the slaves to her room in order to give them strands of her hair and reminds them that

'Each one of you can become angels. And be angels forever . . . If you want to be Christians, Jesus will help you. You must pray to him; you must read –
    The child checked herself, looked piteously at them, and said sorrowfully,
    'O, dear! You can't read, – poor souls!' and she hid her face in the pillow and sobbed, while many a smothered sob from those she was addressing, who were kneeling on the floor, aroused her.
    'Never mind,' she said, raising her face and smiling brightly through her tears, 'I have prayed for you; and I know Jesus will help you, even if you can't read. Try all to do the best you can; pray every day; ask Him to help you, and have the Bible read to you whenever you can; and I think I shall see you all in heaven.'[139]

Eva's Christian vision celebrates the unity of man in the face of material disadvantages, and, if the slaves are encouraged to have the Bible read to them, then the Welsh *seiat* in Hiraethog's novel is depicted as a vehicle for the dissemination of religious doctrine and political education to a peasantry of limited English literacy. Eva's death rekindles the memory of little Joni's simple, childish, faith and leads the pagan Uncle Robert to embrace Christianity. His conversion reaches its climax as he notes that he understands little of religious debates but wishes to embrace 'crefydd fel crefydd F'Ewythr Tomos – un iawn oedd honno' ('a religion like Uncle Tom's – that was a fine one').[140] Hiraethog, in creating Ewythr Robert, has constructed an ideal reader for Stowe's novel; one who has experienced the loss of a child and who, by being exposed to *Uncle Tom's Cabin*, experiences a religious conversion and a new Christian appreciation of human unity.[141]

If Little Eva's death offered a means for the fictional Ewythr Robert to understand the loss of his son in religious terms, the scene also

conditioned the responses of the African American minister Samuel
Ringgold Ward to Wales. Ward's *Autobiography* contains a striking
rewriting of the scene from an African American perspective, in which
the author recalls 'an incident of no small interest to me, which occurred
during my sojourn at Aberystwyth':

> A gentleman named Williams, an agent for one of the wealthiest landlords in
> Wales, lives about a mile from Aberystwyth. I learned that a little boy, a son of
> Mr. Williams, who was ill, was anxious to see me, and that his parents wished
> me to call. The Rev. Mr. Davies kindly consented to accompany me, and we
> drove there. We found Mr. and Mrs. Williams most kind and affable persons;
> and upon being introduced to the chamber where their son lay, we were struck
> with his emaciated appearance; but in spite of this, his eyes beamed with intel-
> ligence, and about his lips a most cheerful smile played constantly. His mother
> told us he had been a great sufferer. His bones were but slightly covered with
> a wasted colourless skin. He could not stand or walk, from lameness; and I
> believe there was but one position in which he could lie. When we saw the
> helplessness of the child, we were glad that we had visited him. He had read
> *Uncle Tom's Cabin*; he felt interested in the slaves, and daily prayed for them;
> he had carefully laid by the little presents of money which had been given
> him, and had a donation to give me, for the cause of the slave. But what made
> the deepest impression upon us was, his mother's telling us that, in the midst
> of the very severe pains which tortured the little sufferer, he would cry out, but
> immediately check himself, saying 'Mamma, I ought not to complain so. How
> much more did Jesus suffer, for me!'
>
> We left that house feeling that we had been highly privileged. We had
> learned the lesson of patient suffering at the bedside of that dear child – had
> seen a babe, as it were, praising God. That the child could long live, seemed
> out of the question; but the wheat of the surrounding fields was no more ripe
> for the sickle, than was that child to be gathered unto God. Since that day, I
> never suffer pain, complainingly, without fancying I see the bright, beaming
> eye of little Williams rebuking me, as he hushes his own cries, in the midst of
> anguish, by the recollection of 'how much more Jesus suffered for him.' That
> child may, ere this, have been called to his rest; he may be with Him whose
> sufferings he learned so early to contemplate: but until I meet him in another
> world, I shall ever remember the lesson learned at his bedside. Since that time,
> some of the severest pangs I ever felt have been mine, both in body and mind;
> but their coming is accompanied by the remembrance of what that beloved
> child learned, in agony. And, blessed be God! the divine consolations which
> lulled his pains are abundant, infinite in efficacy![142]

Ward's scene draws on a well of Victorian sentimentality towards children evident in the works of Dickens and Stowe, and was itself a response
to the fact that the death of a child was a relatively common occurrence.
His reference to *Uncle Tom's Cabin* immediately leads the reader back to

Little Eva's bedside. Eva's face in which 'there was diffused over every lineament . . . that high celestial expression' is replaced by the 'bright, beaming eye of little Williams rebuking me', and Eva's desire to give her hair as a gift to her servants is mirrored in little Williams's wish to pass on 'the little presents of money which had been given him'.[143] The key difference here is that, while Stowe's slaves are illiterate, the African American called to Williams's bedside is himself an esteemed minister of religion, able to offer his own account of the tale. If *Uncle Tom's Cabin* offered a vehicle for the Welsh to engage with the question of slavery within a familiar religious context, it also conditioned a sympathetic African American's responses to Wales. It is worth stressing in this connection that while Ioan Williams argues that the treatment of slaves by their owners would resonate with Welsh peasants living under the control of Tory landlords, there is little sense in Hiraethog's *Aelwyd* or in Ward's *Autobiography* that the Welsh and African American experiences are linked by a common sense of oppression.[144] Hiraethog equates Uncle Tom's material incarceration with F'Ewythr Robert's paganism, and Robert's 'emancipation' is spiritual rather than material, as he converts to Christianity having recalled the death of 'Joni bach'. Likewise, it is a commonality of religious feeling that is stressed by Ward who noted that 'Negroes' were 'the most religious people in the world . . . with perhaps the exception of the Welsh'.[145] Yet, as with Stowe's novel and the slave narratives on which it drew, the division between spiritual and social forms of uplift were never clear cut.

*Uncle Tom's Cabin* had a long afterlife in both American and British culture; its characters continued to appear in minstrel shows, and staged versions continued to be performed into the twentieth century. A striking example of this phenomenon in Wales was D. Griffith's 1877 translation of the *Autobiography* of the Reverend Josiah Henson, advertised as 'Hanes Uncle Tom Ganddo Ef ei Hun' (The History of Uncle Tom written by himself) . The first English version of Josiah Henson's narrative was published in 1849 and sold 6,000 copies in three years, and sales were to increase as he became increasingly identified as the 'real' Uncle Tom on whom Stowe had based her story.[146] Partly due to the connection with Stowe, Henson's narrative was popular well after the end of the Civil War with its publishers estimating that one hundred thousand copies of the various versions of his narrative had been sold by the century's end. In addition to Welsh, it was also translated into French, Swedish, Dutch and German.[147] The first edition to specify that Henson was the 'real Uncle Tom' was edited by John Lobb in 1877, and this was the version translated into Welsh. Yuval Taylor notes that after the Civil War the slave narratives

> underwent a fundamental shift in tone. The righteousness and anger of the classic narratives were muted; the plots ended with the narrator adjusting to newfound freedoms, rather than calling for them from exile; and certain aspects of slave life began to seem quaint, in keeping with the imagery of the Sambo tales and minstrel shows then popular . . . [T]he emphasis on freedom in the classic narratives was replaced by a corresponding emphasis on progress.[148]

Henson's narrative supports this analysis. For example, he describes a desire to seek revenge on his master as follows:

> [M]y eyes fell upon Master Amos, who was nearest to me, my hand slid along the axe-handle, I raised it to strike the fatal blow, – when suddenly the thought came to me, 'What! commit *murder!* and you a Christian?' I had not called it murder before, but self-defence, to prevent others from murdering me. I thought it was justifiable, and even praiseworthy. All at once the truth burst upon me that it was a crime. I was going to kill a young man who had done nothing to injure me, but was only obeying the commands of his father. I was about to lose the fruit of all my efforts at self-improvement, the character I had acquired, and the peace of mind that had never deserted me. All this came upon me with a distinctness which almost made me think I heard it whispered in my ear; and I believe I even turned my head to listen. I shrunk back, laid down the axe, and thanked God, as I have done every day since, that I did not commit that murder.[149]

The key here is that he is able to suppress his murderous intentions and 'recover the self-control and serenity' that are crucial for his efforts at 'self-improvement'.

Serenity and docility were also seen by many as the vehicles for 'self-improvement' in Victorian Wales. Writing on the characteristics of the Welsh people in 1840 the Reverend William Jones was keen to emphasize the fact that the social unrest of his period was the result of external influences, noting that the names of the Chartist leaders Vincent and Frost indicated that they were English, and drawing attention to the fact that

> Bu y corff mawr o bobl Cymru yn llonydd, er dyddiau Owain Glyndŵr, er y gorfu arnynt oddef gormesdeyrn chwerw, ac ennill eu cynnaliaeth drwy lafur caled.
>
> [The great body of Welsh people have been docile since the days of Owain Glyndŵr, despite the fact that they suffered a bitter and oppressive overlordship, and that they had to earn their living through hard labour].[150]

At the Aberystwyth Eisteddfod of 1865 the poet Caledfryn celebrated the fact that no one could recall a time when the Welsh rebelled against their just rulers, and in making the case for royal support for the Eisteddfod the Welsh newspaper *Y Cymro* described the Welsh as 'aelodau mwyaf heddychol a theilwng y deyrnas' ['the most peaceable and worthy members of the Kingdom'].[151] Josiah Henson's autobiography returns continuously to the need for temperance and self-control in order to achieve social advancement and the new emphasis on progress, that was characteristic of post-war slave narratives, spoke to the Welsh experience more directly than the earlier emphasis on freedom from bondage. The Welsh translation of Henson's autobiography ends, significantly and appropriately, with an account of his visit to Windsor Castle for a meeting with Queen Victoria. Quoting the *Birmingham Daily Mail*, the account concludes the autobiography as follows:

> Un o'r gweithredoedd ardderchocaf a wnaed gan unrhyw bobl erioed oedd ysgubo ymaith gaeth-drefniant y De; ac nid oedd y tân a'r cleddyf yr oedd yn rhaid i'r diwygwyr fyned drwyddynt yn ddim amgen na threialon cysegredig eu cenhadaeth ardderchog. Y mae yr hybarch Uncle Tom wedi byw i weled cydraddoldeb cenhedloedd, lle, ychydig amser yn ol, nad oedd dynion o'r un lliw ag ef ond eiddo gwerthadwy i'r rhai a'u perchenogent. Cafodd ef, y caethwas ffoedig, fyw i gael ei groesawu gan y Frenhines Victoria, yn ei chastell breiniol ei hun. Y mae chwyrn-gerbyd Amser yn dwyn oddiamgylch ei ddialeddau, ac nid y lleiaf o honynt yw y seremoni raslawn a dyddorol a gyflawnid ddoe yn Windsor.

> The sweeping away of the slave system of the South was one of the noblest works ever achieved by any people; and the fire and sword through which the reformers had to pass were the hallowing trials of their noble mission. The venerable Uncle Tom has lived to see the equality of races where, a little while since, men of his colour were but chattels of their owners. He, the runaway slave, has lived to be entertained by Queen Victoria in her own royal castle. The whirligig of Time does indeed bring about its revenges, and not the least of them is the gracious and interesting ceremony performed at Windsor yesterday.[152]

To be welcomed by Victoria herself represented a fitting climax to an autobiography that traced an individual's progress from slavery to respectability. This narrative trajectory, and its celebratory conclusion, would resonate with Henson's Welsh readers.

If the denigration of Welsh culture in the Blue Books of 1847 set the tone for much English commentary on the Welsh in the nineteenth century, the Welsh responded by seeking to 'resurrect the old country' in terms that countered the slanderous tongues of English commissioners and journalists, while also living up to a British ideal of sobriety, moderation and docility. Similarly, but in a far more unpromising and uncompromising environment where behaviour was literally a matter of life or death, African American spokespersons sought, in Henry Louis Gates's phrase, to 'reconstruct the image of the black' in the face of the 'Sambo' figures popularized in the minstrel shows.[153] In describing the late nineteenth-century context Kevin Gaines argues that, for African Americans, '[t]he exaltation of domestic virtue, symbolized by home, family, chastity and respectability, all infused with an ethic of religious piety, provided the moral criteria for uplift's cultural aesthetic'.[154] If Henson's narrative spoke directly to these values, it also resonated with the Victorian Welsh, described colourfully by Hywel Teifi Edwards as being '[d]riven by utilitarianism' and 'coated in *hwyl*':

> [Wales] clattered towards its place in the imperial sun sounding aloud all the while its belief in the redemptive power of English, its incomparable loyalty to the Crown, its pre-eminent religious fervour, its deep, moral earnestness, its genius for choral singing (strictly oratorio), and its innocent love of home.[155]

The contemporaneous acts of ethnic reconstruction embarked upon by the Welsh and African Americans in the nineteenth century are brought into an uneasy relationship in the Welsh-language translations of slave narratives. Drawing on the success of Uncle Tom, it seems that for both groups Josiah Henson offered a model of individual self-control as the basis for uplifting the race. In attending a meeting of the Welsh Calvinistic Methodist Church in Paddington, London, Henson described his pleasure at hearing one of William Williams Pantycelyn's hymns sung by the congregation 'in their native Welsh', and ends his account with his own act of (mis)translation: 'The fire of devotion and harmony of voice overcame us; and "Uncle Tom" will not forget this "happy opportunity", or, to speak in Welsh, "*hwyl*".'[156]


## NATIONALISM, ASSIMILATION AND 'MISCEGENATION'

Contemporary theorists have emphasized the ways in which the act of translation, especially between languages of unequal power, is inherently unpredictable and may contribute simultaneously to a levelling of differences, and to a rejuvenation of local cultures.[157] The translations that I have been discussing can be seen both as vehicles for bringing the Welsh into the transatlantic antislavery movement and as catalysts for the development of new forms in Welsh literary culture. If translations could offer a source of variety and enrichment for a local culture, they could also begin to undermine its existence by opening that culture to the rest of the world. These tensions between the global and the local, the universal and particular, reflected in the juxtaposition of print and oral cultures in Gwilym Hiraethog's creative adaptation of *Uncle Tom's Cabin*, reflected broader tensions in the political situation of the Welsh in the nineteenth century; a stateless people increasingly anxious to be regarded as valued members of the British nation-state, while also seeking to retain a sense of cultural difference in the face of Britain's industrial and geographical expansion. Historians of a nationalist bent have been somewhat perplexed by the fact that Wales did not develop a robust political nationalism in the latter decades of the nineteenth century, especially given that in any consideration of the first step towards nationalism – scholarly activity – the Welsh were ahead of many of Engels's 'non-historic' European nations which would ultimately achieve independent statehood.[158] While some have explained this failure by placing considerable emphasis on the cultural 'inferiority complex' resulting from the Blue Books and its aftermath, others emphasize the lack of educational provision in Wales leading to a situation in which the Welsh 'borrowed their intellectual values from the middle-class Nonconformists of the large towns of England, people who laid great stress on the rights of individuals, but who had scant regard for the natural rights of communities'.[159] To compare the Welsh experience with that of African Americans is to open up other possible explanations relating to the kinds of minority nationalisms engendered in states that as their names – the 'United Kingdom' and the 'United States' – suggest, were themselves not 'unitary' in any straightforward sense. The tension between the multifarious 'many' and the unitary 'one people' has, of course, been a constituent feature of American political history, and in the case of Britain it may be something of a misnomer to describe as 'unitary' a state that was home to at least four distinct languages, three different legal systems (Scotland, Ireland, 'England and Wales') and, following an incessant series of religious struggles throughout the second half of the nineteenth century, came to contain three different 'national' churches within its boundaries.[160] If the creation of the United States was predicated on the annihilation of the indigenous peoples, the continuous waves of immigrants throughout the nineteenth century and the emancipation of African Americans in 1865 meant that the state would define itself primarily in civic and political rather than ethnic and cultural terms.[161] The civic dimension of nationhood was also significant in bringing the ethnicities of the Scots, Irish, Welsh and English under the umbrella of the United Kingdom of Great Britain and Ireland. The 'civic' definition of a nation-state encompassing many people is always, however, in danger of slipping into a cultural definition in which ethnic diversity is eradicated in a process of increasing monoculturalism.[162] Despite the myriad differences of history and formation, both African American and Welsh cultural critics and historians tend to contrast the nationalism that was forged by 'literary men' in the nineteenth century in an effort to preserve the perceived distinctiveness of a people and their culture, with an assimilationism that welcomed the eradication of a provincial culture as a means of entering the dominant narrative of Western 'progress'.[163] While individual thinkers would often incorporate both strains of thought within their writings, the distinction has some validity and helps to illuminate the ways in which the Welsh and African Americans adopted comparable strategies in attempting to carve out viable futures within the expanding British and American nation states of which they were a part.

The majority of the Welsh (with some notable exceptions to whom I shall return) embraced a broadly assimilationist position, expressed in typically forthright terms by the *Cardiff and Merthyr Guardian* in 1866:

> The greater must absorb the less – the weakest must go to the wall, and the prevalence of English is only a question of time to which the Eisteddfodau pose no real obstacle . . . Welsh is dying out – 'let it die' – do not attempt to crush it, which might produce a reaction to be deplored; but let it go out by a gradual process, befitting a venerable and honoured tongue.[164]

While the Welsh language is 'venerable and honoured', its demise is inevitable. The evidence amassed by Hywel Teifi Edwards and D. Tecwyn Lloyd suggests that this argument was being widely advanced both by the Welsh themselves and by those English journalists who ventured into 'the Principality'.[165] It received its most eloquent and influential expression, however, in Matthew Arnold's infamous lectures *On the Study of Celtic Literature*:

> I must say I quite share the opinion of my brother Saxons as to the practical inconvenience of perpetuating the speaking of Welsh . . . Cornwall is the better for adopting English, for becoming more thoroughly one with the rest of the country. The fusion of all the inhabitants of these islands into one

homogeneous, English-speaking whole, the breaking down of barriers between us, the swallowing up of separate provincial nationalities, is a consummation to which the natural course of things irresistibly tends; it is a necessity of what is called modern civilisation, and modern civilisation is a real, legitimate force; the change must come, and its accomplishment is a mere affair of time. The sooner the Welsh language disappears as an instrument of the practical, political, social life of Wales, the better; the better for England, the better for Wales itself.[166]

If Arnold has become associated with those Victorian social critics who evoked 'culture' as an alternative source of values to industrial society, here he deems 'modern civilisation' to be a 'real, legitimate force' and the source of welcome changes in society. Culture is not opposed to modern civilization, for the latter creates the context for the dissemination of the former. Arnold, as Her Majesty's Inspector for schools in Wales, was in a position to realize his vision. While his conception of a common British culture was democratic in the sense that he sought to construct a shareable, accessible, common culture rooted in the 'best knowledge and thought of the time', that culture was ultimately based on the belief that society's 'best knowledge' could only be disseminated through the medium of English.[167] Such ideas were broadly welcomed in Wales, where they were already a part of religious and national thought. If Arnold was willing to invite the Celts into the world of 'Culture', the Welsh themselves were inclined to connect their ethnic particularism to a salvationist religion in which the disappearance of a minority culture was an acceptable price to pay in realizing Jesus's vision of the world's people 'all as one' under God. The minister and leading liberal Samuel Roberts was a powerful advocate of such a vision. In an essay written in Tennessee during the Civil War, Roberts advocated the 'mixing of lineages' and argued for the eradication of national differences in the making of an universal Christian culture:

Ni byddai ond ofer i mi ddweyd o hyd 'Cymru fydd,' neu 'Cymro for ever;' oblegyd nid dyna ydyw trefn fawr Rhagluniaeth: ac yn wir, nid yw yr hyn sydd ddyngarol a Christnogol ynwyf am i'r Cymry fod yn Gymry dros byth, nac am i'r Iuddewon fod yn Iuddewon dros byth, nac am i'r Ellmyn fod yn Ellmyn dros byth, nac am i'r Gwyddelod fod yn Wyddelod dros byth, nac am i'r Indiaid fod yn Indiaid dros byth, nac am i'r Negroaid fod yn Negroaid dros byth: ond yr wyf am iddynt gael eu toddi gan wres dwyfol gariad i ffurf fawr ogoneddus yr efengyl, fel y byddont 'oll yn un;' ac yr wyf am iddynt gael eu galw nid ar unrhyw enw cenedlaethol, ond yn hil Adda, neu blant Noah, neu y teulu dynol, neu breswylwyr y ddaear, neu bobl y byd, neu ryw enw cyffredinol i arwyddo eu hunoliaeth, eu bod yn bobl o'r un dechreuad, o'r un

gwreiddyn, o'r un gwaed, o'r un gyfansoddiad, o'r un cyflwr syrthiedig, o'r
un gobaith am iachawdwriaeth, o'r un cyfrifoldeb, ac o'r un anfarwoldeb.

(It would merely be futile for me to declare 'Wales will be' or 'the Welshman
for ever', for that is not the way of Providence; and indeed, that which is
humanitarian and Christian in me does not wish the Welsh to be Welsh for
ever, nor for the Jews to be Jews for ever, nor the Germans to be German
for ever, nor for the Irish to be Irish for ever, nor for the Indians to be Indian
for ever, nor for the Negroes to be Negro for ever; for I wish them to be melted
by the warmth of divine love into the glorious form of the Gospel, so that
they become 'all as one'; and I do not wish for them to be referred to by
some national name, but as the stock of Adam, or the children of Noah, or
the human family, or inhabitants of the world, or the world's people, or some
other general term signifying their oneness, that they are a people deriving
from the same beginnings, from the same root, of the same blood, of the same
constitution, sharing the same fallen state, and the same hope for salvation, the
same responsibility, and the same immortality.)[168]

Thus part of the reason that Arnold's contributionism – where a minority
culture is invited to participate more fully in the development of the
dominant nation – received a warm reception in Wales was that it offered
a secularized form of ideas that were already a part of Welsh cultural
discourse.

Similarly, in discussing the 'roots of African American popular
history', Wilson J. Moses has demonstrated that many black men of
letters embraced an idea of culture that was essentially Arnoldian, based
on the belief that 'the world required only one universal definition of
culture, and that was represented by the arts, sciences and progressive
morality of the Victorian bourgeoisie'.[169] This is reflected in African
American responses to Wales. As I noted earlier, Samuel Ringgold Ward
felt that the Welsh should 'cling with less tenacity to their mother tongue'
if they wanted to be 'more often visited and considered', and Frederick
Douglass had no qualms in encouraging a Boston audience in 1869 to

Look at England, whose mighty power is now felt, and for centuries has been
felt, all around the world. It is worthy of a special remark, that precisely those
parts of that proud Island which have received the largest and most diversified
populations, are today the parts most distinguished for industry, enterprise,
invention, and general enlightenment. In Wales, and in the Highlands of
Scotland the boast is made of their pure blood, and that they were never
conquered, but no man can contemplate them without wishing they had been
conquered. They are far in the rear of every other part of the English realm in
all the comforts and conveniences of life, as well as in mental and physical

development. Neither law nor learning descends to us from the mountains of Wales or from the Highlands of Scotland. The ancient Briton, whom Julius Caesar would not have as a slave, is not to be compared with the round, burly, amplitudinous Englishman in many of his qualities of desirable manhood.[170]

Douglass describes the Britons as a people who are not even fit to be slaves, and offers a powerful case for ethnic 'amalgamation' as the basis for realizing a fully 'masculine' ideal. In the American context, in which race was omnipresent and determinative, Douglass sought a raceless, composite American nationality. 'There is but one destiny, it seems to me, left for us', he noted in 1883, 'and that is to make ourselves and be made by others a part of the American people in every sense of the word'. He concluded that 'assimilation and not isolation is our true policy and our natural destiny. Unification for us is life; separation is death.'[171] In an 1854 attack on the pseudoscientific claims for racial inferiority, Douglass claimed that America was so 'distinguished for industry and enterprise' due to its 'composite character'.[172] Whereas Garrison and Phillips introduced Douglass's 1845 *Narrative* of 1845 as the authentic voice of the slave, his second autobiography *My Bondage and My Freedom* (1855) was introduced by the African American scholar James M'Cune Smith who argued that Douglass's 'versatility and talent' was the result 'of the grafting of Anglo-Saxon on good, original, negro stock'.[173] Assimilation seemed in practice to involve the espousal of a common Americanness at the expense of African American distinctiveness. As the 'representative colored man of the United States', Douglass became a symbolic embodiment of black elevation in the years following the Civil War, accepting such positions as assistant secretary to the commission of inquiry to Santo Domingo (1871) and president of the ill-fated Freedmen's Bank (1874).[174] In the case of Santo Domingo he argued for a humane and enlightened imperialism arguing that 'a large majority of the people of the island' supported annexation. 'They want Saxon and Protestant civilization', he argued unambiguously in a speech of 1873, calling on his audience to 'lift them up to our high standard of nationality'.[175] Nationality thus transcended race, but the dominant, absorbing element within that allegedly raceless national culture was – as it was for many others in Victorian society – 'Saxon and Protestant civilization'.[176] The demotion of African American specificities was a price worth paying, for in Douglass's experience the case for a plurality of cultures reinforced the southern planters' belief that there was a hierarchy of peoples which legitimated the relegation of Africans to the bottom of the social ladder. For Douglass 'states' rights' were inseparable from attempts at continuing the racialist practices of the American South.[177]

Douglass has come to be regarded as 'the nineteenth century's most effective publicist for the doctrines of social equality and racial assimilation', and is thus generally contrasted with those, such as Martin Delany, who espoused a separatist nationalism.[178] Delany, who helped Douglass found *The North Star* in 1847, was a powerful advocate for black emigrationism, and consistently sought to compare the situation of Blacks in America with the minorities of Europe:

> That there have in all ages, in almost every nation, existed a nation within a nation – a people who although forming a part and parcel of the population, yet were from force of circumstances, known by the peculiar position they occupied, forming in fact, by deprivation of political equality with others, no part, and if any, but a restricted part of the body politics of such nations, is also true. Such then are the Poles in Russia, the Hungarians in Austria, the Scotch, Irish and Welsh in the United Kingdom, and such also are the Jews scattered throughout not only the length and breadth of Europe but almost the habitable globe, maintaining their national characteristics, and looking forward in high hopes of seeing the day when they may return to their former national position of self-government and independence let that be in whatever part of the habitable world it may . . . Such then is the condition of various classes in Europe; yes, nations, for centuries within nations, even without the hope of redemption among those who oppress them. And however unfavourable their condition, there is none more so than that of the coloured people of the United States.[179]

While Wales, for Douglass, was presented as a backwater in desperate need of an infusion of English civilization, Delany places the Welsh in a litany of 'nations . . . within nations' who yearn for 'redemption'. Delany was fully aware that a political nationalism was developing among other nationalities and diasporic peoples in Europe whose languages and cultures were not recognized by the states of which they formed a part, and regretted that African Americans were not engaged in the kind of political nationalist movements that were developing in parts of eastern Europe. In the African American context, the political nationalism of Delany would remain subordinate to the assimilationist rhetoric of Frederick Douglass. This pattern was mirrored in Wales.

If Samuel Roberts espoused an assimilationism that was similar to that embraced by Frederick Douglass, the Welsh equivalent to Martin Delany was Michael D. Jones whose nationalism developed in reaction to his witnessing the increasing assimilation of Welsh-American communities during his period as a minister of a Welsh church in Cincinnati from 1848 to 1850. In a letter to the Welsh-American journal *Y Cenhadwr*

*Americanaidd* in 1848 he advocated the creation of a Welsh colony that would take its place in a community of nations:

> Ai nid yw ein hiaith, ein harferion, ein crefydd a'n moesau fel cenedl yn werth eu cadw i fyny? Ac onid yw hanes ein cenedl yr ochr hon i'r Werydd yn gystal a'r ochr draw yn profi fod colli ein iaith yn golli y tri eraill i raddau yn agos ymhob amgylchiad, ac yn llwyr felly lawer tro? Ond beth ydym yn gael gan Saeson yn gyfnewid am ein iaith, ein harferion, ein moesau a'n crefydd? A ydym yn cael gwybodaeth a gwareiddiad? . . . Darllener hanes ein cenedl gan y Saeson a bradwyr llwgrwobrwyedig yn y Llyfrau Gleision, a gwaed pa Gymro all ddal heb ymferwi? . . . Er mwyn ein cysur a'n llwyddiant a'n defnyddioldeb, byddwn o un meddwl am Wisconsin fel lle a allo ymfudo i fyned yno.

> (Is it not worth us preserving our language, our customs, our religion and values as a nation? And does not the history of our nation on this side of the Atlantic, as well as on the other side, prove that to lose our language is also to lose the other three to some extent in most cases, and completely in many instances. And what do we get from the English in exchange for our language, our customs, our values and our religion? Do we gain knowledge and civilization? . . . Is there a Welshman whose blood does not boil upon reading the history of our nation as written by the English and the bribed traitors in the Blue Books? . . . For our solace, success and usefulness, let us decide as one on Wisconsin as the place to which those who can emigrate should go.)[180]

The only literature other than the Bible mentioned in Jones's letter is the Blue Books, a further testament to the fact that modern Welsh political nationalism formed in response to the English commissoners' views on Wales.[181] In witnessing the erosion of Welsh communities in the United States, Jones believed that he was being given a glimpse of the future in Wales itself. If Wisconsin offered the most promising environment for emigration in 1848, he had turned his attention to South America by the late 1850s, a shift that led to the creation of 'Y Wladfa Gymreig' (The Welsh Colony) in Patagonia in 1865. Martin Delany had similarly considered black colonization of Nicaragua before turning his attention to locations in Africa. For both Jones and Delany actual geographical location was less significant than the new form of citizenship that could arise from the creation of an autonomous state. Theirs was the voice of an emergent minority nationalism that argued for political structures that would safeguard and give voice to distinctive cultures.[182]

If Frederick Douglass's assimilationism is usually contrasted by scholars to the black nationalism of his contemporaries Martin Delany

and Alexander Crummell, Samuel Roberts, along with a generation of
Liberal Nonconformist ministers who are seen to have been willing to
abandon Welsh cultural characteristics, is generally contrasted to the
nationalists Michael D. Jones and Emrys ap Iwan. Wilson J.
Moses usefully notes in the African American context that 'the distinction
between nationalism and assimilation is a false one, since the two ideas
are not mutually exclusive', an insight that may be usefully applied to
nineteenth-century Wales.[183] In the very same essay in which he advocated the eradication of national differences, Samuel Roberts stated his
wish

> i'r Cymry fod yn mysg y rhai blaenaf i astudio a derbyn pob egwyddor ag
> sydd o dueddiad i leihau drygau a gofidiau y byd, ac i liosogi ei oludoedd a'i
> gysuron.

> [that the Welsh should be amongst the most progressive of peoples in studying
> and accepting all ideas leading to a lessening of the world's ills and anxieties,
> and to multiply its riches and its comforts.][184]

He was thus striking a tone of ethnic self-assertion. Indeed, having often
made the case for 'Ardderchawgrwydd yr Iaith Gymraeg' (The
Excellence of the Welsh Language) and having been one of the most
vociferous defenders of the Welsh language and religious culture
following the exposes of the Blue Books, Roberts migrated to eastern
Tennessee in 1857 to attempt to create a Welsh settlement, only to return
to Wales in 1867 following its failure.[185] A similar nationalist strain is
also prevalent in Frederick Douglass's writings as he calls for 'authors
and editors as well as orators' to 'arise in our ranks', 'for it is in these
capacities that the most permanent good can be rendered to our cause . . .
Our race must be vindicated from the embarrassing imputations resulting
from former non-success.'[186] Both Frederick Douglass and Samuel
Roberts, despite the myriad differences in background and experience,
can be seen to share a perspective described by Kevin Gaines as 'the
assimilationist cultural aesthetic of uplift', and by Dale Patterson as
'missionary nationalism'.[187] Missionary nationalism, argues Patterson,
'locates ethnic fulfilment at a climactic moment in world history when a
chosen people's capacity to sacrifice its native culture and renovate itself
ushers in the victory of a global order'.[188] For Samuel Roberts, as – in
more unfavourable conditions – for Douglass, the attempt at identifying
an ethnic group with a wider cultural sphere was a means to 'uplift the
race' from a disdained provincialism to a celebrated universalism.

While it might be tempting to follow contemporary trends in cultural theory in exposing the biases and prejudices embedded in the false 'universalism' embraced by Roberts and Douglass, we should not lose sight of the controversial and challenging aspects of their assimilationist position.[189] Their assimilationism did not represent a supine surrender to the dominant order, for it contained elements that were unpalatable to the majority. This is most evident in their belief in 'miscegenation'. Douglass noted in 1886 that

> Two hundred years ago there were two distinct and separate streams of human life running through this country. They stood at opposite extremes of ethnological classification: all black on the one side, all white on the other. Now, between these two extremes, an intermediate race has arisen, which is neither white nor black, neither Caucasian nor Ethiopian, and this intermediate race is constantly increasing.[190]

He proceeded to envisage a future in which the Negro 'will be absorbed, assimilated, and will only appear finally as the Phoenicians now appear . . . in the features of a blended race'.[191] Douglass's second marriage in 1884 to a white woman, Helen Pitts, was no doubt informing the stridency of his views, but his vision of a non-racial America was a consistent element in his thought. He made the case for the equality of 'pure' and 'mixed' races in his essay 'The question of amalgamation' in 1860, for instance, four years before the issue of miscegenation become central to the presidential election of 1864 with the publication of a seventy-page booklet entitled *Miscegenation: The Theory of the Blending of Races, applied to the American White Man and Negro*.[192] On that booklet's first page, the anonymous author attempted to give his work academic credibility by noting that his title, a new word, derived from a combination of the Latin 'miscere', to mix, and 'genus', race or lineage. Packed with very dubious scientific theories, the booklet encouraged its readers

> to embrace our black brother . . . The ideal type-man of the future will blend in himself all that is passionate and emotional in the darker races, all that is imaginative and spiritual in the Asiatic races, and all that is intellectual and perceptive in the white races.[193]

The booklet was intended as an intervention in the 'war election' of 1864 in which Abraham Lincoln was seeking a second term against a stern challenge from the Democrat George McClellan. The author of *Miscegenation* encouraged 'the leaders of progress to urge miscegentic reform . . . The party of abolition must become the party of Miscegenation. The Republican Party will not perform its whole mission till it throws aloft the standard of miscegenation.'[194] The booklet was sent to the era's leading abolitionists and generated a fierce debate in the national and state newspapers, and in the Congress itself. Indeed, the historian Sidney Kaplan has suggested that 'miscegenation' was one of the key issues of the 1864 election.[195]

The *Miscegenation* pamphlet was welcomed by radical abolitionists. Frederick Douglass's long-time German partner, confidant and friend, Ottilie Assing, wrote a piece responding to the pamphlet for the *Morgenblatt* in January 1864, in which she advocated racial mixing. While criticizing the fact that *Miscegenation* had been published anonymously she was pleased that someone had been brave enough to raise an issue that even the abolitionists she knew were reluctant to discuss.

> Its significance . . . lies in the fact that there is someone today who dares to champion a cause that hitherto has been considered to be the most contemptible, offensive and disgraceful, even immoral idea banished from society. A woman who left her husband with another man has a greater chance of being graciously readmitted into this society than she who marries the most respectable and educated colored man out of love and by respecting all legal formalities.[196]

Similar sentiments were expressed by the Welsh radical minister Samuel Roberts. Writing from the Welsh settlement that he had attempted to establish in Tennessee, he welcomed the publication while lamenting the fact that he had not published his own thoughts on the matter.

> Yr wyf newydd weled cyfeiriad mewn newyddiadur at draethodyn Seisnig a gyhoeddwyd yn ddiweddar yn New York ar 'Gymysgu Achau:' ac yr wyf yn deall fod y llyfryn hwnw yn gwneud argraff dwfn ar feddyliau rhai o ddyngarwyr blaenaf yr oes. Buasai yn dda iawn genyf gael cyfle i weled y llyfryn hwnw. Digon tebyg fod ei awdwr yn gallu rhesymu yn fanylach dros y pwnc nag yr wyf fi wedi allu wneud; ond carwn i'r darllenydd gofio fod fy nhraethawd i wedi cael ei ysgrifenu er ys pum mlynedd, ac y buasai wedi cael ei gyhoeddi er ys tros bedair mlynedd, oni buasai fod genyf sail i ofni y buasai yn enyn teimlad i'm herbyn ag a fuasai yn niweidiol i mi . . . Y mae Sais wedi cael yr anrhydedd yn awr o 'dori y garw' a gwnaf finau fy ngoreu i'w gefnogi yn ei lafur i symud effeithiau galarus rhagfarnau culion y naill genedl yn erbyn y llall, ac i'w derchafu o gulni oer afiach eu sectyddiaeth cenedlaethol i ryddid ac undeb a chariad yr Efengyl.

> (I have just seen a newspaper reference to an English language essay that has recently been published in New York on 'Miscegenation', and I understand that this work is having a profound impression on the minds of our age's

leading humanitarians. I would like to see it. Its author, in all probability, can expound in greater detail on the subject than I have been able to; but I would like the reader to remember that my essay was completed five years ago, and that it would have been published more than three years ago if I did not believe that it would provoke strong reactions that could have caused me harm . . . An Englishman has now had the privilege of breaking new ground, and I will do my best to support him as he endeavours to remove the regrettable effects of the narrow prejudices of one race against the other, and raise them from the unhealthy cold narrowness of their national sectarianism to the freedom, and unity and love of the Gospel.)[197]

Neither Ottilie Assing nor Samuel Roberts realized that the booklet on *Miscegenation* was a hoax. It was not written by radical abolitionists but, rather, by two journalists working for the pro-slavery newspaper, *The New York World*. Their intention was to link abolitionism with miscegenation, thus taking advantage of a widespread fear that freeing the slaves would result in sexual relations across the colour line. The intention was to suggest that all abolitionists were secret promoters of interracial sexual relationships. As Elise Lemire notes, despite its apparent message, the miscegenation pamphlet actually reminded readers of all the most popular reasons voiced in the previous five years that black political equality should not coincide with social equality with whites.[198]

The Civil War had ended and Lincoln had been shot during his second year in office by the time that 'Cymysgiad Achau' appeared in Roberts's controversial volume *Pregethau a Darlithiau*, published by T. J. Griffiths of Utica, New York, in late 1865. Welsh Americans were mourning for the sons and fathers who had been killed in the war, and for their recently deceased president, and Roberts's ideas – on the needlessness of war, on the North's central role in the slave trade, and on the need to compensate Southerners for the loss of their slaves – were unlikely to receive a warm reception in this historical context. Indeed, Roberts became a vilified figure on the pages of Welsh America's leading newspaper *Y Drych* (The Mirror), and as late as 1882 he felt the need to defend himself in book form against the accusation that he was sympathetic to the South and that he was even a slave owner himself. In his *Hunanamddiffyniad yng Ngwyneb y Camddarlunio Fu Arno Drwy Adeg Cynddaredd y Rhyfel Cartrefol yn America* (A Self-defence in the face of the false portrayal made during the unrest of the Civil War in America) (1882) Roberts noted that he had argued passionately for abolition while residing in a Southern state, which was more than could be said for any of the 'giants' of *Y Drych*, and claimed that the primary motivation in writing

'Cymysgiad Achau' was 'i godi y rhai gorthymedig i fod yn gyd-stad a'u gorthrymwyr' (to raise the oppressed to the same level as their oppressors).[199] Roberts's essay is thus informed by his abolitionist zeal. I will quote at length from 'Cymysgiad Achau' in the following discussion as it is a striking example of the ways in which the language of Welsh religious nonconformity could be moulded and adapted to engage with the explosive issue of racial difference.

The first and primary reason that Roberts gives for the mixing of races testifies to the truth of Werner Sollors's observation that 'it was a small step from religion to ethnicity' in nineteenth-century American racial discourse.[200]

Y mae deddf y priodasau anachaidd dan oruchwyliaeth yr Hen Destament yn sail i ymresymu dros gymysgiad achau. Ceir y ddeddf hono, sef deddf y priodasau anghyfreithlawn yn y ddeunawfed benod o Lefiticus, ac y mae ei geiriad yn gryf, yn fanwl, yn ddifrifol. Ei hamcan ydyw gwahardd i rai briodi eu cyfneseifiaid; a'u rhybuddio i wylio yn erbyn pob cydymlosgach teuluaidd: ond y mae yn gadael y ffordd yn gwbl rydd i rai ymbriodi â rhai o'r achau pellach . . Ac y mae yn dysgu yn eglur ac yn bendant fod teuluoedd hen genedloedd tir Canaan, drwy ymgyfathrachu yn llygredig â'u ceraint, neu â'u cyfneseifiaid, wedi ymhalogi ac ymwanychu gymaint, nes oedd y wlad megys yn eu 'chwydu' allan o'r ffordd.


(The law of forbidden marriages under the dispensation of the Old Testament is a foundation for arguing the case for miscegenation. That law, which is the law of illegal marriages, can be found in the eighteenth chapter of Leviticus, and its wording is strong, detailed and earnest. Its intention is to forbid marriage to one's kin; and to warn against familial incest; but it allows total freedom for marriage with distant relations . . . And it teaches us clearly and unambiguously that the families of the old nations of the land of Canaan, by having unclean intercourse with their loved ones or their next of kin, became so polluted and weakened, that the land may be said to have 'vomited' them out.)[201]

Roberts's words suggest that the question of 'miscegenation' was related to the incest taboo.[202] An editorial article of 1864 responded to the *Miscegenation* pamphlet by noting that 'if marriage between a white man and a black woman begetting his children is now recommended as miscegenation, then the same may be asked in relation to incest, or any other abomination which the progressivists have not yet dubbed with a euphemistic name' and in 1880 a law was passed banning miscegenation in Mississippi that stated that marriages between whites and blacks were 'incestuous and void'.[203] Marc Shell goes some way to explaining the correspondences made between miscegenation and incest in late nineteenth-century racial discourse when he suggests that the Christian universalist view that 'All men are brothers' – a view widely held by abolitionists – is not as comforting as it seems, for the figural can lead to one of two literal results: either that any act of sexual intercourse between two human beings is incestuous, or that only those I consider my siblings are human while all others are sub-human.[204] The figural could, of course, prove all too literal in the American South where enforced relationships between white masters and their slaves would be common. Roberts engages with this conflation of miscegenation and incest by arguing that the former is in fact a way of avoiding the latter, an argument that is in keeping with his broader call for mankind to fuse into 'one people'.

Y mae egwyddorion ac ordinhadau, ac addewidion a holl ddylanwadau goruchwyliaeth ogoneddus y Testament Newydd wedi cael eu hamcanu i gydweithio er cael cenedloedd y byd i fod 'oll yn un,' yn un corf, yn un genedl . . . Yr oedd awgrym Iesu ei hun ar hyn yn nodedig o eglur, er fod ei ddis-gyblion ar y cyntaf yn methu ei ddeall. 'A defaid eraill sydd genyf, y rhai nid ynt o'r gorlan hon: y rhai hyny hefyd sydd raid i mi eu cyrchu, a'm llais i a wrandawant; a bydd un gorlan ac un bugail' . . . Dywedai Paul wrth ysgrifennu at y Rhufeiniaid, 'Pwy bynag sydd yn credu ynddo Ef ni chywilyddir: canys nid oes gwahanieth rhwng Iuddew a Groegwr: oblegyd yr un Arglwydd ar bawb sydd oludog i bawb sydd yn galw arno' . . . Wrth ysgrifenu at y Galatiaid, dywedai, 'Nid oes nac Iuddew na Groegwr, nid oes na chaeth na rhydd, nid oes na gwryw na benyw; canys chwi oll un ydych yn Nghrist Iesu'. Ac ardder-chog o rymus ac o gynes yr oedd ei enaid mawr nefol yn ymresymu dros y pwnc pan yr oedd yn ysgrifennu at yr Ephesiaid . . . 'Canys efe yw ein tang-nefedd ni, yr hwn a wnaeth y ddau yn un, ac a ddatododd ganolfur y gwahaniaeth rhyngom ni; ac a ddirymodd drwy ei gnawd ei hun gelyniaeth, sef deddf y gorchmynion mewn ordinhadau, fel y creau y ddau ynddo ei hun yn un dyn newydd, gan wneuthur heddwch . . .' Y mae yn amlwg fod Duw'r heddwch wedi anfon ei anwyl Fab, Tywysog Tangnefedd, i fod yn Gymodwr, neu yn Dangnefeddwr rhwng Iuddewon a chenedloedd, a rhwng y naill genedl â'r llall: a'i fod am ddirymu y gelyniaeth oedd rhyngddynt drwy 'gnawd' neu ymgnawdoliad ei Fab: a bod holl duedd yr efengyl i ddatod canolfur y gwaha-niaeth rhyngddynt; a'u cymodi â'u gilydd 'yn un corff,' drwy eu cymodi â Duw drwy'r groes.

(The principles, laws, prophesies and influences of the glorious dispensation of the New Testament have been designed to work together towards making the world's peoples to be as one, one body, one nation . . . Jesus' words on this are notably clear, although, in the first instance, his disciples did not

understand him. 'And other sheep I have, which are not of this fold: them also
I must bring, and they shall hear my voice; and there shall be one fold, and one
shepherd.' Paul said in writing to the Romans, 'Whosoever believeth in him
shall not be ashamed. For there is no difference between the Jew and the
Greek: for the same Lord over all is rich unto all that call upon him.' In writing
to the Galatians he said 'There is neither Jew nor Greek, there is neither bond
nor free, there is neither male nor female: for ye are all one in Christ Jesus.'
And his heavenly soul was magnificently powerful and warm when reasoning
on this issue in writing to the Ephesians . . . 'For he is our peace, who hath
made both one, and hath broken down the middle wall of partition between us;
Having abolished in his flesh the enmity, even the law of commandments
contained in ordinances; for to make in himself of twain one new man, so
making peace . . .' It is clear that the God of peace sent his dear Son, the Prince
of Peace, to be a reconciler, or a Peacemaker between Jews and Gentiles, and
between the one nation and the other: and that he wishes to annul the enmity
that existed between them through the flesh or being of his Son: and that the
whole intention of the Gospel is to undo the dividing wall of difference
between them; and to come to a reconciliation with each other as 'one body',
through their reconciliation with God through the cross.)[205]

These words are a powerful articulation of the ways in which 'Christ as
the type of ethnic fusion and universalism emerges most clearly in
diverse passages from Paul's letters'.[206] While the idea of a 'melting pot'
of races and ethnicities did not become widespread until the success of
Israel Zangwill's 1905 play of that title, there was a long and complex
intellectual tradition informing that image. Sollors traces how Puritan
traditions of typology came to be applied to American racial issues and
describes the ways in which Jesus Christ became a model of the 'Biblical
new man' – a type who created a unity of the world's diverse peoples.
Paul's letters became crucial documents in making this case, and the
passages included in the quotation above were widely quoted in
nineteenth-century periodicals.[207]

If Roberts makes his argument for miscegenation in biblical terms, in
turning to 'rhai gwrthddadleuon cyffredin a ddygir yn erbyn y drefn gari-
adlawn o gymysgu y cenhedloedd' ('some common counter-arguments
against the beneficent law of miscegenation') he develops his case in
relation to Welsh culture:

Os daw y byd oll i fod yn un pobl, ac felly i fod o'r un iaith, y mae lle i ofni y
bydd i'r hen iaith Gymraeg enwog, ac anwyl, gael ei gosod o'r neilldu. Yr wyf
yn ofni mai felly y bydd: ac os hyny ydyw trefn fawr Rhagluniaeth, nid oes
ond plygu i'w threfn gyda gwylder, ac ymfoddloni heb rwgnach. Buasai yn
dda iawn genyf i'r hen iaith Gymraeg allu ennill y flaenoriaeth, a dyfod yn

iaith gyffredinol. Buasai yn dda genyf allu gweiddi – 'Oes y byd i'r iaith Gymraeg;' a buaswn am gael i ganol ei thrysorau, dduwinyddiaeth iachaf y byd, a Philosophi uchaf y byd, a'r esboniadau llawnaf ar bob gwyddor a phob celfyddyd; a phe buasai rhyw obaith am ei chael i'r blaen, yn iaith gyffredinol, buaswn yn gweithio fy ngoreu dros hyny hyd fy medd. Gwnaethum fy rhan, gyda brodyr anwyl eraill, drwy holl ddyddiau fy mebyd; ond yr wyf yn gorfod ofni y bydd ein llafur yn ofer. Y mae yn deg iawn i ni, ar yr un pryd, gofnodi ein cwyn fod Dysgedigion Lloegr, – dysgedigion ei Senedd-dai a'i Llysoedd, a dysgedigion ei hargraffwasgau a'i hathrofau, naill ai yn ei rhagfarnu, neu o'u hanwybodaeth, wedi esgeuluso a difrio yr hen iaith ystwyth, enwog, gyfoethog Gymraeg, mewn dull hollol annheilwng o'u sefyllfa ac o'u dysg, mewn dull hollol annheilwng o'u cymeriad fel boneddigion ac fel ysgolheigion, a hollol annheilwng o enwogrwydd eu gwlad, ac o yspryd eu hoes. Y mae dysgedigion ac ieithwyr penaf Ffrainc a Germany wedi cyhoeddi y tystiolaeth cryfaf ac anrhydeddusaf am hynafiaeth ac ardderchawgrwydd yr iaith Gymraeg: ac os ydyw i gael ei rhoddi o'r neilldu, caiff huno dan ei choron; ac astudir ei theithi amrywiaethol, a'i nerth darluniadol gan ysgolheigion dyfnaf yr oesau a ddaw.

(If the whole world comes to be one people, and therefore of one language, there is reason to fear that the famous and dear old Welsh language will come to be put aside. I'm afraid that is how things will be; and if that is the Providential order then we must submit to that order with humility, and accept it without complaint. I would very much like the old Welsh language to become dominant, and to become the universal language. I would very much like to shout – 'Long live the Welsh language'; and I would like her treasures to include the world's best theology, the world's highest Philosophy, and the fullest explanation of all the sciences and all the arts; and if there was some hope of her taking the lead as a general language, I would work to achieve this until I die. I have played my part, with other dear brothers, throughout the years of my youth; but I am afraid that our labours have been in vain. At the same time, it is wholly appropriate for us to note our complaint that learned Englishmen – the learned in her Parliaments and Law courts, the learned in her presses and academies, either through prejudice, or through ignorance, have ignored and dismissed the flexible, famous and enriching old language in a way that is wholly unworthy of their status as gentleman and scholars, and completely unjustified when we consider the status of their nation, and the spirit of their age. The leading intellectuals and linguists of France and Germany have published the strongest and most honourable evidence of the antiquity and excellence of the Welsh language: and if she is to be put to one side, may she die under her crown; and may her various characteristics and her illustrative power be studied by the profoundest scholars of the future.)[208]

Here, Roberts strikes the key notes of Patterson's 'missionary nationalism' (discussed earlier).[209] While accepting that the Welsh language
must ultimately wither, and that struggles on its behalf are largely futile
as it will never become the language of science and progress, Roberts, in
an argument that would be repeated by Matthew Arnold three years later,
nevertheless argues that the culture expressed in that language deserves
wider recognition by Englishmen. Unlike Arnold, however, British
imperial values seem to play no part in Roberts's argument, and if the
Victorian Welsh's willingness to jettison their language has been traced
by some to an 'inferiority complex' (a term that is often invoked as a
simplistic explanation for complex motivations) Roberts's words call for
a more nuanced interpretation.[210] It is likely that the failure of Roberts's
attempt to create a Welsh settlement in Tennessee is informing his argument, but his analysis is clearly a part of his wider desire to see racial and
ethnic differences transcended in the making of a common global culture
based on the very American idea of the people as one. In describing
nationalism as 'cul, cenfigenllyd ymffrostgar, cynhengar, rhyfelgar, a
llofruddiog' ('narrow, jealous, boastful, quarrelsome, warmongering and
murderous'), Roberts rejected all attempts at holding on to cultural and
ethnic differences in order to argue for the unity of the human race.[211]

It is here that we encounter the most significant correspondence in the
social thought of Samuel Roberts and Frederick Douglass. In his 1869
plea for a 'Composite Nationality' Douglass argued:

> We shall spread the network of our science and our civilization over all who
> seek shelter, whether from Asia, Africa, or the Isles of the Sea. We shall mould
> them all, each after his kind into Americans; Indian and Celt, negro and Saxon,
> Latin and Teuton, Mongolian and Caucasian, Jew and gentile, all shall here
> bow to the same law, speak the same language, support the same government,
> enjoy the same liberty, vibrate with the same national enthusiasm, and seek
> the same national ends.[212]

Douglass's resistance to notions of ethnic and national difference is
evident in his second autobiography *My Bondage and My Freedom*,
where he depicts the 'Wye' plantation on which he grew up. The plantation, he notes, was 'situated on Wye river – the river receiving its name,
doubtless, from Wales, where the Lloyds originated.'[213] He evokes the
place in Gothic terms, emphasizing the plantation's 'isolation, seclusion,
and self-reliant independence'. Colonel Lloyd's plantation, he notes,
'resembles what the baronial domains were, during the middle ages in
Europe. Grim, cold, and unapproachable by all genial influences from
communities without, *there it stands;* full three hundred years behind the

age, in all that relates to humanity and morals.'[214] Following the fabrica-
tions of early romantics such as Gray and Macpherson and the evocation
of the Gaelic culture of feudal Highland society in Walter Scott (from
whose books, as noted above, Douglass adopted his name) the tendency
to exoticize the Celtic peripheries as the site of Gothic otherness was
well established by the mid-nineteenth century. Douglass evokes the
plantation's and family's Welsh origins in order to reinforce this sense. If
he was later to wish that the Welsh had been conquered in order that they
may join the advance of civilization, Douglass evoked the plantation, in
revealing terms, as a space isolated from wider influences:

> Public opinion seldom differs very widely from public practice. To be a
> restraint upon cruelty and vice, public opinion must emanate from a humane
> and virtuous community. To no such humane and virtuous community is Col.
> Lloyd's plantation exposed. That plantation is a little nation of its own, having
> its own language, its own rules, regulations and customs. The laws and institu-
> tions of the state, apparently touch it nowhere. The troubles arising here, are
> not settled by the civil power of the state. The overseer is generally accuser,
> judge, jury, advocate and executioner. The criminal is always dumb. The over-
> seer attends to all sides of a case.[215]

The plantation is thus remade in Douglass's imagination into an isolated
nation with its 'its own language, its own rules, regulations and customs'.
Paul Gilroy notes perceptively that 'the state's lack of access to the plantation illustrated the plantation's general inaccessibility to the varieties
of modern, secular political reason necessary to its reform'.[216] The logic
of Douglass's argument in relation to the plantation was later to be replicated in his encounters with other nations that he deemed to have been
disablingly isolated – such as Wales and Santo Domingo above – and
informs his argument for a 'composite' nationality. While Douglass's
writings contain elements of cultural nationalism and claims for the
distinctiveness of black culture, his social and cultural philosophy is
primarily integrationist. He rejected African American separatism,
African American colonization whether within or beyond America's
borders, schemes for African repatriation and all forms of social segregation. 'A nation within a nation', he declared, 'is an anomaly'.[217]

If I argued in the previous section that translation, in the realm of
culture, could be viewed as a stepping stone from provincialism to the
riches of universalism for some, while being a means of continually
revivifying a minority culture for others, nationalism could also be
perceived in similarly divergent terms in the realm of politics.
Nationalism, like translation, could be a means of conserving difference,

or could offer a way out of a perceived provincialism to the riches of universalism. What we might call the 'conservationist nationalism' of Michael D. Jones and Martin Delany sought to preserve what they deemed to be valuable in their people's cultures, while the 'contributionist nationalism' of Samuel Roberts and Frederick Douglass saw the characteristics of their peoples as significant ingredients in the making of a human civilization envisioned in universalist terms. The common contrast made between nationalism and assimilationism is too simplistic to account for the positions adopted by Roberts and Douglass. Caught in the 'double bind' that Michael Cronin argues faces the minority writer 'forced to choose between the false universalism of a world culture . . . and the romanticism of the particular', Douglass and Roberts embraced a position that would later be described accurately by W. E. B. Du Bois as 'assimilation through self-assertion'.[218]

## CONCLUSION

Looking towards the ocean on an autumnal evening 'on the North Welsh coast' in 1865, Julia Griffiths noted in a letter to her 'dear friend' Frederick Douglass that nothing reminded her of him 'so much as the sea'.[219] The Welsh coast in 1865 led Griffiths to 'think of the Chesapeake Bay', which she had never seen but which had been evoked memorably by Douglass in his *Narrative* of 1845 as follows:

> Our house stood within a few rods of the Chesapeake Bay, whose broad bosom was ever white with sails from every quarter of the habitable globe. Those beautiful vessels, robed in purest white, so delightful to the eye of freemen, were to me so many shrouded ghosts, to terrify and torment me with thoughts of my wretched condition. I have often, in the deep stillness of a summer's Sabbath, stood all alone upon the lofty banks of that noble bay, and traced, with saddened heart and tearful eye, the countless number of sails moving off to the mighty ocean. The sight of these always affected me powerfully. My thoughts would compel utterance; and there, with no audience but the Almighty, I would pour out my soul's complaint, in my rude way, with an apostrophe to the moving multitude of ships:–

> You are loosed from your moorings, and are free; I am fast in my chains, and am a slave! You move merrily before the gentle gale, and I sadly before the bloody whip! You are freedom's swift-winged angels, that fly round the world; I am confined in bands of iron! O that I were free! O, that I were on one of your gallant decks, and under your protecting wing! Alas! betwixt me and you, the turbid waters roll. Go on, go on. O that I could also go![220]

The sea is a recurrent image in Douglass's writings. He recalled that in his youth the 'shipyard was more to us than to many others. It was our schoolhouse, where we learned to read and count.' If the ocean and its traditions had offered a mode of education for the slave, he was also dressed as a sailor, and equipped with a free black sailor's papers, when he escaped northwards.[221] In his second autobiography *My Bondage and My Freedom* this connection between the sea and freedom culminates in an account of his first visit to Britain. In connecting Douglass with the sea, north Wales with Chesapeake Bay, Julia Griffiths's letter was inadvertently evoking the journey Douglass had himself made more than twenty years earlier. Now, with the Civil War over, he may have recalled that his own visit to north Wales had occurred during a British sojourn which had served a dual purpose. Firstly, it had offered him an escape from America at a time when the publication of his autobiography threatened him with re-enslavement. Secondly, it allowed him to make his voice heard within the transatlantic abolitionist movement. If, as Richard Blackett has argued, the 'thirty years of black involvement in the movement were the foundation and the precedent for black activism in the twentieth century', that involvement also brought African Americans to Wales during a crucial period in the nation's modern history, and laid the basis for future instances of transatlantic exchange.[222]

# 2

# 'In the Wide Margin': Modernism and Ethnic Renaissance in Harlem and Wales

2. Tommy Farr and Joe Louis before their World Championship Fight, New York, 30 August 1937.

'The Schmeling fight against the Englishman Tommy Farr, should be presented as a world championship fight', argued Joseph Goebbels, the Reich minister of public enlightenment and propaganda, in 1937.[1] Tommy Farr, born in Blaenclydach into the large family of an immigrant miner from Cork, was no Englishman, and his fight with Max Schmeling never took place. The American James Braddock had held the world heavyweight boxing title since 1935, and the expectation was that the emerging African American 'brown bomber', Joe Louis, would take it from him. Schmeling frustrated those expectations for, having knocked Louis out in the twelfth round in 1936, he awaited a title shot. Schmeling's links to the Nazis, and the fact that there was more money to be made from Braddock versus Louis, saw the German marginalized. Louis beat Braddock to become world champion in June 1937, and Goebbels spoke the words above as a furious Schmeling – with the backing of Hitler – planned a showdown with Farr that was to be labelled as the 'real world championship'. American fight promoter Mike Jacobs had other ideas, however, and stepped in with a big-money offer to Farr, guaranteeing the Welshman a dream date with Joe Louis in Yankee Stadium, New York, on 30 August 1937.[2]

Having been eclipsed in the annals of sporting history by the far more significant fights with Schmeling in 1936 and 1938, Louis's first defence of his title takes on a symbolic significance in this chapter as it marks a moment when Wales and African America met within the confines of the boxing ring. For a tantalizing moment Welsh and African American communities were gathered, simultaneously, around their radio sets. In

Selwyn Griffith's sequence of poems *Arwyr* ('Heroes') of 1989 the poet recalls being woken as a child to hear the fight 'yn clecian fel cesair / o berfedd y Phillips' ('hitting like hailstones / from the innards of the Phillips').

> Y gwyn a'r du
> yn colbio'i gilydd
> yn Saesneg,
> a'r dyrfa'n genllysg o sŵn.

> [Black and White
> pummelling each other
> in English,
> and the crowd a hailstorm of sound.][3]

Jazz trumpeter Miles Davis recalled, no less poetically, that in the East St Louis of his childhood 'we'd all be crowded around the radio waiting to hear the announcer describe Joe knocking some motherfucker out'.[4] Boxing was rarely merely a sport in African America or in Wales. Lawrence Levine suggests that Joe Louis was 'so important' because he was 'never perceived' as an isolated man but, rather, as a part of an entire network of black culture.[5] In describing his upbringing in Lansing, Michigan, Malcolm X recalled that

> every Negro boy old enough to walk wanted to be the next Brown Bomber . . .
> A negro just can't be whipped by somebody white and return with his head
> held up to the neighborhood, especially in those days, when sports and to a
> lesser extent show business, were the only fields open to Negroes, and when
> the ring was the only place a Negro could whip a white man and not be
> lynched.[6]

Louis was the first African American fighter to be given a shot at the title since the flamboyant and controversial original black heavyweight champion, Jack Johnson, lost to Jess Willard in 1915. Johnson's victories were often followed by race riots, fuelled by white anger at the African American fighter's audacity in openly courting white women, in verbally assaulting his aggressors and in challenging social conventions at every opportunity. No African American challenger was given an opportunity to fight for the world heavyweight championship in the 1920s, and when Louis emerged on the scene his handlers were determined to learn from Johnson's example. Louis was given lessons in table manners and elocution. Whereas Johnson was vocal, Louis was quiet. Where Johnson lived in the public eye, Louis shied from publicity.

Whereas Johnson challenged social conventions, Louis was seen as an embodiment of decency and respectability.[7] Louis was, nevertheless, also celebrated as the creation and embodiment of African America as illustrated in the lyrics of the celebratory blues 'King Joe', written by novelist Richard Wright, and recorded by Count Basie and Paul Robeson in 1940:

> Black-eyed peas asks cornbread what makes you so strong,
> Cornbread says I come from where Joe Louis was born.[8]

If Louis's demure behaviour made him acceptable to the white establishment, the political and cultural changes that had occurred during the years of the 'New Negro Renaissance' of the 1920s and 1930s were also factors in his reception. When Jack Johnson fought a white, notes Gerald Early, 'all whites wanted to see Johnson defeated, but Louis fought Schmeling as the favourite among the whites as well as the blacks. Louis was the American hero, the symbolic integration of the black folk hero with the American popular hero.'[9] Early suggests that the 'New Negro Renaissance' – often referred to by the more geographically limiting term Harlem Renaissance – can be dated in relation to boxing. The renaissance begins when Jack Johnson beats the white hope Jim Jeffries in Nevada in 1910 to become the first black heavyweight champion and ends in 1938 with Louis's victory over Schmeling.

Following Early's lead, we might also date the Welsh Renaissance in relation to boxing. For Dai Smith, Tommy Farr played a symbolic role in depression ravaged Wales:

> If Tommy Farr, battered yet unbowed after fifteen rounds against one of the greatest heavyweights ever, had not lost on points, the Welsh would have had to invent the defeat. By losing, Farr remained, in a symbolic sense, integrated in his community. By surviving with such conspicuous courage he embodied the stricken coalfield . . . They, too, had worked in the mines, skivvied in hotels, walked to London with holes in their shoes, sought work in the trading estates of Slough, and even scrapped in fairground boxing booths.[10]

Reports suggest that Farr continually drew attention to his Welshness, with *Time* magazine reporting his statement after the fight: 'I've got plenty of guts – that's old Tommy Farr, you know. I'm a Welshman.'[11] He recalls in his autobiography *Thus Farr* that his trainer Joby Churchill – 'a little Welsh-speaking man straight from the mountain' – would yell instructions in Welsh so that the opposing fighter and his team would not understand him.[12] If the Jewish boxers of the United States fought in order 'to express ethnic pride, settle ethnic scores, refute ethnic stereotypes' and often, as David Margolick notes, wore Stars of David on their trunks, Farr entered the ring at Yankee Stadium wearing a yellow robe with the red dragon stitched on its back.[13] That dragon had been to New York before, stitched on the robe of the lightweight boxer Freddie Welsh. Welsh (who initially wished to call himself 'Fred Cymry' before being persuaded to use the English term for his nationality) was the first boxer to win an official world championship for Wales in 1914.[14] Farr was, therefore, placing himself within, and helping to define, a Welsh boxing tradition. Thus if the Harlem Renaissance starts with Jack Johnson and ends with Joe Louis, the contemporaneous Welsh Renaissance can be seen to begin with Freddie Welsh's winning the first world championship for Wales in 1914, and ends with Farr's valiant defeat to Louis in 1937. While accepting the impossibility of imposing strict time frames on cultural movements, there may be some legitimacy in turning to boxing in this instance, for Louis and Farr seemed to symbolize and dramatize their own people's passage into modernity.

In the 6 September 1937 edition of *Time Magazine*, Farr was described 'as a colliery boy in Wales, who once was a "booth fighter" earning five shillings a week boxing with yokels at country fairs'.[15] In earning $50,000 for his fight with Louis the suggestion seemed to be that the Welsh yokel had become a prizefighter, thus anticipating one of the most famous passages on boxing in African American literature. In his seminal novel *Invisible Man* (1952) Ralph Ellison (the subject of chapter 4 of this volume) describes a 'prize fighter boxing a yokel':

> The fighter was swift and amazingly scientific. His body was one violent flow of rapid rhythmic action. He hit the yokel a hundred times while the yokel held up his arms in stunned surprise. But suddenly the yokel, rolling about in the gale of boxing gloves, struck one blow and knocked science, speed and footwork as cold as a well-digger's posterior. The smart money hit the canvas. The long shot got the nod. The yokel had simply stepped inside his opponent's sense of time.[16]

The passage is based on the juxtaposition of an untrained, rural yokel with an efficient, scientific, urban and urbane prizefighter. If it is by now commonplace to note that the writers and artists of the early twentieth century – the age of 'modernism' in literature, art and music – sought to capture the sense of speed, motion and rapidity made possible by trains, trams, cars and other modern modes of transportation, then in stepping into the scientific prizefighter's sense of 'time' the yokel may be seen to be stepping into modernity itself. In his study of boxing and literature, *The Culture of Bruising*, Gerald Early uses this passage as a basis for exploring the uneasy relationship between white and black boxers in American culture. He notes that 'virtually every white champion has been, despite his style, a yokel: Sharkey, Braddock, Schmeling, Baer, Carnera, Marciano'. In contrast, black prizefighters have been regarded as 'tricksters of style: Jack Johnson, Muhammad Ali, Sugar Ray Robinson, and Sugar Ray Leonard'. Against black opponents, states Early, 'white yokels were not even really fighters; they were more like preservers of the white public's need to see Tricksters pay the price for their disorder'.[17] Few of the white boxers whom Early mentions were actually from rural areas, and Farr's Rhondda valley was itself the powerhouse of Welsh modernity. But Early seems right in describing the ways in which white and black boxers were perceived, as reinforced in *Time Magazine*'s description of Farr as yet another white 'yokel' defeated by a black stylist.

Ellison did not define the 'yokel' and 'prizefighter' in racial terms, for the yokel's step into the modernity of the boxing ring was experienced by many ethnic groups and peoples. It was certainly a step taken by both the Welsh and African American peoples as processes of emigration and industrialization led to a decisive shift from the country to the city. Some, within both the Welsh and African American traditions, resisted the cultural changes bred by urbanization. For them, boxing was an aberration. In Wales, the Reverend Gwilym Davies believed that the Louis versus Farr bout was a manifestation of the 'lowering of the public taste' to the point where 'it revels in commercialized brutality between black and white on a scale hitherto unknown'.[18] W. J. Gruffydd, professor of Welsh and editor of *Y Llenor*, claimed:

> Yr wyf yn cofio adegau yn hanes y genedl pan oedd y pulpud a'r eisteddfod yn llwyfannau i'r ysbryd [cystadleuol] hwn, – pwy oedd y pregethwr gorau, pwy oedd wedi ennill y gadair, pa gôr a gurodd, pa un o ddau dwrne a oedd yn mynd i ennill yr etholiad. Gwelaf heddiw – ym Morgannwg o leiaf – mai'r hyn sy'n anfeidrol bwysig i ni fel cenedl o Gymry ydyw siawns Jac Petersen neu Tommy Farr neu ryw Sais arall a aned yng Nghymru i roi cweir â dyrnau i Sais a aned yn Lloegr neu i ddyn du o America.

> (I remember times in the history of the nation when the pulpit and the eisteddfod gave [the urge to compete] great scope – who was the best preacher, who had won the chair, what choir had won, which of the two lawyers was going to win the election. Today, I notice – in Glamorgan at least – what is of over-riding significance for us as Welshmen are the prospects of Jack Petersen or Tommy Farr, or some other Englishman born in Wales to overcome with his fists an Englishman born in England or a black man from America.)[19]

Similarly, on 16 July 1910, twelve days after Jack Johnson had defeated the 'white hope' Jim Jeffries in Reno, Nevada, the editorial column of the African American newspaper *The Washington Bee* remarked exasperatedly: 'What the colored people can find to go wild over *The Bee* fails to see.'[20] Kevin Gaines notes that 'lest they be confused with newly arrived' folk from the south, the urban African American elite 'extolled Victorian and European cultural ideals and looked with disapproval, if not covert and guilty pleasure' upon black cultural forms such as ragtime, blues, jazz and, in the sporting realm, boxing.[21] Alice Dunbar-Nelson, for example, attempting to buttress her status as a member of the emergent black bourgeoisie in 1920s Harlem, found her more snobbish friends disdaining her acquaintance with members of the boxing fraternity.[22] For the majority, however, the yokel's journey from Blaenclydach (Farr) or the Buckalew Mountains of east-central Alabama (Louis) to Yankee Stadium seemed to embody the cultural trajectory of the Welsh and African American peoples themselves. The boxers symbolized the journey into modernity and, by the 1930s, the peoples' resilience during a period of economic depression.

Marshall Berman offers a memorable description of the modernity into which the rural yokel was stepping:

> [A]n environment that promises us adventure, power, joy, growth, transformation of ourselves and the world – and, at the same time, that threatens to destroy everything we have, everything we know, everything we are. Modern environments and experiences cut across all boundaries of geography and ethnicity, of class and nationality, of religion and ideology: in this sense, modernity can be said to unite all mankind. But it is a paradoxical unity, a unity of disunity: it pours all into a maelstrom of perpetual disintegration and renewal, of struggle and contradiction, of ambiguity and anguish. To be modern is to be part of a universe in which, as Marx said, 'All that is solid melts into air'.[23]

'Disintegration and renewal', 'ambiguity and anguish', describe, despite the myriad differences, the African American and Welsh experience of industrialization. Between 1861 and 1911, as a result of the explosive growth of the coal industry, the population of the county of Glamorgan grew by 253 per cent, and, in the decade preceding the First World War, Wales was ranked second to the United States as a centre for immigration. In 1850, 20 percent of the Welsh population lived in towns. That percentage increased to a little under 50 in 1861, and 60 by 1911. Wales, an agricultural land of about 500,000 people in 1800, was transformed into an urban nation of 2,500,000, with the majority packed into the coalfields of the south by 1911.[24] If the Welsh, along with English, Irish, Italians and Jews, were moving into the industrial valleys of south Wales, African Americans were also, according to *The New York Age*, 'a race changing from farm life to city life' as they moved in large numbers out of the south to the urban centres of the north.[25] Between 1910 and 1920 the Negro population of New York increased by 66 per cent (91,709 to 152, 467) and from 1920 to 1930 it increased by 115 per cent (152, 467 to 327, 706). In 1930 less than a quarter of New York City's African American population was born in New York state.[26] Alain Locke famously suggested that Harlem would have 'the same role to play for the New Negro as Dublin has had for the New Ireland or Prague for the New Czechoslovakia', and James Weldon Johnson asked his readers to 'think what the future of Harlem will be . . . It will be the greatest Negro city in the world . . . And what a fine part of New York City [the Negro] has come into possession of!'[27] By the late 1920s, however, Harlem's former 'high class' homes offered, in the words of one expert on housing, 'the best laboratory for slum clearance . . . in the entire city'.[28] Indeed, one of the most curious aspects of the Harlem Renaissance, according to Henry Louis Gates Jr, was that it occurred at a time 'when Harlem was turning into the great American slum'.[29] The rate of childhood death was higher in Harlem than any other part of New York City even before the economic crash of 1929, when death due to tuberculosis was four times higher amongst African Americans than for any other group, and unemployment was over 50 per cent in the African American community.[30]

The remarkable flourishing of Welsh literature (in both main languages) in the 1930s also occurred within an unpromising context. Between 1921 and 1936, 241 coal mines closed down in south Wales and in 1936 the numbers of miners decreased from 271,161 to 126,233, creating large pockets of unemployment. By the end of 1939, unemployment in Merthyr – for so long the heart of industrial south Wales – was 69.1 percent.[31] For the historian Gwyn A. Williams, the 'social disruption and identity crisis' caused by the depression played 'the same role in Welsh history as the famine in Irish'.[32] What the poet Idris Davies described as 'the great dream and the swift disaster' could be applied with equal relevance to the history of the Welsh and the African Americans in the first forty years of the twentieth century.[33] The boxing ring came to represent this experience of modernity in both cultures; a rapidly transforming society in microcosm, where, as in the industrial and urban crucibles of south Wales and Harlem, 'yokels' were transformed, violently, into modern men. Boxing stands in a metonymic

relationship to the broader social context in which African American and
Welsh modernisms were forged.

To describe boxing in this way may seem somewhat incongruous
given that, for many cultural critics, modernist art's most salient characteristic is its contempt for popular culture. For Theodor Adorno, the most
influential Marxist proponent of this view, capitalism breeds an 'affirmative art' which appeals to the masses and, rather than challenging the
system, 'affirms' or reinforces its dominance.[34] For Adorno, jazz fans
and sport enthusiasts are similar in that they invest their passions in
activities which actually reinforce their human debasement and aesthetic
regression. The admirer of jazz 'pictures himself as the individualist who
whistles at the world. But what he whistles is its melody.' This is a
process which Adorno sees reflected in the mass responses to film and
sport in early twentieth-century society:

> The assent to hit songs and debased cultural goods belongs to the same
> complex of symptoms as do those faces of which one no longer knows
> whether the film has alienated them from reality or reality has alienated them
> from the film, as they wrench open a great formless mouth with shining teeth
> in a voracious smile, while the tired eyes are wretched and lost above. Together
> with sport and film, mass music and the new listening help to make escape
> from the whole infantile milieu impossible.[35]

The only hope for cultural resistance lies in the deliberately complex,
and thus autonomous, realm of modernist art, as embodied in the patently
challenging atonal music of Schoenberg that Adorno admired and later
attempted to compose. The Third Reich's use of boxing and advertising
as means of propaganda (as manifested in Goebbels's words on Farr
versus Schmelling with which I began this chapter) informs Adorno's
analysis, where the regressive aesthetic responses of the masses in capitalist societies make them susceptible to fascist propaganda and
mobilization. The modernist art work stands, for Adorno, as a final
redoubt of political resistance, anxiously fearing, in Andreas Huyssen's
words, 'contamination by its other, which in this case was an increasingly consuming and engulfing mass culture'.[36] Adorno's reference to
the spectator's or listener's 'formless mouth with shining teeth' and
'voracious smile' in the quotation above suggests that another fear of
'contamination' haunts his musing on popular culture. The imagery in
the passage seems to derive from minstrelsy (discussed elsewhere in this
book), the conventions of which informed Hollywood cinema produc-
tions throughout the 1920s and 1930s, and suggests a conflation of
modernism's cultural 'other' with an equally debased 'racial' other. This

symbolic conflation is significant in that amongst those spheres of cultural production which Adorno isolates for his most bitter condemnations are those that had a significant black presence in the late nineteenth and early twentieth centuries: jazz and sport. Thus if, as Andreas Huyssen has argued, 'mass culture' was often gendered female by those seeking to fortify the boundaries of an authentic, masculine, high art against the seductive encroachments of 'mass culture', the popular could also be marked racially as 'black'.[37]

It should, therefore, not be surprising that the challenge to the binary conception of a high modernism defined by its resistance to popular tastes has been mounted most forcefully by those who have attempted to place the literature, art and music of African Americans at the heart of their definitions of the period's culture. Houston Baker has sought to define a distinctive African American modernism against the hegemony of the 'Anglo-American-Irish' canon, George Hutchinson, amongst others, defines 'African American modernism' as part of a wider 'American modernism' which drew significantly on 'low' vernacular forms for inspiration, and Ann Douglas gives jazz, cabaret, boxing, baseball and film a central role in her revisionist account of 'Mongrel Manhattan' in the 1920s.[38] Such readings suggest that the dichotomy between high and popular art ultimately proves inadequate to account for the complexity of cultural exchange and circulation not only in relation to African Americans in 1920s New York, but also in modern civil society more generally. This revisionism is part of a wider shift in contemporary criticism from a 'once monolithically conceived Modernism' to a 'variety of modernisms', which leads to a questioning of the sweeping, overarching theories of the past in the light of contradictory examples unearthed by new research in an increasingly widening range of literary traditions. Thus a modernism once described in cosmopolitan and internationalist terms is replaced by a plurality of geographically located 'provincial' modernisms.[39] A modernism once seen to offer a far-ranging critique of 'bourgeois civilization' is seen in some cases to have contributed to the construction of a bourgeois class.[40] A modernism seen to turn away from the social to a reflexive exploration of the material element of its existence (pigment in art, language in literature) is seen in fact to have retained a mutually influential relationship with, and concern for, its social context.[41] A modernism conceived as the art of the city and metropolis, is seen to coexist with a range of modernisms characterized by a 'return to the folk'.[42] An accepted canon of European modernists (Pound, Eliot, Joyce) is replaced by a range of ethnic modernisms often aligned to various nationalisms.[43] An essentially masculine canon is challenged by an awareness that modernist art exists in an ambivalent dialogue with the first wave of feminism consolidated in the women's suffrage movement.[44] Perhaps most significantly for this chapter on the modernisms of Wales and African America, the notion that modernism disdained the mass market gives way to a contemporary emphasis on the ways in which modernist artists courted the market and on 'the extent to which those shoddy cultural goods that once seemed just the opposite of the gleaming artefacts of modernism may in fact not have been so very different after all'.[45]

This revisionism serves to highlight the fact that the opposition of 'high culture' and 'mass culture' is itself a modernist construction. The critiques of modernity developed within that period itself – from both the political right (Eliot, Pound, Wyndham Lewis) and the left (Adorno, Marcuse) – constituted, according to Raymond Williams, 'a highly selected version of the modern which then offer[ed] to appropriate the whole of modernity'.[46] In attempting to offer a more pluralist account of modernism, Williams focused on two primary areas of debate. The first addressed the question of language. Williams argued that the post-structuralist critiques of realism and representation had resulted in a 'flattened' reading of early twentieth-century artists and writers, which was designed to reinforce 'contemporary theoretical and quasi-theoretical positions'.[47] Unlike many contemporary theorists Williams did not detect 'a common rejection of the representational character of language' in modernism, but observed a diversity of positions ranging from a Brechtian view of language 'as material in a social process' to the surrealist sense that language was 'blocking or making difficulties for authentic consciousness'.[48] Thus, in opposition to a singular account of the modernist rejection of realism and mimesis, Williams emphasized the inherent plurality of positions that coexist within the modernist 'formation':

> [W]hat we have really to investigate is not some single position of language in the avant-garde or language in Modernism. On the contrary, we need to identify a range of distinct and in many cases actually opposed formations, as these have materialised in language.[49]

This pluralist approach was also evident in the second key issue addressed by Williams, that of the location of modernism. While Williams accepted that the 'metropolis of the second half of the nineteenth century and the first half of the twentieth century moved into a quite new cultural dimension', resulting in the emergence of new themes and forms, his reiterated insight was that 'the metropolitan interpretation of its own processes as universals' resulted in a highly selective reading of modernist art and culture.[50] This was particularly the case when considering the 'very marked unevenness of development', not only between imperial and colonized countries, but also 'within particular countries, where the distances between capitals and provinces widened, socially and culturally, in the uneven development of industry and agriculture'.[51]

Raymond Williams presented his claims for the legitimacy of mass culture and for a more plural conception of modernism as a critique of a 'confined' and 'highly selective' definition of early twentieth-century literature.[52] This chapter seeks to substantiate this desire for an account of modernism which addresses internal differences. The aim is to 'identify a range of distinct and in many cases actually opposed formations', and to trace the ways in which 'these have materialised in language'.[53] Marcus Klein, in his discussion of ethnic modernism in the United States, identifies two such formations when he notes that the 'culture that had been formulated by the great modernists enabled them to propose the idea of an elite against the presumption of a rabble' before proceeding to argue that this elitist presumption was opposed in the United States by those who conceived of the rabble itself as a culture, 'and not only that, but the basic, emblematic integer of society'.[54] Thus an 'elitist' modernism bred, in reaction to it, 'an entirely different aesthetic' which sought to celebrate rather than disdain the masses.[55] In Welsh and African American culture this turn away from bourgeois aesthetic values took different forms; some writers identified with the urban proletariat, while others rooted their aesthetic experiments in the experiences of a rural folk. Thus, for the purpose of comparative analysis, I have sought to isolate, within a varied and complex field, three divergent strains of thought that I take to be characteristic of Welsh and African American literature in the era of aesthetic modernism; the bourgeois, the proletarian and the folk. These three strains of modernism offer a useful way of identifying significant comparable aesthetic and intellectual trajectories in African American and Welsh modernisms.

## MODERNISM, DOUBLE CONSCIOUSNESS AND THE BOURGEOISIE

The two 'great modernists' of the African American and Welsh traditions, who did indeed propose the 'idea of an elite against the presumption
of a rabble', were, respectively, W. E. B. Du Bois and Saunders Lewis. In
his revisionist account of *Modernism and Harlem Renaissance*, Houston
A. Baker argues that

> Afro-American scholars, intellectuals and activists of the late nineteenth
> century and early twentieth century were faced with a task substantially
> different from their Anglo-American, British and Irish counterparts. Rather
> than bashing the bourgeoisie, such spokespersons were attempting to create
> one. Far from being rebellious dissenters against existent Afro-American
> expressive forms, they sought to enhance these forms and bring them before a
> sophisticated public.[56]

Baker's argument is similar to that made by Andreas Huyssen, who
claims that the distinctiveness of American modernism derives from its
emergence in a context where the artistic heritage did not play as central
a role in legitimizing bourgeois domination as it did in Europe.[57] Perhaps
the distinction that should be made is not between Europe and the United
States, as Huyssen would have it, nor between African American and all
other Anglo-American modernisms as Baker suggests but, rather,
between the literary modernisms of nation states with established bourgeoisies and the literary traditions of minority groups whose primary
objective is the construction of a bourgeois class within the context of an
emergent nationalism that is still in active process. In the writings of Du
Bois and Lewis this process of bourgeois class formation is profoundly
connected to the issue of cultural, and political, authority.

Du Bois believed that 'a Negro middle-class' would 'usher in
co-operation' and counted 'on the fact that not all of the young Negro
leaders are selfish and stupid exploiters. At any rate, either we get leadership from the best part of this class, or we get nothing'.[58] Du Bois began
his famous lecture on 'The Talented Tenth' (1903) by noting that 'The
Negro race is going to be saved by its exceptional men' and he was in no
doubt as to who should set the terms of cultural advancement:

> Who are today guiding the work of the Negro people? The 'exceptions' of
> course ... A saving remnant continually survives and persists, continually
> aspires, continually shows itself in thrift and ability and character. Exceptional
> it is to be sure, but this is its chiefest promise; it shows the capability of Negro
> blood, the promise of black men ... Can the masses of the Negro people be in

any possible way more quickly raised than by the effort and example of the aristocracy of talent and character? Was there ever a nation on God's fair earth civilised from the bottom upward? Never; it is, ever was and ever will be from the top downward that culture filters.[59]

If the first item on Du Bois's political agenda can be seen to have been the 'enlarging and uniting' of the African American middle class, Saunders Lewis also emphasized that 'ar sylfaen ddiogel cymdeithas bourgeois y mae'n rhwyddaf cynnal bywyd yr artist' ('it is on the safe foundation of bourgeois society that the artist's life can be most easily maintained').[60] In an article on literary criticism he argued that the 'common man' had no capacity to understand the unusual or uncommon aspects that were central to the development of great art and thought, and when introducing his translation of Molière's *Le Médécin Malgré Lui* (1924) he argued that the source of the French dramatist's genius was his bourgeois upbringing.[61]

> Plentyn dinas, mab i siopwr cefnog ym Mharis, oedd Molière. 'Bourgeois' gan hynny . . . Fe ddigwydd hefyd fod nifer o'r disgleiriaf ym mysg disgyblion celf yn blant 'bourgeois'. Y mae'r dosbarth canol o gymdeithas yn feithrinfa dda i'r artist canys gall roi addysg iddo a moethau gwâr ac arian – pethau sy'n anhepgor – a'i gadw serch hynny o fewn terfynau y byddo diwydrwydd yn fantais iddo.

> (Molière was a child of the city, the son of a wealthy shop owner in Paris. He was therefore 'bourgeois' . . . It happens also that a number of the most brilliant disciples of art have been children of the bourgeoisie. The middle class of society is a good nursery for an artist, for it can give him an education, the luxuries of civilized life and money – things which are essential – and can keep him, nevertheless, within the bounds of diligence which will be to his advantage.)[62]

Du Bois's call for an 'aristocracy of talent' is mirrored in Lewis's confession that he would be happy to forget about political nationalism if it were possible to sustain '[c]wmni bach aristocrataidd Cymreig a gadwai lên a chelf yn ddiogel' ('a small Welsh elite who would safeguard literature and art').[63] While, as Dafydd Glyn Jones notes, many of the bourgeois writers of the modernist era wanted to be aristocrats and while there are passages in the works of Du Bois and Lewis where they critique the narrow-minded philistinism of the middle class from an 'aristocratic' viewpoint, neither Du Bois nor Lewis followed Pound, Eliot and the other high modernists in rejecting Western bourgeois civilization as an 'old bitch gone in the teeth'.[64] Rather, they can be seen to have been primarily engaged in a process of fostering and developing a national bourgeoisie for Wales and African America. Gareth Miles describes Lewis as a 'one-man national bourgeoisie for Wales' faced with the problem that his bourgeois ideals had no economic basis in a land of 'common folk and petit bourgeois'.[65] Several critics have similarly noted that with a little over 2,000 out of almost 9 million African Americans having a college degree in 1900, Du Bois's conception of a 'talented tenth' was somewhat fanciful.[66] But actual numbers or economic realities were less significant for Du Bois and Lewis than their desire to engage in a process of developing a confident bourgeois class that would function as a cultural, political and spiritual élite.

Born in the town of Great Barrington, in western Massachusetts, Du Bois recalled that, due to his essentially middle-class upbringing, he 'had little contact with crime and degradation' and while the 'slums in the town were not bad' they 'repelled' him 'because they were inhabited by the foreign-born'.[67] Later in his life Du Bois would fear for his family's lives during a racial pogrom in Atlanta, and would shudder at the sight of an African American's hands being displayed in a butcher's shop after a lynching, but his first experience of racism, as described in his seminal *The Souls of Black Folk*, is not an atrocity perpetuated in the South, but is rather a schoolyard incident which is recalled as follows:

> I was a little thing, away up in the hills of New England . . . In a wee schoolhouse, something put it into the boys' and girls' heads to buy gorgeous visiting-cards – ten cents a package – and exchange. The exchange was merry, till one girl, a tall newcomer, refused my card, – refused it peremptorily, with a glance. Then it dawned upon me with a certain suddenness that I was different from the others; or like, mayhap, in heart and life and longing, but shut out from their world by a vast veil.[68]

Du Bois's first encounter with racism involves a white girl's rejection of the black boy's visiting card. The young Du Bois's shock at the refusal of his gift allies him with the values of his New England society, for the refusal of his visiting card shatters the veneer of gentility embodied within the children's imitation of a social custom. The girl, it is noted, is a 'newcomer', thus placing the source of racism outside Du Bois's New England community and thus safeguarding the values of his own upbringing and his adherence to them.[69] If Du Bois tended to locate the geographical centre of his imagined African American 'nation' within the 'Black Belt' of the Southern states – 'Not only is Georgia . . . the geographical focus of our Negro population', states Du Bois, 'but in many other respects, both now and yesterday, the Negro problems have seemed to be centered in this State' – this was a place to which he had to travel in an act of conscious immersion.[70] The black belt of the South, where one can ride 'ten miles' without seeing 'a white face', was another country for the Massachusetts-born intellectual.[71] His future collaborator, Rayford Whittiford Logan, expressed his frustration at Du Bois's tendency to describe his racial identity as something he discovered at Fisk University.[72] Within a racially bifurcated society, it seems to have been significant for Du Bois that he could present his racial allegiance as a conscious choice, as an existential act.

Much has also been made of Saunders Lewis's status as an outsider. He was born in Seacombe, on the Wirral, and was thus brought up amongst the extensive Welsh community inhabiting Liverpool's Merseyside. While Lewis himself emphasized that there was 'somewhere in the region of a hundred thousand Welsh-speaking Welshmen in Liverpool throughout my boyhood' and that 'at least half of these were monoglot Welsh speakers', it is nevertheless the case, as Gareth Miles argues, that Lewis's upbringing was very different to that of the children of rural and industrialized Wales.[73] Miles notes that while the 'secular and religious leaders' of Wales during the late nineteenth and early twentieth century were 'cultured shopkeepers, farmers, artisans and common folk' – (he does not mention teachers, intellectuals and preachers) – the leaders of the Welsh community in Liverpool were the 'merchants, financiers, and wealthy industrialists' who constituted 'the only strong, self-conscious bourgeoisie which the Welsh nation has ever had'.[74] Thus, despite Lewis being the son of a prominent Welsh minister, his education at Liscard High School for Boys, his attainment of a first-class degree in English at Liverpool University and his employment as an officer by the British Army in France during the First World War meant that the majority of the formative influences on his life were English. His first attempt at writing for the stage was in English, and it was in France, under the influence of Maurice Barrès's trilogy of novels, *Le Culte de Moi*, that Lewis decided to return to his family's Welsh roots.[75] Thus for Lewis, as for Du Bois, his dedication to a cultural nationalist programme was conceived as a choice, as a decision to identify with the moral and intellectual values of the struggle for Welsh cultural distinctiveness.

In seeking to carve out a social space in which they could claim to speak for 'the Welsh' or for 'the Negro', Du Bois and Lewis needed to define the parameters of their imagined constituencies. Du Bois's description of his talented tenth as a 'saving remnant' and as an 'aristocracy of talent and character', has much in common with Coleridge's

notion of a 'clerisy', and with the 'disinterested aliens' of Matthew
Arnold's *Culture and Anarchy* and the 'cultured remnant' of his American
lectures.[76] Similarly, in naming his series of two books on leading Welsh
Victorian authors *Yr Artist yn Philistia* (The Artist in Philistia), and in his
emphasis on 'swyddogaeth' ('the function') of literature and criticism in
his essays, there were clear Arnoldian resonances in Lewis's writings.[77]
Arnold had argued that the 'highly-instructed few, and not the
scantily-instructed many, will ever be the organ to the human race of
knowledge and truth', and, just as Arnold sought to develop a role for the
educated man of letters between the philistine arrogance of the middle
classes and the potential anarchy of the working class, the ideal of
middle-class leadership developed in the writings of Du Bois and Lewis
was predicated on the construction of an unruly and culturally bereft
proletariat, and an illiterate, primitive, rural folk.[78]

In 1928 Du Bois, famously, offered a searing critique of Claude
McKay's novel *Home to Harlem*, accusing the author of having 'used
every art and emphasis to paint drunkenness, fighting, lascivious sexual
promiscuity and utter absence of restraint in as bold and as bright colors
as he can'.[79] Du Bois believed that McKay had followed the model set by
the novel *Nigger Heaven*, written by the white primitivist and patron of
African American culture Carl Van Vechten, in writing a novel that set
out to 'cater for that prurient demand on the part of white folk for a
portrayal in Negroes of that utter licentiousness which conventional
civilization holds white folk back from enjoying'.[80] In response to novels
such as Van Vechten's *Nigger Heaven* ('an affront to the hospitality of
black folk and the intelligence of whites') and Julia Peterkin's *Black
April* ('a veritable cesspool of incest, adultery, fighting and poverty'), Du
Bois argued that the 'overwhelming majority of black folk' in Harlem
'never go to the cabarets. The average colored man in Harlem is an
everyday laborer, attending church, lodge and movie and as conservative
and as conventional as ordinary working folk everywhere'.[81] Although
he wrote on African American literature and the arts throughout the
1920s, Du Bois never discussed jazz musicians such as Louis Armstrong
and Duke Ellington who were spearheading a revolution in music. Even
his late conversion to communism did not affect Du Bois's elitist
aesthetic sensibilities as, in the late 1950s, he compared the 'startling
miracle' of Sputnik to the degeneracy of capitalism as represented in
Elvis Presley's 'motions of copulation on the public stage'.[82]

Similarly, in his apocalyptic vision of 'Y Dilyw 1939' (The Deluge,
1939) Saunders Lewis described the

> . . . frau werinos, y demos dimai,
> Epil drel milieist a'r *pool* pêl droed,
> Llanwodd ei bol â lluniau budrogion
> Ac â phwdr usion y radio a'r wasg.

> [. . . the frail rabble, the halfpenny demos,
> The issue of the dogs and the football pools,
> It filled its belly with pictures of sluts
> And with the rotten husks of radio and newspapers.][83]

Mass culture was also an anglicizing force from Lewis's perspective. He lamented the extent to which the 'English idiom enters unconsciously into Welsh speech today. It is all about us, even in the remotest country-side, in radio set and television screen and daily newspaper. Inevitably there's a landslide of deterioration. Even literary standards seem lost.'[84] Industrialism, for Saunders Lewis, was 'the destroyer of all nationhood, reducing men to hands and community to a mass'.[85] Echoing the views of English Catholic distributists such as G. K. Chesterton and Hilaire Belloc, Lewis argued that for the 'moral health of Wales' the south should be 'de-industrialised'.[86] Despite assisting members of Plaid Cymru to run soup kitchens in Merthyr during the depression years, Lewis dismissed the industrial societies of south Wales for both their politics and their culture. Labour, the dominant political force in south Wales, was 'the devil himself', argued Lewis, 'and in south Wales is destroying language, nationality and traditions. In fact, with the sweep of south Wales by Labour, I look on this part as lost to Welsh civilisation.'[87] While English, argued Lewis, had established itself in Ireland in the eighteenth century and had developed a 'traditional idiom and folklore' in an 'uncommercialised' milieu 'untouched by industrialism', English in Wales was the product of industrialization, an amalgam of the 'Cockney dialect' of Labour politicians and 'railways from Lancashire carrying the vowels and idioms of Manchester'.[88] 'From these, and the newspapers we have formed our Anglo-Welsh speech', argued Lewis, 'and no feebler stuff is spoken in these islands'.[89] In 1923 – the year of the attempted Munich putsch, of de Valera's arrest by the army of the newly formed Irish Free State, of Mussolini's ban on all anti-Fascist parties in Italy, of Charles Mauras's and the Action Française's support for the attacks on left-leaning newspaper publishers by the right wing Camelots du Roi, and of an increase in proletarian militancy in south Wales – Saunders Lewis argued the case for conservative nationalism as a defence against the potential anarchy unleashed by a rising proletariat:

O Ddeheudir Cymru y daw'r ddamchwa a fwria'n yfflon Ymerodraeth Brydain. Dynion heb atgofion na pherthynas â'u cydgenedl yn difetha a dinistrio popeth ag iddo hanes a hynafiaeth. A'r pryd hwnnw, fe wêl dynion mai ymwrthod â chenedlaetholdeb a fu achos y terfysg a'r cwymp.

(The explosion destroying the British Empire will originate in south Wales. Men without memories or any relationship with their fellow countrymen will destroy everything related to history and antiquity. And at that time, men will see that the rejection of nationalism was the cause of the violence and the fall).[90]

While it may seem curious to find a Welsh nationalist seemingly criticizing those who would destroy the British Empire, Lewis's fear is that social change is being led by the wrong class. A people with no understanding of its own past, or of its nation's history, was clearly in no position to offer social leadership. Lewis's words underscore the importance he attached to the role of a nationalist elite and his lack of sympathy for the industrial working class.[91]

Du Bois was also inclined to envisage urban African Americans as people with no communal or historical consciousness. He argued that 'the Negro people need social leadership more than most groups; that they have no tradition to fall back upon, no long established customs, no strong family ties, no well defined social classes. All these things must be slowly and painfully evolved.'[92] While this was the result of slavery, the suffering of African Americans in the past was no reason to condone unacceptable behaviour in the present.

> Simply because the ancestors of the present white inhabitants of America went out of their way barbarously to mistreat and enslave the ancestors of the present black inhabitants, gives those blacks no right to ask that the civilization and morality of the land be seriously menaced for their benefit.[93]

If thirty years had not been sufficient time to escape from the legacies of slavery then African Americans could still be expected to 'make themselves fit members of the community within a reasonable length of time'.[94] Du Bois's notion of 'the talented tenth' was thus developed in relation to a 'submerged tenth' – a phrase that he used in his study of *The Philadelphia Negro* to describe the 'class of criminals, prostitutes and loafers' living in that city's Seventh Ward.[95] In making his case for fostering a class of black leaders in *The Souls of Black Folk*, Du Bois invokes the danger of civil unrest:

> [N]o secure civilisation can be built in the South with the Negro as an ignorant, turbulent proletariat . . . [A]s the black third of the land grows in thrift

and skill, unless skilfully guided in its larger philosophy, it must more and more brood over the red past and the creeping, crooked present, until it grasps a gospel of revolt and revenge and throws its new-found energies athwart the current of advance.[96]

While Du Bois is less dismissive of the black majority than is Lewis towards the Welsh proletariat (and, unlike Lewis, Du Bois would move decisively to the left from the 1930s onwards), the two cultural nationalist leaders shared an early belief in cultural guidance from an educated elite as a means of avoiding the potential social unrest caused by a 'turbulent proletariat'.

If their dislike for the working masses is clear enough, Lewis and Du Bois did not turn to the rural folk for salvation. Indeed, rather like Matthew Arnold's Victorian 'remnant', if the members of Lewis's and Du Bois's cultural nationalist elite were to function as humanizing agents in a world threatened by working-class anarchy, they were also destined to function as mediators between a nascent nationalism and the natural, if unrefined and directionless, spirituality of the folk.[97] The Victorian resonances in the thinking of Lewis and Du Bois are striking. As I have argued elsewhere, the value of 'the greater delicacy and spirituality of the Celtic peoples' for Arnold was that it proved to be a counterbalance to the hard-headed materialism of English philistine society, and such ideas were replicated in the United States by writers such as William Dean Howells who detected in the 'childish simple-heartedness' of African Americans a source of regeneration for an 'over-civilised' United States.[98] These conceptions of Celtic and African-American uniqueness became influential within those groups themselves. Drawing on W. B. Yeats, who followed Arnold in considering the Irish a 'conquered race' with a particular insight into 'charms, dreams and visions', Lewis argued that 'the Celtic peoples have an inherent inaptitude for industrial capitalism, being incapable of organising social life on such a basis'.[99] Lewis noted that his first play *The Eve of St John* was based on the practice of 'conjuring', along with 'other beliefs – such as in the efficacy of the holy bell to ward off evil spirits, and in the dogs of Hell – which lingered until very recently, and may still exist in quiet corners of the land'.[100] If the proletarian novel in vogue in the 1930s was to take a Welsh form, argued Lewis, it would be 'a study of a native society with some richness of tradition and characteristic institutions struggling to preserve these their [*sic*] inheritance against the levelling pressure of the cosmopolitan industrial machine. It would be the story of the struggle of spirituality to survive'.[101] Similarly, W. E. B. Du Bois believed that African Americans were 'the sole oasis of simple faith and reverence' in an America described as 'a dusty desert of dollars'.[102] The African American, noted Du Bois, is

> a religious animal, – a being of that deep emotional nature which turns instinc-
> tively toward the supernatural. Endowed with a rich tropical imagination and
> a keen, delicate appreciation of Nature, the transplanted African lived in a
> world animate with gods and devils, elves and witches . . .[103]

The ideology of Victorian contributionism (discussed in chapter 1) was predicated on the belief that the cultural primitivism of the Celts and African Americans prescribed their amalgamation into the dominant English and American national cultures. That primitivist distinctiveness was adopted by Lewis and Du Bois (in this respect the heirs to Victorian nationalists such as Emrys ap Iwan and Martin Delany) to form the basis for conservationist ethnic movements that challenged the very idea of common national cultures in the United Kingdom and the United States.

The problem, evident in the writings of both Du Bois and Lewis, was that their encounters with the actual African American and Welsh 'folk' on the ground somewhat contradicted their primitivistic ideals. Du Bois's short story 'Of the Coming of John' centres on the experiences of (the intriguingly Welsh-sounding) John Jones, a black native of Altamaha who leaves home to gain a college degree in the North, and is thus a representative of the 'talented tenth'. In returning home to his southern home town, John turns to the Baptist church that he attended as a child as the site where he may present his vision of racial uplift to the masses. He speaks 'slowly and methodically . . . of the rise of charity and popular education' and goes on to sketch 'in vague outline the new Industrial School that might rise among these pines':

> he spoke in detail of the charitable and philanthropic work that might be
> organised, of money that might be saved for banks and business. Finally he
> urged unity and deprecated especially religious and denominational bick-
> ering. 'To-day,' he said, with a smile, 'the world cares little whether a man be
> Baptist or Methodist, or indeed a churchman at all, so long as he is good and
> true . . . Let's leave all that littleness, and look higher'.[104]

John's words amount to the philosophy of the 'talented tenth' as expounded by Du Bois, but his words are met with a total silence by the congregation. Eventually, a church elder gets to his feet, and the following description conveys the religious fervour, bordering on the irrational, that Du Bois identified with the agrarian masses:

> Then at last a low suppressed snarl came from the Amen corner, and an old
> man arose, walked over the seats, and climbed straight up into the pulpit. He
> was wrinkled and black, with scant gray and tufted hair; his voice and hands

shook with palsy; but on his face lay the intense rapt look of the religious fanatic. He seized the Bible with his rough, huge hands; twice he raised it inarticulate, and then fairly burst into words with rude and awful eloquence. He quivered swayed and bent; then rose aloft in perfect majesty, till the people moaned and wept, wailed and shouted, and a wild shrieking arose from the corners where all the pent-up feeling of the hour gathered itself and rushed into the air. John never knew clearly what the old man said; he only felt himself held up to scorn and scathing denunciation for trampling on the true Religion, and he realized with amazement that all unknowingly he had put rough, rude hands on something their little world held sacred.[105]

John's sense of distance from the black folk's culture, mirrors the sense of alienation from black religious practices that Du Bois himself expresses in his chapter 'On the faith of the fathers'. Following an invocation of the 'quiet and subdued' church services of his native Berkshire, Du Bois is alarmed by a 'sort of suppressed terror' that hangs in the air of the southern revival meeting, 'a pythian madness, a demoniac possession' that 'lent terrible reality to song and word'.[106] The intensity of the experience, the 'scene of human passion such as I had never conceived before', forces him back to the relative security of the northern visitor's viewpoint which the narrator shares with the majority of his readers.[107]

> Those who have not thus witnessed the frenzy of a Negro revival in the untouched backwoods of the South can but dimly realize the religious feeling of the slave; as described, such scenes appear grotesque and funny, but as seen are awful.[108]

Whether perceived as 'grotesque and funny' or 'awful', Du Bois's alternative adjectives underline the observer's distance from the activities and cultural values of the observed. The distance between the educated saviour of his people and the folk themselves is thus powerfully invoked.

A similar structure of feeling can be seen to inform Saunders Lewis's writings. Despite being the son of a Methodist minister, Lewis defined his own thought in opposition to that of his Nonconformist ancestors, converting to Catholicism in 1933. In letters to his future wife Lewis expressed a wish to have 'lived in the fourteenth century' before Wales had succumbed to what he referred to as the 'black barbarism of . . . Nonconformity'.[109] He argued further that 'Nonconformity and English landlordism have made us what we are, and it will take many generations, a century perhaps, to recover', and in a speech at the Celtic Congress of 1929 he described the way in which Nonconformist worshippers 'bend down sitting as though they were vomiting. It is sadly appropriate.'[110] Such views amounted to sacrilege in a Welsh-speaking

Wales that continued to be influenced by the nineteenth-century attempts
to 'resurrect' the nation following the attacks upon it in the 1847 Royal
Commission into the State of Education in Wales (the 'Blue Books'
discussed in chapter 1). As I noted in the previous chapter, 'Welshness',
rooted in a pious, literate, cultured and responsible 'gwerin' or 'folk',
became associated with a moral struggle for the hearts and minds of the
people and reached its apotheosis in the writings of O. M. Edwards who
located a genuine Welshness in the egalitarian and highly moral culture
of a rural, Nonconformist, Wales that contrasted with the debased character of the more populous industrial districts of the south.[111] Saunders
Lewis, as Richard Wyn Jones has argued, sought to replace O. M.
Edwards's vision of a liberal, classless and Nonconformist Wales, with a
conservative, hierarchical and Catholic Wales.[112] 'Pwy yw y werin?'
(Who are the folk?) he asked in a revealing letter, published in 1921.
Writing as one 'newydd ddyfod i Gymru' ('who has recently come to
Wales') Lewis noted the extent to which a notion of 'the folk' was being
celebrated, and of the attendant widespread fear that writers receiving
higher education were finding themselves increasingly alienated from
the folk sources that were deemed to be the basis for Welsh literature. He
proceeded sarcastically:

> Pwy yw 'y werin', a pha fodd y'i hadwaenir? Pa faint o addysg sy'n
> anghymwyso dyn i fod yn un o'r werin? . . . Gan gymaint y perygl sydd mewn
> addysg, a wna rhywun gynllunio'n ddoeth i atal y beirdd rhag gwybod
> 'manylion y Gymraeg' a rhwystro i'r colegau daenu diwylliant sydd
> anwerinol? . . . Teithiais lawer yn nyffrynoedd Aberteifi y misoedd diwethaf i
> chwilio am y werin. Disgrifiad llenor y Geninen o'r dosbarth yw 'darllenwyr
> syml sydd yn caru cân a chwedl a llyfr Cymraeg'. Chwiliais am rai felly ac nis
> cefais; 'chwilio gem a chael gwymon'. Cefais aml i fachgen o goleg a chanddo
> sêl ryfedd am gân a llyfr, ond yr oedd ganddo addysg. Pa le y mae'r werin yn
> ymguddio?

(Who are 'the folk', and how does one recognize them? How much education
precludes one from being a member of the folk? Given the dangers of education, will someone develop an intelligent plan to hinder our poets from
developing a detailed knowledge of Welsh, and to prevent our colleges from
disseminating un-folk like culture? . . . During these past months I have travelled widely in the vales of Cardiganshire, looking for the folk. The writer in
*Y Geninen* describes them as 'simple readers who love song and legend, and
books in Welsh'. I searched, but did not find them; 'search for a pearl and find
seaweed'. I came across more than one young man with a zeal for books, but
also college educated. Where are the folk hiding?)[113]

Whereas Du Bois's 'Of the Coming of John' describes the process of disillusion encountered by the educated member of the talented tenth when faced with the reality of rural life, Lewis's letter is written from the perspective of one who harbours no illusions when it comes to folk culture.

Thus, while sharing a high modernist dislike of industrialism and modernity, both Du Bois and Lewis also recoiled from what Marx and Engels had described as 'the idiocy of rural life'.[114] But having expressed their rejection of both the proletariat and the folk, the escape into an autonomous artistic realm as enacted by many high modernists, and as theorized by Adorno, was not an option for these cultural nationalists. Both Lewis and Du Bois were members of newly emergent bourgeoisies within Wales and African America respectively, and thus faced the 'double challenge' which, according to Tom Nairn, faced the 'new middle classes'.

> They have to get rid of an anachronistic 'ancien regime' as well as to beat 'progress' into a shape that suits their own needs and class ambitions. They can only attempt this by radical political and social mobilisation, by arousing and harnessing the latent energies of their own societies. But this means, by mobilising the people. People is all they have got.[115]

What we encounter, then, in the writings of Du Bois and Lewis is a tension between a high modernist rejection of modern industrial society, and a cultural nationalism which requires social engagement for its success. This tension can be viewed as one source for the 'doubleness' which is the famous reiterated trope that unites the diverse chapters in Du Bois's *The Souls of Black Folk*:

> The Negro is a sort of seventh son, born with a veil, and gifted with a second-sight in this American world – a world that yields him no true self-consciousness, but only lets him see himself through the revelation of the other world. It is a peculiar sensation, this double-consciousness, this sense of always looking at oneself through the eyes of others, of measuring one's soul by the tape of a world that looks on in amused contempt and pity. One ever feels this two-ness – an American, a Negro; two Souls, two thoughts, two unreconciled strivings; two warring ideals in one dark body, whose dogged strength alone keeps it from being torn asunder.[116]

The passage evokes the distinct, but not wholly incompatible strivings, deriving from Du Bois's liminal position. The reference to 'an American' suggests an African American self that is recognized as having been wholly assimilated into the dominant culture, of having fulfilled the

Victorian era's promise of 'uplift' to a civil equality. 'A Negro' represents the preservation of difference, an unwillingness to allow the
assimilationist process to extinguish cultural distinctiveness. The term
'double-consciousness' may be regarded as Du Bois's attempt to recon-
cile the two forms of identity. Critics have debated the intellectual
lineage of Du Bois's famous concept exhaustively, noting that it appears
in Emerson's essay 'Fate', in Goethe and in writers as diverse as Whittier,
Wordsworth, George Eliot and William James.[117] Shamoon Zamir strikes
a note of caution when he argues that 'to note that both Hegel and James
have some idea of a divided self tells us nothing about their respective
theories, and even less about Du Bois's relation to these theories', and
Kenneth Warren notes that Henry James's use of the phrase 'double
consciousness' testifies only to the 'teasing repetition' of this term during
the period.[118] The Victorian resonances of Saunders Lewis's early
writing, for example, are evident from the ways in which the teasingly
repeated phrases of Victorian social criticism are reformulated in his
letters to his future wife Margaret Gilcriest. When recalling a 'night we
walked along the shore' he confesses to have written a note which 'I did
not mean to show you until I had understood more clearly myself the
thoughts you had given me'. He proceeds to 'write out' his earlier
thoughts:

> May there not be a double consciousness in each of us; the individual
> consciousness which best realises itself by contrasting itself with other lives
> and beings just as you felt the contrast between your passing self and the
> eternal sea and shore; and then the great universal consciousness which makes
> us all things and realises not separateness but unity, which never distinguishes
> 'you' and 'I', but in everything feels 'I' (compare Shelley's 'Adonais') and
> which is only vaguely and fleetingly felt by our 'minds', though perhaps the
> deepest part of us. And finally, may not the first of these consciousnesses be
> but a reflection of the second, so that the universal soul best realises itself in
> the separate consciousness of each one.[119]

If the notion of 'double consciousness' takes on a complex and social
significance in Du Bois's writings, Lewis's emphasis on the self's being
defined against nature draws attention to the romantic lineage of the
term. The relationship between the particular and the universal is an
abiding concern in the work of both men. While it takes the form of a
philosophical meditation on the relationship between the individual and
an 'universal soul' in Lewis's letter, this structure of thought was
expanded in his later writings as a means of reconciling Welsh distinctiveness with a broader anti-modern movement that sought to defend the

values of a universal 'civilization'. 'Civilization', argued Lewis, 'must be more than an abstraction. It must have a local habitation and a name. Here, its name is Wales.'[120]

If Lewis's use of the term 'double consciousness' is particularly interesting in the context of this comparative analysis, it is also a concept that can be usefully applied to his dramatic works. 'Doubleness' afflicts many characters in Saunders Lewis's plays which often involve characters moving between incompatible worlds.[121] In *Blodeuwedd* (The Woman Made of Flowers), for example, a nationalist desire to imagine a community based on place and tradition is challenged by a modernist aesthetic which questions all such forms of fusion and reconciliation. *Blodeuwedd*, drawn from the twelfth-century sequence of stories known as the Mabinogi, tells the story of Llew Llaw Gyffes who is cursed never to find a wife. Taking pity on his nephew, the magician Gwydion makes him a wife of flowers, a plan which backfires drastically as his creation Blodeuwedd has no respect for social conventions and takes another lover while plotting to murder her husband. The play is generally seen to revolve around the tension between Lleu's respect for tradition, convention and roots and Blodeuwedd's unfettered sexuality and lack of historical moorings.[122] This is to somewhat oversimplify things, for both Blodeuwedd and Lleu are 'double conscious' in that they are able to see the attraction of the opposite viewpoint. Blodeuwedd can celebrate her unfettered sexuality:

> Gyda mi
> Nid oes yn ddiogel ond y funud hon.
> A'm caro i, rhaid iddo garu perygl
> A holl unigedd rhyddid . . .
> . . . Ond cawod fel fy ngwallt
> A leinw ei synnwyr dro, a'm bronnau dwfn
> A'i cudd ef ennyd rhag murmuron byd,
> A'r eiliad fydd ei nefoedd . . .


> (With me there is
> No security except this point of time.
> Whoever loves me must love danger
> And all the loneliness of freedom. In his time
> He'll have no friends, children will not escort
> Him to his secluded grave. But the heavy flood of my hair
> Will fill his senses for a while, and my breasts
> Hide him for a moment from the murmurs of the world,
> And the instant shall be heaven . . . )[123]

But she can also yearn for those familial and national connections that she sees shared by those around her:

> chwilia Wynedd draw
> A Phrydain drwyddi, nid oes dim un bedd
> A berthyn i mi . . .


> (search through Gwynedd
> And the lengths of Britain, not a single grave
> Belongs to me . . .)[124]

Blodeuwedd, a woman made of flowers who has never experienced childhood, seeks familial connections on the one hand, while needing to quench her uninhibited sexuality on the other. If Lewis is clearly expressing a fear of female empowerment, he is also reconstructing a figure from Welsh myth in order to comment on the ideology of nationalism itself: at once given by ancestry and history, but needing to be created anew; present in the reconstructive imagination of the cultural nationalist, but absent from society; caught in 'a tension between actual and ideal'.[125] Blodeuwedd literally has no past or origins, and her focus is predominantly on the present. For Lleu, the future can be constituted only through the reclamation of the past, and thus for him our origins tell us who we are and determine the choices that we can make in life. Yet both the abandoned Lleu and the created Blodeuwedd are 'dieithr . . . i frechiau mam' (strangers to a mother's arms), a key similarity which suggests that ultimately, for both, tradition is a process of invention and choice, a notion which can be traced throughout the work of the Liverpool-born author who discovered his Welshness and constructed a nationalist politics on the foundation of his imagined Wales.[126] Although Lewis the politician had already dedicated himself to the nationalist cause by the 1920s and completed the first two acts of *Blodeuwedd* in 1925, he failed to complete the play until 1948. It would seem that, for Lewis the playwright, it was not clear in the 1920s how the struggle between modernist fragmentation and nationalist reconciliation would play itself out.

*Blodeuwedd* dramatizes a clash between two modes of historical interpretation that can be seen to struggle for dominance throughout the course of modernism. These modes are famously represented in Samuel Beckett's *En Attendant Godot* of 1952. In Beckett's play Estragon, like Blodeuwedd, is not interested in origins. Vladmir, like Lleu, wishes to hold on to memory. It is then not surprising that Lewis translated

Beckett's play into Welsh (*Wrth Aros Godot*) in 1970, for in doing so he was returning to a set of issues that had troubled his own dramatic works from the outset.[127] If, for Du Bois, African Americans constituted a 'nation without grandfathers', Lewis was to make a revealing, if problematic, comparison when describing the situation of Wales after the acts of union of 1536.[128]

> Wynebwn y gwir amdanom ein hunain: yr oeddem ni, nyni ein tadau ni, nyni'r genedl Gymreig, yr oeddem ni yn union yn yr un cyflwr â Negroaid yr Affrig wedi eu trosglwyddo i'r America. Yr oeddem yn cyfrif cyn lleied â hwythau. Nid oedd inni gyfle o gwbl i ymgynefino â dim a berthynai i lywio na gweinyddu bywyd cymdeithasol. Yr oeddem hefyd wedi colli pob hanes am ein gorffennol ein hunain. Ni wyddem – ni wyddom heddiw – am ein gwareiddiad gynt.

> (Let's face the truth about ourselves: we were, we of our fathers, we of the Welsh nation, we were in exactly the same state as the Negroes of Africa after they'd been transplanted to America. We mattered as little as did they. We had no opportunity to get used to any aspect of the government of social life. We had also lost our history and our past. We did not know – and we do not know today – about our past civilization.)[129]

Saunders Lewis and W. E. B. Du Bois shared Vladimir's commitment to roots and tradition, but tended to view the people whom they hoped to lead as Estragons in that they lacked a historical awareness. Their reactions to the working masses and peasantry is best understood as part of their desire for cultural authority; the construction of a social space from which to speak. Located between a primitivist folk and an unruly proletariat these men of culture could function as humanizing agents in a world threatened by working-class anarchy, and as the mediators between the natural, if unrefined and directionless, spirituality of the folk, and an emergent cultural nationalism.

## MODERNISM IS ORDINARY

By the 1930s, in keeping with Marcus Klein's analysis which I quoted earlier, a generation of writers had emerged who turned to the popular culture, despised by Saunders Lewis and W. E. B. Du Bois, as a basis for their art. If Du Bois and Lewis shared a broadly elitist, high-bourgeois, attitude towards the masses, the poets Langston Hughes and Idris Davies rooted their works within the vernacular popular culture of proletarian communities. For Langston Hughes, Countee Cullen's expressed desire to make his Black identity 'incidental' to a 'universal' poetry was an attempt at 'pour[ing] racial individuality into the mould of American standardisation'.[130] In responding to the emergent bourgeois nationalism of intellectual leaders such as Du Bois, Hughes, in his famous statement of 1926 'The Negro artist and the racial mountain', drew attention to

> the low-down folks, the so-called common element, and they are the majority may the Lord be praised! The people who have their nip of gin on Saturday nights and are not too important to themselves or the community, or too well fed, or too learned to watch the lazy world go round . . . Their joy runs, bang! into ecstasy. Their religion soars to a shout. Work maybe a little today, rest a little tomorrow. Play awhile. Sing awhile. O, let's dance! These common people are not afraid of spirituals . . . and jazz is their child. They furnish a wealth of colorful, distinctive material for any artist because they still hold their own individuality in the face of American standardizations . . . Most of my own poems are racial in theme and treatment, derived from the life I know. In many of them I try to grasp and hold some of the meanings and rhythms of jazz. I am as sincere as I know how to be.[131]

'I believe that poetry should be direct, comprehensible and the epitome of simplicity', stated Langston Hughes, so that it could engage with and depict the lives of what he described as 'the low-down folk'.[132] The central tenets of Hughes's poetic vision were shared by his Welsh contemporary, Idris Davies, who responded in the following terms to English poet Geoffrey Grigson's harsh review of his work in the influential literary journal *New Verse*:

> In the current issue of NEW VERSE you have a word or two about my book of verse, *Gwalia Deserta*. I did not, of course, expect any favourable comment upon it in NEW VERSE, and I certainly was not surprised to see it called 'simple'. I wish it were simpler than it is, for even now it is too 'difficult' for some folk in South Wales – the folk for whom I have tried to write about, the folk who have never heard of NEW VERSE and literary cliques. Without any hesitation, I admit that Gwalia Deserta is simple, but I think you do me an injustice when you say it is superficial. I have written about coal-miners, employed and unemployed, in as realistic a way as I possibly could. I did not try to be pretty-pretty about them. I tried to give an objective account of the whole show. When I tell you that I worked for 7 years in the coal-face, I think you will agree that I had some practical knowledge of my subject. It would have been very easy to make *Gwalia Deserta* obscure . . . I did what I could do, openly and honestly, and I let the book take any chance it had.[133]

While both Hughes and Davies aimed to write a literature of 'simplicity' and direct engagement with an urban, industrialized folk, they did not merely wish to satisfy a mass audience, nor to allow the expression of proletarian sympathies to descend into propaganda. Hughes stated that:

> We younger Negro artists who create now intend to express our individual dark-skinned selves without fear or shame. If white people are pleased we are glad. If they are not, it doesn't matter. We know we are beautiful, and ugly too . . . If colored people are pleased we are glad. If they are not, their displeasure doesn't matter either . . . We stand on top of the mountain, free within ourselves.[134]

The apparent tension here between the poet who wishes to engage in the lives and tribulations of the 'low-down folk' while remaining free within himself on top of the racial mountain, is reflected in Idris Davies's writings. While expressing a qualified enthusiasm for W. H. Auden, Davies dismissed the works of the New Signature poets (Stephen Spender, C. Day Lewis and Louis MacNeice) as propaganda:

> I am a socialist. That is why I want as much beauty as possible in our everyday lives, and so am an enemy of pseudo-poetry and pseudo-art of all kinds. Too many 'poets of the Left', as they call themselves are badly in need of instruction as to the difference between poetry and propaganda. Like many of the pansy poets, they are half-baked and semi-illiterate when it comes to genuine appreciation of English poetry. These people should read Blake on Imagination till they show signs of understanding him. Then the air would be clear again, and the land be, if not full of, fit for song.[135]

Davies drew on a nineteenth-century strain of idealistic socialism often described as 'utopian', 'ethical' or 'religious', which, as M. Wynn Thomas notes, 'unlike its politically aware and economically minded twentieth-century successor, particularly honoured the figure of the artist'.[136] Much the same could be said of Langston Hughes, and both poets combined a broadly socialist commitment to the struggles of the working class, with an aestheticist valorization of the artist. If the aestheticist desire to find an alternative home to a debased society in the alternative world of art was transformed into an identification with an imagined pre-industrial national community in the work of Du Bois and Lewis, Hughes and Davies sought to reject bourgeois materialism by creating works of aesthetic beauty which spoke to the dreams and aspirations of the economically exploited and culturally disdained. This desire to identify with the poor is manifested in the African American tradition by a poet such as Sterling Brown or performer such as Paul Robeson (discussed in detail in chapter 3), who located an alternative to what they perceived to be the alienations of modernity in the 'popular' forms

– work songs and spirituals – of an essentially rural 'folk' who were seen to reside outside the crass debasing effects of mass culture. Hughes and Davies, however, while drawing on the older forms of folk song, blues and hymns (as I shall discuss later), also engaged and utilized the language, rhetoric and discourse of mass commercial culture, and drew on the cultural activities of an industrial proletariat. Hughes combined and juxtaposed 'high' and 'low' cultural forms to the extent that contemporary critic James Smethurst describes him as a 'premature post-modernist'.[137]

Mass culture in the form of sport and music (considered by Malcolm X as the only fields open to the majority of Negroes) feature prominently in the writings of Hughes and Davies.[138] Hughes's 'Prize Fighter', in a poem of that name, comes to the realization that 'Only dumb guys fight', while Davies's 'Ambitious Boxer' punches left and right in his sleep before 'one dawn ended every bout – / His angry wife had lain him out'.[139] Hughes's sequence of 1927, *Fine Clothes to the Jew*, and Davies's *The Angry Summer* are saturated with musical references.[140] Davies's brass bands 'in all the valleys / Blaring defiant tunes', his chapel congregations and visitors to Barry Island singing the 'sweet hymns of Pantycelyn', his violin-playing miners marching to London, his jazz bands and the sopranos and tenors at the penny concerts arranged to raise funds for the striking miners, are mirrored in Hughes's collection where the narrator begins by feeling the blues 'a comin' ('Hey!'), and proceeds to 'sing' a sequence of blues stanzas ('Hard Luck', 'Bad Man', etc.) punctuated by the 'cornets' of the cabaret ('Closing Time'), the beating drums of the jazz club ('Saturday Night'), the black woman who 'croons – De Dawn's a-comin' ('Prayer Meeting'), Minnie who sings her blues ('Minnie Sings Her Blues') and the 'Jazz Band in a Parisian Cabaret'.[141] There are other interesting parallels in terms of theme and content between Hughes's and Davies's poems: Davies's 'Unemployed Miners' finds its equivalent in Hughes's 'Out of Work'; Davies's attack on British neutrality in 'Spain' is mirrored in Hughes's 'Song of Spain'; Hughes's imagined 'Air Raid over Harlem' is thematically connected in its concern for civilian deaths during wartime with Idris Davies's 'Air Raid'.[142] Some release from social suffering can be gleaned from the knowledge in Davies's *The Angry Summer* that 'Lizzie the Barmaid is rippling with fun' in the 'Admiral Nelson' where 'on Saturday night the beer is good' as it is also in Harlem where, in Hughes's poem 'Saturday', Charlie the gambler and Sadie the whore call upon their fellow revellers to 'shake 'em up an'shake 'em up'.[143]

Where the bourgeois modernists lamented the cultural debasement represented by mass culture and sought to forge a language uncontaminated by the discourses of popular culture (Du Bois's Victorian diction and Lewis's self-consciously literary language can be considered examples of this), Hughes and Davies sought an alternative modernism that would function as a vehicle for creating a sense of ethnic solidarity in the creation of a common vernacular. Ann Douglas argues that for many ethnic writers in the United States the creation of a distinctively modern art meant 'undoing dispossession, making inventive use of one's buried or censored cultural and linguistic origins', and much the same can be said for the linguistic minorities within the older nation states of Europe.[144] Seamus Deane's claim that Irish literature tends to dwell in modernist fashion on the medium in which it is written 'because it is difficult not to be self conscious about a language which has become simultaneously native and foreign' can be applied, with added force, to the case of Welsh modernism, for between 1901 and 1951 the numbers of Welsh speakers declined calamitously from 50 per cent to 29 per cent of the population.[145] Deane's phrase can also be applied in modulated fashion to African American writers who, like their Jewish contemporaries in America, found that if their hopes of achieving upward social mobility through linguistic assimilation to a standard norm was always limited, they could turn instead to what 'they already possessed, Yiddish-American and African American vernacular speech'.[146] The 'linguistic revolt' of minority modernist writers was thus quite different to that of modernists within majoritarian traditions, for, whereas the latter sought to forge a language deliberately foreign and estranging to what they perceived to be a degenerate and materialist society, minority writers sought to broker a sense of communal and ethnic solidarity in the poetic reconstruction of the vernacular.

Linguistic choices are particularly significant in this respect. Ann Douglas argues that the black vernacular voice in Hughes's poems was a voice that he 'chose to speak'.[147]

> His lower-class idiom was an earned achievement, not a natural attribute; he had appropriated his black idiom as surely as he'd appropriated the white, and he'd done it far more self-consciously . . . He learned Black English not at home or at school but from outsiders, the dispossessed of his race.[148]

This 'learning' process is enacted in the development of Hughes's 1920s blues poetry. The title poem of his first collection, *The Weary Blues* (1926), begins with the narrator speaking in a standard English which, while alliteratively resonant ('Droning a drowsy syncopated tune'), contains few signs of African American diction as the reader is led into Harlem:

> I heard a Negro play.
> Down on Lenox Avenue the other night
> By the pale dull pallor of an old gas light.[149]

The African American pianist is a vehicle for the speaker's own immersion in the language and sounds of Negro culture. 'O! Blues' exclaims the narrator as the musician makes the 'piano moan with melody'. Ultimately the listener is rendered speechless and can do no more than quote the blues lyrics, themselves framed by quotation marks in the body of the poem:

> 'Ain't got nobody in all this world,
> Ain't got nobody but ma self.
> I's gwine to quit ma frownin'
> And put ma troubles on the shelf.'[150]

By placing the blues lyrics within inverted commas the poem constructs its own hierarchy of discourses, and in *The Weary Blues* most of the poems are spoken in an overtly authorial voice which, if not precisely 'high', is nevertheless clearly distinguishable from the voices of Hughes's African American characters.[151] The vernacular voice, used to represent the blues lyrics, is framed by the standard poetic voice of the poem's narrator. The poem thus enacts the process by which Hughes gains access to a Black vernacular which is not his own, and offers a poetic re-enactment of the poet's own process of learning the language and world view of the 'low-down folks' through immersion in their musical culture. That process has been completed by Hughes's second collection *Fine Clothes to the Jew* (1927), where blues stanzas are represented without the framing voice of the narrator. Rather than enacting the process of listening to the blues, the poems are blues performances in their own right. Listen, for example, to 'Homesick Blues':

> De railroad bridge's
> A sad song in de air.
> De railroad bridge's
> A sad song in de air.
> Ever time the trains pass
> I wants to go somewhere.
> [. . .]

> Homesick blues, Lawd,
> 'S a terrible thing to have.
> Homesick blues is
> A terrible thing to have.
> To keep from cryin'
> I opens ma mouth an' laughs.[152]

While the laughing, open mouth of the final line may be reminiscent of minstrelsy, and while the dialect performance is itself evocative of minstrel conventions, Hughes's blues are not performed for white entertainment nor to denigrate their black subjects. Rather, Hughes is elevating the vernacular in the belief that it offers a source for the reinvigoration of the poetic tradition and is a worthy basis for art. His early poems move between voices, often juxtaposing the assimilationist impulse of a dominant standard English with a distinctive Black urban vernacular. It is this dimension of Hughes's poetry that led Ann Douglas to describe him a 'bilingual' writer.[153]

If the term 'bilingual' foregrounds Hughes's use of dialect and standard voices, it is an accurate description of Idris Davies who wrote his earliest poems in his native Welsh. Seventy per cent of the inhabitants of the industrial township of Rhymney into which Idris was born in 1905 were Welsh speakers, but that percentage was already declining. Davies was overstating the case when he recalled that

> I lost my native language
> For the one the Saxon spake
> By going to school by order
> For education's sake,

for he continued to speak Welsh with family members throughout his life.[154] But the stanza, and the use of the word Saxon, is clearly designed to suggest that his English-language poetic persona is the result of an essentially colonial educational system. Davies was in fact, as Dafydd Johnston has noted, a member of one of the first generations of children in his native Rhymney who would be bilingual, not least as a result of the exclusive use of English in the Board schools set up by the Education Act of 1870.[155] The social trend was towards greater anglicization, and it is perhaps revealing that Davies's earliest published poem describes his difficulty in expressing himself in his native tongue:

> Crwt o gartref Cymreig oedd
> A lliw hen Gymru arno,
> Ond eto aeth i'r ysgol nos
> I ddysgu iaith y Cymro!

Sut y bydd yn dysgu hon,
Ond amser a ddywedai,
Gadewch e'n llonydd yr awrhon –
Mae'r ferf yn methu chwareu.[156]


(He was a boy from a Welsh home,
And had the colour of old Wales upon him,
And yet he went to night school
To learn the Welshman's tongue!

How well he will learn it,
Only time alone can tell,
Leave him in peace this hour –
The verb just will not play.)

The 'struggle over the nature of reality' in Davies's work, embodied in his poetic commitment to depict the realities of working-class life, was also a struggle over language.[157] While a poet such as D. Gwenallt Jones in the less linguistically anglicized Swansea Valley to the west could write a powerful poetry rooted in the experiences of the working class through the medium of Welsh, Davies saw that his desire to write of and for 'the folk in South Wales', demanded that he write in the primary language of that south-Walian experience: English.[158] Davies's poetic development – beginning tentatively in Welsh before he established his mature expression in English – stands witness to the passing of a Welsh-speaking proletarian culture in the Rhymney Valley. If Hughes consciously learned the Black vernacular English practised in many of his most famous poems, then Davies's approximation of south-Walian English was also the result of choice. The decision to write in English was the first significant choice and later, having left the pit for a teachers' training course which allowed him to study English and history courses at Nottingham University, that decision was the basis for crafting multi-voiced sequences that sought to capture the expressiveness of his native community.

The multi-voiced, dialogic, nature of Hughes's and Davies's poetry is best illustrated with reference to specific poems. Hughes's 1936 poem 'Broadcast on Ethiopia' is particularly notable for its juxtaposition of divergent discourses.[159] The poem begins in a formally conservative manner, with the rhyme, iambic rhythm, and slightly clichéd evocation of Mark Anthony in Shakespeare's *Julius Caesar*, all signifying a serious, solemn engagement with a politically turbulent context:

> The little fox is still.
> The dogs of war have made their kill.

Hughes varies the lengths of his lines in the section that follows, and the shift to a more vernacular voice conveys a society's response to Heile Selassie's condemnation of the use of chemical weapons at the League of Nations in 1936:

> Haile
> With his slaves, his dusky wiles,
> His second-hand planes like a child's,
> But he has no gas – so he cannot last.
> Poor little joker with no poison gas!

The final lines move us close to the diction of a grim nursery rhyme or child's doggerel, and this impression is intensified by a quotation from a popular song, associated with Fats Waller, which seems to offer a seemingly playful but thematically profound African American revision of America's myth of foundation: 'MISTER CHRISTOPHER COLUMBUS'. The song is interrupted by a news bulletin regarding Selassie's escape from the 1935 Italian invasion, before being resumed: 'HE USED RHYTHM AS A COMPASS'. These lines are followed by two lines which seem to evoke the nineteenth-century world of the runaway slaves –

> Hunter, hunter, running, too –
> Look what's after you:

– which are themselves followed by a further news bulletin announcing communist electoral success in France. 'France ain't Italy!' shouts a vernacular voice in response to the radio broadcast, to be answered by another passionate voice engaging in debate:

> No, but Italy's cheated
> When *any* Minister anywhere's
> Defeated by Communists.
> Goddamn! I swear!
> Hitler,
> Tear your hair!
> Mussolini,
> Grit your teeth!
> Civilization's gone to hell!

Following this continual juxtaposition of voices, the poem returns to the solemnity of the opening lines as a standard diction returns to reflect on the League of Nation's abandonment of Ethiopia in the face of Mussolini's invasion:

> The British Legation stands solid on its hill
> The natives run wild in the streets
> The little fox is still.

> Addis Ababa
> In headlines all year long.
> Ethiopia – tragi-song

While Idris Davies is less formally innovative, his long sequences *Gwalia Deserta* and *The Angry Summer* are based on shifts of voice, form, rhythm, rhyme and diction that are very close in spirit to Hughes's work. The formal, objective voice that Hughes utilizes at the beginning and end of 'Broadcast on Ethiopia', is reflected in Davies's evocation of the political class during the miners' lockout of 1926:

> The telephones are ringing
> And treachery's in the air.
> The sleek one,
> The expert at compromise
> Is bowing in Whitehall.
> And lackey to fox to parrot cries:
> 'The nation must be saved.'[160]

In the course of his sequence, Davies, like Hughes, juxtaposes the language of newspapers –

> 'These are your children begging for bread,
> You foolish miners!' the newspaper said[161]

– with a social commentary that, as in Hughes, occasionally approximates a grim nursery rhyme, such as in the following revision of 'Oranges and Lemons':

> Oh what can you give me?
> Say the sad bells of Rhymney.

> Is there hope for the future?
> Cry the brown bells of Merthyr.

> Who made the mineowner?
> Say the black bells of Rhondda

> And who robbed the miner?
> Cry the grim bells of Blaina.[162]

Hughes's vernacular voice commenting on Fascist dictators is mirrored in Davies's evocation of Hitler –

> The thug of all thugs, he ranted till he fell
> And even his dust went screaming into Hell[163]

– and, like Hughes, the music of hymns (*Angry Summer*, 31, 47), marching songs (*Gwalia Deserta* XXVII, *Angry Summer*, 44) and American popular culture permeate Davies's sequences:

> Let us dance tonight in Tredegar,
> Jazz to a lively tune . . .[164]

The key thematic concerns of Davies's work are combined when he juxtaposes political memory, communal activities, popular culture and metropolitan misrepresentation in asking:

> Do you remember 1926? The slogans and the penny concerts,
> The jazz-bands and the moorland picnics,
> And the slanderous tongues of famous cities?[165]

If Hughes drew on a wide range of literary references in his work, his allusion to Shakespeare's *Julius Caesar* in 'Broadcast to Ethiopia' is mirrored in Davies's suggestive, and characteristically allusive, reference to 'slanderous tongues'. The phrase appears in Shakespeare's comedy of misrepresentation *Much Ado About Nothing*, where Leanto's daughter, Hero, is 'Done to death by slanderous tongues'.[166] This individual slander is generalized to represent a whole generation in one of W. B. Yeats's most specifically Decadent poems 'Into the Twilight' where

> hope fall from you and love decay,
> Burning in fires of a slanderous tongue.[167]

'Into the Twilight' was initially titled 'The Celtic Twilight' and both the Decadent movement and the Celtic nationalism of the late nineteenth century shared a hostility to what was perceived to be a philistine industrial society. The hostility to human exploitation is shared by Davies and Hughes, but unlike the *fin de siècle* aesthetes and the high modernists of the early twentieth century, neither blamed the members of the proletariat themselves for their suffering and both accessed the modes of resistance and affirmation which they detected in popular urban culture. While Davies's conventional verse forms and occasional lapses into triteness and bathos have led some critics to view the poetry as enacting 'his own cultural disinheritance', the truth is that, as for Hughes, the range of forms and allusions in the poetry – from Blake to Yeats,

Houseman to Eliot, Welsh hymnology to jazz lyrics – draws on his profound and wide knowledge of the English literary tradition as well as popular culture.[168]

Indeed, Langston Hughes and Idris Davies can be seen to play a pivotal role in the shifting cultural landscapes of twentieth-century African America and Wales respectively: in their allusions to hymns and spirituals, their biblical references, their nostalgic evocations of 'Gwalia' and 'Africa' respectively, their poems mark the passing (or residual persistence) of one culture; in their references to jazz, to popular dances, to proletarian consciousness, to Dalí, Picasso, Charlie Chaplin and Barry and Coney Islands, they mark the emergence (and dominance) of another. In the poetry of Hughes and Davies there are clear nineteenth-century influences (manifested in Davies's admiration for the Welsh poet Islwyn and Hughes's indebtedness to Paul Lawrence Dunbar), fused with an experimentation with proletarian vernaculars. Both poets juxtapose voices and points of view, 'high' and 'low' cultures, and in the fragmentary, heteroglossic, form of their poetic sequences both can be seen to manifest a number of characteristics that are today recognized as distinctively 'modernist'. James Smethurst's description of Hughes as a poet who took 'up the problem of a usable past of African-American expressive culture, as well as the problem of a usable present of African American popular culture within the limitations of a mass African-American audience' are equally applicable, when trans-posed to a Welsh context, for Idris Davies.[169] The twentieth-century literatures of Wales and African America develop, in Raymond Williams's terms, from the conflicts, tensions and rapprochements of the emergent and residual cultural forces embodied within the poems of Davies and Hughes.[170]

The tension between the old and the new, the inherited and the chosen, the residual and emergent, is particularly evident in the poets' treatment of religious belief. Writing as socialists, both Hughes and Davies believed that religion encouraged the working classes to displace their worldly concerns into a wholly ineffective religious passion. Davies calls on the miner to 'Come out of your Methodist dream, boy bach / And fight in your sorrow in the sun', and, speaking in the first person, Hughes's poetic consciousness turns to greet Christ himself:

> Listen, Christ,
> You did alright in your day, I reckon –
> But that day's gone now.
> They ghosted you up a swell story, too,
> Called it Bible –

> But it's dead now,
> The popes and the preachers've
> Made too much money from it.[171]

The 'popes and the preachers' in Hughes's poetry of the 1930s are the religious equivalents of industrial capitalists, seeking ultimately to 'make money' and having little sympathy or understanding for the struggles of working people. In describing the 'cyrddau mawr' (day-long series of sermons by renowned preachers), Davies recalls the preacher 'belching behind the biggest Bible':

> And all would be so embarrassed if Jesus Christ
> Came with pick and shovel to the colliery yard,
> Seeking a stent in the four-foot face.[172]

Davies consistently views the miner as not only a 'slave' (a recurring keyword in his poetry) to industry but also as the 'trembling slave' of an intellectually restrictive 'theology' which commits its followers to 'crawl' in a 'barbarous gloom'.[173] The critique of religion cuts both ways, however. For if, Hughes and Davies reject the Christian tradition that had so moulded the culture of their nineteenth-century forebears (as discussed in chapter 1), and seek to expose the hypocrisy of Christian masters, politicians and industrialists, they nevertheless do so within an intellectual terrain made possible by a distinct, if elusive, notion of a genuine Christianity. It seems from the quotations above that the poets' quarrel is less with the gospel itself than with the institutional forms of religion. Idris Davies recalls being told by the deacons 'That I would be roasted and pronged and tossed like a pancake', not for having rejected Jesus altogether but for having 'tried to picture Jesus crawling in the local mine'.[174] If the cast out, vilified and crucified Christ returns as a miner in Davies's imagination, he returns as an African American in one of Hughes's tersest poems:

> Christ is a Nigger
> Beaten and black –
> O, bare your back.
>
> Mary is His Mother –
> Mammy of the South
> Silence your mouth.
>
> God's His father –
> White Master above,
> Grant us your love.

> Most holy bastard
> Of the bleeding mouth:
> Nigger Christ
> On the cross
> Of the South.[175]

Cary Nelson describes it as 'a poem of searing truths uttered by ambiguous speakers' and, while the call and response pattern is clear enough, there is an ambiguity as to who shouts the italicized orders at the end of each stanza – white racists or African American Christians urging a Christ-like turning of the other cheek?[176] The brevity of the lines and absence of designated speakers makes 'Christ in Alabama', written in 1931 as a response to the Scottsboro case, a meditation on the inherent instability of Christian symbolism.[177] The poem meditates obliquely on the Christian roots of Southern racism, and of Black activism. Thus, while seeming to be a critique of religion, the poem seems also to suggest that Christian universalism, in which Christ is a type for the wretched of the earth, has also formed the most powerful basis for challenging racist practices. This tension is embodied within the form of the poem itself with its clear call and response pattern suggesting a sermon or spiritual.

Idris Davies also drew upon the forms and imagery of religious Nonconformity, while seemingly deliberately distancing himself from his parents' beliefs. Tony Conran was perhaps the first to note that poems such as 'Gwalia Deserta XXV', often dismissed as simplistic, should be sung as hymns.

> Who seeks another kingdom
> Beyond the common sky?
> Who seeks the crystal towers
> That made the martyrs sigh?
>
> On earth alone your towers,
> By human strength, shall stand,
> And the waters of your mountains
> Alone shall save the land.
>
> Your cities shall be founded
> On human pride and pain,
> And the fire of your vision
> Shall clean the earth again.[178]

This is a secular, socialist answer to the romantic hymnody of Methodism, with the kingdom in the sky, the fire of divine vision and the emphasis on waters and cleansing evoking the symbolism and imagery of the works of the greatest of all Welsh hymn writers, Williams Pantycelyn. If Davies and Hughes rejected the aestheticist and modernist belief in artistic autonomy, replacing it with a poetry that sought to fuse beauty with social commitment, then a similar logic is displayed in their use of religion. The imagery of Welsh and African American Christianity is transformed in their works from focusing on a kingdom in the sky, to transforming the reality, and infusing the political struggle, on the ground.

The use of popular forms, of hymns, jazz, the vernacular, may lead us to think of the works of Hughes and Davis as being in opposition to a dominant experimental modernism which celebrated the autonomy of the art work. James Smethurst notes, however, that on the left 'writers and readers associated with journals such as *New Masses* saw themselves as proceeding out of modernism'.[179] Idris Davies seems consciously to draw attention to the fact that his poetry does not follow modernist conventions. 'Crossing the Waste Land behind the back streets of Aberglo', he thinks of T. S. Eliot and then of 'Ianto bach Rees who had never heard of T. S. Eliot', and in the playful 'Dai to Dali', Davies's Welsh proletarian everyman asks the leading surrealist to 'Come down and see our crooked, crowded valleys'

> For truth is stranger than any surrealistic art
> Where the slag-heaps hold a mirror to the heart.[180]

If Davies's awareness of modernism is expressed primarily through the content of his poetry, Hughes seems to comment obliquely on modernist practices through the use of montage, parody and pastiche as governing principles in his works. In 'Broadcast on Ethiopia', discussed above, for instance, the modernist juxtaposition of voices coupled with the characteristic high modernist belief that 'Civilization's gone to hell' can be seen as a deliberate attempt on Hughes's part to engage with the aesthetic and political legacies of high modernism. Modernist poetic practice and political commitment combine in Hughes's 'Cubes' where the juxtaposition of black and white on the primitivist canvasses of Picasso mirror the cultural juxtapositions resulting from French colonialism: 'In the days of the broken cubes of Picasso', the French 'Amuse themselves bringing to Paris / Negroes from Senegal'.[181] The result of this is that the 'young African' carries back from Paris 'A little more disease / To spread among the black girls in the Palm Huts'. While Europeans may delight at the cubist primitivism of Picasso's famous portrayal of five nude prostitutes,

*Les Demoiselles d'Avignon* (1907), the 'three old prostitutes' forced on Africa are 'Liberty, Fraternity, Equality'. In a subtle but profoundly far-reaching critique of the modernist claim to aesthetic autonomy, Hughes explores the ways in which the African influences on cubism are based on an exploitative imperial relationship between France and her colonial territories.

If 'truth is stranger than any surrealistic art' for Davies, and cubism is built on a history of imperial exploitation for Hughes, then both can be seen to reject all claims to aesthetic autonomy. Both saw poetry as part of a struggle over the definition of reality, and for both Davies and Hughes mass culture could be turned to as a resource in the struggle against the distorting forms of racism and class exploitation. While many writers on the left, including Kenneth Fearing and Nathaniel West in the United States and D. Gwenallt Jones in Wales, mirrored the Frankfurt School's tendency to view mass culture as a vehicle for the further indoctrination and exploitation of the masses, Idris Davies and Langston Hughes are part of another tradition which saw culture as 'ordinary' and mass culture as the arena for social and aesthetic possibilities.[182] For Davies and Hughes, the making of a culture is a collaborative process drawing in as wide a range of people as possible, and this perhaps is the key difference between their views and those of Saunders Lewis and W. E. B. Du Bois. For Du Bois and Lewis, culture is defined by the educated few who pass it down for acceptance by the majority. For Hughes and Davies, a common culture is one that is continuously recreated and remolded by the collective practice of its members. The high-modernist definition of culture as the preserve of a privileged minority is challenged in the populist modernism of Davies and Hughes by a definition of culture as something that is collectively made, and communally expressed, through a diversity of voices.

## GENDER, ANTHROPOLOGY AND THE FOLK

Du Bois and Lewis considered the proletariat to be a threat to social cohesion and to bourgeois leadership, while Langston Hughes and Idris Davies based their art on the experiences of the industrial working class. A third distinctive strain of modernism, manifested in both the Welsh and African American literary traditions, rooted itself in that other constituency against which Du Bois and Lewis had defined their roles as members of an intellectual elite; the 'primitive and unrefined' rural 'folk'. While sharing a desire to ground their search for new forms of cultural expression in the vernacular and dialect characteristic of Hughes's and Davies's populist modernism, Zora Neale Hurston and Margiad Evans turned to the rural folk of the American South and of rural Wales, rather than an urban proletariat, for their sources. And, while sharing the dislike of urban mass culture characteristic of Du Bois's and Lewis's elitist modernism, Hurston and Evans were not beholden to 'positive' and 'uplifting' images of racial and national vindication.

Hurston referred dismissively to Du Bois's 'talented tenth' as 'the Negrotarians'.[183] In several articles in the 1930s she rejected notions of racial 'uplift' and argued that African American folk expression was not subordinate to Anglo-American high art. She repudiated those who thought that acquiring degrees and losing their dialect were marks of intelligence and deplored 'the intellectual lynching we perpetrate on ourselves; in emulating white': [184]

> Fawn as you will. Spend an eternity standing awe struck. Roll your eyes in ecstasy and ape his every move, but until we have placed something upon his street corner that is our own, we are right back where we were when they filed our iron collar off.[185]

Education, Hurston argued, should not be seen as a vehicle for assimilation, and she suggested that an African faculty be brought to America to teach music and dancing to black Americans:

> You see, no matter how much talent a Negro may have, if he is sent to a white conservatory he is ruined. He gains technique, yes. But he loses the flavor and quality that sets him apart from white artists. What should happen is that this native quality be increased rather than obliterated. That is the only way we can ever hope to add anything to Western arts.[186]

In keeping with this philosophy, Hurston was the only major black writer to attack the first important Supreme Court decision for integration, Brown vs The Board of Education in 1954. She controversially wrote a piece opposing integrated schools in a white Southern newspaper. Werner Sollors suggests that Hurston's position derived from the fact that 'segregation' was for her a 'marginal' issue.[187] It is surely less that 'segregation' was 'marginal', than that for Hurston the desire to preserve cultural differences was paramount. The core of her position was that what black and white liberals had legislated was actually an insulting assimilationism that implicitly said the best way to educate blacks was to whiten them. Hurston lamented 'the white majority's indifference, not to say scepticism' to the 'internal lives' of minorities.[188]

The 'internal life' of 'minorities' was also an issue of central concern for Margiad Evans. In reviewing a volume of English translations of Welsh-language stories by Kate Roberts, the English critic H. E. Bates had wondered why Roberts would bother writing 'in a language that is more foreign to Englishmen than most languages of western Europe'.[189] Margiad Evans noted in response that the 'Welsh will understand me when I say that their great language is an island. Its difficulty makes it remote and few of us who are not born there have the patience and the daring to land on its fervent rocks.'[190] Evans argued that an 'imaginative intensity' compressed into the nation's 'small actual heritage in land' resulted in a creative vitality that gave the Welsh 'a start over the Cosmopolitan tongues'.[191] An anglophone conception of 'Culture' – conceived in 'universalist' terms but predicated on the erasure of difference – held no appeal for Hurston or Evans. If the ideology of racial uplift towards a 'common culture' determined the choices available to women in the Victorian era, Hurston and Evans represent an early twentieth-century commitment to difference manifested in the return to those folk cultures that had been left behind in the drive towards assimilation.

That modernist writers coveted the primitive is a frequently acknowledged fact. In a typically complicating and qualifying analysis Raymond Williams describes the different political implications of this 'recourse to a simpler art':

> As in the earlier case of the 'medievalism' of the Romantic Movement, this reach back beyond the existing cultural order was to have very diverse political results. Initially the main impulse was, in a political sense 'popular': this was the true or the repressed native culture which had been overlain by academic and establishment forms and formulas. Yet it was simultaneously valued in the same terms as the exotic art because it represented a broader human tradition, and especially because of those elements which could be taken as its 'primitivism', a term which corresponded with that emphasis on the innately creative, the unformed and untamed realm of the pre-rational and the unconscious, indeed that vitality of the naive which was so especially a leading edge of the avant-garde.
>
> We can then see why these emphases went in different political directions as they matured. The 'folk' emphasis, when offered as evidence of a repressed popular tradition, could move readily towards socialist and revolutionary tendencies . . . On the other hand, an emphasis on the 'folk' as a particular kind of emphasis on 'the people' could lead to very strong national and eventually nationalist identification, of the kind heavily drawn upon in both Italian and German Fascism.[192]

If this 'vitality of the naive' could form the basis for avant-gardist and fascist tendencies, it could also, as in the writings of Margiad Evans and Zora Neale Hurston, coexist with a self-conscious literary attempt at giving voice to repressed and marginalized female consciousness.[193] If, for Freud, Western civilization was based on the excessive suppression of instinct, modernist writers, as many critics have noted and analysed, were attracted to those aspects of human experience that had been suppressed. The search for the primitive and the exploration of female sexuality thus emerge as being amongst the most central, and widely discussed, themes of modernist art. Neither the return to the 'primitive', nor the interest in female experiences, is unique to modernism, of course, and the conjunction of the discourses of race and gender has a long history. However, the rise of psychology and anthropology as vehicles for understanding human behaviour, the political struggles of first wave feminism and the emergence of regional nationalisms during the era of literary modernism had far-reaching effects on the ways in which writers depicted folk cultures and imagined female experience in the early twentieth century. The works of Evans and Hurston ask us to explore the ways in which the literary representations of 'the people' are affected when marked by developments in ethnography, and by the specificities of women's history.

The shift from a nineteenth-century universal, 'Arnoldian', concept of 'Culture' to a modernist, pluralist, definition of lower-case 'cultures', is well established in intellectual history, where it is often based on a rather simplistic contrast between the Victorian concept's complicity with racism, sexism, classism and imperialism and the modernist attempt to delineate an anti-hierarchical and comparative account of culture. The characteristic nineteenth-century commitment to a universal culture to which all people should aspire, is seen to give way to the twentieth-century's anthropologically informed awareness of cultural difference and pluralism. In registering the problems with this generalizing narrative (which ignores the fact that belief in plural cultures did not eradicate the tendency, prevalent in the works of many modernists, to make invidious comparisons between groups of people, for instance), Susan Hegeman sees the early twentieth-century change in the definition of 'culture' not as a shift from the universalism of 'sweetness and light' to the pluralism of 'anthropology', but in terms of a transformation in the 'axis of categorisation and differentiation from the evolutionary-teleological' to the 'geographical-spatial'.[194] 'Conveniently for the ethnographer or the modernist artist (living in an era of increasingly easy and efficient travel)', notes Hegeman, 'such a spatial reconception of one's relationship to the past makes its objects, and its physical and human representatives, newly tangible, and finally appropriable'.[195] The significance of this 'spatial turn' in anthropology was that it questioned teleological Victorian evolutionary and historical narratives, insisting instead 'on the simultaneity of the primitive with (and within) the civilised'.[196]

The anthropologist Franz Boas is generally viewed as the intellectual catalyst for this shift away from teleological narratives of development. Invited by Du Bois in 1906 to deliver the commencement address at Atlanta University, Boas spoke on the past greatness of African cultures. Du Bois recalled that in a year that had witnessed a vicious anti-Black pogrom in the city, Boas told his audience that they 'need not be ashamed' of their African past.

> [T]hen he recounted the history of black kingdoms south of the Sahara for a thousand years. I was too astonished to speak. All of this I had never heard and I came then to realise how the silence and neglect of science can let the truth utterly disappear or even be unconsciously distorted.[197]

Working within a context of rising immigration and virulent Anglo-Saxonsim, Boas, a German-Jewish emigrant to America, dedicated his life to attacking racist intellectual paradigms and social policies. By dismissing the notion that racial continuities could be analysed by measuring heads and contending that there were no racial differences in intelligence, his work marked the culmination of what George Stocking describes as a 'paradigm shift' in the social sciences.[198] Human behaviour after Boas's intervention would be analysed in terms of environment and culture rather than in biological terms. In the papers of the Universal Races Congress, with which I began this book, Boas compared the physical shapes of European groups and first-generation immigrants to the United States. He noted that head shapes varied even in children of first-generation immigrants. This, Boas suggested, was a result of the fact that that 'mechanical treatment of children in America differs from their treatment in Europe. The European child is swaddled while the American child is allowed to lie free in the cradle.' While Boas noted that such practices could not account for all physical differences, his conclusion was unambiguous: 'The old ideas of absolute stability of human types must, however, evidently be given up, and with it the belief in the hereditary superiority of certain types over others.'[199]

Boas's rejection of skull measurement as a useful classificatory tool for races brought him into conflict with one of Britain's leading anthropologists, the professor of geography and anthropology at the University College of Wales, Aberystwyth, H. J. Fleure.[200] From the 1910s onwards Fleure dedicated himself to the exploration of racial types in Wales. Though Fleure was an outspoken critic of racism, he nevertheless based his analyses of British racial types on a distinction between 'Nordic', 'Alpine' and 'Mediterranean' stocks. While explicitly noting the dangers of applying the linguistic designation 'Celtic' to physical anthropology, he nevertheless believed that the 'little dark people' – the fundamental 'Mediterranean' type found in mid Wales – were ill disposed to industrialism and had cultivated religion, music and poetry while leaving commercial enterprises to the Nordic types. Born in Guernsey and concerned about the alienation bred by urban industrial societies, Fleure argued for the retention of those rural values that he believed persisted among the racial remnants on the more remote western areas of Wales. He viewed Wales as the 'ultimate refuge' of 'old thoughts and visions that had been lost to the world' and hoped that once the 'fever of industrialism' had subsided, the riches of the Celtic tradition would be rediscovered.[201] In order to sustain this world view, he insisted on the persistence of head forms, and believed that human types were not wholly cosmopolitan, for 'whenever different climatic zones have been invaded, the intruders have failed to secure a permanent footing, perished outright, or disappeared by absorption'.[202] For Fleure, Franz Boas's findings on the virtual instant modification of head form amongst European immigrants in America, as presented at the Universal Races Congress of 1911, had to be countered for they would 'destroy the foundations' of the 'anthropological research for the elucidation of race history' to which he had dedicated his life's work.[203] Fleure believed that craniometry was leading to 'a stage at which it is possible to outline something of the process of race development'. This desired 'outline' would be predicated on an interpretation of racial heredity and Fleure, therefore, rejected Boas's opinions on 'the rapid modifiability of type'.[204]

Despite their disagreement regarding craniometry, there are some striking similarities in the thought of Franz Boas and H. J. Fleure when placed against the dominant liberal universalism of the Victorian era.[205] In opposition to the Arnoldian, universalist conception of 'Culture', both Boas and Fleure sought to foster cultural diversity. In a revealing English-language foreword to a collection of Welsh-language essays on prehistoric Wales, Fleure celebrated the fact that this 'group of students' (which included the poet and ethnologist Iorwerth Peate) have sought 'to express their loyalty to their country' by attempting to 'dissipate the

opinion that Wales before the Romans was the home of mere uninter-
esting savagery'.[206] The reassessment of the Welsh past is seen to have a
relevance for the present, for as he noted in an article of 1918 which
echoes Franz Boas's sentiments on African continuities in America,

> instead of looking upon the Celtic tradition as the poor keepsake of a conquered
> people, all but exterminated by the Anglo-Saxon conquerors, we might with
> more truth look upon it as an heirloom, a precious ancient phase of our own
> tradition, to lose which would impoverish the British peoples forever.[207]

The Welsh language was key to this process of cultural appreciation and
preservation. Fleure embarked on a study of regional dialects, relating
them to physical types, and encouraged the recording of folk tales and
stories as a record of historical change and 'racial' memory.

> The hill countries of Europe keep alive inheritances from the remote past,
> though in most cases the languages of the plains have spread up the valleys
> and have ousted ancient forms of speech save for a few words used in the
> farmyard or the kitchen. There are, however, a few old tongues surviving here
> and there, Basque on the Franco-Spanish frontier in the west, Romansch,
> Ladin and Frioul in the Eastern Alps. In none of the cases just mentioned does
> the ancient language gather around it powerful emotional associations
> affecting large numbers of people, but this is the case in Wales. We may say
> that in many ways Wales is the refuge and repository of ancient heritages
> England once possessed, but we must also say that associations gathering in
> comparatively recent times around the Celtic language, still widely spoken
> and possessing a growing literature, have helped to keep up and even in some
> ways to accentuate distinctions that are rooted in a long and involved history.[208]

David Livingstone notes that Fleure's resort to a notion of 'survivals'
was indicative of his 'disinclination to see human culture as treading a
predetermined evolutionary path'.[209] Franz Boas, like Fleure, rejected
the notion that peoples could be rated on an evolutionary scale. Evolution,
for Boas and Fleure, was not equivalent to 'development'. Indeed,
departing from the concept of a universal 'Culture', Boas talked in terms
of cultures and illustrated his beliefs by arranging museum exhibitions
according to 'culture area' as opposed to a unitary plot of civilization's
evolution. Boas believed that a 'primitive' fish hook should be properly
displayed alongside other products of the culture to which it belonged –
baskets, weapons, jewellery etc. – rather than next to other more
'advanced' fish hooks.[210] He insisted that artefacts be analysed and
discussed in relation to their cultural context and in their own terms and,
like Fleure, advocated the collection of folklore and the material culture
of an area, seeking to arrange it 'according to the canons of interpretation

used by the culture itself'.[211] If Fleure's work often seems to establish an organic relationship between the 'folk' and the 'soil', he was equally interested in the cultural contacts and historical changes that were the focus of Boas's work. Both anthropologists emphasized the importance of language to culture and society, rejecting the idea that one language could be superior to another, and, in Fleure's work on Welsh and Boas's on Native American languages and African American dialects, linguistic pluralism was valued and promoted.[212] Both Boas and Fleure insisted that cultures developed in their own terms, in their own languages. Fleure saw that distinctiveness as being rooted in race, while Boas emphasized ever changing cultural practices, but despite their disagreements both can be seen to be proponents of cultural pluralism. They rejected the Victorian, 'Arnoldian', monistic, conception of 'Culture' which different groups were striving to reach and, concurrently in New York and Aberystwyth, replaced it with an 'anthropological' conception of pluralism.

Zora Neale Hurston was a student of Franz Boas at Columbia University, and actually played a role in his campaign to undermine the practice of craniology. Langston Hughes recalled that Hurston was not one to flaunt her education, noting that she did not 'let college give her a broad a' and 'had great scorn for all pretensions, academic or otherwise'.[213]

> Almost nobody else could stop the average Harlemite on Lennox Avenue and measure his head with a strange-looking, anthropological device and not get bawled out for the attempt, except Zora, who used to stop anyone whose head looked interesting, and measure it.[214]

Boas himself felt that the merit of Hurston's anthropological work lay in its sincerity. '[P]itched headforemost into . . . a crib of negroism' upon her birth in Eatonville, Florida, Hurston knew African American folklore from her childhood.[215] The authenticity of this background led Boas to encourage her return to the South to collect 'Negro folklore'.[216] In the revealing preface that he wrote for her anthropological volume *Mules and Men* he described the way in which

> she entered into the homely life of the southern Negro as one of them and was fully accepted as such by the companions of her childhood. Thus she has been able to penetrate through that affected demeanor by which the Negro excludes the White observer effectively from participating in his true inner life.[217]

It is Hurston's 'insiderness' that is of significance to Boas, her ability to access an 'inner' dimension of African American life inaccessible to the 'White observer'.

Margiad Evans's connection to anthropological discourse is not as direct as Hurston's, but anthropological thought was an influential presence within the writing and publishing milieu of 1930s Wales. The October 1939 edition of Keidrych Rhys's innovative literary journal *Wales* includes a piece on 'The Welsh people' in which H. J. Fleure reports on his most recent findings following the cranial measurements of '4000–5000 adult men of ascertained localised ancestries'.[218] This piece appears alongside reviews by Margiad Evans of P. Thornesby Jones's *Welsh Border Country* and G. Jekyll and S. R. Jones's *Old English Household Life*.[219] While Evans laments the way in which 'whole towns are crinkled into a sentence and villages are crumpled almost to a word' in Thornesby Jones's book, she finds *Old English Household Life* to be a satisfying 'dictionary of candle and shovel, kettle, chimney and hovel: it is the majority of things gone, a corner cupboard history, a deliberate envocation, a summary of man's odd needs' which unfortunately omits to mention 'the kiddle for baking bread, the methods of de-lousing heads and bedding, witchcraft, and the effect on household life of the dispersal of monasteries'.[220] Evans writes as an insider in both cases, chastising Jones for attempting to 'demolish the might of Glyndwr' who 'to us was a prince', and needing only to 'lift up' her eyes from *Old English Household Life* to see the objects listed: 'a white earthenware horse who with us stands on the dresser and is dusted every alternate Friday. This one might say, puts one in the book without any further trouble.'[221] If Boas valued Hurston's 'insiderness', it seems that Keidrych Rhys assumed that Evans would be an appropriate reviewer of two books recording the material objects of rural life due to her familiarity with the people and places described.

However, if Boas believed Hurston to be a participant in the folk life being observed, Hurston's own view was that the acquired skills of Boasian anthropology allowed her to adopt a necessary analytical distance from the culture of her upbringing which was 'fitting me like a tight chemise'.

> I couldn't see it for wearing it. It was only when I was off in college, away from my native surroundings, that I could see myself like somebody else and stand off and look at my garment. Then I had to have the spy-glass of Anthropology to look through at that.[222]

There is a revealing difference between Boas's view of Hurston as a full participant in the culture being studied, and Hurston's own description which, as Barbara Johnson has noted, describes an opposition between inside and outside which is dramatized in her works as anthropologist and imaginative writer.[223] A similar insider/outsider duality is also central, for somewhat different reasons, in the case of Margiad Evans. Born Peggy Whistler in Uxbridge, London, she developed a strong attraction to the border country between Wales and England during childhood visits and eventually settled in Herefordshire, on the English side of the border.[224] Her authorial pseudonym is a Welsh form of Margaret (from which Peggy is derived), coupled with the surname of her paternal grandmother, Ann Evans, who was 'believed to be of Welsh extraction'.[225] While Stephen Knight views Evans as a writer who was 'Welsh by choice', Evans noted in a revealing letter to Gwyn Jones that

> I'm not Welsh: I never posed as Welsh and it rather annoys me when R[obert H[erring] advertises me among the Welsh short stories because I am the border – a very different thing. The English side of the border too; I don't speak fretfully: you know how I honour the Welsh writers and how hospitable they have been to me.[226]

The affirmative and confident 'I am' is somewhat undermined by the hybrid border context in which that identity is located, and the passage draws our attention to what Tony Brown has described as Margiad Evans's 'acute awareness of the liminality of her situation'.[227] That 'liminality' is embodied in the reference to the 'hospitality' of Welsh writers, suggesting that Evans views herself as an outsider seeking refuge, or domicile, with another family or group to which she does not fully belong. Rhys Davies, in one of the earliest accounts of Evans's work, described her as an 'authentic seer', thus combining a sense that Evans was a prophetic visionary of future literary developments with an emphasis on the act of 'viewing' which is a feature of her work noted by several contemporary critics. Stephen Knight, for instance, explores Evans's adaptation of the late nineteenth-century trope of the metropolitan traveller's journey to an exotic 'wild Wales', and refers to her 'ethnographic treatment' of the border communities in her early work.[228]

Evans and Hurston can be usefully compared as minority women novelists of the 1930s who drew on anthropological conceptions of culture to reveal, what they perceived to be, the inner lives of rural folk. Amongst the significant similarities between their writings are their attempts to capture the dialects spoken by their characters; their detailed accounts of folk dances (compare the description of the Cakewalk in Hurston's play *Color Struck* to Margiad Evans's description of dancing 'The Black Nag' at a rural fête in *Country Dance*); their interest in folk superstitions and beliefs (Hurston's interest in hoodoo rituals is similar to Evans's repeated evocation of Welsh superstitions); and their descriptions of manual farm labour by individuals 'broken from being poor'.[229] In their emphasis on the life and customs of rural societies both authors share an ethnographic impulse to document ways of living and thinking. The ways in which anthropology 'developed the ethnographic paradigm' in 1920s and 1930s literature has been explored by George Marcus and Michael Fisher who argue that 'ethnographies as a genre had similarities with traveller and explorer accounts, in which the main narrative motif was the romantic discovery by the writer of people and places unknown to the reader'.[230] This is clearly part of the motivation behind Margiad Evans's *Country Dance*, published by the major British publishing house Basil Blackwell, and Hurston's books of the 1930s which appeared under the imprint of J. B. Lippincott. For Marcus and Fischer, ethnography mounted a critique of Western civilization by contrasting modern man unfavourably with a primitive man who had retained a 'respect for nature', 'sustained close, intimate, satisfying communal lives' and 'retained a sense of the sacred in everyday life'.[231] This notion of the primitive as the source of revitalization for an industrialized and mechanized centre can be traced at least as far back as the Romantic movement and, as I have argued elsewhere, was central to the construction of 'Celticism' in the Victorian era. What is remarkable is the longevity of such ideas, which were reinforced and given a new lease of life in the 1930s.[232] Hazel Carby quotes another of Boas's students, Ruth Benedict, on the loss of African American distinctiveness in the cities of North America, and argues that anthropology provided Hurston not only with a 'spyglass' but with a 'theoretical paradigm that directed her toward rural, not urban, black culture and folk forms of the past, not the present'.[233] Fleure's student Iorwerth Peate similarly saw an essential 'Welshness' disappearing in the cities and felt that urban influences on rural areas were disrupting traditional crafts and mores; he referred, for instance, to the way in which an influx of 'Woolworth spoons' was 'destroying the remnants of the turner's trade'.[234]

   The impact of modernity on rural life is represented in the writings of Evans and Hurston by rooted, traditional, female characters who are fooled by inauthentic, predatory salesmen. The salesman in their work represents the more unstable and strategically negotiated sense of identity promoted by capitalist modernity. In his wide-ranging analysis of ethnic modernism in the United States, Werner Sollors notes that 'one way in which the confrontation of the premodern world with modernity was represented in literature was through the figure of a seductive stranger, typically a salesman of sorts, who brings modern commercial leisure culture to remote, traditional settings'.[235]

This is precisely what happens in *Country Dance* and in Hurston's 1933 story, 'The Gilded Six Bits'. The community in Evans's *Country Dance* is disturbed by a 'china and hardware' salesman who is travelling with his little girl. Mary's initial response is to send him away, but she becomes sympathetic when he states how 'good it is to hear English again! The folk here have a tongue that we cannot understand.'[236] Mary buys cough mixture and a scrubbing brush from him. Ten minutes after the salesman's departure a neighbour runs to the door describing how a salesman has just won her mother's confidence by claiming that he's happy 'to be among his own people' and asking who 'won the prize for singing at the Eisteddfod this year'.[237] The salesman's ability to perform 'Welshness' and 'Englishness' introduces a contingent sense of identity into the novel, and seems to contradict the opening statement that 'the struggle for supremacy in her mixed blood is the unconscious theme of Ann Goodman's book'.[238] In Hurston's 'The Gilded Six Bits', Joe, a factory worker, returns home with nine silver dollars every Saturday afternoon but on one occasion finds his wife in bed with ice cream salesman Otis D. Slemmons.[239] Slemmons has gold pieces for jewellery, a mouth full of gold teeth, and speaks 'Chicago talk'. Joe beats Slemmons, who is driven away leaving a gold piece on a watch chain behind him which Joe uses to remind his wife, Misie May, of her unfaithfulness. After a reconciliatory bout of lovemaking with Joe, Misie May finds Slemmons gold piece to be gilded, and the story revolves around the symbolism of Joe's authentic pieces of silver and Slemmons's gilt pieces. The intrusion of salesmen into the stories of Evans and Hurston represents a loss of innocence, and an awareness that character and identity, as manifested in language and behaviour, can be performed and can function as deceptive masks.

Literary critics have tended to align Hurston and Evans with the more rooted and stable identities of their traditional characters. Hazel Carby's critique of Hurston's ruralism can be applied with equal relevance to Margiad Evans. Whereas Carby valorizes Langston Hughes's role in shaping a 'discursive category of the folk in direct response to the transformative social process of migration to urban cities and industrialisation', she accuses Hurston of having 'constructed a discourse of nostalgia for a rural community'; and, whereas Hughes's use of the blues, jazz and popular cultural forms 'represented a communal sensibility . . . embodied in the conditions of cultural transformation', Hurston 'assumed that she could obtain access to, and authenticate, an individualised social consciousness through a utopian reconstruction of the historical moment

of her childhood in an attempt to stabilize and distance the social contradictions and disruptions of her contemporary moment'.[240] Margiad
Evans's idealization of the year she spent, at the age of eleven, on her
aunt's farm at Benhall, near Ross-on-Wye, has been seen to be the
personal experience informing *Country Dance*, and the terms of Carby's
contrast between Hurston and Hughes could be applied with equal
validity to Margiad Evans and Idris Davies.[241] Both *Country Dance* and
*Their Eyes Were Watching God* can be seen as literary manifestations of
the various movements which aimed to shift the orientation of society,
both politically and physically, 'back to the land'.[242] However, if the
works of Zora Neale Hurston and Margiad Evans may be criticized for
constructing 'a discourse of nostalgia for a rural community', these
authors were not merely longing for a lost past, for their meditations on
their own positions as women and as members of ethnic minorities lead
to a fictional questioning of the anthropological gaze which their works
simultaneously enact and problematize. There can be 'no persuasive
representation of a distinctive "native" mode of expressivity', notes Dale
Patterson in a discussion of African American and Russian writers,
'without creative experiments that replicate an unbridgeable gap – those
linguistic lacunae and cognitive lapses that emanate from exchanges
between literate outsiders and indigenous insiders'.[243] It is this interpretive conflict that lies at the heart of the anthropologically inflected works
of Margiad Evans and Zora Neale Hurston.

The writings of Evans and Hurston offer particularly striking examples of the kind of 'ethnically marked' texts described by the critic Doris
Sommer: texts which 'can sting readers who feel entitled to know everything'.[244] In her revisionist theory of minority writing, Sommer urges us
to move beyond the notion of universalism as a measure of literary worth
(that is the assumption that the study of literature exposes us to the
universals of the human condition) and to turn to the tropes of particularism (the ways in which a text may resist meaning, holding the reader
at arm's length and refusing intimacy). In *Mules and Men*, Hurston
warns her readers that

> Folklore is not as easy to collect as it sounds. The best source is where there
> are the least outside influences and these people, being usually under-
> privileged, are the shyest. They are most reluctant at times to reveal that which
> the soul lives by. And the Negro, in spite of his open-faced laughter, his
> seeming acquiescence, is particularly evasive. You see we are a polite people
> and we do not say to our questioner, 'Get out of here!' We smile and tell him
> or her something that satisfies the white person, because, knowing so little
> about us, he doesn't know what he is missing.[245]

The shift from 'these people' to a 'we' who address a distanced 'you' is significant in this passage as the tone shifts from scientific objectivity to identification, from 'speaking of' to 'speaking for'. Neutral objectivity is abandoned as the paragraph proceeds and the characteristically anthropological gesture of peeling away the surface appearances to reveal a hidden truth is frustrated. Indeed, as Barbara Johnson has noted, it is difficult to know whether the narrator is describing a strategy or employing one.[246] The conclusion of Margiad Evans's *Country Dance* can be discussed in similar terms. Following the end of the diary that constitutes the novel the third-person narrative voice returns with her final thoughts:

> All old stories, even the authenticated, even the best remembered, are painted in greys and lavenders – dim, faint hues of the past which do no more than whisper of the glory of colour they once possessed. Yet live awhile in these remote places where these pale pictures were painted, and something of their first freshness will return to them, if only in the passing of a homestead or the mowing of a field. You will come to know how the dead may hold tenure of lands that were theirs, and how echoes of their lives that are lost at a distance linger about their doorways. Here among the hills and valleys, the tall trees and swift rivers, the bland pastures and sullen woods, lie long shadows of things that have been.
>
> But new furrows are ploughed in old fields, harvests are sown and gathered, and names that sprang from the red earth itself have died away to a faint murmur which only native ears attuned may hear.[247]

Hurston's notion that folklore is not as easy to 'collect' as it 'sounds' would seem to comment obliquely on the limitations of the documentary strategy of her anthropological discipline. The relationship between the 'sounding' of a story and its representation in words or paint is also central for Margiad Evans who seems to argue that familiarity with a place will slowly lead to an appreciation of a past that can only be dimly perceived in greys and lavenders, in whispers and murmurings. If Hurston shifts from a position of objectivity to identification in the course of her paragraph, Evans retains a sense of intellectual distance, yet seems to assume greater knowledge than the 'you' being addressed. Both passages thus construct a reader who is an outsider, less attuned to and less acquainted with the worlds described by the authors. How would Evans know that 'native ears' hear the 'faint murmur' beyond the perception of others if she were not, to some extent, a native herself? Both passages seem, simultaneously, to engage and deflect the 'you' being addressed. Is this a form of self-promotion on the part of the writer, suggesting that her own privileged positions as an African American, or a native of the border, makes her our only source of reliable information, or are we being warned against useless prying in the world of 'long shadows' and of smothering 'laughter and pleasantries'? 'If reliable knowledge cannot be gotten', notes Doris Sommer, 'control is impossible'.[248]

Both Hurston and Evans frustrate the reader's desire to 'know' and to 'control' by respecting the play of cultural differences within their novels. They do so by not only describing differences of language and dialect between insiders and outsiders, but by dramatizing the effects of language and dialect difference within the texts themselves. At the levels of both content and form Margiad Evans's *Country Dance* can be read as a meditation on the effects of linguistic difference. The folk song which forms the novel's epigraph, in the original Welsh followed by an English translation, tells the reader that:

> Ti gei glywed os gwrandewi
> Sŵn y galon fach yn torri.
>
> (Thou shalt hear if thou listen
> The sound of the little heart breaking.) [249]

These lines resonate with the reference to 'native ears attuned to hear' in the novel's penultimate sentence discussed above, but also alert us to the bilingualism of the world that we are about to enter. Margiad Evans uses a range of devices to convey linguistic difference within her text. Occasionally, Welsh appears in an untranslated form – 'Cythraul', 'Winllan', 'Nos Da', 'Ffarwel'. More commonly, Welsh appears in the text followed by a translation – 'Ni fedrwch gael ei debyg yn Lloegr' (In England you will not find the like).[250] At other times, English is used, but we are told that Welsh is being spoken:

> Then he comes, leans his elbow on the wall, and says in his tongue:
> 'Good day, my proud girl.'[251]

In more developed passages of dialogue it is unclear whether the characters are speaking Welsh or not. Given that Ann tells us that the master 'always speaks to me in Welsh', and given the use of 'thee' and 'thou' to suggest the Welsh *ti* and *chi* respectively, it would seem that a Welsh dialogue is being conveyed through the medium of English in the following passage, but we are not told that this is the case and it is possible that an English dialect, influenced by the Welsh language, is being spoken here:

'Now, Ann, art thou vexed with me?'
    'I've reason to be.'
He draws his brows together, as he does when he is angered.
'Thou art very saucy for a shepherd's daughter: very high and haughty thou art, Ann Goodman.'[252]

In a text which, at the level of both content and form, is centrally concerned with linguistic tensions, these literary representations of bilingualism are notable. 'The literature of ethnic soul', notes Dale Patterson, 'must not demystify the aura of something intangible and inexpressible even as it provides narrative access to the other within the body of a nation'.[253] This is one way of explaining the reasons why Margiad Evans is not consistent in her use of Welsh in her text. As Kirsti Bohata has suggested, the persistent use of the Welsh language in the text frustrates that metropolitan audience's desire for complete knowledge of life on the border.[254]

The text's resistance to complete comprehensibility is reflected not only in its inherent bilingualism, but also in the suggestive understatement that characterizes Margiad Evans's elliptical prose style, making *Country Dance* (while uncharacteristic of Evans's other more gothically inflected novels) reminiscent of other modernist attempts at stripping sentences down to their basic constituents. Delmore Schwarz has suggested that Ernest Hemingway's 'reticence, intensely emotional understatement' is partly derived from 'the simplified speech which an American uses to a European ignorant of English' in the context of an ethnically diverse and multilingual America, and there may be some legitimacy in suggesting that Evans's style is the product of a bilingual environment, for its simplicity may be seen to approximate the language an English person would use when communicating with monolingual Welsh speakers.[255] Margiad Evans had stayed for some weeks in the summer of 1930 in the village of Pontllyfni in north-west Wales, an area with a high concentration of monolingual Welsh speakers at that time, and referred to that period in a letter to Kate Roberts: 'I know not one word of Welsh (now) and very little of Wales, but I have never forgotten the fact that thousands of men and women and little children speak nothing else.'[256] The border area in which the novel is set was virtually wholly English speaking by the time Evans was writing the novel in the 1930s, but the transposition of names from north Wales, coupled with the sense of linguistic tension, suggests that Evans's actual experiences in Pontllyfni informed the reconstruction of the mid-nineteenth-century border community. *Country Dance* can be seen, then, to engender a process of linguistic dialogue made possible by Evans's bicultural experiences and border identity. In the nineteenth-century border landscape of *Country Dance*, characterized by a persistent ethnic struggle between the Welsh and the English, Ann Goodman's familiarity with the dominant and multiple subdominant discourses of the novel's ethnically divided and gendered society seems to equip her uniquely with the burden and the gift of speaking in tongues.

Margiad Evans's concern with linguistic difference is paralleled in the often troubling relationship between voices and linguistic registers (if not actual languages) in the writings of Zora Neale Hurston. Henry Louis Gates Jr's powerful argument for Hurston's centrality in the African American canon rests on his Bakhtinian, 'dialogical' reading of *Their Eyes Were Watching God* that proclaims it the first example of a 'speakerly text'.[257] The free indirect discourse of Hurston's novel (that is those moments where the third-person voice of the omniscient narrator expresses the thoughts or feelings of another character) is not written in the standard English of classic realism but is shot through with vernacular sayings and forms, blurring the boundaries between the dialect of the characters and that of the traditional narrator's standard English. The novel abounds in examples of this technique, such as the following passage where the narrator is conveying Janie's thoughts about her partner, Tea Cake:

> Tea Cake wasn't doing a bit more harm trying to win hisself a little money than they was always doing with their lying tongues. Tea Cake had more good nature under his toe-nails than they had in their so-called Christian hearts. She better not hear none of them old backbiters talking about her husband! Please Jesus, don't let them nasty niggers hurt her boy. If they do, Master Jesus, grant her a good gun and a chance to shoot 'em.[258]

When read aloud, it would seem that much of this passage is a direct quotation, but there are no quotation marks here. Hurston's use of this 'bifocal' utterance which contains 'elements of both direct and indirect speech' results, for Gates, in a 'written manifestation of the aspiration to the oral'.[259] Hurston thus triumphantly 'resolves the implicit tension between the literal and the figurative . . . between standard English and black dialect', between observer and observed.[260] Approached, however, in the light of Hurston's statements regarding anthropology, in light of the relationship between languages in the text, and in light of the fact that, while Janie does indeed gain a voice at various stages in the narrative, there is nevertheless a third-person narrator who dominates proceedings, the novel may be seen to embody an anxiety concerning narrative point of view and a self-referential problematizing of language and representation. In Hurston's African American retelling of Exodus, *Moses, Man of the Mountain*, the great leader of the Hebrews becomes exasperated at the fact that he has to rely on his brother Aaron to speak on his behalf. Realizing that Aaron 'don't seem to pacify' the increasingly unhappy grumbling Hebrews, Moses concludes that:

> It's no use for me to try and talk any high court language to these people. I might as well get right down with them, and you don't need to talk for me anymore Aaron. I'll just talk to the people myself.[261]

This particular tension between being spoken for by others, and of speaking for oneself, is dramatized in *Mules and Men* when an informant, Robert Williams, tells the story of a young woman who goes to college. Upon her return to Eatonville, Florida, she is asked to transcribe a letter dictated by her illiterate father. As the educated daughter transcribes the story she finds that she is unable to convey on paper the clucking sound that her father uses to coax a mule to work. To the father's question 'Is you got dat?' she answers

> 'Naw suh, Ah ain't got it yet.'
> 'How come you ain't got it?'
> 'Cause Ah can't spell (clucking sound).'
> 'You mean to tell me you been off to school seben years and can't spell (clucking sound)? Why Ah could spell dat myself and Ah ain't been to school a day in mah life. Well jes' say (clucking sound) he'll know what yo' mean and go on wid de letter.'[262]

The scene is clearly a self-reflexive consideration of the problem of ethnographic representation, but also, as Alice Gambrell argues, 'contributes to Hurston's career-long, highly self-conscious consideration of her scripted role as a female medium'.[263] The fact that the transcriber is a daughter is significant in this respect. Just as Ann is the female protagonist able to move between linguistic communities in *Country Dance*, it is Hurston, the female anthropologist, who has the ability to give voice to African American folklore in *Mules and Men*, and Janie who speaks of both female and African American experiences in *Their Eyes Were Watching God*. For Evans and Hurston, the representation of, and meditation on, differences in language and dialect, are related to the processes of giving voice to a suppressed female subjectivity.

This is particularly the case in scenes depicting the deaths of mothers. In Hurston's autobiography, *Dust Tracks on a Road*, her mother's death is described as follows:

> I had left Mama and was playing outside for a little while when I noted a number of women going inside Mama's room and staying. It looked strange. So I went on in. Papa was standing at the foot of the bed looking down on my mother, who was breathing hard. As I crowded in, they lifted up the bed and turned it around so that Mama's eyes would face the east. I thought that she looked to me as the head of the bed was reversed. Her mouth was slightly open, but her breathing took up so much of her strength that she could not talk. But she looked at me, or so I felt, to speak for her. She depended on me for a voice . . .
>
> Somebody reached for the clock, while Mrs. Mattie Clarke put her hand to the pillow to take it away.
>
> 'Don't!' I cried out. 'Don't take the pillow from under Mama's head! She said she didn't want it moved!'
>
> I made to stop Mrs. Mattie, but Papa pulled me away. Others were trying to silence me. I could see the huge drop of sweat collected in the hollow at Mama's elbow and it hurt me so. They were covering the clock and the mirror.
>
> 'Don't cover up that clock! Leave that looking glass like it is! Lemme put Mama's pillow back where it was!'
>
> But Papa held me tight and the others frowned me down. Mama was still rasping out the last morsel of her life. I think she was trying to say something, and I think she was trying to speak to me. What was she trying to tell me? What wouldn't I give to know! Perhaps she was telling me that it was better for the pillow to be moved so that she could die easy, as they said. Perhaps she was accusing me of weakness and failure in carrying out her last wish. I do not know. I shall never know.[264]

That the mother should 'depend' on the author for a voice suggests that a past has been muted and needs to be given articulate form by the present generation. The fact that 'Papa held me tight' and the 'others frowned me down' suggest that, while being positioned several generations after slavery, Hurston's own generation will still have to struggle against embedded traditions of patriarchy and submissiveness. The community, while often the source of a valuable folk wisdom in Hurston's writings, is here a coercive power that has to be resisted if Hurston is to remain faithful to her mother's wishes. Here the mother's wishes pose a challenge to folk customs, but the daughter's inability to fulfil those wishes leaves her in a state of confusion. The passage ends in doubt, for without understanding the mother's speech the daughter has no hope of comprehending her thoughts.

Communication is also a central concern in a similar scene from Evans's *Country Dance*, though here it is the father rather than the daughter who has difficulty in understanding the mother's wishes.

I take my father his tea in the bottom meadow, where he is loading hay with
the rest: when I come back there is my mother on the floor beside her bed,
gasping for breath.

'What is it? What have you' I cry, running to her.

'My heart!' she answers.

I lift her up in my arms and lay her on the bed. Her face is grey like ashes
and damp with sweat; every minute it seems to me that she must die under my
hands.

'Mae arnaf eisiau gweld John,' she gasps.'I want to see John'. She has
fallen into her own tongue, that she has not spoken since she was married.

There is no time to lose: from the window I can see my father down in the
meadow, working by the gate. I lean out with my fingers to my mouth and give
the shepherd's whistle; he looks up.

'Father!'

He throws down his fork. I wait but a moment to see him start on the way
before going back to my mother, who is groaning.

. . . [W]hen he comes to her bed and tries to speak to her, she does not seem
to know he is there.

'What is she saying? What does she want?'

'She is asking for you, Father.'

'Myfanwy, Myfanwy, I am here. Speak to her, Ann! Can't you? Speak her
own tongue!'

'Father is here,' I tells her.

She grasps my wrists.

'Oh, be quick, Ann dear, be quick, I am dying.'

'He is here,' I cry over and over.

At last I tells my father to say:

'Rwaf [*sic*] yma wrth eich ymyl' . . .

He tries, word for word, after me, and she smiles as best she can . .

There is nothing we can do to hinder her, but she is still alive when the
doctor comes into the room. He looks at her once, and a minute after we see
that she is dead. Without a word or another glance my father pulls the curtains
and goes away downstairs.[265]

The narrating daughter is a cultural mediator in this scene. She can speak
and understand the Welsh that her mother 'has not spoken since she was
married', and can thus translate her dying mother's words to her monolingual English father. Marriage has literally meant the silencing of one
dimension of the mother's identity in a striking equation of linguistic and
gender suppression. The mother's last gesture is to smile 'as best she
can' (whether ruefully or with pleasure is not clear) at the father's belated
attempt at speaking her own language, and the whole passage meditates
self-reflexively on the problems inherent in representing the Welsh

experience through the medium of English. The Welsh language (printed with some revealing spelling errors) is the realm of the female, of unuttered and unutterable feelings repressed by marriage, while the English language belongs to the patriarchal realm of the husband and doctor.

If the mother's native voice and language have been rendered silent in the patriarchal and often violent world of *Country Dance*, Ann Goodman literally writes herself into being in the form of the diary that constitutes the novel.[266] The diary begins with its author noting that 'Gabriel gives me the book, telling me to write in it all I do, for him to see, until we shall be married'.[267] Language is here a form of surveillance. The question of language difference, and representation of linguistic difference carries a charged significance, and it is upon reading the accounts of her encounters with Evan ap Evans that Gabriel explodes in a fit of jealousy, throwing the diary 'in to the brambles and nettles' while exclaiming:

> 'I know Welsh,' he cries, 'I understand why you looked on the ground when that man passed you, speaking his dirty tongue. Get away you little bitch, and find your Welshman!'[268]

In the novel's first representation of masculine violence against women Gabriel 'pushes' Ann 'on the ground'. Following his departure, Ann retrieves her diary, and notes that 'it is mine now. Farewell Gabriel.'[269] From that moment she is writing for herself, an unambiguous representation on Evans's part of a woman's claim to the words she writes and a reclamation of her own expressivity. This act of authorial control within the diary mirrors the process of discovering and publishing described by Margiad Evans in the novel's introduction. Ann's writing of her own self into being is re-enacted in Margiad Evans's reclamation and re-presentation of Ann's voice for history.

> Circumstances have dimmed the memory of this woman and ironically accentuated that of the rivals, Gabriel Ford and Evan ap Evans, shepherd and farmer, Englishman and Welshman. The glare which at her death picked them out with horrible distinctness has left her curiously nebulous and unreal, a mere motive of tragedy. Even today, nearly seventy years later, anyone of our countryside will describe either of them from hearsay. Only one very old man remembers her face because as a boy he loved it.[270]

Ceridwen Lloyd-Morgan describes *Country Dance* as an 'act of recovery of women's lost history', and it is interesting to note that one of Henry Louis Gates Jr's claims for the significance of *Their Eyes Were Watching God* is that the novel enacts the voicing of a culturally muted expressivity.[271] Gabriel's attempt to control Ann's language and behaviour, and violent response to her expressed thought, in *Country Dance* finds its equivalent in the relationships between Janie and Joe Starks in *Their Eyes*. Janie responds to the growing sense of restriction that she feels in their marriage in the following terms:

'You sho loves to tell me whut to do, but Ah can't tell you nothin' Ah see!'

'Dat's cause you need tellin',' he rejoined hotly. 'It would be pitiful if Ah didn't. Somebody got to think for women and chillun and chickens and cows. I god, they sho don't think none theirselves.'

'Ah knows uh few things, and womenfolks thinks sometimes too!'

'Aw naw they don't. They just think they's thinkin'[272]

Their dialogue revolves around the question of who is allowed to 'tell' what they 'see', and to 'think' what they 'know'. Joe's increasing authoritarianism results in his hitting Janie when 'the fish wasn't quite done at the bone, and the rice was scorched'.[273] Janie responds by internalizing her feelings and her thoughts:

She stood there until something fell off the shelf inside her. Then she went inside there to see what it was. It was her image of Jody tumbled down and shattered. But looking at it she saw that it never was the flesh and blood figure of her dreams. Just something she had grabbed up to drape her dreams over. In a way she turned her back upon the image where it lay and looked further. She had no more blossomy openings dusting pollen over her man, neither any glistening young fruit where the petals used to be. She found that she had a host of thoughts she had never expressed to him, and numerous emotions she had never let Jody know about. Things packed up and put away in parts of her heart where he could never find them. She was saving up feelings for some man she had never seen. She had an inside and an outside now and suddenly she knew how not to mix them.[274]

If the internalization of feeling is seen as a female act of withdrawal, the distinction between the 'inside' and 'outside' is also, as noted earlier, central to Hurston's embrace of anthropology which allowed her to 'see myself like somebody else' and to 'stand off and look' at the 'garment' of her native culture.

The threat of physical violence against women and the forced repression of the female voice are powerfully evoked in *Their Eyes Were Watching God* and *Country Dance*, and surely undermine the claim that these novelists base their work on 'a discourse of nostalgia for a rural community'.[275] As Mary Helen Washington argues persuasively, 'when Hurston chose a female hero for *Their Eyes Were Watching God* she faced an interesting dilemma: the female presence was inherently a critique of the male-dominated folk culture and could therefore not be its heroic representative'.[276] Much the same can be said of Margiad Evans's choice of Ann Goodman as the narrator of *Country Dance*, where again the apparent valorization of rural life is undermined by an awareness of the way in which female subjectivity and autonomy is suppressed. The representation of hidden – oppressed or repressed – experiences revolves around issues of linguistic and gender difference in the writings of Hurston and Evans. Their form of ethnographic modernism resists what Doris Sommer describes as the 'liberal embrace' of 'well meaning readers' which seeks to 'reduce otherness to sameness'.[277] As women novelists writing from a minority experience, Hurston and Evans not only allow the subaltern to speak, but challenge their readers to listen.

## CONCLUSION

This chapter has been an attempt at substantiating Raymond Williams's desire for an account of modernism which addresses internal differences, and turns to some revealing works produced in what he referred to as 'the wide margins of the [twentieth] century'.[278] My discussion of the bourgeois, proletarian and folk strains within Welsh and African American modernisms is informed by Williams's suggestion that modernism be analysed from 'a standpoint not its own . . . from the deprived hinterlands, where different forces are moving'.[279] This desire to adopt an outsider's position is a characteristic of Williams's criticism, and is a tendency which he himself traced to his upbringing 'outside the metropolis' in his economically, if not communally, 'deprived hinter-land' on the Welsh border. Williams was to note that his native village, Pandy, was a place that was 'so marginal a case', that 'there were so few places like that I subsequently went to'.[280] The particularity of this experience may be seen to inform Williams's questioning of metropolitan universalism, and his insistence that the study of any cultural formation would have to 'attend to individual differences inside it'.[281]

Nevertheless, just as Williams tended occasionally to dramatize his sense of isolation or marginality, there is a sense in which Pandy was less marginal than he suggests. Williams notes that, while Pandy was a rural village, the 'very fact of the railway' on which his father, Harry, worked as a signalman, meant that he was aware of 'the trains passing through, from the cities, from the factories, from the ports, from the collieries', and 'by the fact of the telephone and the telegraph' the signalmen 'had a community with other signalmen over a wide social network, talking beyond their work with men they might never actually meet but whom they knew very well through voice and opinion and story, they were part of a modern industrial working class'.[282] Rather than lamenting the debasing effect of radio and television on the 'masses', Williams consistently argued for the opportunities offered by such technologies and their potential to develop enriching means of entertainment and encourage an 'outward looking' attitude in which even the most marginal communities could take 'their own best knowledge to a wider and more active society', bringing cultures into positions of dialogue and exchange.[283] This was a truth that Raymond Williams would have known from his childhood, as documented in the moving diaries of his father, Harry. The entry for 31 August 1937 offers a fitting conclusion for this chapter. It was Raymond's sixteenth birthday, and Harry's scribbled note in his 'National Union of Railwaymen' diary tells us that the day started with father and son rising early 'to listen to fight – Tommy Farr v Joe Louis'.[284]

# 3

# 'They feel me a part of that land': Paul Robeson, Race and the Making of Modern Wales

3. *The Proud Valley* (1940).

Paul Robeson's death on 23 January 1976 was one of the first significant events to take place in America's bicentennial year. A few months later a group of poets from the United States marked the two hundred years of their nation's independence by embarking on a tour of the British Isles. The poets visited several major cities, but in an improvised detour to their itinerary the African American poet Michael S. Harper accompanied Denise Levertov to the Welsh village of Abercanaid.[1] Harper's 'Visit to Abercanaid' is dedicated to Denise, but is addressed to her mother, Beatrice, who was born in Abercanaid but is now

> gone from this valley for eighty years,
> alive, blind and going deaf in Oaxaca,
> her eighteen years in a Mexican family
> loomed in the lovely embroidery of her daughter's peasant clothes.[2]

The poem is truly transnational, moving from Oaxaca back to Abercanaid via London and Cardiff. Perhaps the most significant journey in the poem, however, is 'down the road' from Abercanaid to

> the shrine
> of Aberfan, site of the schoolhouse
> where children died in the arms
> of their teachers in great avalanches
> of rock . . .

If it was two hundred years since American independence, 1976 also marked a decade since the morning in October 1966 when a large part of one of the waste tips above the small mining village of Aberfan, south of

Merthyr Tydfil and a few miles from Abercanaid, started to move, engulfing Pantglas Junior School and killing 144 people, 116 of whom were children. 'The world reacted to the disaster with shock, horror and perhaps a guilty conscience for a hundred years of cheap coal', stated the author of the most authoritative study of the disaster.[3] In terminal decline by the final decades of the twentieth century, much of the mining industry was already history by the time of Harper's visit in 1976. He notes the 'green covering the mine openings' and the 'bright stream' that 'purifies after decades / of coal-smoke', before offering an evocation of the landscape and culture of south Wales which, despite its references to zigzagging gullies and rugby crowds, never collapses into mere stereotype due to the striking choice of verbs – 'grunt', 'wailing' – and the final reference back to the 1966 disaster:

> We walk up a small gully zigzagging to the smell
> of roses and faint gardenias in summer sun;
> the chopped hills grunt in their green capes
> toward the Cardiff docks twenty miles away,
> the rugby stadium, the poetry of crowds
> wailing in victory and defeat as the rains
> fertilize the gravesites of taught children.

'Taught' may be the most important word in the poem. It only occurs once, at the close of the second stanza – the halfway point – and binds the first two stanzas tightly to the two stanzas that follow. It is a word that conveys, simultaneously, a teacher's occupation and the heightened emotional response to tragedy; a word that foregrounds the process of cultural communication, whilst also conveying the immanence of a cultural break as the threads that tie the present to the past are pulled tight in response to an event that threatens to defy poetic representation.

The next stanza begins with the poet greeting Denise Levertov's mother:

> Beatrice Levertov: hearing your daughter
> read your poem of childhood, of valley reveries
> of 'shop' and 'doctor' as your own father ran out
> with his collar to catch the local train, I send you
> message-greetings in homage to Denise
> whose images rise into clouds as triumph-trumpets
> in the spoken utterance of growth and change,
> for she has come home in her backtracking of you.

Barbara Johnson, speaking generally of apostrophe, notes that this style of address reveals 'the desire for another's voice' and Harper's greeting suggests a desire for mutual recognition and continuity, a desire to open lines of communication in the face of tragedy and death.[4] Time ceases to be linear as Denise's 'backtracking' of her mother opens possibilities for movements across chronological, geographical and emotional limits. Kimberly Benston has described Harper's poetry as a space where 'history is defined not by death or its henchmen but by the refigurative energy of those who see and hear resonances of resistive will'.[5] These figures of resistance are often jazz musicians in Harper's work and Benston's observations on the poem 'Dear John, Dear Coltrane' are equally applicable to 'A Visit to Abercanaid': 'Far from excluding the possibility of renewal, the violence threatening cultural and genealogical continuity . . . is possibly enshrined as the enabling agent of an histori- cally "witnessed" and specifically located "Black Orphic" descent and return.'[6] The 'violence threatening cultural and genealogical continuity' in 'A Visit to Abercanaid' is the 1966 disaster at Aberfan, and the 'Black Orpheus' who has travelled into the valleys to witness the suffering of the mining communities, and who returns with his regenerative music, is Paul Robeson. In the penultimate stanza Denise carries a rock from the river Canaid, to give to her mother 'in the darkness of August' whilst 'listening to . . . the giant basso of Paul Robeson / who joined you for tea when she was seven'. The poem's meditations on lines of kinship and communication are concluded in the final stanza where Beatrice is described as smiling 'in Oaxaca over aerogram' with the 'Mark Abercanaid' whilst 'listening to lullabies of Robeson'. Robeson func- tions in the poem as a means for Harper to bridge the African American experience – which forms a consistent point of origin in his work – and the particular bonds of kinship informing Denise Levertov's own iden- tity. Beatrice's movement out of Wales to Mexico is mirrored in Robeson's international travels which are embodied in the geographical spaces traversed in the poem itself. Denise Levertov described how, given the absence of a firm sense of place and community in her own diasporic life, the 'inherited tendencies and the influence of the cultural milieu of my own family' had a heightened bearing on her sense of self.[7] Harper's 'Visit to Abercanaid' is simultaneously a tribute to Denise and Beatrice Levertov, a poetic response to the Welsh landscape and an elegy for Robeson whose music seems to connect the geograph- ical and historical fragments that constitute the poem, enacting what Robert Stepto has described as 'kinship-in-process' – the persistent teasing and tracing of familial continuity in the 'the grace notes' of human experience.[8]

In greeting Beatrice Levertov directly and describing an imagined scene where she opens an aerogramme from Abercanaid, Harper is foregrounding that activity of exchange between poet and reader, speaker and subject, performer and audience, that is at the heart of the poem's meditation on loss, kinship and perpetuation, a meditation that concludes appropriately by evoking the life and legacy of Paul Robeson. Harper makes no direct reference to Robeson's relationships with Wales in the poem, but the setting is itself suggestive and by having the poem published in the *Anglo-Welsh Review* in 1977 he could assume that his readers would make the connection, for Robeson's visits are revered in Wales as being amongst 'the most resonant moments in Welsh political and cultural history'.[9]

Robeson's connections with Wales are said to have begun in 1928, when he impulsively joined a group of marching Welsh miners singing in London's West End. The next ten years saw him donating money to, and visiting, Talygarn Miners' Rest Home, appearing in many concerts across Wales including an appearance at the Caernarvon Pavilion the night after an explosion had claimed 266 lives at the Gresford Pit near Wrexham, and, most famously, a visit to Mountain Ash in 1938 for the 'Welsh National Memorial Meeting to the Men of the International Brigade from Wales who gave their lives in defence of Democracy in Spain'.[10] The 1930s also saw Robeson establishing connections with the multi-ethnic community in Cardiff's Butetown, which was also home to the political activist and Pan-Africanist native of Philadelphia, and uncle by marriage to Robeson, Aaron Mosell.[11] 1939 saw Robeson playing the role of David Goliath, an African American seaman who settles in a Welsh mining village, in one of the few movies which he did not later disown, *Proud Valley*. Hounded during the McCarthy era for his communist sympathies, Robeson had his passport confiscated from 1950 to 1958. The persistent invitations made throughout the 1950s for Robeson to appear at the Miners' Eisteddfod in Porthcawl, led to the 'Transatlantic Exchange' of 1957 which allowed the Eisteddfod audience to hear Robeson's voice via a telephonic link from New York. Following the return of his passport in 1958, he visited the National Eisteddfod at Ebbw Vale, where he was introduced by Aneurin Bevan, and presented with a Welsh hymn book by the leading Welsh modernist poet, T. H. Parry-Williams. In the October of that year he finally appeared in person at the Miners' Eisteddfod in Porthcawl. His last significant contact with Wales occurred in 1960 when he appeared with the Cwmbach Male Choir at a Movement for Colonial Freedom concert in the Royal Festival Hall, London.[12]

Robeson's visits have come to play a significant part in narratives of Welsh history. Neil Evans has argued that the tendency to overestimate the extent of Welsh tolerance towards minorities was given academic support in the 1970s and 1980s by a school of social historians who viewed the proletarian internationalism and cosmopolitanism of the south Wales valleys as being rooted 'in the plural experience of the coalfield'.[13] Dai Smith, for example, identifies the emblematic resonances of 'Robeson', while reinforcing the established view of cosmopolitan, international, south Wales:

> South Wales, at its provocative best, contradicted the curtailers of human interaction anywhere and everywhere it could. The ideal was, perhaps, often merely, though movingly, emblematic as when south Wales miners arranged a transatlantic radio link so that Paul Robeson, deprived of his civil liberties and his passport in the USA, could sing at their Eisteddfod; or when Nye Bevan . . . welcomed Robeson to the National Eisteddfod in Ebbw Vale in 1958. Yet if this south Wales was an ideal or even an abstract idea it was also its actual representation which was readily understood, in human terms, by those who came across it.[14]

Elsewhere Smith views the appearance of Bevan and Robeson on the Eisteddfod stage in 1958 as a 'symbol of what could be done if Wales spoke to the world', and Hywel Francis referred to the event as the meeting of 'two great internationalists and champions of humanity united at Wales' "prif ŵyl", its premier cultural festival'.[15] In the years following the granting of some measure of Welsh political autonomy with the establishment of the National Assembly for Wales in 1999, Robeson emerged again as a significant cultural marker; a symbol of the internationalism that characterized the best of Wales's past and the signifier of a cultural tolerance which a devolved Welsh nation should seek to develop. The new millennium saw a striking exhibition (sponsored by the National Assembly amongst other bodies) entitled 'Let Robeson Sing; a celebration of the life of Paul Robeson and his relationship with Wales', which travelled to universal acclaim around the nation. The accompanying book sought to 'remind Wales of an old friend who learned much from us and still has much to teach us, as a people and as a nation'.[16] The exhibition's title evoked the 1950s campaign for the return of Robeson's passport and reappeared in 2001 as the title of a chart hit in which the Welsh rock band The Manic Street Preachers sought to 'learn to live' and 'learn to sing' like their African American hero who possessed 'a voice so pure – a vision so clear'.[17] While the exhibition, the accompanying booklet, and The Manic Street Preachers' single sought, successfully, to appeal and engage a wide general audience, discussions of Robeson's relationship with Wales never seem to move beyond well-meaning, but very limited, commentaries. As an 'honorary Welshman', a 'gentle giant', an 'old friend', a 'voice so pure', a 'champion of humanity' for whom 'we'll keep a welcome in the hillsides', Robeson is burdened by a legacy of affectionate but ultimately simplistic stereotypes in the Welsh imagination.[18] It seems that, to adapt M. Wynn Thomas's discussion of a very different public figure, 'a comfortable, affectionate familiarity with a "known" public identity' prevents us from recognizing any longer the turbulent originality of Robeson's work, and 'the troubling and troubled nature of his gifts'.[19]

In evoking 'the giant basso of Paul Robeson' and concluding his 'Visit to Abercanaid' with the act of listening to 'lullabies of Robeson', Michael Harper inadvertently offers a fairly accurate reflection of the way in which Robeson is remembered in Wales. For, in listening to 'lullabies of Robeson' we are in danger of falling into a complacent sleep. The Czech novelist Josef Škvorecký may jar us out of a self-satisfied slumber. In 'Red Music', which appeared in the same year as Harper's 'Visit to Abercanaid', Škvorecký describes the ways in which jazz, suppressed under the Nazis, continued to offer a means of anti-authoritarian expression in Soviet-controlled Czechoslovakia where 'the lives of individuals and communities' were controlled 'by powers that themselves remained uncontrolled'.[20] While modern jazz was rejected as the 'degenerate' music of a 'vanishing class', the communist authorities

> pushed Paul Robeson at us, and how we hated that Black apostle who sang, of his own free will, at open-air concerts in Prague at a time when they were raising the Socialist leader Milada Horáková to the gallows, the only woman ever to be executed for political reasons in Czechoslovakia by Czechs, and at a time when great Czech poets (some ten years later to be 'rehabilitated' without exception) were pining away in jails. Well, maybe it was wrong to hold it against Paul Robeson. No doubt he was acting in good faith, convinced that he was fighting for a good cause. But they kept holding him up to us as an exemplary 'progressive jazz man', and we hated him. May God rest his – hopefully – innocent soul.[21]

Robeson's 'innocence' is a subject of controversy. During a visit to the Soviet Union in 1949 Robeson had become increasingly aware of the persecution of Jews. Among Paul and Essie Robeson's closest Russian friends was the Yiddish actor and impresario Soloman Mikhoels, whose brutal murder in 1948 (on Stalin's personal order it later transpired) had stunned the Russian Jewish community. The Robesons had entertained

Mikhoels along with the Yiddish writer Itzik Feffer on a sponsored visit to the United States in 1943, and Robeson was keen to meet Feffer again during his 1949 visit. After repeated urgings Robeson was allowed to see Feffer alone in a hotel room. Drawing a finger across his own neck and writing on scraps of paper in a room that was assumed to be bugged, Feffer, who was under arrest, communicated to Robeson that Mikhoels had been murdered by secret police and that the country was witnessing a purge of Jewish culture.[22] Introducing his encore at Tchaikovsky Hall in Moscow a few days later Robeson spoke of the 'deep emotional ties between American and Soviet Jews, a tradition continued [by] the present generation of Jewish writers and artists'.[23] He proceeded to sing the 'Song of the Warsaw Ghetto Rebellion', 'Zog Nit Keynmol', in Yiddish. While most commentators have noted that following a moment's silence 'the stunned audience, Great Russians and Jews alike, responded with a burst of emotion', David Levering Lewis argues that the response was actually divided.[24] Loud booing is clearly audible on recordings of the concert, partly stimulated no doubt by the presence of KGB agents scattered about the hall. 'Those who approved courageously redoubled their applause', notes Lewis, 'while the objectors shouted their disapproval more loudly'.[25] While this confrontation between Muscovites must have displeased the Kremlin, upon his return to the United States Robeson categorically denied any knowledge of Soviet anti-Semitism. His silence is particularly damning given that, unlike many other Western supporters of the USSR, he had definitive knowl-edge of an anti-Yiddish, if not anti-Semitic, campaign. Such tensions were to reoccur as Robeson continued in his unwavering support for the Soviet Union. Although he remained silent about Khrushchev's 1956 revelations of Stalinist atrocities, several intimates have since revealed that he was profoundly shaken.[26] While the Manic Street Preachers are the most recent of many plausibly to present Robeson's suicide attempt in a Moscow hotel in March 1961 as the result of his being drugged by the CIA, Robeson's careful biographer also draws attention to the fact that the singer had become increasingly agitated that night as people attending a late-night party in his room begged for his assistance in locating imprisoned relatives.[27]

Such disturbing, unsettling and paradoxical elements in the African American performer's life are completely ignored in the imagined 'Robeson' of the Welsh. Discussions of Robeson and Wales may benefit from the bracing (if at times excessive) revisionism that Robert Stradling brings to bear on Welsh history.[28] Stradling has suggested that historical narratives that see south Wales as the centre for the emergence of a highly developed internationalist class-consciousness are often predicated on exaggerated accounts of the allegedly unique commitment of Welsh miners to the Republic in the Spanish Civil War, and it could be added that Robeson – closely associated in the Welsh historical imagination with the cause of the International Brigades – plays a similar talismanic role in such narratives. Whereas Hywel Francis sees Paul Robeson's presence at the National Memorial Meeting at Mountain Ash as a symbol of 'the cause of internationalism which the Spanish struggle represented', Stradling notes that the Welsh support for the Spanish Republic was also informed by a virulent strain of anti-Catholicism, and while Ireland and Scotland sent men to Spain in greater numbers than did Wales, neither of these nations felt the need to 'manufacture a history of popular struggle' based on the 'deathless list of Wales's glorious dead' that had begun to be memorialized in the Mountain Ash meeting.[29] In his revisionist polemic, *Wales and the Spanish Civil War*, Stradling discusses those Communist Party members who had spent time in Moscow studying for a year in the Lenin School and notes that

> the commitment of hardened loyalists to the Soviet Union arose out of and was driven by a fierce concern for the working classes in general and for their own communities in particular. Nevertheless, in the last analysis, such men, and many other party members who never made it to Moscow, were emissaries of the Comintern and thus (in effect) not so much 'internationalists' as single-minded agents of the totalitarian Stalinist state.[30]

Stradling's account is marred by the unnecessary (and unfortunately characteristic) insertion of 'in the last analysis' – a coercive cliché that assumes that there comes a moment when all that has gone before is rendered irrelevant, that there is a rhetorical and historical vantage point from which, to quote Stefan Collini, 'all that matters is the outcome or reigning state of affairs at a posited moment of judgment, as in the logic of a game or war or contest of some kind'.[31] The suggestion seems to be that as these men were 'single-minded agents of the totalitarian Stalinist state' their 'commitment . . . for the working classes in general and for their own communities in particular' is rendered irrelevant. While a post-Cold War perspective will inevitably condition our responses to twentieth-century history, it is crucial that we are able to engage our historical imaginations in a way that allows us to understand the meaning of the Soviet Union for leftist activists in the past. In registering the destructiveness of the Soviet experiment as it degenerated into Stalinist debasement, we should not ignore its role in offering an alternative, a narrative of possibility, for political activists of the left around the world. For many African American and Welsh socialists in the mid-twentieth century the Soviet Union offered the only challenge to Western capitalism and imperialism that seemed powerful enough to matter. 'If Soviet internationalism is interpreted as primarily definable by its destructiveness to Soviets', argues Kate Baldwin, 'it is occluded as a narrative of possibility for non-Soviet others'.[32]

These tensions – between emancipation and incarceration, the critique of inequality and a willing blindness to social atrocity – are embodied in the life and career of Paul Robeson. I have no intention of offering a totalizing account of that life here. In what follows I seek to reconstruct the role that Wales played in the evolution of Robeson's political and cultural thought in the 1930s, before going on to explore the extent to which his cultural views were in some ways reflected, and in others frustrated, in his performance as a miner in his 'Welsh' movie *Proud Valley*. The inadequate, but significant, engagement with questions of racial difference in that film led me to revisit the 1930s context from which it emerged and to offer a reading of the Welsh industrial fiction of the period that sees it not as the representation of a society that 'contradicted the curtailers of human interaction anywhere and everywhere it could', but as a fiction structured along lines of race and class, reflecting a society profoundly troubled by questions of ethnic difference. I argue that 'Robeson' in 1930s Wales is a much more complex and ambiguous figure than previous analyses have suggested, and that his presence should obligate us to fashion more nuanced and adequate accounts of the Welsh culture with which he engaged.


## ROBESON'S POLITICAL AND CULTURAL THOUGHT: NATIONALISM AND INTERNATIONALISM

In July 2003, at the National Library of Wales, Aberystwyth, Hywel Francis concluded a lecture entitled 'Paul Robeson: his legacy for Wales' with the apparently rhetorical question: 'Mae e'n rhan o'n gwlad fach ni – pa wlad arall yn y byd all ddweud shwd beth?' ('Robeson is a part of our small nation – what other country in the world can make such a claim?')[33] The answer is that many nations can, and do, make such a claim. Much is made of Robeson's statement that 'there is no place in the world I like more than Wales', and his sense that 'Welsh hymns are the closest thing to Negro spirituals'.[34] While we need not question the sincerity of such assertions, they do need to be evaluated in the context of what Jonathan Karp has described as Robeson's 'ethnic two-timing'.[35] For instance, Robeson quoted Frederick Douglass's observation that 'nowhere outside dear old Ireland, in the days of want and famine, have I heard sounds so mournful' as those of Negro songs, and he described 'the countryside in and around Cork' for *The Irish Democrat* as a place 'where the people understood me . . . because of their long history of British oppression'.[36] Similarly, he drew attention to Marjory Kennedy-Fraser's suggestion that Negro songs were direct products of Scottish folk songs – a cultural connection that took political form when the Scottish Trade Union Congress passed a resolution in support of returning Robeson's passport in 1954, thus giving rise to the 'Let Robeson Sing' campaign.[37] Robeson detected in the music of Russian serfs a 'note of melancholy, touched with mysticism' that was also prevalent in Negro spirituals, and asserted that he had on occasion 'found whole phrases that could be matched to Negro melodies'.[38] Moreover, the 'sigh and tear' of Yiddish folk songs also testified to the fact that 'these people are closer to the traditions of my race' than the peoples of imperial nations such as France, Italy and Germany, and in Egypt, the only African nation that Robeson visited, he informed his auditors of the unique cultural and linguistic relationships that existed between Egyptians and African Americans.[39] Robeson described his belief in the 'oneness of humankind' as deriving from 'the simple, beautiful songs of my childhood, heard every day in church and every day at home in the community – the great poetic song-sermons of the Negro preacher and the congregation . . . [were] in the tradition of the world's great folk music'.[40] In combining the folk songs of different nations, and audiences from different cultural backgrounds, he was using the black congregational model of his youth to forge new connections, new bases for identification among people who may never before have conceived of their experiences in a comparative context.

Robeson argued that his encounters with the British Labour movement in general, and the Welsh miners in particular, played a key role in the development of the internationalism that he espoused in his concerts.[41] He spoke of having 'learned my militancy and my politics from your Labour Movement here in Britain' and remembered travelling 'all over the British Isles, visiting with the Welsh miners, railwaymen, dock workers and textile workers – sharing their griefs and little triumphs, learning their songs, basking in the warmth of their generous friendship and hospitality'.[42] In linking the African American experience to that of other peoples through performance, Robeson was consciously rekindling and regenerating the transatlantic connections forged by the abolitionists in the nineteenth century for the battle against capitalism in the twentieth century.[43] This active forging of alliances on the political left was perceived to be against the national interests of the United States and, unwilling to testify that he was not a member of the Communist Party, Robeson, as noted earlier, was barred from travelling and had his passport confiscated for eight years from 1950. Not only was he banned from going overseas, he was also barred from travelling within the Americas. Unable to give an arranged concert in Vancouver in 1952, Robeson responded by singing to over 40,000 Canadians at the Peace Bridge Arch at the western extremity of the Canadian–American border. During that concert Robeson referred to an invitation that he had just received to appear at the Miners' Eisteddfod – 'I just couldn't receive an invitation that could mean more' – before going on to note that it was in Wales that he 'first understood the struggle of white and Negro together':

> When I went down into the coal mines – into the Rhondda Valley – went down in the mines with these workers, lived among them – later did a picture, as you know, called 'Proud Valley' – and I became so close that in Wales today, as I feel here, they feel me a part of that land. And I have just received an invitation to appear at a festival in October to be given by the miners and by the workers of Wales, and I hope to be able to get there to do that. (Applause).[44]

It would be another six years before Robeson would be allowed to travel overseas. Shortly before the lifting of his passport ban in 1958, Robeson was interviewed by Pacifica Radio, San Francisco. He was asked whether 'your commitment to the political scene' resulted from 'your feeling about your own people . . . or did it have other overtones or political convictions?' He answered revealingly:

> First it starts as an American Negro, interested in my own people. The other great change is very constant in my mind. I was in the Welsh valley, and the Welsh people sing very much like we do – the Negro people – in many of our songs – beautiful songs. And I was one of the few outsiders who sang at their national festival, which has gone on since the time of the Druids. And I went down into the mines with the workers, and they explained to me, that 'Paul, you may be successful here in England [sic], but your people suffer like ours. We are poor people, and you belong to us. You don't belong to the bigwigs here in this country.' And so today I feel as much at home in the Welsh valley as I would in my own Negro section in any city in the United States. I just did a broadcast by transatlantic cable to the Welsh valley, a few weeks ago, and here was the first understanding that the struggle of the Negro people, or of any people, cannot be by itself – that is, the human struggle. So I was attracted

by and met many members of the Labour Party, and my politics embraced also
the common struggle of all oppressed people, including especially the working
masses – specifically the laboring people of all the world. That defines my
philosophy. It's a joining one. We are a working people, a laboring people –
the Negro people.[45]

This passage is significant in that it traces several shifts in Robeson's
thought; an initial nationalist commitment to 'my own people' develops,
through encountering the Welsh, into an internationalist commitment to
'the human struggle' which leads ultimately to a redefinition of 'the
Negro people' as 'a working people'. While Robeson's relationship with
Wales was, therefore, far from unique, and needs to be placed in the
context of his internationalist connections with many other nations and
peoples to be understood, his own words testify to its significance. Each
of the stages that Robeson describes in the evolution of his thought
merits further commentary, and it is through exploring the continuities
and contradictions of his work and career that the significance of his
Welsh connections can come into focus.

Robeson began his career espousing the characteristic Harlem
Renaissance notion that racial uplift could be achieved through cultural
accomplishment. In 1918 W. E. B. Du Bois celebrated Robeson's
achievements as one of an emerging class of race leaders: 'the best foot-
baller in the country today' who 'won the class oratorical prize for two
years' at Rutgers, is also a 'varsity debater, plays guard in basketball,
throws weight in track, catches baseball, and is a baritone soloist'.[46] By
the mid-1920s Robeson was a major contributor to the cultural renaissance of Harlem, having abandoned a brief career as a lawyer for a future
as an actor and singer who espoused and embodied the Du Boisian belief
'that until the art of the black folk compels recognition they will not be
rated as human'.[47] But artistic achievements proved a limited vehicle for
social advancement, for African American art was often celebrated for
its primitive, non-Western qualities. Just as Victorian men of letters such
as Matthew Arnold and William Dean Howells had viewed the poetic,
feminine temperament and childishness of primitive peoples such as the
Celts and African Americans as sources of reinvigoration for their own
philistine, materialist societies, so white critics of the 1920s celebrated
the contribution that African Americans could make to a mechanized,
spiritless American culture.[48] Even a writer such as avant-gardist Waldo
Frank, who was critical of those modernist works in which 'the negro is
not a negro at all' but is merely 'a healing and resolving norm within the
white man's soul', was unable to overcome such conventions in his own

writings. In his short story 'John the Baptist' the main protagonist tells his black cleaning lady, 'Nigger woman . . . you are all one!'[49] The African American was seen to offer the possibility of unity in a world of modernist fragmentation. In a 1926 issue of *New Republic*, Elizabeth Shepley Sergeant suggested that

> Unlike most moderns, Paul Robeson is not half a dozen men in one torn and striving body. The sureness of essential being takes him across the concert stage, as it did across the football field, with the fine, free movement of his strong athletic body, which is the reflection in action of an inward goal. [50]

Robeson's external appearance and movements are read as manifestations of an internal essential being that contrasts with the chronic fragmented consciousness of 'most moderns', and his presumed 'unity of being' make him a symbol of black authenticity. His first performances of the spirituals in the Greenwich Village Theatre, New York, in 1925 were seen by a *New York Times* critic as voicing 'the sorrows and hopes of a people' and, according to the white promoter of black culture Carl Van Vechten, Robeson's performances of 'these simple, spontaneous outpourings from the heart of an oppressed race ranks with the best folk music anywhere and with a good deal of the second-best art music'. [51]

Robeson was happy to be regarded as the cultural voice of his people, and it is perhaps somewhat surprising to find that he also tended to view his own work in the primitivist terms of the dominant society. He described the spirituals as the 'expression and yearning of a child-like people', referred to African Americans as 'a people upon whom nature has bestowed, and in whom circumstances have developed, great emotional depth and spiritual intuition', and referred to himself as 'an African' who finds it easier to 'feel things rather than comprehend them'. [52] Sterling Stuckey notes that Robeson 'did not hesitate to affirm without a trace of shame some of the very qualities that whites thought stamped blacks as inferior', and what we witness in Robeson's early writings is the adoption of a strategy that we also witnessed in the writings of Du Bois and Saunders Lewis; a primitivist anti-industrialism does not stamp Blacks as an inferior people unsuited to the challenges of modern society but, rather, forms the basis for a valued sense of cultural distinctiveness. [53] Thus, just as Du Bois argued that African Americans were 'the sole oasis of simple faith and reverence in a dusty desert of dollars', Robeson argued that, while Western men had 'brought misery with their machines' and had 'made a fetish of intellect', the

negro feels rather than thinks, experiences emotions directly rather than inter-
prets them by roundabout and devious abstractions, and apprehends the
outside world by means of intuitive perception instead of through a carefully
built up system of logical analysis. No wonder that the negro is an intensely
religious creature and that his artistic and cultural capacities find expression in
the glorification of some deity in song.[54]

As in Du Bois's *The Souls of Black Folk* – a volume that Robeson greatly
admired – the African American has a particular role to play in the development of American society and a specific spiritual and emotional
contribution to make in alleviating the excessive materialism and mech-
anization of industrial society.

With the Renaissance reason and intellect were placed above intuition and
feeling. The result has been a race which conquered Nature and now rules the
world. But the art of that race has paid the price. As science has advanced, the
art standards of the West have steadily declined. Intellectualised art grows
tenuous, sterile . . . Is there no one to bring art back to its former level? This, I
think, is where the Negroes and the great Eastern races come in . . . The race
which first learns to balance equally the intellectual and the emotional – to use
the machine and couple them with a life of true intuition and feeling such as
the Easterns know – will produce the supermen.
    No one can tell from what root the race will come. Probably all will
contribute – when he learns to be true to himself the Negro as much as any
man.[55]

Some of the contradictions of Robeson's early thought are encapsulated
in this passage. While clearly not an assimilationist who welcomes the
disappearance of cultural distinctions in the melting-pot culture of the
United States, Robeson, like Du Bois, always retained a commitment to
human universality. The internationalist vision is reflected in the belief
that 'all will contribute' in the making of a social order in which 'the
machine' and the 'life of true intuition' will be in balance. Thus, while
Western man had developed his powers of abstraction 'at the expense of
his creative faculties', this did not lead to a desire to 'discount' the
'achievements' of Western society. Robeson argued that one would not
wish to

retrogress in terror to a primitive state. It is simply that one recoils from the
Western intellectual's idea that, having got himself on to this peak over-
hanging an abyss, he should want to drag all other people – on pain of being
dubbed inferior if they refuse – up after him into the same precarious
position.[56]

From T. S. Eliot's fertility cults to W. B. Yeats's Celtic mysticism this turn towards the resources of the pre-modern in order to move backwards into a future that has transcended modernity altogether is a characteristic modernist strategy. In order for the African American's distinctive contribution to be made, however, the Negro, according to Robeson, needs to learn to be 'true to himself'. In envisioning a role for African Americans in the development of human civilization, Robeson (again like Eliot, Yeats, Du Bois, Saunders Lewis and many others) is forging a position for himself as an artist, seeking in this case to promote a characteristically cultural nationalist agenda of making African Americans conscious of their own culture, and their own distinctiveness. He develops this argument by comparing African Americans with Jews:

> [The Jews] like a vast proportion of Negroes, are a race without a nation; but, far from Palestine, they are indissolubly bound by their ancient religious practices – which they recognize as such. I emphasize this in contradistinction to the religious practices of the American Negro, which, from the snake-worship practiced in the deep South to the Christianity of the revival meeting, are patently survivals of the earliest African religions; and he does not recognize them as such. Their acknowledgement of their common origin, species, interest, and attitudes binds Jew to Jew; a similar acknowledgement will bind Negro to Negro.[57]

Robeson, therefore, sought to make African Americans aware of their African heritage in order to counter an 'acute inferiority complex' which led to a desire 'to become as nearly like a white man as possible'.[58] 'In my music, my plays, my films, I want to be African', he declared in 1934: 'Multitudes of men have died for less worthy ideals; it is even more eminently worth living for.'[59] This declaration of an African identity was somewhat at odds with the growing emphasis on class in the depression years of the 1930s, but it reflected both Robeson's roots in the cultural nationalism of the Harlem Renaissance and the growing strength of nationalist currents in the political discourse of the period, on both the left and the right.

Interestingly, Robeson stated that he discovered Africa in London. The Robesons were largely based in London from the end of 1927 to 1939, and from the outset both he and his wife Eslanda were struck by the opportunities they had to engage with African cultures. In her book *African Journey* (1946) Eslanda recalled that

> [i]n America one heard little or nothing about Africa. I hadn't realized that, consciously, until we went to live in England. There was rarely even a news

item about Africa in American newspapers or magazines. Americans were not interested in Africa economically . . . politically, or culturally. Practically nothing was or is taught in American schools about Africa . . . In England on the other hand, there is news of Africa everywhere: in the press, in the schools, in the films, in conversation . . . There are courses on Africa in every good university in England; African languages are taught, missionaries are trained, and administrators are prepared for work 'in the field'. Everywhere there is information about Africa.[60]

It was in London, 'the centre of the British Empire', notes Paul Robeson in *Here I Stand*, that 'I came to consider that I was an African':

> Like most of Africa's children in America, I had known little about the land of my fathers, but in England I came to know many Africans. Some of their names are now known to the world – Nkrumah and Azikiwe, and Kenyatta who is imprisoned in Kenya. Many of the Africans were students, and I spent long hours talking with them and taking part in their activities at the West African Student Union building. Somehow they came to look upon me as one of them; they took pride in my successes; and they made Mrs. Robeson and me honorary members of the Union. Besides these students, who were mostly of princely origin, I also came to know another class of Africans – the seamen in the ports of London, Liverpool and Cardiff.[61]

Robeson, an American member of the African diaspora, is thus recognized as one of 'their own' by Africans residing in the metropolitan centre of the British Empire.

Edward Said has described the movement from the colonized 'margin' to the imperial 'center' as a 'voyage in' which results in the erasure of 'the separations and exclusions' of 'divide and rule' as 'surprising new configurations spring up'.[62] While the problems of thinking of the colonial relationship in such binary terms have been widely debated, the formation of a diasporic African consciousness – which could encompass princely students and Cardiff dockers – in 1930s London, can be regarded as an example of the 'new configurations' described by Said. Robeson mentions Nkrumah, Azikiwe and Kenyatta, and these African figures were engaged alongside Afro-Carribeans such as George Padmore and C. L. R. James and Indian nationalists such as Jawaharlal Nehru and Krishna Menon (both friends of Robeson's), in forming an anti-colonial politics rooted in Marxist, or more broadly leftist, thought.[63] Raymond Williams offers a basis for discussing this phenomenon in the chapter entitled 'Formations' in his curious, but often suggestive, book *Culture* (1981). Williams begins by discussing guilds, professions, clubs and movements and then proceeds to the more complex issues of schools,

factions and dissident groups. All these, he states, 'relate to developments within a single national social order'.[64] In the twentieth century,
however, new international formations have emerged and these have
tended to be perceived as radical within the metropolitan centre.
Contributors to the various avant-garde artistic formations, notes
Williams, were often 'immigrants to such a metropolis, not only from
outlying regions but from other and smaller national cultures, now seen
as culturally provincial in relation to the metropolis'.[65] Williams is
primarily concerned with mapping the emergence of literary modernism,
but his ideas, as Edward Said has noted, have a particular relevance to
the development of anti-colonial political programmes in cities such as
London where 'the sociology of metropolitan encounters' fostered associations between immigrants and mainstream formations which created
'especially favourable supportive conditions for dissident groups'.[66]

Robeson took full advantage of such supportive conditions, and
sought to formulate, through 'patient enquiry', the foundations for a new
consciousness of Africa amongst his people. He described the way in
which his linguistic studies and readings in the legendary traditions, folk
songs and folklore of west Africa led him into 'the core of African
culture':[67]

> As I plunged with excited interest, into my studies of Africa at the London
> School of Oriental Languages, I came to see that African culture was indeed a
> treasure-store for the world. Those who scorned the African languages as so
> many 'barbarous dialects' could never know, of course, the richness of those
> languages and of the great philosophy and epics of poetry that have come
> down through the ages in these ancient tongues.
>
> I studied many of these African languages, as I do to this day: Yoruba, Efik,
> Twi, Ga and others. Here was something important, I felt, not only for me as a
> student but for my people at home . . .[68]

His studies informed his performances of the spirituals and in a series of
interviews made during the 1930s he developed and elaborated an
Afrocentric cultural nationalist philosophy, arguing that a meaningful
future for African Americans could be forged only through an engagement with, and an understanding of, African languages and customs.
Thus, just as Saunders Lewis sought to 'take away from the Welsh their
sense of inferiority. . . to remove from our beloved country the mark and
the shame of conquest', and Du Bois sought to encourage the Black Folk
of the South to embrace their 'African fatherland' in the formation of a
'race solidarity' and 'race unity', so Robeson's 'first concern' was to
'dispel the regrettable and abysmal ignorance of the value of its own

heritage in the Negro race itself', and he even expressed a wish to 'go to Africa and reveal to the blacks their own historical mission'.[69] Robeson's Afrocentric cultural nationalism exemplified a significant element in African American thought in the 1920s and 1930s that was embraced by some and ridiculed by others. Gertrude Stein 'did not like hearing [Robeson] sing spirituals', arguing that 'they do not belong to you any more than anything else'.[70] Hers was a view espoused from within the African American community by figures such as George Schuyler who argued that the Harvard- and Berlin-educated 'dean of the Aframerican literati', W. E. B. Du Bois, the 'former student of Rodin', Meta Hardwick Fuller, and the 'dean of American painters in Paris', Henry O. Tanner, produced work that was 'no more "expressive of the Negro soul" – as the gushers put it – than are the scribblings of Octavus Cohen or Hugh Wiley'.[71] Others within the black community would wonder how grateful the perennially degraded sufferers of inferiority complexes would actually be to receive the advice of their would-be African American benefactors, with Ralph Ellison chuckling in the 1930s 'about the appearance of neo-Garveyism from a wealthy singer' such as Robeson, and writing later to Richard Wright that 'as for the Davises, Fords, Wilkersons, Yergans, yes, and Robesons, we can laugh those clowns to death'.[72]

As Robeson is firmly embedded in the Welsh historical imagination as the internationalist champion of human brotherhood, it is somewhat surprising to find him espousing a cultural nationalist philosophy rooted in language and legend in his writings of the 1920s and 1930s. While Robeson's connections with Wales are seen to be emblematic of that internationalist working-class consciousness that rejected an idea of Welshness based on the Welsh language and its culture, Paul Robeson's life and thought foreground the inherent limitations of basing histories of the Welsh or African Americans on the simplistic binary distinctions of cultural particularism versus universalism, traditionalism versus modernity, reactionary versus progressive, rural versus urban, ethnic versus civic. For if Robeson's travels led to his 'discovery' of Africa in London, it was his espousal of an 'African' identity, rooted in language and cultural distinctiveness – and not a rejection of a racial or national identity – that led to his admiration for, and direct connections with, the Soviet Union. Robeson described his first visit to the Soviet Union in 1934 as evolving 'through my interest in Africa', and his main interest was 'to study the Soviet national minority policy as it operates among the people of Central Asia'.[73] He recalled in 1955, during the period of his passport ban, that it was an African who directed my interest in Africa to something he had noted in the Soviet Union. On a visit to that country he had travelled east and had seen the Yakuts, a people who had been classed as a 'backwards race' by the Czars. He had been struck by the resemblance between the tribal life of the Yakuts and his own people of East Africa.

What would happen to a people like the Yakuts now that they were freed from colonial oppression and were a part of the construction of the new socialist society? I saw for myself when I visited the Soviet Union how the Yakuts and the Uzbeks and all the other formerly oppressed nations were leaping ahead from tribalism to modern industrial economy, from illiteracy to the heights of knowledge. Their ancient cultures blossoming in new and greater splendour. Their young men and women mastering the sciences and arts.[74]

This connection between Robeson's increasing interest in African cultures and in the Soviet Union is reflected in the fact that 1934 saw his first efforts at studying African languages and cultures at the London School of Oriental Languages, and his first visit to the USSR. Amongst those with whom Robeson spent a great deal of time during his two weeks in Russia was the film director Sergei Eisenstein, who was keen to include the African American actor in a number of his projects. Robeson confided to Eisenstein that he had some reservations before his visit, but was struck by 'the warm interest the . . . expression of sincere comrade-ship towards me, as a black man, a member of one of the most oppressed of human groups'.[75] Soviet Russia was a place in which he felt 'like a human being for the first time since I grew up. Here I am not a Negro but a human being. Before I came I could hardly believe that such a thing could be.'[76]

Upon returning to London, Robeson stated that his interest in the Soviet Union 'was, and is, completely non-political'.[77] Such a statement is only tenable if politics is defined in the narrowest sense and, in making such a declaration, Robeson was following a number of prominent African American writers (with novelist Richard Wright as a notable exception) who, while being deeply interested in the Soviet Union and the communist left, were unwilling to appear in public as acknowledged members of the Communist Party.[78] Many African American artists were attracted to the vision of Stalin's Soviet Union as a model for anti-racism and the fair treatment of minorities. Both Langston Hughes and Louise Thompson praised the Soviet treatment of the dark-skinned workers of the Central Asian soviet republics, Alain Locke endorsed 'the cultural minorities' art programmes being consistently and brilliantly developed in the Soviet Federation for the various racial and cultural folk traditions

of the vast land', and Richard Wright recalled his excitement at encountering Stalin's *The National and Colonial Question* in the 1930s:[79]

> Stalin's book showed how diverse minorities could be welded into unity, and
> I regarded it as a most politically sensitive volume that revealed a new way of
> looking upon lost and beaten peoples. Of all the developments in the Soviet
> Union, the method by which scores of backward peoples had been led to unity
> on a national scale was what enthralled me. I had read with awe how the
> Communists had sent phonetic experts into the vast regions of Russia to listen
> to the stammering dialects of peoples oppressed for centuries by the czars. I
> had made the first total emotional commitment of my life when I read how the
> phonetic experts had given these tongueless people a language, newspapers,
> institutions. I had read how these forgotten folk had been encouraged to keep
> their old cultures, to see in their ancient customs meanings and satisfactions as
> deep as those contained in supposedly superior ways of living. And I had
> exclaimed to myself how different this was from the way in which Negroes
> were sneered at in America.[80]

Stalin's views on national minorities had been preceded by Lenin's
'Theses on the National Colonial Question', and the application of these
texts to the United States led to the passing of the 'Black Belt nation
thesis' by the Communist International in 1928. The largely rural African
American communities stretching from Virginia to Mississippi were
believed to meet all the requirements of nascent nationhood as defined
by Stalin: 'a historically evolved, stable community of language, territory, economic life and psychological make-up manifested in a
community of culture'.[81] Notwithstanding its impracticality and incon-
sistent applications, the thesis, as William Maxwell notes, 'pointed
hundreds of African Americans to Communism during the 1930s'.[82]
Thus, despite the widely observed universalism at the heart of Soviet
communism, Robeson, like Wright, was attracted to communism as it
offered an international basis for the recognition of a distinctive African
American folk culture. Maxwell argues further that 'the African-American
left could see non-Russian Soviet republics in much the same way that
[Zora Neale] Hurston saw Eatonville: as guarantors of the continued
value of minority culture in the midst of modernization'.[83] It is worth
noting that Hurston saw no such connection, and felt that Robeson and
other leading African American communists had been duped. The
communists 'did not love us just because our skins were black', she
argued: 'The USSR was bent on world conquest through Asia. They saw
in us a shoe-string with which they hoped to win a tan-yard. A dumb, but
useful, tool.'[84]

If there was a range of positions regarding communism within the African American community, Kenneth Mostern usefully draws our attention to the different positions that black members of the Communist Party could take concerning racial identity. First, they could 'deny the significance of racial subjectivity to the politics of anti-capitalism altogether'. Secondly, they could take a 'national socialist' position, in which 'autonomous black nationalist organizing by the Negro proletariat – not the middle class – is a necessary moment of cultural and economic development'. Thirdly, they could 'take a more strictly nationalist line, whereby being Negro was already identical to being "proletarian"'. Mostern notes that the US Communist Party (CPUSA) is widely assumed to have insisted upon the first option, 'quite without any knowledge or research on the part of those who make the assumption'.[85] Robeson, like many on the African American left, actually embraced the third of Mostern's positions; from the mid-1930s onwards he sought to fuse the very idea of being a Negro with being proletarian; ethnic-consciousness with class-consciousness. He would state that he was from 'a working class people'.[86]

It is probably due to the fact that Robeson's connections with Wales are seen to emblematize south Walian internationalism that the connection between nationalist and socialist discourses in Robeson's thought, and in the African American milieu from which it arose, have been ignored in Wales. That Welsh commentators have paid little attention to the contradictions and complexities of Robeson's thought can be partly explained by the binary terms in which a generation of historians have narrated the history of Wales as a crude struggle waged between a 'privileged minority' of 'self-blinded visionaries' who espoused a 'linguistically exclusive "Welshness"', and a 'collectivist, universalist' working class who promoted 'an inter-meshing of class and community solidarities whose horizons were truly international'.[87] Kenneth Mostern has observed a similar trend in African American studies, where intellectual historians tend to assume that the Communist Party in the United States denied the significance of racial subjectivity to the politics of anti-capitalism.[88] A comparative approach to the relationship between nationalism and socialism in Welsh and African American cultural politics reveals interesting parallels. While there are cases of a robust rejection of nationalism by writers and politicians on the left, little work has been done on the intellectual connections between the various cultural and political strands that co-existed uneasily in 1930s Wales. I shall return to the connection between working-class consciousness and nativist sympathies in the Welsh industrial novel later in this chapter, but a few examples should suffice to suggest the cultural complexities that have been obscured by historical polemics. George Ewart Evans, a product of the industrial settlement of Abercynon, nurtured as a writer in the communist milieu of the *Left Review*, found a way out of the 'war-ridden bourgeois reality' of his times through communist politics and the painstaking recording of a 'prior culture' which he believed was still salvageable in the language and customs of the peasantry of rural Suffolk.[89] That Ewart Evans should have been in sympathetic correspondence with the advocate of a rural, monoglot Welsh-language Wales, Iorwerth Peate, suggests something of the surprising connections that were formed across what may appear, superficially, as the most insurmountable intellectual fault-lines in mid-twentieth-century Wales.[90] The same point may be made from a different perspective by looking at the key publication produced by Welsh communists, who were riding a wave of self-confidence in the second half of the 1930s. Idris Cox's *The People Can Save South Wales* offers a programme for the reconstruction of communities ravaged by the depression; a programme made all the more appealing in presentation by the invocation of a partly historical, partly mythic, Welsh past.

> Centuries ago Welsh chieftains roused the people of Wales to arms against the English Kings and their invaders who set out to oppress the Welsh nation and to make them slaves of their English masters. The flag of revolt was hoisted on the Welsh mountains and our ancestors laid down their lives in the fight for freedom and liberty.
>
> Today it is not the military invaders who threaten the people of Wales. It is the profit-making system of capitalism which is sucking the life-blood of our people.[91]

This is not a communist internationalism that rejects, on principle, all appeals to national identity. It is a discourse that reflects the particular privilege accorded to the 'folk', on the political left and right, in the 1930s, allowing a mythic fight against English oppressors to be transposed into the proletarian struggle against a vampiric, blood-sucking, capitalism. Indeed, the British Communist Party recognized the right for Welsh self-determination in 1939.[92] Welsh political and cultural thought in the 1930s was similar to that of African America, in witnessing a convergence of two highly influential, but distinct, conceptions of 'culture'; a sociological definition in which an universal 'culture' referred to the non-economic spheres of society, and an anthropological definition in which particularist 'cultures' were the unique possessions of pre-industrial peoples. If communists may be seen to veer more towards the former, while nationalists identify primarily with the latter, in both Wales and Black America there are cases where the nationalist and communist strains in 1930s thought converge in a shared challenge to the notion that Western modernization and capitalist accumulation are beneficent, and in a defence of pre-modern societies as sources of alternative values in a materialist world.

This fusion of ethnic particularism and socialist universalism informed Robeson's responses to Wales. If Robeson admired the internationalist socialism of the Welsh miners, as expressed eloquently in his words at the Mountain Ash Memorial Meeting where he noted that those who had joined the International Brigade 'fought not only for Spain but for me and the whole world', he was also attracted to what his biographer Martin Duberman describes as the 'ethnic insistence' of the Welsh.[93] This is a dimension of Robeson's thought that has been ignored by commentators in Wales, with the notable exception of T. J. Davies. In his Welsh-language biography, *Paul Robeson* (1981), Davies draws on Robeson's 1935 comment that 'Negroes the world over have an inferiority complex because they imitate whatever culture they are in contact with instead of harking back to their own tradition', to argue that the African American singer touched

gwïthien ddofn ynom. Ninnau fel y Negroaid wedi cefnu, i fesur, ar ein diwylliant brodorol a mabwysiadu un Seisnig; eto, ym mêr ein hesgyrn yn gwybod bod ynddo rin a gwerth, a phan ddeuai Paul Robeson i'n mysg, yn lladmerydd huawdl i ddiwylliant dirmygedig, caem ynddo un a roddai lais i gri a foddwyd yn ein hisymwybyddiaeth . . . Bid siwr, y mae elfen o dristwch yn y sefyllfa, y miloedd ym mhabell yr Eisteddfod yng Nglyn Ebwy yn ei gymeradwyo am eu bod yn cael boddhad mawr yng nghanu gŵr a gyflwynai ei ddiwylliant ei hun heb ymddiheuro; eto, yr un rhai, er yn gweld yr hyn a wnâi Paul Robeson ac yn falch o'i genhadaeth, yn methu cymryd y cam gwleidyddol i roi i'w cenedl hwy yr urddas y credent y dylai'r Negro ei gael.

(a deep vein within us. Like the Negroes, we have turned our backs, to a degree, on our indigenous culture and adopted an English culture; yet, in the marrow of our bones we are aware of its worth and value, and when Paul Robeson came to us, an eloquent spokesman for a derided culture, we found a voice for a cry that had been submerged in our subconsciousness . . . There is certainly an element of sadness in the scene; the thousands in the Eisteddfod pavilion in Ebbw Vale applauding and enjoying the singing of a man who presented his own culture without apology; yet, those same thousands, despite seeing what Paul Robeson was doing and welcoming his message, were unable to take the political step that would give their nation the status that they believed should be granted to the Negro.)[94]

While a familiar form of cultural nationalism (based on a belief that language is the essential underpinning of Welsh culture, and thus implicitly dismissive of the English-speaking communities and cultures of south Wales) is being deployed in this analysis, Davies draws attention to an overlooked aspect of Robeson's connection with Wales. Robeson himself viewed language as the foundation for distinctive cultures, and in 1951 recalled learning languages in order to sing the folk songs of 'the African, the Welsh, the Scotch Hebridean, the Russian, Spanish, Chinese, the Yiddish, Hebrew and others'.[95] While Robeson, during the filming of *Proud Valley*, expressed a desire to 'please the people of Wales by singing to them properly in their language, it is wonderfully rich and well suits my voice', there is no evidence that he ever did learn Welsh: when he performs the national anthem, 'Hen Wlad fy Nhadau' (Land of My Fathers) at the conclusion of *Proud Valley* and in the 'Transatlantic Broadcast' to the Miners' Eisteddfod of 1957, he sings it in English translation; 'Dafydd y Garreg Wen' is listed as 'David of the White Rock' in his programmes and presumably sung in English; and the final line 'Ar Hyd y Nos' is the only Welsh heard in his performances of the Welsh tune 'All Through the Night'.[96] 'The Welsh language', stated Robeson at the Ebbw Vale Eisteddfod in 1958, 'is a language not to be trifled with and unless I could be perfect at it I would not attempt to sing in Welsh'.[97] Robeson was certainly interested in the Welsh language. Charles L. Blackson, writing of Robeson as a bibliophile, draws attention to a Welsh-language grammar in his collection and when asked to suggest an appropriate gift to mark his visit to the 1958 Eisteddfod, Robeson requested a Welsh-language hymnbook.[98] J. Beverley Smith, whose father Cecil Smith was chairman of the Ebbw Vale Eisteddfod of 1958, recalls that when Robeson stayed overnight with his family he was particularly interested in the collection of Welsh-language literature at the house and asked detailed questions regarding Welsh folk singing and the ways in which Welsh-language culture was supported financially.[99] 'You may not know it', Robeson told the Eisteddfod audience, 'but I was brought up in traditions very similar to yours. My father was a Wesleyan minister; my brother is one, and almost every Sunday I have taken part in similar hymn-singings to those you are enjoying tonight.'[100]

Robeson's concert performances offered a creative expression for the fusion of ethnic particularism and socialist universalism that informed his responses to other people and places. His increasing engagement with Marxist thought in the 1930s led not to the rejection of a racial identity in favour of class identity but, rather, a redefinition of class identity made possible by the black nationalist interpretation of Lenin's and Stalin's definitions of colonial peoples. From the early 1930s onwards Robeson expanded his repertoire beyond the spirituals to embrace the folk songs of other peoples. The programme of his 25 March concert in Wrexham testifies to his inclusion of the Russian 'O Ivan , You Ivan', the English 'O, No, John! No!' and the Welsh 'David of the White Rock' in his repertoire, and Martin Duberman notes that Robeson included performances of Russian songs arranged by Gretchaninov, the Scottish 'Turn Yet to Me' and the Mexican 'Encantadora Maria' in his British concerts of that year.[101] Robeson argued that he could interpret folk songs from around the world because of the fact that 'I came from a working-class people'.[102] Kenneth Mostern notes that the very category 'folk song' positions 'class identity' onto 'groups rather than individuals'.[103] Perhaps more significantly, this fusion of 'folk' and 'class' results in a view of class identity which is not the product of historical forces, of social position or of active engagement in common cultural practices but is, rather, a factor determined, ultimately, by race. Robeson argued that he failed

> to see how a Negro can really feel the sentiments of an Italian or a German, or a Frenchman, for instance . . .I believe that one should confine oneself to the art for which one is qualified. One can only be qualified by understanding, and this is born in one, not bred.[104]

Nature ('born in one') it seems is more significant than nurture ('bred') in the making of a cultural sensibility, a view that Robeson reiterated unequivocally in 1934.

> I would rather sing Russian folk-songs than German grand-opera – not because it is necessarily better music, but because it is more instinctive and less reasoned music. It is in my blood.[105]

Robeson's 1920s primitivism is not wholly rejected in the 1930s, for the key constituents of character and culture seem to be predetermined 'in my blood'. What occurs in the 1930s is that Robeson's racial conception of identity is generalized to encompass other oppressed peoples. This fusion of 'race' and 'class' allows the son of an ex-slave who has become solidly bourgeois through the success of his concert performances to identify with working people due to his membership of an oppressed race. Robeson suggested, as I noted earlier, that this particular fusion of class and ethnic identity, this 'understanding that the struggle of the Negro people, or of any people, cannot be by itself – that is, the human struggle', emerged as a result of his experiences in Wales.[106] Robeson's performances of Welsh hymns and Negro spirituals emphasized cultural particularity while drawing on a tradition of Christian universalism, modulated into the secular terms of a Leninist internationalism that valued cultural distinctiveness. Roland Grigor Suny has argued that, in spite of later attempts to curb internal, minority nationalist impulses, the earlier policies inspired by Lenin and Stalin laid the groundwork for a flourishing of national cultures in the Soviet Union that was not stopped by the later repeal of cultural support.[107] The appeal of communism to Robeson was that it offered a universal context for the preservation of cultural particularity. As Kate Baldwin notes, it was the 'transnational formations of a Leninist tradition that Robeson strove to foster in his performances of national folk songs'.[108]

There are, then, significant shifts taking place in Robeson's thought from the late 1920s through the 1930s. In the late 1920s and early 1930s he tilted towards a strong racial identification, advocating the tenets of cultural pluralism. By the end of the 1930s, following his engagement with socialist thought, his identification with the working classes of the British Isles and his experience of the Spanish Civil War, he embraced revolutionary internationalism. Later, in the 1950s, he would renew his cultural nationalist roots with a reaffirmation of his primary identification as a Negro. As Martin Duberman notes:

> All of Robeson's shifts were subtle, none sudden or complete. For most of his life he managed to hold in balance a simultaneous commitment to the values (sometimes competing, but in his view ultimately complementary) of cultural distinctiveness *and* international unity.[109]

The way in which Robeson responded to the, often conflicting, forces of cultural distinctiveness and political universalism within Welsh society testifies to the accuracy of this analysis.


## ROBESON'S IMAGE: FROM *THE EMPEROR JONES* TO *THE PROUD VALLEY*

If Robeson's concert repertoire of international folk songs placed the African American experience within a transnational context and offered a practical expression of his cultural thought, the creation of a screen persona that embodied his cultural and political views proved more diffi-cult. From his first celluloid appearance as the deceitful Reverend Jenkins in Oscar Micheaux's *Body and Soul* (1924), to his final appear-ance as a black sharecropper in *Tales of Manhattan* (1942), Robeson struggled with a legacy of racial stereotypes that gave rise to 'the painful entanglement between cultural self-determination and racist domina-tion'.[110] Robeson's struggle had proved a futile one in most cases, with Alexander Korda's production, *Sanders of the River* (1935), being the most infamous example. Having agreed enthusiastically to play the part of an African chieftain given that the film was to incorporate African dancing and music shot and recorded on location, Robeson was ulti-mately dismayed to find that the film had been edited into a celebration of British imperialism. Robeson attempted, unsuccessfully, to suppress the film by buying all the available prints. Having been criticized for pandering to primitivism in *Sanders of the River*, and for reinforcing the image of the 'happy darkie' in *Showboat* (both on stage in 1928 and on film in 1937), Robeson defended his acceptance of these roles by noting with some justification that to 'expect the Negro artist to reject every role with which he is not ideologically in agreement . . . is to expect the Negro artist under the present scheme of things to give up his work entirely'.[111] By the 1950s, however, he seemed willing to disown all his film appearances with the exception of his Welsh-based movie *Proud Valley* (1940), of which he stated that 'it was the one film I could be proud of having played in'.[112]

*The Proud Valley* was based on an idea by Ealing director and commu-nist, Herbert Marshall, who in 1938 had directed Robeson in London's left-wing Unity Theatre's *Plant in the Sun*; an innovative play that promoted a collective ethos by making all actors anonymous and calling upon them to play any part without notice.[113] Aware of Robeson's connections with Wales, and himself a pupil and later translator of Eisenstein, Marshall conceived of the film as embodying aspects of his, and Robeson's, political vision. This led to problems, for Ealing Studio boss Michael Balcon wished to emphasize entertainment rather than politics, and Marshall's original conclusion – in which the miners ran their own mine as a cooperative – proved unpalatable to the coal owners in Wales who, without exception, refused to allow the film to be shot on their premises. The outbreak of war during production also led Balcon to urge his film-makers to emphasize national unity, rather than class soli-darity. Marshall was thus ousted as director to be replaced by the Russian

Sergei Nolbandov, and the producing duties were handed to Pen
Tennyson, the Eton-educated socialist and great-grandson of the
Victorian poet. Despite these changes, the film remained a vehicle for
Robeson and was tailored around his vocal talents. David Berry draws
attention to the 'number of cut-aways to close-ups of the star', but what
is in fact more striking, especially when compared to Robeson's other
films, is the number of medium shots that emphasize his relationships
with others.[114] In the important modernist film, *Borderline* (1930), Paul
is filmed in close up as though he were a giant.[115] Described by Essie
Robeson, who co-starred in it with her husband, as 'a dreadful high-
brow', *Borderline* was a collaboration between the film-maker Kenneth
Macpherson, the poet and magazine editor Bryher and the poet H.D.[116]
McPherson's stated aim was to reject 'the method of externalised observation' and in its place create a film which 'delved into the minds of the
people in it'.[117] Robeson became the subject of this psychological gaze.
'Like a dream, the great negro head looms disproportionate and water
and cloud and rock and sky are all subsidiary to its being', H.D. wrote in
a lengthy pamphlet written to accompany and explain the film: '[l]ight
has been, it is obvious, created by that dark daemon conversant with all
nature since before the time of white man's beginning'.[118] The overt
primitivism here needs no explication. If the effect of the modernist
aesthetic of *Borderline* was to create a wholly asocial, ahistorical view of
the African American male then, as Hazel Carby notes, the 'images of
Robeson sitting at the dining table and around the hearth as an integral
part of a white family' in *Proud Valley* suggested a very different
aesthetic practice.[119]

*Borderline* was an avant-garde silent film, produced after sound had
been introduced to the cinema. Robeson's famous voice is, therefore,
silenced and the lack of sound foregrounds the film's intense emphasis
on the image and the individual psyche. *Proud Valley* is the polar opposite of *Borderline* in this respect, for the film's emphasis on society and
community is reflected in the centrality given to music and song. If
Robeson famously sought to suggest a connection between the world's
peoples in his performances of folk songs, it is initially by singing that
the unemployed African American seaman, David Goliath (played by
Robeson), introduces himself to the miners of Blaendy and begins to be
incorporated into their community. Walking through the streets of the
mining village David hears a choir practising Mendelssohn's *Elijah* for
the forthcoming Eisteddfod, and joins them by singing the baritone aria
'Lord God of Abraham, Isaac and Israel' from the street below the

practice room window. The genial conductor, Dick Parry, is impressed and runs to the window calling on David to join the choir before taking him home and finding him a job at the pit. If Mendelssohn's canonical oratorio is the initial vehicle for integration – suggesting a high, European, cultural realm that is the rightful inheritance of all (a notion given added significance at a time when Mendelssohn's music was banned by the Third Reich) – the film also suggests a correspondence between African American and Welsh cultures through the juxtaposition of musical performances.[120] At the Eisteddfod, which has been post-poned for a month due to the death of Dick Parry in a pit disaster, David sings the spiritual 'Deep River' in respect to his friend. This is 'one of the most emotional sequences ever seen in British film', according to Stephen Bourne, to be surpassed only perhaps by Rachel Thomas's rendition of the Welsh hymn 'Yn y Dyfroedd Mawr a'r Tonnau' ('In the deep and mighty torrent') later in the film as a group of anxious women and men await news of casualties following a pitfall.[121] 'Deep River' and 'Yn y Dyfroedd Mawr a'r Tonnau' share similar imagery, with the final stanza of the Welsh hymn describing the way in which a vision of Christ makes 'me sing / In this deep river' ('golwg arno wna i'm ganu / yn yr afon ddofon hon').[122] The novelist Jack Jones, who plays the role of a miner in the film (and whose role in co-writing the script I shall discuss later) recalled that when he suggested this particular hymn and hummed its melody, Sergei Nolbandov misrecognized it as a Russian folk song, thus no doubt reinforcing the connection between the world's folk cultures that Robeson sought to evoke in his performances.[123] It could be argued, then, that Robeson retained a liking for *Proud Valley* due to the fact that of all his screen appearances it is as David Goliath that he came closest to embodying on celluloid the cultural and political values promoted by his concert performances.

Jeffrey C. Stewart argues that towards the end of the 1930s Robeson had become 'increasingly sophisticated about his image' on screen, and that 'he began to pose his body in ways that maximised its power as a signature of moral and political leadership, rather than as a fetish of aestheticizing modernist gazes'.[124] This shift from an apolitical aesthetic modernism to a politically engaged art can be seen to occur concurrently with the shift in emphasis in Robeson's thought discussed earlier; from a primitivist cultural nationalism rooted in an African motherland to an universalist socialism that venerated an idea of a common humanity rooted in distinctive folk cultures. *Proud Valley* reflects these shifts, and the first dialogue of the film can be seen as a humorous, self-referential

commentary on Robeson's cultural status. The film opens with David
Goliath sitting on a wall, contemplating a worn-out shoe before jumping
onto a moving train and hoisting himself into an empty coal truck. He
lands on Bert, a cockney hobo on his way to the mining village of
Blaendy. Their dialogue sets the scene. We are told that David has
worked underground in the United States, that he was 'laid up at Cardiff
three months ago' and has been unemployed since. Bert tells him of 'a
coloured bloke' who had a job in the Glen Colliery, 'Blackie Ellis they
called him', and in doing so informs the film's audience that there is no
colour bar in south Wales. More significantly, Bert earns a living during
the depression years by travelling around British villages singing various
folk songs very badly; 'I pick a well known tune and I murder it.' The
Welsh, who are 'daft about their music and open-hearted as the sun', are
more than happy to pay him to leave them alone. Bert describes his occupation as 'Art related to psychology. You touch people's feelings by
offending their ears.' 'Why don't you join me eh?' he asks David. 'No
thanks', states the African American. 'I'd rather work for my living.' The
comedy of the scene relies on the audience's awareness that David
Goliath is in fact Paul Robeson. The dialogue actually encourages
viewers not to suspend their disbelief but to revel in the incongruity of
having a singer of international stature playing the role of an unemployed miner who would prefer to 'work' than to 'sing' for a living.
Bert's 'occupation' is similar to Robeson's in real life in that he travels to
various locations singing folk songs; the difference being that Bert is
paid to leave rather than to perform, and he conceives of his singing in
modernist terms as a fusion of 'art' and 'psychology'. That this opening
scene from *Proud Valley* may be read as both a commentary on the image
of 'Robeson' and a humorous critique of modernist aesthetics is reinforced by the fact that it contains intertextual references to American
playwright Eugene O'Neill's celebrated modernist play *The Emperor
Jones*.

While the initial version of O'Neill's *The Emperor Jones* opened in
Greenwich Village in 1920 and starred the African American actor
Charles Gilpin, the play was firmly associated with Robeson by the late
1930s due to the film version of 1933. Robeson had first taken on the role
of Brutus Jones, an African American emperor of an island in the West
Indies, in 1924 following a disagreement between Gilpin and O'Neill,
and his performances helped establish his reputation as a stage actor.[125]
With the exception of the opening scene the whole of the play is
concerned with Jones's internal, psychological struggles. The play

enacts a descent into Jones's subconscious as we see his past careers as a Pullman porter, a convict, a gambler and a murderer. Jones's unconscious takes the form of a primeval forest on stage, and as he makes his way through the undergrowth of his past he is slowly stripped of the paraphernalia of authority and begins to question his own status as a civilized being in a language that is O'Neill's approximation of black vernacular:

> Lawd! Keep dem away from me! And stop dat drum soundin' in my ears! Dat begin to sound ha'nted, too. [He gets to his feet, evidently slightly reassured by his prayer – with attempted confidence.] De Lawd'll preserve me from dem ha'nts after dis [Sits down on the stump again]. I ain't skeered o'real men. Let dem come. But dem odders – [He shudders – then looks down at his feet, working his toes inside the shoes – with a groan.] Oh, my po' feet! Dem shoes ain't no use no more 'ceptin to hurt. I'se better off widout dem. [He unlaces them and pulls them off – holds the wrecks of the shoes in his hands and regards them mournfully.][126]

Even a brief excerpt conveys the primitive qualities that O'Neill imposes on the African American, as Jones loses his bearings on reality. Drawing on Freud's arguments in *Totem and Taboo* (published in English in 1918) that primitive peoples were closer to spiritual impulses, and on a nineteenth-century tradition of racial thought, O'Neill's innovative exploration of complex human psychology is undermined by the racist dichotomies of white reason versus black irrationality that permeate the play, and that are endemic to nineteenth-century colonial discourse and widespread in modernist literature. Hazel Carby notes that the 'cultural effect of the creation of Brutus Jones is a fundamental questioning of the possibility of rational black leadership', and, while O'Neill gestures at a history of exploitation in the Caribbean, by concentrating wholly on the workings of Jones's mind he ignores the history of colonialism.[127] Social conflict is thus replaced by psychological conflict and, in his 'fascination with the dangerous potential for violence and anger within the black male body, at the expense of concern with the violence and anger acted upon it' O'Neill, argues Carby, 'shared the dissecting gaze of the lynch mob'.[128]

This, however, was not how the majority of African American commentators viewed the play in the 1920s. George Schuyler was in a minority in regretting that 'even when [the African American] appears to be civilized' in the works of white artists, 'it is only necessary to beat a tom tom or wave a rabbit's foot and he is ready to strip off his Hart Schaffner and Marx suit, grab a spear and ride off wild-eyed on the back of a crocodile'.[129] W. E. B. Du Bois, Sterling Brown and Rudolph Fisher all spoke approvingly of O'Neill's works, and perhaps this is not surprising given that white playwrights before O'Neill tended to have African American parts played by white actors in blackface.[130] The most robust defence of O'Neill came from Robeson who in a 1924 article, 'Reflections on O'Neill's Plays', described *The Emperor Jones* as one of 'the great plays – a true classic of the drama, American or otherwise'.[131] In 1925 he argued that O'Neill 'has got what no other playwright has – that is, the true, authentic Negro psychology. He has read the Negro soul, and has felt the Negro's racial tragedy.'[132] In describing the experience of playing the role of Emperor Jones, he noted that

> One does not need a long racial memory to lose oneself in such a part . . . As I act, civilization falls away from me. My light becomes real, the horrors terrible facts. I feel the terror of the slave mart, the degradation of man bought and sold into slavery. Well, I am the son of an emancipated slave and the stories of old father are vivid on the tablets of my memory.[133]

O'Neill's vision of African American primitivism was in accordance with Robeson's own views on the racial distinctiveness of African Americans in the 1920s (discussed above). Fredric Jameson has argued that the

> most influential formal impulses of canonical modernism have been strategies of inwardness, which set out to reappropriate an alienated universe by transforming it into personal styles and private languages: such wills to style have seemed in retrospect to reconfirm the very privatization and fragmentation of social life against which they were meant to protest.[134]

This analysis is certainly relevant to Macpherson's *Borderline*, discussed earlier, and may also be applied to *The Emperor Jones*. Jameson also draws our attention to those aspects of modernist aesthetics that are consciously rejected in *The Proud Valley*.

The way in which the Emperor Jones contemplates his shoes and his 'po' feet' in the quotation above is replicated in the very opening of *Proud Valley* as David Goliath sits on a wall observing his worn shoes as he waits for a train to pass. He teams up with the Cockney, Bert, in the coal truck, and the scene in which a Cockney and an African American are located in a country that is foreign to them evokes the opening scene of *The Emperor Jones*, where the African American emperor is simultaneously admired and mocked by the Cockney trader Henry Smithers. Such parallels could be read as light-hearted gestures of acknowledgement at Robeson's past achievements, but the tone, marked most obviously by Bert's description of his vocal performances as 'art related to psychology', is ironic, and suggests that *Proud Valley* is a film that deliberately rejects modernist strategies of inwardness for an art that is committed to political education and social transformation. Robeson had argued at the Mountain Ash Memorial Meeting of 1938 that in 'the struggle we are waging for a better life, an artist must do his part', and by the late 1930s he rejected any division between art and politics.[135] Jeffrey C. Stewart argues that in the 1930s and 1940s 'Robeson reappropriated some of the postures and poses he created in the 1920s and adapted them to his more activist career', and illustrates his argument by noting the way in which the military jacket worn as a cover hiding primitive instincts in *The Emperor Jones* was redeployed as an 'emblem of authority' when Robeson portrayed a leader of white men in *Song of Freedom* (1936).[136] A further illustration of the way in which the 'aestheticizing modernist gazes' of the 1920s were transformed into the 'moral and political' imperatives of the 1930s can be made by comparing scenes from *The Emperor Jones* and *The Proud Valley*.[137]

In illustration 4, a scene from the stage version of *The Emperor Jones*, Robeson's nakedness conveys an erotic exoticism. Stripped to the

4. Paul Robeson in *The Emperor Jones*, London, 1925.

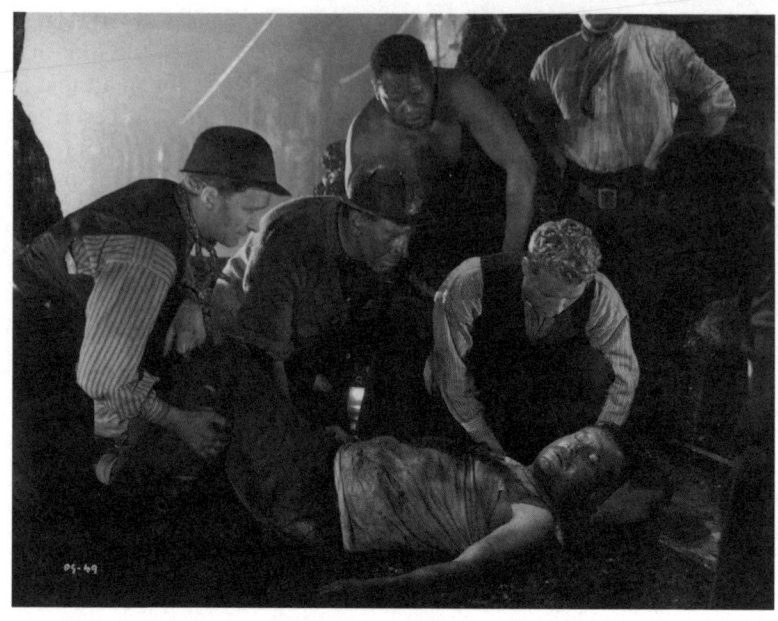

5. Paul Robeson and fellow miners in *The Proud Valley*, 1940.

trousers of his military uniform, his subconscious is also stripped to its irrational and atavistic core, symbolized on stage in the form of the witch doctor on whom Robeson's eyes are firmly focused. In illustration 5, from *Proud Valley*, the primitive exoticism of the Emperor Jones is replaced by a communal camaraderie evoked by a group of working males. Robeson's black manhood is seen to be integrated into the communal life of the Welshmen. Indeed, it is male bonding that the film seeks to emphasize for Robeson's sexuality is suppressed throughout and he never appears alone with any white women, with the exception of children, in any frame. Just as Robeson's voice blends with that of the choir upon his first arrival in Blaendy, the medium-range shots that predominate in the underground sequences emphasize David's role as one of a team. In figure 5 he is neither the closest to Dick Parry's dead body, nor the tallest figure in the scene, but is incorporated fully into the men's communal concern for their dying 'butty'. If Robeson self-consciously used his body to promote his shifting cultural and polit-ical agendas, then what we witness here is a transformation in Robeson's use of his own nakedness; from symbolizing black primitivism to representing working-class collectivism.

However, if there are significant shifts in the way in which Robeson is represented in *The Emperor Jones* and *Proud Valley*, there are also striking continuities. While *Proud Valley* largely rejects the image of Robeson as a black primitive, David Goliath remains trapped in a number of simplistic stereotypes. Indeed, while the Emperor Brutus Jones could take advantage of his position to assert himself consciously against whites in O'Neill's play, David Goliath, despite his integration into the community, is never the agent of change and is never called upon to take any decisions. The African American trade unionist A. Philip Randolph feared that the picture would exert a 'bad influence' in that 'the Negro worker in the film was excluded from consultations with management' and was shown as a 'mendicant' whose death did not result in a 'collective expression on the part of the workers of sympathy and remorse'.[138] Reviewing *Proud Valley* in 1940, Grahame Greene expressed similar doubts, noting his dislike of the final 'patriotic speeches and crisis posters and miners dying for England [*sic*]', and reserving his greatest opprobrium for Robeson whose 'fat sentimental optimism' was 'a little revolting', especially as manifested in his 'big black Pollyana' of a part, 'keeping everybody cheerful and dying nobly at the end'.[139] David Berry notes that although he is 'nominally the film's hero' David Goliath is never seen 'as an active force in decision-making'; he stays behind when the men enter the pit-owners' office in London, it is Ned who warns of the build up of gas in the seam, and Emlyn is the one who strives to arrange a meeting between the miners and their bosses.[140] David, as I noted above, is also wholly desexualized and is 'strangely passive' in domestic scenes.[141] Richard Dyer notes that Robeson's role in *Proud Valley* is 'akin to the servant role, constantly tidying up after others'.[142] This is somewhat harsh as David is integrated into the society as an equal, and the hierarchical relationships of slave society are in fact reversed as the Parry family become wholly dependent on him when he takes on the burden of primary breadwinner following Dick Parry's death. Ultimately, however, David sacrifices his life so that his white brothers may live, and the fact that the *Los Angeles Examiner* could announce in February 1940 that Universal Studios were hoping to persuade Robeson, following his return to the United States, to play the role of Uncle Tom in a film version of Stowe's novel foregrounds the extent to which the African American actor was expected to play stereotypical roles with their roots in the nineteenth century.[143]

If the African American miner is represented in comfortingly stereo-typical terms, then *Proud Valley* also perpetuates stereotypes of the Welsh.[144] If Welsh-language chapel culture was in retreat in the face of secularization by the early twentieth century, and the 1920s and 1930s had seen an intensification of labour radicalism in the coalfield, the miner as portrayed in *Proud Valley* draws on a wholly outmoded Victorian idealization of the pragmatic, godly, collier, as analysed by Hywel Teifi Edwards.[145] In the second half of the nineteenth century, argues Edwards, the 'Welsh collier was to crystallize the strengths of the common people whose worthiness would provide a sound foundation for a redeemed Wales' following the attacks on the morality of the Welsh in the renowned Blue Books of the government's commissioners inquiring into 'the State of Education in Wales' in 1847 (discussed in chapter 1).[146]

> Welsh literature fashioned a stereotypical goodly collier, appealingly pathetic, to stand in that defensive line of worthy working people who were to help restore the good name of Wales which the Blue Books had traduced. His was a particularly important role, representing as he did the industrial South, that populous, heterogeneous, dangerous part of Wales that was most likely, as was feared, to bring further obloquy on 'Cymru lân, Cymru lonydd' ('Pure Wales, docile Wales').[147]

In the keynote anthem of *Proud Valley* the miners boast that 'You can't stop us singing'. This use of music as a vehicle for conveying stoicism, courage and godliness drew specifically on the tradition of mythologiza-tion described by Edwards. With its roots in the 1850s, this image of the miner took definitive form, in Wales and beyond, following the Tŷ Newydd pit disaster of 1877. On 11 April that year, flood water from an old pit burst into Tŷ Newydd imprisoning two groups of five miners, the youngest being 14 years old. By the following morning the first group had been reached, with four of them being successfully rescued. The second group spent ten days underground before being reached by the rescue party who had, by then, hewn their way through 114 feet of coal under constant danger from floods, lethal gases and explosions. Daily reports on the development of the rescue mission appeared in the British press, and papers such as the *Telegraph* and *Times*, having been wholly contemptuous of the miners during the 1875 strike, celebrated the valour of the 'humble men' of Tŷ Newydd and praised their 'intense exercise in self-devotion, patience and deliberate courage – a concentration as it were of qualities which could only be acquired by the habitual exercise of these qualities in every day life, and perhaps their cultivation through many generations'.[148] The Welsh press emphasized the fact that these colliers were Welshmen, and the faith in God that had resulted in their miraculous deliverance. The emphasis on Christian brotherhood was underlined by the fact that the first group had been located when the rescuers heard them singing Dafydd Williams's eighteenth-century hymn, 'Yn y dyfroedd mawr a'r tonnau' (In the deep and mighty torrent). This image of the Welsh miner as God-loving Christian fused with the growing view of Wales as 'Gwlad y Gân', the 'Land of Song'. The large choirs that formed the basis for that invented tradition grew in the industrial valleys of south Wales, and their performances of choruses by Bach, Beethoven, Handel and Mendelssohn were embraced with enthusiasm in the 1870s. In 1872 and 1873 the Côr Mawr (Great Choir), led by Caradog (Griffith Rhys Jones) had competed victoriously in a choral competition at the Crystal Palace in London, a key moment in creating the image of the Welsh collier as soulful, yet disciplined, singer.[149] The personal stories of the Tŷ Newydd disaster connected with the emergence of Welsh choral culture. One of the trapped miners, William Morgan, in his desire to be released had been sucked by a violent rush of air into the hole that was being cut to release him. The 28-year-old member of Caradog's Côr Mawr broke his neck and died. Amongst the rescuers was Gwilym Thomas, a powerful baritone who, as 'the Gallant Rescuer', embarked on a concert tour around Britain following the disaster and was the soloist with the Rhondda Glee Society in the Chicago World's Fair in 1893. As a 73-year-old soloist at the 1916 Aberystwyth Eisteddfod he was still known as the 'gallant rescuer' of Tŷ Newydd.[150]

'Yn y dyfroedd mawr a'r tonnau' was known as the 'collier's hymn' following the events at Tŷ Newydd and was incorporated by Joseph Parry, the foremost Welsh composer of his day, into the anthem 'Molwch yr Arglwydd' ('Praise the Lord') which he composed to thank God for the miners' deliverance.[151] This hymn is heard towards the end of *Proud Valley* as Rachel Thomas leads the crowd in a rendition at the pit head as the community waits for news. The film then cuts to the trapped miners, where Ned (played by Jack Jones) is singing the same hymn, thus conveying the umbilical connection between the trapped miners and the anxious community, and between the scenes depicted in *Proud Valley* and the heroic story of Tŷ Newydd.

The image of a singing mining community is fused in this scene with another late nineteenth-century stereotype – that of the 'Welsh Mam'. Jane Aaron has traced the emergence of this image in the periodicals of the nineteenth century where the Welsh mother is invariably characterized by her religious devotion, thrift, temperance, stoicism, respectability and is often figured as Debora, the 'mother of Israel' from the Bible's Book of Justices.[152] Deirdre Beddoe notes that 'these ideas had taken firm root in Wales' by the 1870s and 1880s and

> it is in the mining valleys of south Wales that we see the most complete adoption of separate spheres and women's absorption of the domestic ideology in the emergence of that archetypal stereotype – the Welsh Mam . . . That such a complete working-class incarnation of the doctrine of separate spheres should emerge in the coal-mining areas is no accident. The heavy burden of her labour within the house took up all her time and, even if she had wished to work outside the home, there was no waged work for women in these areas anyway.[153]

Of all Welsh actresses it is Rachel Thomas, the Welsh-speaking daughter of an active trade-union miner from Alltwen in the Swansea Valley, who in her own words 'put the Welsh Mam on the map'.[154] *Proud Valley* was her first film appearance, and her portrayal of Mrs Parry, a pillar of her community who faces the death of her husband with a stoic strength, offers a distillation of nineteenth-century stereotypes of Welsh motherhood.[155] The respectable collier and the Welsh Mam would continue to percolate into the Welsh imagination for much of the twentieth century. Rachel Thomas herself would play the role that she established in *Proud Valley* again in *Blue Scar* (1949), *Undercover* (1943), the television version of *How Green Was My Valley* (1959–60) and, alongside the quintessential 'good collier', Amanwy (David Griffiths), in the film *David* that gave the Welsh mining communities a respectable place and image in the Festival of Britain celebrations of 1951. Constructed largely in response to the attacks mounted by Victorian England on Welsh sobriety, chastity and respectability, the 'good collier' and 'stoic Mam', having given their country almost a century's service as comforting stereotypes, were given a new lease of life at the outset of the Second World War by *Proud Valley*.

It is difficult not to follow Graham Greene in viewing *Proud Valley* as a film disablingly reliant on an array of outmoded stereotypes of both the African Americans and the Welsh. In a highly suggestive account of the uses of stereotypes in film the critic James Snead argues that

> One of the prime codes surrounding blacks on screen . . . is an almost metaphysical stasis. . . [O]ne may formulate the history of black film stereotypes as the history of the denial of history in favour of an artificially constructed mythology about unchanging black 'character' or 'nature'. The problem is

that, especially, in film, stereotypes and codes insulate themselves from historical change, or actual counterexamples in the real world.[156]

The code of stasis arises, argues Snead, in order to justify the continued
economic disadvantage of blacks. Poverty is not the effect of history or
exploitation but the result of the African American's racial 'ineptitude
and shiftlessness'.[157] Matthew Arnold was only one of the most influential figures to associate the Celt with certain enduring racial traits,
depicting the Welsh as a people characterized by stasis. 'The Celtic
genius', noted Arnold, has 'sentiment as its main basis, with love of
beauty, charm spirituality for its excellence . . . ineffectualness and
self-will for its deficit'.[158] The Celt is 'always ready to react against
despotism of fact', is 'sensual' and is 'particularly disposed to feel the
spell of the feminine idiosyncrasy; he has an affinity to it; he is not far
from its secret'.[159] This inevitably, and crucially, made the Celt 'ineffec-
tual in politics'.[160] It is significant that stereotypes of the Welsh and of
African Americans, while having long pre-histories, emerge in their
most enduring and pervasive forms in the second half of the nineteenth
century. It has been argued that blacks were most intensely caricatured,
on stage and in print, during the 1840s, when northern opposition to anti-
slavery was particularly violent, and the 1890s, when the progress of
reconstruction was being destroyed by anti-black violence and legal
restrictions. Gerald Early also notes that the United States in the 1840s
and 1890s

> went through a period of expansion through conquest (the Mexican War, the
> Spanish American War) and augmented population (European immigration)
> that was directly tied to how white America saw its mission and destiny in
> relation to darker races. In short, these particularly distressing periods
> occurred when whites were thinking about their own identity and the meaning
> of race and nationality.[161]

These were also periods in which African Americans, in the slave narratives of the 1840s and the slowly emerging body of poetry, novels and
autobiography in the 1890s, sought to engender what Henry Louis Gates
describes as 'the reconstruction of the image of the black'; an attempt to
define their own roles in a world of economic and geographical expansion.[162] The pre-eminent black 'reconstructor', Booker T. Washington
sought to placate white southerners in creating an image of the
hard-working African American who had 'without strikes and labour
wars, tilled the fields, cleared your forests, builded your railroads and
cities', who could be compared to 'those of foreign birth and strange

tongue and habits'.[163] In Wales, 'a nation that craved commendation' sought to construct an image of itself that would underline its role as a valuable contributor to the expanding British Empire.[164] The 1870s, the decade of the heroics of Caradog's Côr Mawr and the Tŷ Newydd miners, also saw the Welsh celebrating the role of the '24th Welch' in defeating the Zulus at the battle of Rorke's Drift, winning a record eleven Victoria Crosses in the process. 'The imperial sun', as Hywel Teifi Edwards notes, 'shone on the Welsh', illuminating a race of valiant fighters, industrious workers and powerful singers.[165]

Despite the best intentions of its producer and writers, *Proud Valley* ultimately recycled the static stereotypes of the nineteenth century in order to underline the role that the mining communities of Wales were expected to play in the British war effort. Reaching back beyond the recent years of militancy and political mobilization in south Wales, the film draws on an older stereotype of the pragmatic miner who is willing to collaborate with the owners for the national cause. The sequence where the miners march to London enacts a shift in their consciousness of war, and their role in the war effort. The question asked by one of the miners soon after their departure from Blaendy – 'What has Hitler to do with us?' – is answered as their march is punctuated by newspaper head-lines which become increasingly threatening as they near their destination. By the time they get to London they are more than willing 'to pull together with the pit-owners', having eavesdropped on a meeting 'in which the despairing bosses are discussing the impossibility of increasing coal output to meet the government's latest demand'.[166] While the film emphasizes a folksy Welsh ethnicity, it is clear that London is the place where the real decision making takes place. With the exception of David Goliath's reference to the 'Darren Valley Armaments Factory' in the film's opening scene, the German threat is not referred to in the first half of the film. The film's conclusion had to be amended to account for the outbreak of war and, as David Berry has noted, the 'last sections of *Proud Valley* betray the hasty script revisions to meet the new war situation'.[167] Nevertheless, from Robeson's initial performance of Elijah's call to God for assistance in his hour of need, to David's final act of martyrdom, it is difficult not to see *Proud Valley* as a British wartime appeal for American assistance. The result is a film set in one of the major world centres of a militant working-class consciousness that makes no mention of unions, or unionization. While Herbert Marshall's original script had the miners taking control of their own pit, the revised version had the pit reopening due to the demands of war. The film's united front ethos is captured most powerfully in the engineer, Mr Lewis, a symbol of the well-meaning pit representative, who leaves London with the miners to supervise the pit's reopening and ultimately dies by throwing himself in front of a tram in order to save the workmen supporting the roof. Workers and owners work in harmony, all the protests and initiatives, as Peter Stead notes, 'are prompted by the spontaneous brainwaves of individuals', and working-class radicalism is sublimated in song.[168] 'Welshness' offers an appealing dimension of local colour, but the bus intended to take the choristers to the Eisteddfod is decked out in Union Jacks and (improbably) St George's Crosses without a Red Dragon in sight. The film's conclusion in which pastoral scenes of the Welsh countryside appear over Robeson's translated rendition of the Welsh national anthem (where the call for the preservation of the native language in the original is replaced by an anodyne 'longing for Wales') serves to underline the fact that the respectable miners of Blaendy – like the miners of Tŷ Newydd before them – are the backbone of Great Britishness.

*Proud Valley*'s apparent pro-war message was undercut by Robeson upon his return to the United States. Having kept a judicious peace while in Britain, Robeson announced to American journalists that he supported the Soviet–Nazi pact as a defensive measure by Russia in the face of a desire by the West to mount a crusade against the Soviet Union.[169] He was also to defend the Soviet advances into Poland and Finland as defensive reactions to British influence in Scandinavia and the potential realignment of powers in western Europe in which the 'purified' regimes expected to replace Mussolini and Hitler would combine with Britain and her allies to challenge the threat of Bolshevism.[170] While Robeson always expressed his liking for *Proud Valley*, especially its depiction of a black working man integrated into a Welsh working-class community, his image was again being used to promote beliefs that he did not espouse. Following his final appearance on celluloid in 1943 Robeson concluded that there was no escape from black stereotypes while the South remained 'Hollywood's box office'.[171] Tired of having his image exploited he decided 'no more films for me'; a statement that evoked the spiritual 'no more auction block for me' and thus equated the silver screen with the slave market.[172]

## 'AREN'T WE ALL BLACK DOWN THAT PIT?': RACE AND THE WELSH INDUSTRIAL NOVEL

The proletarian male bonding portrayed in *Proud Valley*, as a bare-chested Paul Robeson is visually integrated into the working lives of his fellow miners, had been anticipated in B. L Coombes's proletarian classic *These Poor Hands: The Autobiography of a Miner Working in South Wales* (1939). Towards the end of his book Coombes hears the sound of music coming from 'the public house next door' as he is about to put on his work clothes:

> I recognise that it is Paul Robeson singing 'Old Man River'. If I have to run with my clothes in my hand I will not start dressing until he has finished. To do anything else except listen would be to insult one whom I count as one of the greatest men of all time.
> You can feel the suffering of the negroes in his voice as he sings:
>
> > 'I'm so weary, and sick of trying;
> > I'm tired of living, and scared of dying'.
>
> He is singing of a distant river and of slaves, but he might almost be singing of the mountains here and of us. I'm very tired of trying, but I am not so scared of dying; only of dying under the mountain and of being brought out looking like one of the cockroaches that has been crushed by a working-boot.[173]

The narrator's lack of clothing may evoke a latent eroticism, but his naked exposure to Robeson's voice is also a mark of respect, for to 'do anything . . . except listen would be to insult one whom I count as one of the greatest men of all time'. The attraction to forms of black masculinity evoked by Coombes was a significant aspect of Paul Robeson's reception in Wales, and my aim in the final part of this chapter is to read the industrial fictions of the 1930s as a means of exploring the cultural and political circumstances that made Wales so receptive to Robeson's persona and performances. For while 'Old Man River' emerges from a specific context of 'distant rivers and of slaves', it is transformed in Coombes's empathetic imagination into a song about 'the mountains here and of us'. While some African American commentators were dismayed at the way in which Robeson's performance as Joe in Oscar Hammerstein and Jerome Kern's *Showboat* reinforced the stereotype of the servile, Uncle Tomming, Negro, his performance of the musical's keynote song 'Old Man River' established Robeson's international reputation in the late 1920s. By the late 1930s, despite Hammerstein's objections, Robeson – singing to raise money for the International

Brigades in Spain – transformed his signature tune into a protest song as the original's 'I'm tired of livin'', and 'feard of dyin'' became 'I must keep fightin'', until I'm dyin''.[174] If the image of 'Old Man River' could be moulded to fit different contexts, then so, increasingly, could the image of 'Robeson'. The connection between a Welsh miner and the African American singer evoked in Bert Coombes's autobiography takes a slightly different form in Jack Jones's 1937 overview of 'Nofelau'r Cymry Seisinig' (The novels of the Anglo-Welsh) in the journal *Tir Newydd*. Jones concludes his article by noting that he will leave it to others to offer assessments of his own work, and warns any would-be critics that

> Y mae fy nghynnyrch yn enfawr i ddyn a ddechreuodd sgrifennu yn hwyr ei ddyddiau, gyda ychydig gymwysterau, os dim, ganddo at yrfa lenyddol. Ond fel 'old man river', yr wyf wedi dal i ymlusgo yn fy mlaen.

> (I've produced a considerable body of work for a man who began writing late in life, and who has little, if any, qualifications for a career in writing. But, like old man river, I've kept rolling along.)[175]

The Welsh novelist, and ex-miner, thus imagines himself to be 'Old Man River', a figure firmly associated with the figure of Paul Robeson. Three years later Jones, as noted above, was to play the role of Ned in *Proud Valley* and to co-write the film's screenplay. Indeed, the film's cinema release had been preceded by a radio version, broadcast in February 1940, directed by the Welsh-language novelist T. Rowland Hughes and written by Jack Jones.[176] Both radio and film versions include *Proud Valley*'s most famous line, which is spoken by Dick Parry in response to an intolerant miner's opposition to having a 'black-man to work down the pit': 'Damn and blast it, man, aren't we all black down that pit?' In both cases the hearty laughter that follows Dick Parry's quip releases the tension provoked by the script's evocation of racial conflict. While David Berry notes that a contemporary perspective should not blind us to the fact that the film broaches the subject of race 'openly and coura- geously enough for the 1940s', what has not been noted by critics is that Dick Parry's words – evoking a connection between the black masks of Welsh miners and the black skins of African Americans – are the most famous expression of a trope that reoccurs with a surprising, suggestive and problematic, regularity in the industrial novels of 1930s Wales.[177]

In an unsurpassed chapter on 'The Welsh industrial novel', Raymond Williams describes the ways in which a south-Walian society that was 'black with miners', gave rise to a remarkable body of fiction that traced the rise of industrial society and the emergence of a powerful working-class consciousness. Williams argues that the Welsh industrial novel is distinctive in the lateness of its emergence – crystallizing in the 1930s – and is characterized by the fact that, 'unlike the English nineteenth-century examples', the Welsh industrial novels 'are, in the majority, written from inside the industrial communities; they are working class novels in the new and distinctive twentieth-century sense'.[178] Williams also notes that in attempting to develop fictional forms suited to the societies that they sought to portray writers often reverted to 'the story of a family'.[179] A tension between the particular and the general ensues, for the 'family has then to be typical, carrying the central common experiences, but in relationships, in a bonding, which are in the whole experience much wider'.[180] In developing Williams's analysis we may note that each of his observations impacts on the representation of race in the Welsh industrial novel. Emerging belatedly as a body of novels in the 1930s, Welsh industrial fictions reflect that period's concern with questions of race and eugenics; written from inside the societies depicted, the novels draw upon an intimate knowledge of working-class culture and reflect the racial attitudes and pervasive influence of American popular culture; and, in so far as the family becomes the site and embodiment of communal and national identity in these novels, nationality becomes rooted in an ancestral, racial, identity. Indeed, one characteristic of what Raymond Williams described as the 'new crystallization' and 'new form of the industrial novel' that emerged in 1930s Wales is its persistent engagement with questions of race and ethnicity.[181] Reconstructing the nature, form and extent of this engagement sheds further light on the Welsh reception of Paul Robeson, and the ambivalent role that Robeson played within Welsh culture in the 1930s.

In his discussion of 'race and the making of the American working class', David Roediger registers the crucial contribution made by the 'new labour historians' of the 1960s, 1970s and 1980s in showing the extent to which workers, even in periods of economic depression or political oppression, were historical actors who made their own political choices and created their own cultural forms. He notes, however, a hesitancy on the part of leftist historians to explore 'working class "whiteness" and white supremacy as creations, in part, of the white working class itself'.[182] We might not expect a similar argument to be relevant in Wales where ethnic tensions have generally been more muted than in the United States, and where the number of 'visible minorities' has always been below 2 per cent of the population. When Sir Alfred Zimmern, briefly professor of international politics at Aberystwyth, described the south Wales coalfield as 'American Wales' in 1921 he did so in order to emphasize 'what a joy' it had been 'to pass even a too fleeting and infrequent week-end among men and women who really care for ideas and love the search for truth'.[183] The historian Dai Smith adopted both Zimmern's metaphor and his optimism in reconstructing a south-Walian society, the photographs of which continued to emit 'the sounds, defiant and plaintive, of the fancy-dress gazooka parties in the jazz carnivals and the silver bands, mingling American popular music with the beat of a drum or the minor key melancholy of a hymn made bearable by the sheer triumph of people walking together'.[184] Smith sees the Welsh working-class embrace of American cultural forms as an inherent rejection of bourgeois versions of Welsh respectability – based in the Welsh language and religious Nonconformity – and notes, for instance, that cinemas 'sprang up all over South Wales and were rightly seen as intrinsically subversive of social quiescence'.[185] Smith, like the new American labour historians described by Roedigger, argues that working-class societies were not unthinking victims of political or cultural hegemonies. Yet, as the Wales-based African American ethnographer Glenn Jordan has noted, the cultural forms and political values that emerged from those societies were not always progressively subvervise:

> South Wales miners, and mining communities, are famous for their socialist traditions and internationalism, including their virtual hero worship of Paul Robeson. But there is another, long-established tradition in the south Wales Valleys: the working-class community as breeding ground for racism.[186]

It might be worth keeping Jordan's words, and Roediger's observation that 'even in an all-white town, race was never absent', in mind when considering the following dialogue from Gwyn Jones's novel *Times Like These* (1936).[187]

> 'When was I last in the pitchers, mam?'
>    'I can't say I'm sure. Was it that there *Birth of a Nation*?'
>    'No. We been since then.'
>    'It was that there Charlie Chaplin film, wasn't it?'
>    'That's right, Luke. We did. Ay – remember that, mam?'
>    Polly laughed. 'Yes, indeed. He was real funny old Charlie was!'
>    'Ay – like that darky me and Olive seen in Bournemouth. He was a proper case, he was!'[188]

Informing this brief dialogue from *Times Like These* are two widely disseminated versions of blackness that have been described by Donald Bogle as the threatening, lascivious 'black buck' of *Birth of a Nation*, and the comic 'coon' of minstrel shows.[189] Welsh-American David Llewellyn Wark Griffith's virulently racist milestone in cinema history, *Birth of a Nation*, was released in 1915. It was periodically revived, in 1921, in 1924/5 and then again with sound in 1930, which is probably the version referred to by Gwyn Jones's characters.[190] The first half of Griffith's film, in which two friendly families, the Southern Camerons and Northern Stonemans, become enemies with the coming of the Civil War, fits the paradigm of the Civil War genre that flourished in the American cinema from 1908 to 1917. The second half of the film introduces a new icon in American cinema; the intimidating, violent 'brutal black buck' who aims to marry a white woman.[191] While the Stonemasons and Camerons continue to be divided for a time by the war's bitter legacy, they eventually unite to defend a white heritage (symbolized by white womenfolk) that is perceived to be threatened by black political advancement during the post-war years of reconstruction. The film proceeds to offer a heroic depiction of the Ku Klux Klan riding to the defence of white civilization against what is presented as a looming black threat. It is possible to dismiss Gwyn Jones's reference to the film as a mere reflection of the period's popular discourse, but an earlier passage in the novel, where Shelton, the colliery agent, expresses his fear of miners suggests that the reference to *Birth of a Nation* is deliberately suggestive.

> To his mind came the picture of Louise undressing – cool, wonderful; shimmering silk, mother-of-pearl flesh – exquisite, exquisite, thrice exquisite – and then, as though all the colliers were one, a bestial, slobbering, black-jowled mask leering at her, a monstrous phallic thumb jerking at her, and the mask now with lips bubbling up to a wet puffiness of lust, now pulling thin in the most grotesque convulsions of hate. As though through and across his wife's shoulders and petally breasts he saw this foulness. If only he had an axe to smash right into it! If only he had a hatchet, big-bladed, big-bladed, to bring smashing down on it! Pulp it all up together, in a cream of blood and bones and flesh and brains. He'd down those bloody miners. By God, he'd down them![192]

The mother-of-pearl flesh of Shelton's wife is compared to the 'black-jowled mask' of the miners. A class anxiety is figured in terms of racial and sexual anxieties in this passage as the miners take on the form of a 'monstrous phallic thumb jerking at her' in Shelton's mind. Indeed, as he picks up his hatchet in a fantasized revenge killing it seems that Shelton has also been watching *Birth of Nation*.

The evocation of the miners' 'black mask' in Shelton's fantasy resonates with *Proud Valley*'s claim that 'we're all black down that pit', and draws on an image that is fairly widespread in 1930s literature. In going *In Search of Wales* in 1932, the travel writer H. V. Morton described the miners rising from their shifts as 'pitch black devils . . . For a second the cage looked like a prison full of Negroes'.[193] The same comparison seems embedded in the very title of Jack Jones's novel *Black Parade* (1935), which begins as follows:

> Two stark-naked young men in the living room of the cottage singing a duet from one of Dr. Parry's operas as a middle-aged woman picked up and hung away the pit clothes they had shed. They had both washed white the upper halves of their coal-blackened bodies, and the elder of the two was standing in the tub half filled with water washing his lower part . . . 'How many times have I told you about standing about naked and showing all you've got in front of Marged. Cover up for shame's sake.'
>
> 'Oh Marged don't mind, tisn't as if she was a slip of a girl. You're not particular are you Marged?' . . .
>
> They went on washing and dressing and singing. They were a handsome pair of young men, now that they could be seen free of the disguise of the coating of coal dust.[194]

Stephen Knight has perceptively suggested that the theatre is never far from Jack Jones's fiction, and the opening sentence of *Black Parade* sounds like a stage direction.[195] Jones's reference to the 'disguise . . . of coal dust' resonates with the *Black Parade* of his title and may be connected imagistically to Shelton's evocation of a 'black mask' in *Times Like These*, and with the 'darky' that Gwyn Jones's family saw in Bournemouth who was probably not actually black but was, rather, like the lead African American characters in *Birth of a Nation*, a white in blackface.[196] Thus, in addition to evoking the theatre, Jones's novel seems to be informed by blackface conventions. The combination of singing, a humorous sexuality and bodies clothed in a black 'disguise', present the characteristic constituents of minstrelsy at the novel's opening. During the course of the novel the central character, Saran (based on Jack Jones's mother), makes several visits to the theatre, and amongst the performances mentioned in the text we find *Uncle Tom's Cabin*, *The Octoroon* and, when the theatre is converted into a cinema, *The Singing Fool*.[197] *Uncle Tom's Cabin* refers to the hugely popular stage production of Harriet Beecher Stowe's anti-slavery novel which, as I noted in chapter 1, was translated into Welsh no less than three times during the nineteenth century and was the source of several African American stereotypes.[198] *The Octoroon* was an abolitionist play by Irish American Dion Boucicault, first performed in the 1850s. The play centres on a relationship across the colour line in pre-Civil War America, and interestingly, while the American version ended with the tragic death of the Octoroon (a person with one-eighth of black blood and thus deemed to be black in Southern law), the British version ended with a happy marriage between the Octoroon and her white suitor.[199] *The Singing Fool* was the most successful talkie ever upon its release in 1928, and was blackface performer Al Jolson's sequel to *The Jazz Singer*.[200] The 'blacking' on which all these performances relied involved the use of facial greasepaint or burnt cork to darken the skin and derived from a mid-nineteenth-century American tradition of impersonation that continued well into the twentieth century.[201] Jones's fictional evocation of blackface performances is not merely a suggestive, if problematic, metaphor for ethnic, linguistic and cultural changes in Welsh society (I will return to this aspect of his work), but also reflected a historical truth; for minstrelsy was remarkably popular in Wales from the mid-nineteenth century until the Second World War.

While Jack Jones's novels have been dismissed as 'a compilation of the "Hundred Best Known Facts about South Wales"', some of the facts that form a basis for his fiction are less well known than others.[202] Jones is not being fanciful when a character in *Bidden to the Feast* (1938) returns to Merthyr and notes how 'grand it is to be home' with the 'children crying for more bread and butter and talking about the Christy Minstrels'.[203] Edwin P. Christy's minstrel troupe had an extraordinary eight-year run at New York's Mechanics' Hall before touring Britain and inspiring a string of imitators, and are here evoked, along with bread and butter, as a characteristic of the 'home' to which the Welsh exile returns.[204] In chapter 1 I discussed the ways in which Ieuan Gwyllt used the pages of his journal *Y Cerddor Cymraeg* (The Welsh Musician) as a pulpit for cultivating his nation's musical tastes in the nineteenth century. He feared that 'sensation music' imported from England and Europe would subvert the religious morality and respectability of Wales's musical culture, and warned against popular music's ability to 'borthi y nwydau mwyaf llygredig' (feed the most debased instincts).[205] The popularity of minstrelsy, as noted by William Dean Howells on his visits to Wales, continued into the twentieth century, as illustrations 6 and 7 suggest. During the long month of the miners' lockout in 1926

6. The Pontardawe Carnival, Glanrhyd tinplate works, 2 September 1933.

communities sought escapism in bands such as the 'Seven Sisters Black Natives', the 'Carolina Coons' and the blackfaced 'Graig Miners'. Dai Smith and Hywel Francis note that, during the 1926 strike and lockout, the carnivals of 'jazz' and 'comic bands' 'became as important as the Federation in maintaining morale'.[206]

Despite the apparent seriousness of the Pontardawe minstrels in illustration 6 and despite its morale-boosting features during the depression years (see illustration 7), minstrelsy was fundamentally based on trivializing black aspirations to full citizenship, and offered white travesties and imitations of black culture. The popularity of minstrelsy was not unique to Wales, for minstrelsy reinforced a widely held view of the hierarchy of races that justified imperial conquest and arguments for racist beliefs. It is no coincidence that the miners' 'obscene jokes and smutty yarns' in Lewis Jones's novel *Cwmardy* (1937) remind Big Jim of his 'adventures in the Boer War' where he encountered

a black 'ooman, naked as a dog, on a tump 'bout hundred yards away. Duw, duw, she was the first 'ooman us had seen for years, and the sun that hot we was full of tickles all the time. We all winked to her, but she take no notice, mun. Then I shout, 'Dera-ma. Argllwydd [*sic*] mawr.' She didn't half run then. All of us did race after her like mad. But I was a good runner then, and did

7. A south Wales Jazz Band, 1930s.

soon leave 'em all standing. But funny thing, mun, she did leave me standing. I did go like hell, but all I could see was her little black arse shining in the sun like a brass button, before she did turn round and shout, 'Toodle-oo'.[207]

Eric Lott notes that minstrelsy, while being based on racist stereotypes and the exploitation of a crude distortion of black culture for white entertainment, was also a 'derisive celebration of the power of blackness; blacks, for a moment, ambiguously on top'.[208] The white male's desire for the black woman in Jim's narrative is converted into harmless humour with his 'butties', the woman playing the role of the minstrel clown who escapes her white suitor, but ultimately poses no threat to the white Briton's position of dominance. If Big Jim's story is recounted within the context of British imperialism, minstrel conventions were also adapted to Welsh conditions. Between 1861 and 1911, as a result of the explosive growth of the coal industry, the population of the county of Glamorgan grew by 253 per cent, and in the decade preceding the First World War Wales, in relative percentage terms, was ranked second to the United States as a centre for immigration.[209] Wales, an agricultural land of about 500,000 people in 1800, was transformed into an urban nation of over 2,500,000 by 1911.[210] In a society that saw major changes in the make-up of its ethnic composition the question of who was native and who was foreign, brother and other, became a question of some concern.

Within this context, blackface 'assures its audience that difference is visible, always encoded in the same way, skin deep'.[211] While minstrelsy in America reflected white anxieties over urbanizing trends amongst blacks, Susan Gubar argues that race-changing conventions 'enabled artists from manifold traditions to relate nuanced comparative stories about various modes and gradations of othering'.[212] As the novelists of 1930s Wales attempted to 'understand the social experience that had also held their individual lives in thrall' they evoked the racial imagery of American popular culture to comment obliquely on the changing ethnic composition of their societies.[213]

Indeed, a striking characteristic of the Welsh industrial novel is that social changes are often linked to changes in the racial composition of society. This is famously and unambiguously the case in a scene from Richard Llewellyn's bestselling *How Green Was My Valley* (1939) where the community hears that a local child, Dilys Pritchard, is murdered. In response, Mr Gruffydd the minister forms the men into what approximates a lynch mob:

'Beasts live among you' he shouted, 'working with you shoulder to shoulder, who will kill your children and go their way unpunished . . . Such beasts you shall exorcise . . . Are we in one mind?'
'Yes' said the crowd.
'Then come,' Mr. Gruffydd said, 'let us cleanse ourselves.'
Down from the rock and out in front of the crowd, striking up a hymn as he went, down toward the village Mr. Gruffydd led us. The boots of the men beat time upon the ground, and their voices flung the anthem before them, and the blaze of torches lit their bearded faces and struck sparks from their eyes . . . Around each public house, and all around the three rows of houses where the half-breed Welsh, Irish and English were living, the men took a stand, almost elbow to elbow, so that none could go in or out . . . Up to the rows of houses where the dross of the collieries lived. These people did the jobs the colliers would never do, and they were allowed to live and breed because the owners would not spend money on plant when their services were to be had so much the cheaper . . . Their houses were bestial sties, where even beasts would rebel if put there to live, for beasts have clean ways with them and they will show their disgust quick enough, but these people were long past such good feeling. They were a living disgust.[214]

The alliterated 'b' in the repeated words 'beasts' and 'bestiality' evokes something of the menace induced by the sound of the men's boots beating time as they march, and John Harris is surely right to suggest that the scene offers an uncomfortable reminder of other nationalisms of the 1930s based on racial purity and on idealizations of a rural folk.[215] In light of this scene it is perhaps not surprising to find that John Ford, who played the role of a Clansman in *Birth of a Nation*, went on to direct the Best Picture Oscar-winning version of *How Green Was My Valley* in 1941.[216] Ian Bell, Hywel Teifi Edwards and Dai Smith have all commented in various ways on the intensity of the racial anxiety in this scene, and all tend to follow John Harris in regarding Llewellyn's virulently racist sentiments as 'unique in Anglo-Welsh literature'.[217] Given the alleged uniqueness of Llewellyn's racial anxieties it is perhaps surprising to find that the novel's reviewers, while voicing widespread misgivings about the work, 'made no reference to its dubious politics'.[218] Had George Ewart Evans reviewed the novel perhaps he would have picked up some of its worrying political aspects, as he did when appraising novelist Rhys Davies's 'new style guidebook' *My Wales* in 1937:

> Rhys Davies attempts to take a detached view of the conflict between miners and owners since the beginning of the last century. He sees the struggle isolated in South Wales, not a world-wide phenomenon. As a result he has startling theories of its cause. The strife in South Wales is a natural outcome of the presence of mixed breeds in the coalfield. What a notion! Comic of Bill Bristol, Mike and Dai working together in the same seam. But is fascist-fodder comic?[219]

George Ewart Evans was responding to passages such as the following where Davies offers a colourful overview of the history of south Wales:

> In the early part of the nineteenth century the Rhondda Valley was occupied by about a hundred people, living a comfortable if austere life among its woods, wild precipices and green fields. Within a hundred years 114,000 people had found accommodation there, and they were still arriving in eager droves. Nearly all the trees had been whisked away and in their places long naked rows of dwellings had been built, rigid lines of stone divided into poky little houses overflowing with the invaders . . . Quite early in the nineteenth century there were minor, slovenly – and criminal – attempts by mad agitators to clean up the economic degradations of the times: the hordes of immigrants still arriving in the new Eldorado had made labour very cheap, thousands failing to find work for some time . . . Outside the chapels another section of the industrialized race grizzled and let loose moans and complaints . . . This outside section, some said and still say, was composed of rootless ruffians and barbarous aliens, particularly Irishmen, who were merely stirring up trouble for its own sake, loving a fight, bored with the monotony of work. Any excuse served to call a strike, which might develop into rioting, arson, plundering.[220]

This is not all that Rhys Davies has to say about 'The South Wales Workers' in the longest chapter of *My Wales*, but the passage is indicative of a structure of argument that reappears at several points in Davies's work. The animalistic terms – grizzle, moan – predates Richard Llewellyn's emphasis on the bestiality of the lumpenproletarian 'half-breeds' and conveys a pervasive sense of otherness that is reinforced by the stark juxtaposition of the rural and industrialized visions of the Rhondda Valley.

Similarly, in his first autobiography *Unfinished Journey* (1937), Jack Jones presents a narrative of malign foreign influences destroying Welsh innocence. He describes the area of Merthyr in which he grew up, Tai-Harry-Blawd, as a place where the Welsh were in a minority, mixed with English, Irish and Scotch. 'At first I knew only Welsh', he tells us, '. . . [b]ut I was playing about with children who couldn't speak Welsh from morning till it was time to go to bed at night, and from them I learnt many of their far from harmless tricks'.[221] Lawlessness and 'far from harmless tricks' are associated with outsiders, and this view of Wales is reinforced later in the narrative when Jones describes his experiences as a soldier in the Boer War:

> The Boer prisoners were of three generations, I thought. Boys of my own age, men about my dad's age, with the eldest section about as old as my granser when he died. They were dressed in clothes like those granser and dad used to wear the time granser was alive – and the look in their eyes I had seen in granser's and dad's eyes when they spoke of the 'foreigners', the English, Irish, Scotch and other nationalities who had crowded into Merthyr in the wake of the English industrial adventurers who transformed our more or less peaceful and beautiful country into hell upon earth. I was beginning to understand why Lloyd George had been so pro-Boer.[222]

Jones's identification with the Boers leads to a meditation on the meaning of his father's and grandfather's experiences in Wales. This meditation follows a familiar structure of feeling whereby a 'peaceful and beautiful country' is transformed into a 'hell on earth' by the 'English, Irish, Scotch and other nationalities'. Those 'other nationalities' are frequently evoked in Jones's novels. In *Rhondda Roundabout* (1934) we are told that

> The Jews came to the Rhondda to look for gold whilst Dan was away on holidays . . . [T]he poor Jew . . . took the empty shop next to the Chinese laundryman. (Shoni used to swear that things started to go bad in the Rhondda the day the Chink started washing Rhondda people's clothes.)[223]

Here racist sentiments are voiced by characters and, unlike *How Green was My Valley* and *Unfinished Journey*, are generally not given the

authority of the narrative voice. Thus the nativism that informs parts of
Jones's autobiography is not as prevalent in his novels. In *Bidden to the
Feast* (1938), he describes the ethnic tensions between the Irish and the
Welsh, but does so from a position of some distance, with the narrative
voice drawing the reader's attention to the ironies of a situation in which
two nationalities in servitude to 'English masters' vent their frustrations
upon one another.

> But there were no Eisteddfods or cantatas on the seventeenth of the month, St.
> Patrick's Day for the Irish of the place. Not much singing that day, but plenty
> of old fighting. Then who started it? Some say the Irish did, others say the
> Welsh. Anyway, the English they kept out of it, and the Jews and Scots they
> went about their business as pawn-brokers and credit-drapers, leaving the
> Welsh and Irish to fight if they wanted to . . . Left them to sing 'Hen Wlad fy
> Nhadau' or 'The Wearin' of the Green', whichever they fancied. Welsh who
> lived in Colliers' Row, and Irish who lived in Paddies' Rows, Welsh who
> worked in pits, and Irish who worked in ironworks, Welsh and Irish who had
> slaved to make millions sterling for English masters unto the third and fourth
> generation, now at each other's throats.[224]

In *Bidden to the Feast*, it is the father who subscribes and gives voice
to a nativist narrative of the kind that we find in Richard Llewellyn and
Rhys Davies. The father is no hero, however, but is in fact a brutal
authoritarian who alienates his sons when they marry non-Welsh wives.
When his daughters win a clock for singing he smashes it as punishment
for wasting their time in pleasurable pursuits, and then proceeds to beat
them – leading his wife to suffer a stroke from which she never recovers.
Jones thus questions the idea that everything of value derives from an
earlier, native Wales, a questioning that is pursued more stridently in
communist Lewis Jones's 'novelisation of a phase of working-class
history' in his sequence of novels *Cwmardy* (1937) and *We Live* (1939).[225]
In these novels it is always Big Jim, Shane and the older unionist Ezra
who voice nativist beliefs, whilst the new generation, Len and Mary, see
little of value in such rhetoric. Ezra laments the fact that Len and Harry
Morgan have brought 'your foreign theories into the valley' in *We Live*,
and Big Jim castigates the mine owners for bringing 'non political
foreigners into the pit'.[226] Unlike Richard Llewellyn, Lewis Jones does
not give such views the full authority of the narrative, and the history of
the coalfield is described as follows:

> The village was now more prosperous than it had ever been. The pits never
> ceased their throbbing night or day. The 'foreigners' had inter-married with

the natives, their children, now young adults, creating a new cosmopolitan population in the valley. Street and mountain fights were no longer so frequent, but the continually extending police-station housed more police than it ever had.[227]

By placing quotation marks around 'foreigners' the narrator is clearly revealing that who is and is not a foreigner is no longer self-evident, obvious or readily apparent. Society has moved on. The suggestion remains, however, that ethnic tensions were one of the reasons for mountain fights in the past. Even novelists who generally take a sanguine view of the growing ethnic diversity of south Wales often give a particular prestige to characters who are native to Wales. It may not be surprising that Rhys Davies's fictions are full of long-faced native Silurians and men like Pugh Jibbons in 'Blodwen' who is a man of the mountains who 'had not submitted to industrialism, Nonconformity or imitation of the English', or Reuben Daniels in *The Withered Root* who is of 'the old pure Welsh blood'.[228] Shane in Lewis Jones's *Cwmardy* is also, however, 'proud of the fact that her people belonged to the valley before the pits were even thought of' and Tudur in Glyn Jones's surrealist short story 'Porth-y-Rhyd' is 'a descendant of the first men to light their fires in the coast caves'.[229] Welsh writings of the 1930s are characterized by a racial ambivalence; they document and occasionally celebrate the emergence of a new, cosmopolitan, urban Wales, while also conveying some unease about what the *Welsh Review* described in 1939 as 'the coming of a mongrel race'.[230] Thus, far from being unique in conceiving of Welsh history in racial terms, Richard Llewellyn's *How Green Was My Valley* offered a simplified, bestselling, treatment of a theme that reappears in the period's novels, and reverberates beyond the fiction into other discourses relating to 1930s Wales.

As I discussed in chapter 2, the 1920s and 1930s saw anthropologist H. J. Fleure travelling across Wales measuring the size of people's skulls. Fleure offered an inventory of racial types in the literary journal *Wales*: 'Carmarthenshire has B in abundance, but some A-B transitional and of course large elements of F and some E'. The 'tangle of immigration' that he saw in 'Glamorgan and Monmouth' exposed the limitations of his methodology, for he could only conclude that 'one cannot venture much more than a statement that B was obviously fundamental and F an important coastal element'.[231] For Ernest William McBride, professor emeritus, and previous chair of zoology at the Imperial College of Science and Technology, London, the 'tangle of immigration' and uncontrolled reproduction in south Wales called for the 'Cultivation of the Unfit'.[232]

By 'cultivation' McBride meant the 'compulsory sterilisation as a punishment for parents who have to resort to public assistance in order to support their children'. He knew where to find such parents: 'Dock labourers and miners figure prominently in the over-production of children, and it is worthy of note that in both groups there is a large proportion of the Iberian element in our population from Wales and Ireland.'[233]

That Fleure's research was funded by the Leverhulme Trust, and McBride's article appeared in the respected scientific weekly *Nature*, testifies to the influence of, and respect granted to, racial and eugenicist thought in the 1930s. If the miners would include large numbers of Welsh and Irish, the dock labourers to whom McBride refers constituted the most ethnically diverse communities in 1930s Britain. Butetown, the multi-ethnic community that had formed around Cardiff docklands, was the subject of commentary and reports throughout the 1930s.[234] A *Western Mail* editorial of 10 July 1935 mirrors in language and imagery McBride's January 1936 article in *Nature*. In drawing attention to the 'Problem of Cardiff's coloured community' the editor was alarmed by the 'growth of the half-caste population':

> The number is increasing rapidly because so many seamen are out of work and living on shore – 'in idleness but not in want'. Their way is made easy by the dole system. A coloured man out of work marries, begets a family and may receive more money from the public purse than if he went to sea.[235]

A vigorous debate ensued in the pages of the *Western Mail*, in which the Reverend Stanley E. Watson, who had been a missionary in Guyana and the West Indies, refuted the accusation that black seamen were idle by drawing attention to the fact that a few weeks earlier many had travelled to London to work as extras in Paul Robeson's film, *Sanders of the River*.[236] These debates were to filter into the writings of the 1930s where Butetown, or Tiger Bay, is envisaged as the location of a new hybrid culture that is both appealing and somewhat frightening. Idris Davies reinforces a familiar stereotype in describing 'the colored seamen in the morning mist / Slouching along the damp brown street', but (despite the apocalyptic allusion to Yeats's 'The Second Coming') ultimately admires their ability to curse and laugh in the face of 'the dismal dawn'.[237] The rugby player Ben Fisher in Gwyn Jones's *Times Like These* returns to his mining community bearing sensational stories of his exploits in Cardiff that reinforce the notion of Butetown as a place where social conventions are subverted:

In Cardiff . . . he had adventures other than those of the football fields. Adventures that brought forth names evocative of magic and desire – Bute Street, Tiger Bay, all niggers and Woolworth blondes, I never seen no colour line there, I tell u; the Honolulu and the Pernambuca Cafes, little chinky Chinamen and men with fezzes; dances in Canton, all Jews, college boys, and fancy stuff to do your eye good . . .[238]

While there may have been no colour line in Bute Street, Ben Fisher's description of the place underlines the racial terms in which he sees the world. Butetown had seen the first major British race riot in 1919, and the widely reported accounts of racial tensions in Tiger Bay in the 1930s seem to tap into, and to reflect, a wider racial anxiety that is expressed in the period's fiction.[239]

In Jack Jones's *Black Parade* racial anxieties are played out within the context of a boxing ring. There are two significant boxing scenes in the novel. The first presents the Welshman Harry plastering the Irishman Flannery's 'mug until the nose, moustache and lips were pounded into one piece of blood-soaked hairy flesh'.[240] Glyn, the character from whose perspective we view the fight, is reduced to vomiting violently by the sight. The tone in which the other fight is described is rather different:

'I'll knock that bloody smile off your chops,' muttered Harry as he went for the nigger bald-headed. But when he got to where the nigger had been a split second before the nigger wasn't there. But he soon learnt where he was when a stinging left came from somewhere to almost flatten his nose. 'Damn you,' he muttered, turning and charging in the direction the blow had come from, only to receive a stinger from another direction. And so it went on throughout the round, a round during which Harry saw but little of the coloured man who smiled . . . 'Science, that is,' murmured Billy Samuels proudly as the smiling untouched negro returned to his corner at he end of the second round, by which time Harry was in a very bad way indeed . . . He was carried to his corner, where he was washed and brought to his senses, and after that was done Billy Samuels shook him by the hand and said that never had he seen a gamer chap than Harry had that night proved himself, and the negro boxer also shook Harry by the hand and said that he was the stiffest proposition he had met in any part of the United States of America or here in this country . . .[241]

The black boxer is merely a 'nigger' when the fight begins, but is slowly elevated into the more respectable 'coloured man' and 'negro' in the face of the pounding that Harry receives. The African American is introduced as Joe Wills before the fight, a name that implicitly evokes a widely covered American boxing controversy of the 1920s. The main challenger for the heavyweight championship, held by the white Jack Dempsey, was the African American Harry Wills. A fight between the two men was never arranged, partly because Dempsey's promoter did not believe in interracial fights, and partly due to a fear of race riots of the kind that had accompanied Jack Johnson's victories in the previous decade.[242] Jack Jones splits Harry Wills's name between the Welshman Harry and the African American Wills, a suggestive identification of both the Welshman and African American with the boxer famously denied his chance to fight for the heavyweight title. The difference between the two fights in Jones's novel reflects a difference in the social, and fictional, status, of the Irish and African Americans. Ethnic tensions between the Irish and Welsh, as Paul O'Leary has noted, were common in nineteenth-century south Wales, a reality reflected in the visceral violence of the bout between Harry and Flannery.[243] African Americans posed no such threat and the way in which Jones depicts the scene seems to evoke – to adopt Gerald Early – a culture of clowning more than a 'culture of bruising'. Wills's perpetual smile and ability to disappear whenever Harry tries to land a punch is reminiscent of the trickster figure in African American culture, and the clowning 'coon' of minstrel shows. The minstrel mask is used to hide a submerged hatred and the smiling boxer destroys Harry before patronizing him by claiming that he has never met stiffer opposition. This seems unlikely as, according to Jones's account, Harry never manages to land a punch during the whole fight. While Jones utilizes a heightened realism to depict Harry's bout with the Irishman Flannery, the fight with the African American Wills seems to belong to a symbolic, metaphorical realm where the black boxer represents a model of the 'sly civility' that post-colonial critics have argued is a common strategy adopted by minorities in their relationships with the dominant culture.[244] Eric Lott, in his suggestive account of blackface minstrelsy, notes that to

> put on the cultural forms of 'blackness' was to engage in a complex affair of manly mimicry . . . To wear or even enjoy blackface was literally for a time, to become black, to inherit the cool, virility, humility, abandon, or *gaité de coeur* that were the prime components of white ideologies of black manhood.[245]

This attraction to forms of black masculinity was a significant aspect of Paul Robeson's reception in Wales. In 1922, two prize-fight promoters from Chicago had in fact offered to train Robeson as a challenger to Harry Wills and Jack Dempsey, and it was erroneously reported that Robeson had abandoned a career as a lawyer to 'earn money for his wife and children' in the boxing ring.[246] In Jack Jones's *Black Parade* Joe

Wills embodies the 'cool, virility' and 'abandon' described by Lott. The ambivalence of Welsh responses to African American masculinity is captured in the connection that Jones implies between the two fighters; the Welsh Harry, and African American Wills.

As well as being a response to the changing ethnic composition of south-Walian society, the stark racial differences embodied in the minstrel show also offered a way for individuals to understand the transition from a rural life to industrial wage labour. Faced, as George Rawick has noted in the American context, with 'the imposition of time discipline, the bastardization of crafts, the attacks on holidays, and the attempts to control sexuality and drinking characteristic of capitalist development', white workers began to 'project ambivalent longings for their own past onto purportedly lazy and inhibition-free blacks'.[247] The worker's investment in race allowed him to construct a 'pornography of his former life . . . In order to ensure that he would not slip back into the old ways or act out half-suppressed fantasies. He [had to] see a tremendous difference between his reformed self and those whom he formerly resembled.'[248] The slovenly, unsophisticated, inarticulate 'darky' of the minstrel show could thus be read as an embodiment of rural idiocy. No one was to probe deeper into the inner working of the Welsh industrial subconscious than Rhys Davies, who in *The Black Venus* (1944) seems precisely to explore 'half-suppressed fantasies' of an earlier self, and embodies those fantasies in the 'black venus' of the tale's title; a statue owned by the 'fiercely independent' Lizze Pugh that stands as an incarnation of an uninhibited sexuality and a primitive resistance to industrialized society. The story is set in the rural village of Ayron, a place where 'streams ran pellucid as in the dawn of time', that feels 'a thousand miles from the railway station' and where, beyond the machinery of surveillance developed in industrial settlements, old Welsh customs such as 'courting in bed' – where, in cold houses with few rooms, couples would get to know each other in bed with a bolster laid between them – continue unabated.[249] The racial difference represented by the black Venus mirrors the difference that Davies constructs between the native Welsh and the English who dismiss the indigenous population as 'savages' who go 'prowling about in the night'.[250] The black Venus of Rhys Davies's novel is thus a symbol of both the Welsh self and the Other; an embodiment of a rural past that the author – a native of the industrialized Rhondda – simultaneously longs for and rejects.

Such ambivalence is of the very essence of minstrelsy for, as Eric Lott notes, 'the repellent elements repressed from white consciousness and projected onto black people were far from securely alienated; they were always already "inside", part of "us"'.[251] The shift from rural to urban societies was also a linguistic shift in Wales, from the Welsh language to bilingualism, and ultimately to English; the period from 1931 to 1951 saw the number of Welsh speakers in the Rhondda, for instance, collapse from 45.5 per cent to 29 per cent of the population.[252] If the minstrel represented an earlier, rural, and outmoded civilization, minstrelsy also offered a means for commenting on the linguistic shift from Welsh to English – one of the most charged sites of ambivalence in Welsh culture. Bert Coombes, an Englishman who married a Welsh speaker and knew enough Welsh to sustain a conversation in the language, is particularly sensitive to issues relating to language difference. His autobiography contains a number of scenes involving linguistic mix ups such as the following:

> I knew a Welshman who went to work in the Yorkshire mines and stayed there some years. When he returned to South Wales he brought the new accent with him and settled in a fresh place. Everyone thought he was an Englishman. The women where he lodged and some female neighbours always stayed indoors while he bathed, and among sly glances they had a lot to say concerning his physical capabilities and shortcomings. They spoke freely to one another in Welsh and became more personal as the days passed and he showed no sign of understanding. One day they annoyed him too much and he started to abuse them in fluent Welsh. There was consternation in that circle after that and a definite silence until he found other lodgings.[253]

If the boundaries between 'native' and 'foreigner' were blurred in a rapidly transforming, mobile society, then language differences were also unobservable in real life and could lie beyond the gaze of the realist narrator of industrial fictions. Rhys Davies and Jack Jones often tell us that their characters are actually Welsh speaking.[254] In *How Green Was My Valley* it becomes clear that the family are meant to be speaking Welsh when Huw is told to speak English in school.[255] Even in the case of *Cwmardy* and *We Live* it seems that Big Jim and Shane are meant to be Welsh speakers, although this is never absolutely clear. When Big Jim tells Len in the opening scene of *Cwmardy* that 'this is where King Rhys did have his head chopped off' the narrator tells us that 'the statement was resonant with rolling r's'. There are no r's except in Rhys and 'where' in the English sentence, while the Welsh *brenin* (king) and *torri* (chopped) would, indeed, make it a resonant sentence.[256] Later on, in the inquest scene, the narrator refers to Jim's 'poor grasp of English' and he describes himself as 'not much of an English speaking man'.[257] Just as

'Shane' (transformed to Shân in *We Live*) is meant to denote the Welsh 'Siân', so the English they speak in the novel is a way of making Welsh intelligible to a larger audience. If the discovery or exposure of hidden racial origins is a characteristic of American fiction – from Boucicault's *Octoroon* to Walter Mosely's *Devil in a Blue Dress* – the equivalent in Welsh writing in English may be a form of linguistic passing where one is never sure what language is being spoken, or, as in Coombes's scenario, which languages people speak.

In describing a lodge meeting of the South Wales Miners' Federation, Coombes draws attention to the

> mixture of languages and dialects [that] were there sometimes! Yorkshire and Durham men, Londoners, men from the Forest of Dean, North Welshmen – whose language is much deeper and more pure than the others from South Wales – two Australians, four Frenchmen, and several coloured gentlemen.[258]

This passage is interesting in that Coombes begins by drawing attention to differences in language and dialect, but ends by emphasizing differences in race. Nathaniel Mackey notes that language and race were intimately related on the minstrel stage, for, in poking fun at black people's alleged insecure grasp of English, minstrelsy also commented on the tenuousness of language itself.[259] The minstrel's ability to change accents and to develop a distinctive dialect can be seen to speak directly to the English-language novelist wishing to offer a realist account of mid-nineteenth-century Wales. While the minstrel was a white man blacked up with greasepaint or burnt cork, the novelist who sought to narrate the story of industrialization in Wales from its nineteenth-century beginnings had initially to disguise a Welsh-language culture in English clothing. In a community undergoing a process of linguistic change the minstrel show allowed for apprehensions regarding the tenuousness of language to be expressed. In a multi-lingual and multi-ethnic society blackface performance may be regarded a perfect metaphor for one culture's borrowing from another, and for the inevitable blurring of cultural boundaries. It suggests that identity is not prescribed in the blood, but is in fact a matter of performance. In the specific case of Welsh writing in English blackface performance may be seen to represent, in Eric Lott's words, 'one culture's ventriloqual self-expression through the forms of someone else's'.[260]

In responding to the damning indictment of Wales and the Welsh language that Arthyr Tyssilio Johnson (writing under the pseudonym, Draig Glas) mounted in his book *The Perfidious Welshman* (1910), a writer adopting the title Fluellyn (an anglicization of the Welsh Llewelyn, and a variation on Shakespeare's spelling in *Henry V*) announced that 'Your peculiar critic in "Perfidious Welshman" says "Anglicize yourself as quickly as possible!" Personally, I would as soon take a nigger's advice to blacklead my face.'[261] Language change is equated to race change in this unfortunate passage. This connection between linguistic and racial difference can also be seen in the fact that, when Jack Jones (as I noted above) described himself as 'Old Man River' in his 1937 piece on Anglo-Welsh novelists, he did so in an article that he knew would appear in Welsh; the linguistic change is mirrored in the race change involved in his identification with Robeson. Jones may have had Robeson in mind when, in a remarkable testimony to the African American influence on his work, he composed a story entitled 'The Black Welshman'. In a rambling, largely unstructured narrative that was serialized in the *Empire News* in 1957 and never published as a novel, Jones writes in the first person as an African American boxer who escapes to Wales having killed a white assailant. Known as Tom Ross, but actually named Abraham Dowling, born free in Chicago to a father who had been a slave, the narrator becomes known as 'the black Welshman (y Cymro Du) because in time I spoke the language better than most Welsh people'.[262] Jones's novel lies beyond the boundaries of this present study, but it is worth noting that having used the conventions of black minstrelsy as a vehicle for exploring the social changes that he observed in his own life, Jones ultimately donned the black mask himself in portraying a Welsh-speaking African American inhabitant of the Rhondda Valley.[263]

I hope, therefore, to have demonstrated that Dick Parry's rhetorical question in the most famous line in *Proud Valley* – 'Aren't we all black down that pit?' – drew on a tradition of comparing the miners' mask with 'black' skin. That Robeson's David Goliath should eventually sacrifice himself to free trapped workmates in the pit reflects both the limitations of his integration into the Welsh community and the film's recycling of nineteenth-century conventions where the African American is ultimately akin to a servant, 'consistently tidying up after others'.[264] The film's conclusion – where David Goliath sacrifices his life for the family and community in which he has settled – is an unintentionally accurate metaphor for the uses of the black image in the Welsh mind, for in order for a coherent and politically empowering working-class movement to emerge from the ethnic diversity that characterized nineteenth-century south Wales the black male became an enabling image of otherness.

In the United States and beyond, Paul Robeson found it difficult to escape the pernicious influence of minstrel traditions. He continued to feed his audience's desires by including a remarkable amount of 'Dear-Old-Southland' numbers on his gramophone recordings even if they were ultimately discarded from his active repertory – 'Dear Old Southland' itself, 'Carry Me Back to Green Pastures' and even 'That's Why Darkies Were Born'.[265] A history of attraction to minstrelsy inevitably conditioned Welsh responses to African American performers. It is perhaps revealing that as late as 1958, with his passport ban having just been lifted and the civil rights movement underway in America, Robeson was introduced to the Eisteddfod crowd at Ebbw Vale by Colonel Morgan, chairman of the Cymanfa Ganu, as 'Ole Man River himself' who 'is still rolling along'.[266]


CONCLUSION

In the penultimate chapter of Lewis Jones's *We Live*, Len, the central character, is about to leave his mining village to join the International Brigades in Spain. His girlfriend, Mary, and his parents, Jim and Shân, gather together to 'have a sing-song':

Shân immediately opened her eyes and Mary drew her chair to the piano. 'What shall we have, Len?' she asked.

'Let's have something bright and happy that we all know.'

Mary, her thin shoulders swaying to the rhythm, immediately began playing a jazz tune. When she had finished it she asked: 'Did you know that one, mam?'

'Yes, my gel. Of course I did. It was *Bwthyn bach* with some fancy tra-la's, wasn't it?'

'Duw, duw, no. That was "The Blues", mam.'

'Huh. Never mind, Mary fach. Don't worry. I haven't got my specs on and it is quite easy to make a mistake with my eyes so old as they are.'

Len laughed loudly, but after some more tunes the music got into him and mixed with the wine. He rose from the chair and stood by Mary, lifting his voice to the refrains she played. They went through song after song, and, as they exhausted their repertoire of modern music and the wine took more effect, they unconsciously drifted to the old hymns of the people.

Shân became wide awake when the sad tones moaned through the kitchen. She clothed them in their Welsh words, her low contralto throbbing an accompaniment to the voices of Len and Mary, who eventually stopped singing and left the field clear for the old lady.

> Jim took the pipe from his mouth and used it as a baton to keep time, smiling happily as Shân crooned her way back into the past where they both immersed themselves to the temporary exclusion of the present . . .
>
> [W]hen Shân floated into the plaintive melody of *Dafydd y Gareg* [*sic*] *Wen*, everyone but herself became silent.
>
> The old woman was weeping openly before she had completed the ballad.[267]

Robeson, as I noted earlier, was firmly associated in Wales with the struggle of the Spanish Republic and, while there is no way of proving that Robeson was in the author's mind when composing this scene, it is striking that Shân mistakes Mary's performance of the African American blues for the popular Welsh song 'Bwthyn Bach' (Little Cottage).[268] While Robeson was never associated with the blues, the folk song 'Dafydd y Garreg Wen' was included in his repertoire from the mid-1930s onwards. In both *Cwmardy* and *We Live*, Lewis Jones evokes a residual Welsh-language culture at moments of personal or communal tragedy. While Jim and Shân are transformed in the act of singing into representatives of an older Welsh-language culture to which they are transported in song 'to the temporary exclusion of the present', the scene creates a connection between the African American blues embraced by the new generation, and the Welsh folk music of the past. Residual and emergent cultures, from two distinct traditions, fuse in a scene that seeks, like Robeson's concert performances of the world's folk songs, to fore-ground cultural diversity within the context of the wider, universal, human values that inform Len's decision to go and fight, and ultimately to lose his life, in Spain.

In the twenty-first century, with the Soviet experiment a chapter in history, with Welsh coal mining and the working men's halls and libraries that it spawned preserved in folk museums, and with the international left in retreat, there is a danger that a nostalgic 'immersion' in Robeson's recordings leads to the 'temporary exclusion' of our very different present. Two recent works by Welsh writers testify to Robeson's continued relevance, however. Playwright Greg Cullen suggests in his powerful theatrical exploration of Welsh racial attitudes, *Paul Robeson Knew My Father* (2000), that in responding with righteous indignation to McCarthy's America we are in danger of ignoring the very real elements of racism and intolerance in our own culture, past and present. Cullen's replacement of Lloyd George with Paul Robeson in his reso-nant title suggests the extent to which the African American is embedded in the Welsh national consciousness. In her celebrated autobiography *Sugar and Slate* (2002), Charlotte Williams, the black Welsh daughter of a white Welsh-speaking mother and a black Guyanese father, explores the problems inherent in comparing 'Welsh' and 'Black', for when the 'Welshman' is assumed to be 'a black man at heart', where does that place 'the black man who is Welsh or the Welshman who is black'?

> So are we really all comrades under the skin? It's a curious thought. Perhaps we are in many ways. Paul Robeson in the film *The Proud Valley* isn't a Welsh folk hero for nothing . . . It's a sort of civil rights film for Wales . . . Yet maybe we have woven the connection rather too deep into the mythology of Wales.[269]

As in all acts of mythologization, 'Robeson' seems to emerge fully formed from a cultural vacuum, his political ideas represented as consistent, pure and resistant to change, and his persona made to embody the most valuable of human characteristics. This chapter has sought to problematize the myth; to emphasize the tensions and contradictions in Robeson's thought, to suggest the contradictory ways in which he was perceived in Wales, and to foreground the linguistic, political and cultural complexities of the Wales to which, in significant and revealing ways, he related.

4

# The Invisible Man's Welsh Routes: Ralph Ellison in Wartime Wales

8. Dancers at the American Red Cross in Libanus Chapel, Morriston.

In his introduction to the thirtieth-anniversary edition of *Invisible Man* the African American novelist Ralph Ellison recounted the gestation of his seminal novel as follows:

> I had published yet another story in which a young Afro-American seaman, ashore in Swansea, South Wales, was forced to grapple with the troublesome 'American' aspects of his identity after white Americans had blacked his eye during a wartime blackout on the Swansea street called Straight (no, his name was *not* Saul, nor did he become a Paul!). But here the pressure toward self-scrutiny came from a group of Welshmen who rescued him and surprised him by greeting him as a 'Black Yank' and inviting him to a private club, and then sang the American National Anthem in his honor. [The story was] published in 1944, but now in 1945 on a Vermont farm, the theme of a young Negro's quest for identity was reasserting itself in a far more bewildering form.[1]

Ellison described *Invisible Man* as having 'erupted out of what had been conceived as a war novel', and here he views the 'Negro's quest for identity' in his short story as essentially prefiguring his more extensive engagement with that subject in his most famous work.[2] *Invisible Man* – once described as 'the veritable *Moby Dick* of the racial crisis' – now occupies a central position in the American and African American literary canons, and it is, therefore, not surprising that critics have tended to follow Ellison's lead in reading his short stories of the 1940s as anticipating some of the key themes of his acclaimed masterpiece.[3] In this chapter I depart somewhat from this convention by concentrating specifically on Ralph Ellison's writings set in wartime Wales. Ellison served in the merchant marine as second cook and baker from 1943 to 1945, seeing this as a means of contributing to the war effort without serving in the segregated American army. His period aboard the *SS Sun Yat Sen* in 1943 brought him to the Welsh ports of Cardiff, Barry and Swansea, and it is the latter destination that forms a setting for the story 'In a Strange Country', referred to in his introduction above and published in 1944.[4] Ellison also wrote two other unpublished stories based on his experiences in Wales which exist in several drafts, at various stages of completion, in the Ellison Papers at the Library of Congress: 'A Storm of Blizzard Proportions' and 'The Red Cross at Morriston, Swansea, S.W.' All three of Ellison's Welsh-based short stories explore the ways in which the Welsh 'pressure' an African American 'toward self-scrutiny'.

In an uncompleted draft of 'A Storm of Blizzard Proportions' Ellison suggestively scribbled in pencil on the margin 'love of soil if not of government'.[5] This deceptively simple statement offers a useful basis from which to begin discussing Ellison's responses to the Welsh, for his encounters with a people who retain a national identity without the protective buttressing of an independent state, and who preserve a sense of cultural distinctiveness while contributing to the war effort of a larger nation state, lead to fictional engagements with the 'troublesome . . . aspects' of American and African American identity. This engagement takes on a powerfully personal form in 'A Storm of Blizzard Proportions' which consists primarily of a dialogue between a departing African American merchant marine and his Welsh sweetheart. It is perhaps the most Hemingwayan of Ellison's stories, evoking at its best 'that quality of implying much more than was stated explicitly' that Ellison said he encountered in Hemingway's stories.[6] In keeping with Ellison's marginal scribbling, the story is profoundly concerned with place, seeking to connect a Welsh present with an Ohioan past as the narrator faces an uncertain future. Painful memories are being rekindled as a relationship with both a woman and a country are coming to an end. Faced with the departure of her wartime lover, the Welsh girl imagines an idyllic scene:

'I want a nice house . . . On a hill, where the mist comes down in the winter. With a brass fender where children can play and learn their lessons. And where you can tell them of America – Or' she said with a sudden breathlessness, 'it could even be a house in America. A little house in Ohio . . .'

He watched the dimples steal into her face as she dreamed aloud, watched the soft glint of her teeth in the fireglow. And in his mind he saw the long roll of Welsh hills covered with heather, the browns and greens of the countryside, like fine tweeds beneath the cloud-hidden sun. It would have been a fine life.

For, he realized abruptly, he loved this land, this country, as he had come that distant year to love Ohio – strange he should recall that year. That was the year he lost his mother and had hunted to keep himself alive. It was a wonderful country, he thought, though connected with irrevocable loss, as now this land would be should he never return.[7]

The confined space of the Red Cross Club in which the story takes place contrasts with the narrator's free and imaginative ranging across the geography of Wales, and across the Atlantic to Ohio. This contrast is mirrored in the juxtaposition of the story's focus on a single moment in time, with the narrator's imaginative journeys from the present to the past and onwards to the future. These spatial and temporal shifts are fused powerfully in the tale's conclusion:

> She left hurriedly. And as he waited he watched the dying glow of the fire and thought of the voyage westward. Tomorrow he would sail for home. Weeks of cold, rough seas. A cold crossing he would have of it. And at home there would be the snow. He shivered, hearing the quiet cracking of the coals. A snowstorm of blizzard proportions, the Army newspaper had said, was sweeping the mid-western states. Already the snow was covering the hills of Ohio, already powdering his mother's grave-stone there, and on the brooks and frozen rivers, where quail made tracks in the falling dusk. Snow was sweeping the hills and drifting the briars, and drily shaking the blood-red leaves that hung like bandages snagged on the thorns in flight – an endless snowing all over the snow-whole world of home. Snow sweeping, snow falling, snow drifting down. Snow in the hills and far-away-places. A snow of blizzard proportions. Covering all.[8]

The use of alliteration, the narrative movement westwards and the specific references to the snow, newspaper and graveyard, all suggest the influence of James Joyce's modernist engagement with questions of identity in his short story 'The Dead', which concludes as follows:

> The time had come for him to set out on his journey westward. Yes, the news-papers were right: snow was general all over Ireland. It was falling on every part of the dark central plain, on the treeless hills, falling softly upon the Bog of Allen and, farther westward, softly falling into the dark mutinous Shannon waves. It was falling, too, upon every part of that lonely churchyard on the hill where Michael Furey lay buried. It lay thickly drifted on the crooked crosses and headstones, on the spears of the little gate, on the barren thorns. His soul swooned slowly as he heard the snow falling faintly through the universe and faintly falling, like the descent of their last end, upon the living and the dead.[9]

As with the Red Cross Club that is the setting for 'A Storm of Blizzard Proportions', the bedroom that is the location for the final part of 'The

Dead' is a confined space which contrasts with this final mental journey across Ireland's geography. If, as Benedict Anderson argues, a people's ability to imagine a national community was made possible by the development of 'print-capitalism' and the creation of widely read newspapers, then it is significant that the movement outwards from the confined space of Gabriel's room to the geographical space of the Irish nation itself is prompted by newspaper reports.[10] The conclusion of 'A Storm of Blizzard Proportions' shares a reference to newspapers, and follows the narrative development of Joyce's final tableau in moving from 'the dying glow of the fire' to the 'rough seas' to the 'hills of Ohio' themselves. Both passages use evocatively echoing language, utilizing sibilance ('soul swooned slowly' in 'The Dead', 'snow sweeping, snow falling' in 'A Storm'), and equally resonant repetition of liquid consonants ('soul . . . slowly . . . falling' in 'The Dead', 'sweeping the hills and . . . drily shaking the . . . leaves' in 'A Storm'). Sentences which possess such a phonetically echoic character are more likely to be associated with poetry than prose, encouraging the reader to generate meanings that may not be emphasized semantically. Ellison's allusion to the opening line of T. S. Eliot's 'The Journey of the Magi' – 'A cold coming we had of it' – reinforces this impression.[11] While 'The Dead' moves outwards to encompass a national, Irish, space, 'A Storm of Blizzard Proportions' gestures towards a transatlantic, transnational space, where the Welsh hills are connected to the hills of Ohio, the loss of a Welsh girlfriend is connected to the loss of the narrator's mother, and where relating to Wales leads to a reconnection with the United States. In this respect the narrative development of 'A Storm of Blizzard Proportions' offers an intensely private variation on the narrative development of both 'In a Strange Country' and 'The Red Cross at Morriston, S.W.', for both stories use Wales as a site from which to probe the meaning of the African American experience.

This is most explicitly the case in the story 'In a Strange Country' where Wales forms the context in which the central character, Parker, begins to perceive the possibility of uniting his own 'double consciousness' as – to follow Du Bois – a 'Negro' and an 'American':[12]

'Are there many like me in Wales?'
'Oh yes! Yanks all over the place. Black Yanks and white.'
'Black *Yanks*?' He wanted to smile.[13]

If Parker responds to the notion of a 'black Yank' with a wry smile at the story's opening, it is an identity that he comes to embrace as the story proceeds. This process of increasing identification with 'America' reaches a climax at the story's conclusion:

> When the opening bars were struck, he saw the others pushing back their chairs and standing, and he stood, understanding even as Mr. Catti whispered, 'Our national anthem'.
>
> There was something in the music and in the way they held their heads that was strangely moving. He hummed beneath his breath. When it was over he would ask for the words.
>
> But even while he heard the final triumphal chord still sounding, the piano struck up 'God Save the King.' It was not nearly so stirring. Then swiftly modulating they swept into the 'Internationale', to words about an international army. He was carried back to when he was a small boy marching in the streets behind the bands that came to his southern town . . .
>
> Mr Catti had nudged him. He looked up, seeing the conductor looking straight at him, smiling. They were all looking at him. Why, was it his eye? Were they playing a joke? And suddenly he recognized the melody and felt that his knees would give way. It was as though he had been pushed into the horrible foreboding country of dreams and they were enticing him into some unwilled and degrading act, from which only his failure to remember the words would save him. Only now the melody seemed charged with some vast new meaning which that part of him that wanted to sing could not fit with the old familiar words. And beyond the music he kept hearing the soldiers' voices, yelling as they had when the light struck his eye. He saw the singers still staring, and as though to betray him he heard his own voice singing out like a suddenly amplified radio:
>
> > '. . . Gave proof through the night
> > That our flag was still there . . .'
>
> It was like the voice of another over whom he had no control. His eye throbbed. A wave of guilt shook him, followed by a burst of relief. For the first time in your whole life, he thought with dreamlike wonder, the words are not ironic. He stood in confusion as the song ended, staring into the men's Welsh faces, not knowing whether to curse them or to return their good-natured smiles.[14]

Dai Smith is the only Welsh critic to have discussed the story, and quotes selectively from this conclusion to suggest that 'the story is a sentimental but forceful expression of what south Wales, by the 1940s, had come to stand for in the estimation of others'.[15] Writing from an American perspective John F. Callahan suggests that the 'strange country' of the title stands 'less for Wales than for America, and like many Americans, Parker discovers his Americanness overseas'.[16] I am not inclined to disagree with either of these readings, but neither pays attention to the anthems being sung nor to the different reactions that they elicit. The 'strange country' of the title is deeply ambiguous, referring simultaneously to Wales and the United States. Ellison's Welsh-based short stories emerge from a collision of cultures and world-views that needs to be analysed. If one of the most positive results of the impact of post-structural and post-colonial theories on the field of literary criticism has been the questioning of the national boundaries in which literary studies have traditionally taken place, a genuinely 'transatlantic' perspective should locate texts within the differing cultures which they simultaneously inhabit, while also creating a space for the tensions, ambivalences and similarities between different literary traditions, and cultural contexts, to be discussed. This chapter aims to substantiate such an approach by using the anthems sung at the conclusion of 'In a Strange Country' as a means of structuring a discussion of the ways in which Ellison related to wartime Wales, the broader cultural and political significance of his responses and the ways in which his Welsh experiences led him to refine and reassert one of his central themes: 'a young Negro's quest for identity'.

## 'THE STAR SPANGLED BANNER': 'BLACK YANKS' IN BRITAIN

The narrator of 'A Storm of Blizzard Proportions' is, like Ellison, a member of the American Merchant Marine. The story opens with his having disembarked in south Wales. Standing in a bar he finds himself 'obsessed by Jack Johnson', as reflected in this fragmented soliloquy:

> They didn't praise him as they do Joe, but what I like is that he went where he wanted to go and did what he wanted to do . . . Old Jack Johnson had something Joe Louis doesn't have. Have I? Dog beneath Joe's skin. All chained up inside. In the ring Joe's a controlled explosion. From containing himself. Joe's fight is a machine, Jack's was a dance. Those silent movies. . . Old Jack reached out for life . . . Fought them with his fists, fought them with his grin, fought them with his high-powered car.[17]

In the racially volatile context of the Second World War, Ellison's narrator is drawn to Jack Johnson, as opposed to Joe Louis. This suggests that Gerald Early's argument regarding the responses to Johnson and Louis, discussed in chapter 2, may be open to revision. For Early, the different reactions to Jack Johnson and Joe Louis reflected a shift in the position of the African American within the national culture, for 'when

Johnson fought a white, all whites wanted to see Johnson defeated, but Louis fought Schmeling as the favourite among the whites as well as the blacks'.[18] Louis was a more palatable figure for all Americans in that he was characterized by his humility and eschewed direct criticism of American society. Indeed, during the war years Louis donated the profits of several fights to the Army and Navy Relief Fund, and visited American troops stationed in Britain (including a visit to Bangor, north Wales) to raise morale and to support the Allied effort.[19] If, for Gerald Early, Joe Louis symbolized the 'integration of the black folk hero with the American popular hero', then, in rejecting Louis for Johnson, Ellison's narrator in 'A Storm of Blizzard Proportions' may be signalling the death of a 'certain hope' in the war years as described by James Baldwin in 1963:

> The treatment accorded the Negro during the Second World War marks, for me, a turning point in the Negro's relation to America. To put it briefly, and somewhat too simply, a certain hope died, a certain respect for white Americans faded ... You must put yourself in the skin of a man who is wearing the uniform of his country, is a candidate for death in its self-defense, and who is called 'nigger' by his comrades-in-arms and his officers; who is always almost given the hardest, ugliest, most menial work to do; who knows that the white G.I. has informed the European that he is subhuman (so much for the American male's sexual security); who does not dance at the U.S.O. the night white soldiers dance there, and does not drink in the same bars white soldiers drink in; and who watches German prisoners of war being treated with more human dignity than he has ever received at their hands . . .[20]

Richard Dalfiume described the 1940s as 'the forgotten years of the Negro Revolution', and it is by now commonplace to present the Second World War as a watershed in African American history as the dissonance of fighting against fascism and for democratic principles in the name of a racist, segregated, America led to widespread protests against racial discrimination in the defence industry and the military.[21]

> Looks like to me
> Folks ought to know
> It's hard to beat Hitler
> Protecting Jim Crow

said Langston Hughes in 1943, offering a typically succinct expression of the dilemma faced by African Americans; whether to fight overseas in a Jim Crow army or concentrate on the struggle for equality at home.[22] This dilemma was embedded, and to some extent resolved, in the slogan adopted by *The Pittsburgh Courier* – 'Double V' for victory at home and abroad. While the Socialist Workers Party, with some justification, denounced the 'Double V' as 'a cover for unqualified support of the war', the slogan was enthusiastically adopted by the National Association for the Advancement of Colored People (NAACP) and, according to one black journalist, had the support of 'nearly every newspaper and pulpit'.[23] Nevertheless, at the outset of war, African Americans were barred entirely from the marines and air force, and only allowed to enlist in the navy as messmen. The Second World War saw considerable transformations within the American Army, however, in the form of the first black marines, pilots and tank units. During the worst days of the 'Battle of the Bulge' in December 1944 the army issued a directive requesting African American volunteers for racially integrated combat units. These changes marked the beginning of the end for the Jim Crow army and led ultimately to the formal integration of the American armed forces ordered by Truman in 1948, and confirmed in 1949.[24] Such tangible advances were driven forward by a new radical assertiveness amongst the African American population, embodied most strikingly in A. Philip Randolph's March on Washington Movement, that threatened to mobilize the black masses for a march on the American capital to protest against segregation in the army and in industry.[25] Historian Harvard Sitkoff, however, has suggested that the view of the 1940s as a period of increased black militancy is a myth. He draws attention to the widespread opinion among African Americans that Randolph's planned March on Washington was unpatriotic, to the fact that the black press aimed to bring 'home to the Negro people of America that this is their war and not merely "a white man's war"', and to the relative absence during the war years of the widespread racial rioting seen between 1917 and 1919 or between 1964 and 1968.[26] Sitkoff concludes by arguing that those 'militantly fighting for change in the 1960s would not look at the agenda and actions of World War II blacks and racial organizations as models to emulate'.[27] While Sitkoff's essay offers a useful corrective to exaggerated accounts of wartime militancy, there is no doubt that many fighting for change in the 1960s – as Baldwin's observations above suggest – did indeed look back to the 1940s. The war years did see an increase in the membership of the NAACP, the establishment of the Congress of Racial Equality, the emergence of a zoot-suited youth black subculture, and riots in Detroit, New York and LA.[28] Like Baldwin, Leroi Jones in his nationalistic account of African American music, *Blues People* (1963), argued that 'between the thirties and the end of World War II there was perhaps as radical a change in the psychological perspective of the Negro American toward America as there was between the Emancipation and 1930'.[29]

The continuity between the wartime experiences of African American servicemen and the radicalism of the 1960s may be reinforced when we consider that the dominant boxer of the post war years, Muhammad Ali, would seem to follow Jack Johnson rather than Joe Louis, in challenging white racism through his verbal and physical flamboyance. In later life Ali would become an all-American hero, lighting the Olympic torch at Atlanta in 1996, but during the 1960s when he embraced Islam, changed his name from Cassius Clay, and resisted the draft, he was widely disliked, distrusted and vilified by Americans.[30] While Ali seemed invincible in the ring the fact that the Hollywood dream factory would simulate his defeat in Sylvester Stallone's Oscar-winning *Rocky* (1976) suggests that Early may have overemphasized the changed attitudes towards successful African American boxers in the period between Jack Johnson and Joe Louis. In Stallone's film, Rocky Balboa, an inarticulate Italian-American, is plucked from obscurity to take on the quick-witted and agile African American, Apollo Creed, clearly moulded on Ali (even down to his rivalry with Joe Frazier). Balboa is improbably brought into fighting shape by Mickey, a weathered trainer played by an aging Burgess Meredith. In advising his white protégé on how to deal with a threatening African American, Meredith was actually repeating a role that he had played – in a rather different context and for different ends – thirty years earlier.

*A Welcome to Britain* was made in 1943 by the British Ministry of Information with the support of the American Office of War Information. In it, Burgess Meredith is a GI guide who introduces American soldiers to some of the embarrassing situations that they may encounter while stationed in Britain. A white GI is shown flirting with a barmaid, throwing his money around and making disparaging remarks about a Scotsman's kilt. Having outraged the locals he boards a train and gets into a compartment with an African American GI. An elderly British lady invites them both back to her house for tea and, while the black GI buys some cigarettes, Burgess Meredith confides to the camera that while this sort of thing would not happen at home it is not unusual in Britain.[31] Historical accounts and contemporary reports seem to support this view. Following a period of research in Cardiff the African American anthropologist St Clair Drake reported in 1949 that the 'simple verdict is that the British liked the Brown Yanks tremendously' and, according to historian

Graham Smith, the evidence 'points overwhelmingly to the conclusion that the blacks were warmly welcomed in Britain'.[32]

Ralph Ellison offers a fictional account of this welcome in his short story 'In a Strange Country'. It begins with the main protagonist Parker sitting in a Welsh pub recalling events that have happened earlier that evening:

> Coming ashore from the ship he had felt the excited expectancy of entering a strange land. Moving along the road in the dark he had planned to stay ashore all night, and in the morning he would see the country with fresh eyes . . . Someone had cried 'Jesus H. Christ,' and he had thought, He's from home, and grinned and apologized into the light they flashed in his eyes. He had felt the blow coming when they yelled, 'It's a goddamn nigger', but it struck him anyway. He was having a time of it when some of Mr Catti's countrymen stepped in and Mr Catti had guided him into the pub . . .
>
> At first he had included them in his blind rage. But they had seemed so genuinely and uncondescendingly polite that he was disarmed. Now the anger and resentment had slowly ebbed, and he felt only a smouldering sense of self-hate and ineffectiveness. Why should he blame them when they had helped him? *He* had been the one so glad to hear an American voice. You can't take it out on them, they're a different breed; even from the English.[33]

The passage traces a shift in Parker's perception of the Welsh, from initially including them in his 'blind rage' to his increasing awareness of their ethnic difference. Following an encounter with white GIs, Parker has a literal black eye that functions as a suggestive metaphor in a story preoccupied with issues of sight and self-perception. Upon entering the club with his Welsh hosts the light strikes Parker's injured eye – 'it was as though it were being peeled by an invisible hand' – and the story proceeds to explore the layers of identity that constitute the African American self – the black 'I'.[34]

This Emersonian play between 'eye' and 'I' is also famously present in *Invisible Man*.[35] The 'invisibility to which I refer', states the narrator of the novel's 'Prologue',

> occurs because of a peculiar disposition of the eyes of those with whom I come in contact. A matter of the construction of their *inner* eyes, those eyes with which they look through their physical eyes upon reality. I am not complaining, nor am I protesting either. It is sometimes advantageous to be unseen, although it is most often rather wearing on the nerves. Then too, you're constantly being bumped against those of poor vision. Or again, you often doubt if you really exist.[36]

Henry Louis Gates Jr has discussed the ways in which Ellison's *Invisible Man* parodies the literary structures of Richard Wright's naturalist novel *Native Son* (1940). Whereas Wright's omniscient narrator speaks from a position of all-knowing objectivity, describing characters that are essentially voiceless and powerless, Ellison shifts to the first person creating a narrator who 'shapes, edits and narrates his own tale' thus 'defining reality by its representation'.[37] This process is already underway in the suggestive play between vision ('eye') and identity ('I') in Ellison's 'In a Strange Country'. While the act of seeing is ultimately exposed as being dependent on authorial perspective, the gesture of the 'look' is inseparable from the documentary strategy of Ellison's semi-autobiographical short stories.

'In a Strange Country', retitled as 'Black Yank in Britain' when reprinted in *The Negro Digest* in 1944, traces a shift in Parker's sense of identity; a shift in his perception of 'America'. Having initially smiled ironically at being described as a 'black Yank', he ends the tale listening to the American anthem and realizes 'in dreamlike wonder' that for 'the first time . . . the words are not ironic'.[38] Parker's increasing identification with America reflects a tendency, observed by historians, for returning GIs to feel 'even more American than when they departed'. According to David Reynolds:

> Nineteen thirties America had a keen sense of regionalism and the first effect of Army life was often to enhance the GI's awareness of sectional and ethnic identity. In the training camps of Dixie, Northerners discovered the distinctiveness of Southern values. In their squads or aircrews, Irish met Pole, Italian mixed with Jew, New Englanders rubbed shoulders with men from Texas or Wyoming . . . The uniform, of course, created am impression of uniformity: American soldiers all looked the same. But many GIs, I think, came to accept that they were all Yanks – overseas the similarities outweighed the differences.[39]

Maggi Morehouse argues similarly that 'African Americans returned from war feeling more American', but there is little doubt that black GIs felt considerably more ambivalent about their homeland than their white counterparts.[40] In fact war can be seen to have exacerbated racial tensions. Ellison noted in his introduction to the 1981 edition of *Invisible Man* that 'this nation's conflicts of arms have been – at least for Afro-Americans – wars-within-wars' and African Americans abroad often had more to fear from white Americans than the local inhabitants, as the opening scene of 'In a Strange Country' suggests.[41] While Ellison noted that the attack depicted in the story did 'not lie in any personal

experience of racial difficulties', experiences similar to Parker's – where
the British assisted a black GI being racially abused by white Americans
– were widely reported in the African American press.[42] *The Negro
Handbook* of 1944 reported that the 'British people as a whole resented
the attitude of the American white troops in their treatment of coloured
soldiers', and the African American journalist Roi Ottley noted in
September 1944 that 'the people here have a racial tolerance which gives
them a social lever. Thus the Negro has social equality here in more ways
than theory.'[43] Ottley's account was corroborated in *The Monthly
Summary of Events and Trends in Race Relations*, which reported in
1945 that some 'American officers are apparently interested in bringing
the segregated transportation system to England, at least for the duration'
and illustrated their case with the following story:

> Two coloured American soldiers got on a Cardiff tram. Two American officers
> followed and one told the coloured soldiers to 'Get out.' As they were about to
> leave the conductress stopped them saying: 'you are in Britain. Coloured men
> are not banned from *our* cars. Stay on.' And they stood put.
>
>     When the officers were getting off one said: 'You English [*sic*] are making
> it hard for us; when we get back to America we shall not be able to manage
> these fellows.'[44]

Due to what Roi Ottley described as the Southern belief 'that on his
return the Negro will be mighty difficult to remold into the Jim Crow
pattern', attempts were made to foster racist attitudes amongst the
British.[45] Returning African American soldiers described the ways in
which 'in England a few of the narrow minded possibly Southern white
American soldiers have already poisoned the mind of a few of the British
people toward us' and a Mississippi Black Veteran remembered that the
first obstacle he faced overseas was an idea implanted in the British mind
by white GIs that blacks were so low on the evolutionary scale that they
had tails that appeared at night.[46] Ralph Ellison has one of his characters
recount a similar story in the conclusion to 'The Red Cross'. The narrative shifts from the main narrator to Doc at this point, and this technique
of creating a story within the story creates a sense of dialogue, emphasizes the collective nature of the African American GI's experience, and
suggests the ways in which aspects of that experience were passed on
orally. Doc describes the way in which a group of Welshmen gathered
around him in rural pub:

> I noticed that every time I'd have a round the folks would stand back and
> watch me a while, like they was waiting for something to happen. Finally I
> asked the man what the hell is going on. First he acted embarrassed like, then

he told me to wait a second. And man, next thing I know he's rapping for everybody to be quiet and making a speech. He gave them hell for even believing it.

Believing what? Well, what had happened was that before we were sent to that camp somebody had been around telling them folks not to have anything to do with us. They said that we was bad fellows and not fit to associate with. That was all. They hadn't ever seen any of us and they believed it.

'Oh no, that's not all', somebody else said. 'You know that's not all. Tell him the rest.'

'Why don't you be quiet?' he said. 'Nobody believes the last part noway.'

I asked him what it was people expected him to do.

'That's just it' he said reluctantly. 'They was waiting for me to show my tail.'

'Your tail?'

'See there', he said, 'you don't believe it. But it's the truth. Whoever got there ahead of us told these people that whenever we got a little high we had a long black tail that would stick out behind.'

'Why didn't you show it to the people, Doc?'

Doc didn't say they brought him *that* much liquor.[47]

The humorous conclusion reflects the GIs' high spirits on a night out, but Ellison does not end the story on a comical note. One of the African Americans responds to Doc's story by stating 'seriously' that 'the people must have been mighty ignorant'. 'They wasn't no more ignorant than some of us when the army took us out of Alabama' is Doc's response, suggesting that the army was a source of both education and enlightenment for many African Americans, and was also a means of placing their own experiences in America within a wider, comparative, context.

Ellison's conclusion to 'The Red Cross' suggests that British tolerance towards African American troops should not be overestimated. If the British seemed initially to welcome black GIs, their enthusiasm waned as numbers, and the widely reported fear of miscegenation, increased. Graham Smith suggests that 'the British ceased to view the black soldiers' relations with local girls with equanimity' in 'about March or April 1943', but David Reynolds is probably right to suggest that 'the distinction between civil rights and sexual wrongs had been apparent in British attitudes from the start'.[48] This tension was to become increasingly apparent as the war proceeded, both in the press and in the government.[49] At the outbreak of war the black British community probably numbered somewhere between 8,000 and 10,000, mostly concentrated in the ports of London, Liverpool and Cardiff.[50] Britain, as Roi Ottley suggested in his reports, was primarily a white country, and the government of the time was keen to keep things that way.[51] The British chiefs of staff, for instance, asked in April 1942 for the maximum number of *white* engineer units and Anthony Eden suggested to American Ambassador Winant that 'our climate [i]s badly suited to negroes'.[52] During his short stay in Britain in 1942, General Eisenhower was preoccupied with the problem of maintaining separate but equal policies in a country unused to segregation, and expressed the problem as follows:

> [H]ere we have a very thickly populated country that is devoid of racial consciousness. They know nothing at all about the conventions and habits of polite society that have been developed in the U.S. in order to preserve a segregation in social activity without making the matter one of official or public notice. To most English people, including the village girls – even those of perfectly fine character – the negro soldier is just another man, rather fascinating because he is unique in their experience, a jolly good fellow and with money to spread. Our own white soldiers, seeing a girl walk down the street with a negro, frequently see themselves as protectors of the weaker sex and believe it necessary to intervene even to the extent of using force, to let her know what she's doing.[53]

Racial tensions resulting from the presence of American soldiers in Britain came to prominence when the death penalty meted out in Britain to two African American soldiers accused of rape was a matter of parliamentary debate on 10 May 1944. Rhys Davies (1877–1954), a Welsh-speaking Labour MP, originally from Llangennech but representing the constituency of Westhoughton in Lancashire, played a significant part in proceedings, as reported in the *Daily Telegraph* and summarized in *A Monthly Summary of Events and Trends in Race Relations*:

> *Lt. Lawson* (C.W.) in the House of Commons yesterday called the attention of the Foreign Secretary to the sentence of death recently passed on two coloured American soldiers for rape. He asked if Mr. Eden would inform the American Government that the carrying out of such a sentence would be interpreted by many people in this country as racial persecution and therefore likely to cause bad feeling between the two countries.
>
> *Mr Eden* replied that this question raised an issue on which the Government had no basis for representation to the United States Government.
>
> *Mr Rhys Davies* (Soc.): Is it not an anomaly that a person can be sentenced to death on British soil in this country for an offence for which the same punishment would not apply under our own law?
>
> *Mr. Eden*: The jurisdiction of the United States authorities over their armed forces in this country rests upon the Visiting Forces Act passed by this House in 1942. Therefore I have no locus in the matter.

It was very clearly stated then by the Minister that in some respects American military law was more severe than our own.

*Lt. Lawson*: Has the same sort of sentence ever been passed for similar offence on white American soldiers in this country?

*Mr. Eden*: I must point out that this action has been taken under an Act which the House has passed and under the law of another country which is being administered in accordance with the Houses's decision. I really cannot say more than that.[54]

The above report suggests that there were three primary issues at stake. The first turned on a legal difference between Britain and America, for rape was not a capital crime in the UK. This was a reminder of the second issue relating to the far-reaching legal powers accorded to US forces in Britain following the Visiting Forces Act of 1942. Unlike all other Allied forces in Britain, the US had been accorded exclusive jurisdiction over its own troops. Thirdly was the suggestion of racial discrimination. In June, Eden, under duress, had to reveal more and stated that seven GIs had been executed in Britain – all but one for murder, the other for murder and rape – but he and the Foreign Office stonewalled requests for information on the race of the soldiers in question. Black GIs accounted for forty-one, one-third, of all rape convictions at US Army General Courts-Martial in wartime Britain, despite accounting for less than one-tenth of the total American presence. For James Grigg of the British War Office this was a reflection 'of the natural propensities of the coloured man'. For Walter White of the NAACP, and for Rhys Davies and other MPs, it smacked of racial prejudice.[55] Little coverage was given to the hanging of the two men on 11 August 1944. By then the furore had blown over, but the episode reveals the extent of racial discrimination and segregation within the American army.

Indeed, it was as a result of pressure from US authorities that African Americans were not included in the various schemes to promote GI–British relations in 1943–4, with the War Office noting that 'it had definitely been agreed with U.S. authorities that no coloured troops should be billeted'.[56] The Women's Voluntary Service's offer to run 'additional or alternative facilities in locations where . . . supplementary provision for the convenience of coloured soldiers was required' was welcomed by the British–American Liaison Board, with two of the three such facilities that ultimately opened located in Bala in north Wales and Penarth in south Wales.[57] Even the American Red Cross, according to *The Crisis* in 1943, was 'running a segregated Jim-Crow setup for soldiers abroad'.[58] Rather than merely looking after the casualties of war, the ARC looked after the welfare of soldiers off base in towns, and in effect was operating, in the words of ARC director in Britain Harvey D. Gibson, 'the largest hotel chain in the world'.[59] David Reynolds has drawn attention to the desire among many American GIs and politicians that Red Cross Clubs should, in Gibson's words, 'create a strictly American atmosphere . . . by installing showers and other distinctly American comforts and . . . by preparing and serving food as nearly in American fashion as circumstances make possible'.[60] This 'little America' was run along segregationist lines as reflected in Ellison's 'The Red Cross' where the narrator arrives at the Swansea club only to realize that 'this club was attended principally by white soldiers'. He is then driven out to the club in Morriston, which Ellison recalled in 1977 was 'located a few miles north of Swansea' and was 'frequented mostly by Afro-American GIs'.[61] The depiction given in the story, however, is distinctly interracial:

> Miss Trent was in charge of the Club's activities. Tall, handsome, and in her early twenties, she was the daughter of a Negro college president. She explained modestly that the club was quite popular, and that frequently men stationed as far away as Ireland returned here to spend their furloughs. I asked if it were usual to have so many white troops present, and she said it was; sometimes they even outnumbered the Negroes. Since several boys were obviously from the South I asked if having mixed troops made any special problems.
>
> 'No', she said. 'But at first I thought it might. Then I decided that if there was a problem I would let it come from the boys and not from me. As it turned out the white boys are just like colored boys. They have familiar problems and if they come to me for advice, or just for a talk, I give them as much attention as I do our own.'[62]

While ARC administrators argued that '[w]e have no negro clubs. We have no white clubs. We have negro staff clubs and we have white staff clubs', Ellison's 'The Red Cross' suggests a slightly more complex picture in Swansea with de facto segregation practised in the white club, while the unofficially 'Negro' club was more racially mixed.[63]

If the ARC's Jim Crow practices were a subject of debate in the African American press, that organization was also at the centre of a debate regarding the preservation of blood plasma to be used in transfusions for the war wounded. In 1941, allegedly following requests from army and navy officials, the ARC announced that African American blood would be refused. Following considerable pressure this policy was reversed and during the next several months articles appeared both in the

African American press and in 'white' medical journals maintaining that there was no difference in the blood of races and denouncing the separation policy of the Red Cross. At the end of 1943 a spokesman for the army admitted that there was no scientific basis for the segregation of blood, but noted that there was a disinclination on the part of whites to receive coloured blood:

> Whether that disinclination is the result of ignorance or prejudice it nevertheless exists and is a factor with which this office always reckons in setting up any plasma program for the Army. It is the conviction of this office that disregard of this feeling would greatly militate against the successful conclusion of the program for collecting blood plasma.[64]

Langston Hughes offered a pithy account of the feelings of many in his poem 'Red Cross':

> The Angel of Mercy's
> Got her wings in the mud,
> And all because of
> Negro Blood.[65]

It may also be this controversy that was on saxophonist Charlie Parker's mind when he gave the title 'Red Cross' to one of his finest bebop variations on the chords of Gershwin's 'I Got Rhythm' in 1944. The melody's unusual opening seems to mirror Hughes's poem, as the organization's high ideals are dragged into the mud represented by the two repeated low B flats:

9. The opening bars of Charlie Parker's 'Red Cross'.[66]

'A Storm of Blizzard Proportions' and 'The Red Cross at Morriston, S.W.' are located in an ARC club because this is a setting that would resonate with readers of the African American press, and is a site that explicitly and implicitly addresses some of the charged tensions faced by the African American soldier.

The African American experience in the Second World War was characterized by paradox. For, if segregationist practices and racist attitudes meant that few black soldiers or their families failed to see the irony of fighting tyrannous regimes in the name of a 'Jim Crow' army, many accounts suggest that the war context did lead to a greater identification with 'America'. The narrator of Ellison's 'The Red Cross' hears Count Basie's swing music upon nearing the Red Cross club in Morriston, and during the war years Victory records and the American Forces network used swing – black and white – as if it were *the* national music. Werner Sollors suggests that the concurrent elevation of interracial swing music on the one hand, and the separation of white and black blood on the other, can be seen to reflect the extraordinary contradictions of the war era.[67] These contradictions are embedded in Ellison's 'In a Strange Country' where it is perhaps not surprising that Parker is unsure whether to 'curse them or return their good-natured smiles' when the Welshmen sing 'The Star Spangled Banner' in his honour.


## 'OUR NATIONAL ANTHEM' AND 'GOD SAVE THE KING': WELSH IDENTITIES[68]

If the experience of being a member of a segregated army abroad is one source of Parker's ambiguous self-identification as an American at the conclusion of 'In a Strange Country', the Welsh context also imposes a 'pressure toward self-scrutiny'.[69] In the story's final scene Parker notes that the rendition of 'God Save the King' 'was not nearly so stirring' as the rendition of the Welsh anthem that preceded it, and this intriguing observation offers a basis for exploring the, at times uneasy, relationship between Welshness and Britishness during the war years.[70] If Ellison's 'In a Strange Country' is a story fundamentally concerned with the nature of African American identity, it takes place within a country which is itself the site of contesting forms of national allegiance. The narrator of 'The Red Cross' notes that 'it was not as difficult as [Hayes, the club director] had expected' for 'Negro troops': 'For although American Negro and Welsh historical backgrounds were different, there were also certain cultural and temperamental similarities. Both Welshmen and Negroes loved to sing, to dance, to talk long over drinks, to laugh, to enjoy a good argument.'[71] In a letter to his past lover, Senora Babb, Ellison noted of the Welsh that 'I love them like my own people', and expressed his pleasure 'that hundreds of Negro boys are acquiring their first notions of real democracy among these people who, strangely, are culturally so similar'.[72] If Ellison is here evoking a somewhat romantic sense of attachment between the Welsh and African Americans, his observations in the 1940s offer a useful basis for comparing the two peoples' experience of war.

On the whole both the Welsh and African Americans were very willing participants in the war efforts of the larger nation states of which they were a part. Harvard Sitkoff argues persuasively that anti-war sentiments amongst African Americans were relatively rare, and have been overestimated by many historians, while Kenneth Morgan notes similarly that if the First World War had seen major movements of protest in favour of a negotiated peace in Wales, during the Second World War 'there was virtually no dissent'.[73] If the 'Double V' encapsulated the African American desire to defeat fascism abroad and racism at home, the Executive Committee of the South Wales Miners' Federation also passed a resolution acknowledging that there were fights to be fought on two fronts, while insisting on the primacy of the anti-fascist war over the class struggle.[74] While small groups of nationalists and conscientious objectors resisted the call to arms in both groups, the majority supported the war and those who did fight were often radicalized by their experiences.[75] Armed service led to a heightened sense of injustice and increased militancy for returning African American and Welsh soldiers. Young black GIs in the southern states made a point of registering to vote following their return from military service, for instance, often turning up in military uniform and displaying their medals. By 1950 registration in the state of Mississippi had risen by twenty thousand.[76] War service also led to a greater confidence and desire to control their destinies on the part of the British working class, with twenty-five of Wales's thirty-six constituency seats won by Labour in Attlee's landslide victory of 1945.[77] Wartime experience was to condition post-war expectations and activism, as the following account by a Welsh miner suggests:

> I came back from the war in 1947 . . . [T]he one thing that hit you was the boys coming back from the forces at that time (it was optional whether you wore safety helmets and they used to wear berets and it indicated that there was this influx of miners coming back from the armed forces). And I believe it did a lot to strengthen the role of the NUM after nationalization. Because a lot of these lads then became active, they were not going to go back to the old systems.[78]

The desire to engage in the political process was partly the result of an increasing identification with America for black soldiers, and the historic victory for the Labour Party across Britain consolidated the 'Britishness' that had been fostered during the war years as the primary identity of the Welsh.

John Davies notes that the chief purpose of the government's wartime propaganda machine was to 'disseminate the notion that Britain was totally united'.[79] The Second World War, notes Davies, 'like the First, did much to strengthen Britishness. At the same time, it seemed a death blow to Welshness.'[80] Changes in the cultural landscape are revealing in this respect. If the period of the Second World War was characterized by a common sense of Britishness, the question of Welsh national identity had played a significant role in the years leading up to the war. During the depression years of the 1930s appeals to, and invocations of, various forms of Welshness and of Welsh history were made across the political spectrum, from communists such as Idris Cox and Lewis Jones, to nationalists on the political right such as Saunders Lewis and Ambrose Bebb.[81] While peripheral to the majority experience of the economically pulverized communities of 1930s Wales, the cultural arena saw the dramatic emergence of the Welsh industrial novel (discussed in chapter 3), the modernist experimentation of writers such as Kate Roberts in Welsh and the young Dylan Thomas in English, with this literary activity reflected in the establishment of cultural periodicals such as Keidrych Rhys's *Wales* (1937) and Gwyn Jones's *Welsh Review* (1939) in English, mirrored by Alun Llewelyn-Williams's *Tir Newydd* (1935) and Aneirin Talfan Davies's *Heddiw* (1936) in Welsh.[82] If the depression gave rise to the radical working-class politics discussed in the previous chapter, it also formed the context for a less widespread but widely observed growth in Welsh national consciousness, particularly following the burning of an RAF bombing school in Penyberth, in the Welsh-speaking heartland of the Llŷn Peninsula in 1936 by three leading Welsh nationalists: the dramatist Saunders Lewis (discussed in chapter 2), the author D. J. Williams and the Baptist minister Lewis Valentine. A guilty verdict was achieved only after the case had been transferred from Caernarfon to the Old Bailey in London. This emergent cultural and political sense of Welshness was served a severe blow with the onset of the Second World War. *The Welsh Review* temporarily stopped publication during the war years, *Wales* ceased publication in 1940, to be resumed in 1943, *Tir Newydd* ceased to exist in 1939 and *Heddiw* in 1942. Distinctive programmes for the BBCs 'Welsh region', created after considerable protest in 1937, came to an end from the first day of the war as broadcasts became limited to a unified 'Home Service'.[83] If war transformed the British economy, pulling Wales in particular out of depression, even a staunch supporter of Britain's stand such as W. J. Gruffydd could see the potential cultural devastation: 'England could win the war and Wales could lose it . . . The impact of [this war] on the future of Wales and the Welsh language', he stated, 'will be inexpressibly greater than [the impact of the last war]'.[84]

Ellison's Welsh-based short stories thus take place in a country which is itself the site of conflicting class, national and linguistic allegiances. This cultural diversity is reflected in Ellison's stories. An early scene in 'The Red Cross' evokes the narrator's first encounter with Swansea, and with a wartime blackout:

> At the gates a constable examined my pass and told me how to get the bus for the city. The bus, like those which run on Fifth Avenue but traveling much faster, was filled with people going into town from nearby villages. I settled back, listening to the strange English and to a language which I learned later was Welsh. In five minutes I got off at the bottom of what I was told was Wind Street, paid the conductor four pence as I left and started heading for the Red Cross Club.
>
> Moving along the street by flashlight I sensed rather than saw the wrecked buildings, as when you approach Colorado Springs in the early morning you *feel* the mountains before you see them. Then when a bus flashed by I saw demolished masonry fenced off along the side walk. Those barrage balloons I'd seen from the ship were not for show. In the early days of the war Swansea had been badly blitzed; and unlike London, where the debris is quickly cleared away, Swansea had neither the money nor the facilities to do so. I was told that several bodies were sealed beneath one of the wrecked buildings. Looking up the hill to the intersecting street at the top was like looking at the will-o-wisp glowing of cigarettes around a dark cinema balcony and up ahead, a lot of people were singing. It was Saturday and by the time I reached the top of the hill I felt I had stumbled into a *Mardi Gras* procession. Hundreds of flashlights and cigarettes flickered on and off revealing soldiers' trousers and women's legs as they moved leisurely along.[85]

The experience of encountering a new city in the blackout is conveyed by the fact that the narrator 'listens' and 'senses', before he 'sees' the reality of wartime debris as a bus flashes by. Later in the story we are told that it is 'bad blackout etiquette to flash one's light in another's eyes' (this presumably explains the emphasis on 'legs' in the passage above, which also evokes the simmering sexual desires of soldiers let free having crossed the Atlantic) and are taken on a rather frightening drive from Swansea to Morriston. Elements of Ellison's narrative can be corroborated from contemporary accounts, with the *Daily Telegraph* noting in 1941 that road deaths had doubled in Great Britain since the introduction of the blackout.[86] While the Second World War was less lethal than the first for the British, 60,000 Britons were killed in air raids in the Second World War, compared to 1,117 in the First World War.[87] Of all Welsh cities it was Swansea that suffered most severely during the war years, with forty four raids being mounted on the town between 1940 and 1943. A total of 369 people were killed, including 230 who died in the three-night blitz of February 1941 that destroyed the entire town centre. 'Where is your husband?' a Swansea woman was asked during the height of the bombing. 'In the army, the coward', was the reply.[88] Ellison's narrator senses the mound of uncleared debris resulting from these raids, and his comparison with 'Colorado Springs' evokes the narrator's sense of exile, while also creating an uneasy correspondence between the sublime grandeur of the American landscape and the unfathomable reality of war-torn Europe.

If Swansea's wartime destruction is 'sensed', the strangeness of the new environment is 'heard' in the local English dialect, and in the Welsh language. Ellison's sensitivity to the diverse cultural strands that constitute Welsh culture in the 1940s is striking. Upon arriving at the Red Cross Club 'held in Lebannon [sic] Church Hall' a 'structure erected in the early Eighteenth Century', the narrator comments both on Welsh cultural distinctiveness and on the palpable familiarity of what the political scientist Alfred Zimmern had famously described in 1921 as 'American Wales':[89]

Hayes' reference to a *church* hall completely disarmed me for the loud Count Basie recording I heard as we reached the building. Suddenly it was like coming home. We passed through a small vestibule into a large, bright, room alive with some of the most expert, international, interracial, Lindyhopping I'd ever seen. 'It's not the Savoy,' said Hayes 'but on Saturday night it's the next thing to it.' Young soldiers, Negro and white, were doing everything but tossing the vivacious Welsh girls boogie-nilly to the high pointed ceiling. To the left of the dance floor, couples were drinking 'Pepsis' at tables arranged before a fireplace. Several girls in white aprons were serving a group of service men at an L shaped snack bar. Straight ahead, a stage, the kind you find in high school auditoriums, faced the room. And to our right, men and girls lounged in groups of upholstered chairs, conversing, somehow, over the blare of the phonograph. I asked Hayes why the stage and learned that Welsh drama had developed out of the nonconformist religious movement, which instituted amature [sic] dramatics; thus the stage; thus, at longer range, such contemporary Welsh dramatists as Emlyn Williams and Richard Llewellyn. Even so, I was sure that the hall's original builders would have been more than mildly surprised at the Lindy.

In the room where we went to check our coats two girls were making a last minute inspection of their makeup. Another girl came in behind us, who, judging from her rapid breathing, had just finished a dance.

'Why hello, Iris,' one of the girls greeted her.

'Hello Dylis! [*sic*] You just coming?' she called.

'Oh sure' Dylis said, 'What are you putting down tonight, Iris?'

'Nothing,' said Iris disgustedly 'Nothing but shoe leather.'

'So don't y' worry, darling. Stick around a while, you'll get a play.'

Which, said with full appreciation for subtitles of shading and meaning, was ample evidence that the extent of the boys' cultural contribution to Wales was not limited to American dances. But for the accent – incidentally, they do speak the way you heard in 'The Corn Is Green' – I might have been in Harlem, on Broadway, or, for the matter, in Brooklyn.[90]

Ellison's vivid description of a Red Cross Club reflects the fact that, as Zimmern implied in the 1920s and as Dai Smith has argued more recently, the cultural forms adopted and adapted by south-Walian society from the early twentieth century were profoundly American.[91] While some aspects of the GIs' America would have been new to the Welsh, they would in all probability already be familiar with the swing music of the Basie band and dreamed of dancing at the Savoy Ballroom. If the narrator is struck by the familiarity of the Pepsis and the Lindyhoppers, he also comments on the culturally distinctive development of Welsh drama and the emergence of anglophone Welsh literature.[92] Richard Llewellyn would have been familiar to Ellison probably as a result of John Ford's Hollywood version of *How Green Was My Valley*, which had won the best picture Oscar in 1941, creating a hugely influential exportable version of Welshness – populated by singing miners, faithful mothers and stern Nonconformist deacons – in the process.[93] The references to *The Corn is Green* and Emlyn Williams are more intriguing. In stating that 'they do speak in the way you heard in *The Corn is Green*', Ellison is clearly assuming that his readers are aware of Williams's play. A successful Hollywood film version of the play, starring Bette Davis, was released in 1945, but Ellison had probably composed his story before then. A version of the play had opened in New York with Ethel Barrymore as Miss Moffat in November 1940, however, and went on to win the New York Drama Critics' Circle award for the 'best play of foreign authorship presented in New York during the season 1940–41'.[94] Ellison was living in New York and moving in literary and theatrical circles during the early 1940s, and was clearly aware of Williams's play.

While to speak of an 'influence' between writers is invariably problematic, a 'contrapuntal' reading of Williams's play and Ellison's work
may prove to be illuminating, for if Ellison engages with the duality of
the African American experience, Williams depicts the struggle between
Welsh and British structures of feeling.[95] In the penultimate paragraph of
*Invisible Man* the narrator meditates upon his own invisibility and
comments cryptically that

> In going underground, I whipped it all except the mind, the *mind*. And the
> mind that has conceived a plan of living must never lose sight of the chaos
> against which the pattern was conceived. That goes for societies as well as for
> individuals . . . And there's still a conflict within me: With Louis Armstrong
> one half of me says, 'Open the window and let the foul air out,' while the other
> says, 'It was good green corn before the harvest'.[96]

Jazz trumpeter Louis Armstrong has the ability to transform the 'bad
breath' of city life into art and, while Ellison's narrator seeks to achieve
something similar, he is also drawn back to the folk traditions (the 'good
green corn') of the rural South. The title of Williams's *The Corn is Green*
comes from a similarly structured passage written by the promising
miner Morgan Evans. He wishes to replace the 'carbon monoxide' in the
mine for a 'smell . . . like fresh flowers lying about' and imagines a
surreal scene where he walks 'through the . . . shaft, in the dark' and 'can
touch with my hands the leaves on the trees, and underneath where the
corn is green'.[97] Ellison's 'green corn' may be derived from bluesman
Leadbelly's song of that name, or the agrarian Green Corn Rebellion,
where farmers in Ellison's native Oklahoma plotted to rebel against the
draft during the First World War, but the reference to the 'good green
corn' is particularly resonant given Ellison's references to Emlyn
Williams and his play. The connections are too tenuous for any firm links
to be made, but the characters in the opening section of *Invisible Man*
bear a suggestive resemblance to the characters in *The Corn is Green*,
and a comparative analysis of Ellison and Williams brings new perspectives to bear on their works.

M. Wynn Thomas reflects a broad critical consensus in arguing that
Williams's *The Corn is Green* offers a 'ringing affirmation of
Britishness'.[98] Williams's play is a reworking of the Pygmalion story in
which Miss Moffat, an 'admirable member of the eccentric, philanthropic, programme of the English middle class', educates the bright
miner Morgan Evans out of the squalor and limitations of his Welsh life
and prepares him to take up a place at Oxford University.[99] Thomas

argues that a 'sophisticated people's culture is never hinted at in *The Corn is Green*', and thus 'the transition from one culture to another' is made to seem 'relatively troublefree and completely desirable'.[100] This reading is reinforced by the fact that the Welsh speakers in the play, especially as embodied in the figure of Old Tom, are a backward people speaking a limited local patois.

> *Miss Ronberry.* (nervously): Is there anything you would like to know, Mr Tom?
> *Old Tom.* Where iss Shakespeare?
> *Miss Ronberry.* Where? . . . Shakespeare, Mr Tom, was a very great writer.
> *Old Tom.* Writer? Like the Bible?
> *Miss Ronberry.* Like the Bible.
> *Old Tom.* (looking at her doubtfully) Dear me, and me thinkin' the man was a place. (Following the others, muttering sadly) If I iss been born fifty years later, I iss been top of the class.[101]

Such passages led Russell Stephens to argue that 'Williams's best-known and finest play is also his most colonialist', and Stephen Knight to characterize the play as a work of 'Anglocentric conservatism'.[102] Such readings are reinforced by Williams in what he had to say about his own play. Writing 'of one of Time's Square's Current Hits' in *The New York Times* in February 1941, Williams describes the process of writing the play in the 1930s, and moulds its essential message to reinforce, and engender, American support for the British war effort.[103] He begins by describing the creation of schoolmistress Miss Moffat, based on fond memories of his own inspirational teacher Sarah Cooke, and her class of 'little barbarians'. The Welsh are described in the same terms at the end of his piece where he evocatively recalls coming out of a studio in London 'a few weeks back' having been 'speaking to Ethel Barrymore and the others in New York on a radio program'. There is a 'great glow in the sky', as London is under attack.

> Ethel Barrymore's voice still rang in my ears. Looking at the glow, I remembered (for no reason) that I had a letter from Miss Cooke in my pocket, in which she said she'd give anything to be a rear-gunner. I could see her, too, her gray hair back in the wind, taking pot-shots at a lot of fanatical young barbarians whom (in a saner world) she might be busy turning into good citizens. And then I thought 'Yes, that's what I meant when I decided I wanted Miss Moffat to typify the finest qualities in the British woman . . . and there she is in New York every night, for all America to have a look at, with Ethel Barrymore, one of America's great figures, to tell them exactly what I mean about Miss Cooke'. Yes it's more than just gratification: quite a bit more.[104]

In enlisting his play as part of the British war effort Williams offers a revealing insight into the terms in which he thought of his own people. The passage illustrates Miss Cooke's success in raising the Flintshire-born, Welsh-speaking playwright from his ethnic Welsh provincialism to his position as an internationally successful British playwright, and from the Olympian heights of his own success he equates the ignorant Welsh barbarians of his play, who may become good citizens through the educative efforts of Miss Moffat, with the German 'barbarians' currently being shot at by the good citizens of the British Air Force. The conflation of the Welsh peasants of Williams's play and the German soldiers waging war on Britain is remarkable and calls for some explanation. Stephen Knight has argued persuasively for the adoption of post-colonial paradigms in the discussion of Welsh texts, and, if we adopt the approach towards colonized subjects advocated by Homi Bhabha, Williams's words can be read as those of a hybridized colonial subject whose confident imperial Britishness 'undermines the operation of colonial power by inscribing and disclosing the trace of the other so that it reveals itself as double-voiced'.[105] When we consider that *The Corn is Green* is set in the late nineteenth century, Williams's equation of educational and military imperatives, while laudably seeking to attract American support for the British war effort in 1941, also underlines the connection between the cultural effects of compulsory English-language education and military conquest. There is some truth in Robert Young's observation that it 'is significant that compulsory national education was introduced in Britain in the late nineteenth century, for its rationale shared much of the spirit of colonialism'.[106] As discussed at some length in chapter 1, compulsory national education in Wales was through the medium of English, and social progress involved the abandonment of what was perceived to be an outmoded and inferior Welsh-language culture.

The effects of the ideology of social uplift, that I have argued dominated the thought of the Welsh and African American bourgeoisies in the late nineteenth and early twentieth centuries, was to be long lasting. Both *The Corn is Green* and the opening section of *Invisible Man* are centrally concerned with this process of social and racial uplift through education. The figures of the educationalists Miss Moffat and Miss Ronberry in *The Corn is Green* are paralleled in the figures of the African American educationalist Bledsoe and the white philanthropist Mr Norton in Ellison's *Invisible Man*. Where Morgan Evans is presented as someone who may become 'a great statesman of our country', in *The Corn is*

*Green* (and is widely believed to be partly modelled on Lloyd George, the only Welshman to have become prime minister of Britain), the Invisible Man is believed to be 'a potential Booker T. Washington'.[107] The rustic, virtually Welsh monoglot, Old Tom, who is often 'carried away by the music', finds his equivalent in the figure of Jim Trueblood, the performer of 'primitive spirituals' that embarrass the narrator of *Invisible Man* in their 'earthly harmonies'.[108] In encountering Trueblood the educated narrator gives voice to his prejudices: 'How all of us at the college hated the black-belt people, the "peasants", during those days! We were trying to lift them up and they, like Trueblood, did everything it seemed to pull us down.'[109] If Trueblood represents a 'peasant', he is also abhorred by the Invisible Man for breaking the incest taboo with both his mother and daughter. As the narrative develops, however, the Invisible Man comes to shed his earlier prejudices and to consider Trueblood an embodiment of a distinctive African American consciousness. A critique of the African American ideology of racial uplift is built into the narrative of *Invisible Man*, not least when the narrator sees in his mind's eye the

> bronze statue of the college Founder, the cold Father symbol, his hands outstretched in the breathtaking gesture of lifting a veil that flutters in hard, metallic folds above the face of a kneeling slave; and I am . . . unable to decide whether the veil is really being lifted, or lowered more firmly into place; whether I am witnessing a revelation or a more efficient blinding.[110]

Morgan Evans never comes to realize the alienating effects of his education in *The Corn is Green*, but there are suggestions throughout the play that the results of Miss Moffat's philanthropic efforts are not wholly positive. Morgan, for instance, laments the fact that he is increasingly regarded by his fellow miners as '[c]i bach yr ysgol! The schoolmistress's little dog!' and the play does not end with a final and triumphal farewell as Morgan leaves for Oxford.[111] His departure takes place offstage, while the audience sees Miss Moffat holding Morgan's and Bessie's illegitimate child and noting that 'you musn't be clumsy this time'.[112] It seems that the Welsh future lies in English hands.

M. Wynn Thomas suggests that for 'Old Tom' we may 'read Uncle Tom, perhaps', drawing on African American sources to suggest that Williams portrays Welsh culture in wholly dismissive terms.[113] Interestingly, Ellison was also criticized for creating a central character in *Invisible Man* who, in the words of John O. Killens, 'is a young Uncle Tom . . . obsessed with getting to the top by pleasing the Big, Rich White folks'.[114] While both Thomas and Killens invoke the image of 'Uncle Tom' as the unthreatening and submissive African American type of Harriet Beecher Stowe's anti-slavery novel, Houston A. Baker has traced some of the ways in which African American spokesmen were able to use that minstrel mask in order to promote their political programmes within the white world.[115] Ellison foregrounds the use of such strategies in *Invisible Man*, most notably when the narrator recalls his grandfather's death:

> On his deathbed he called my father to him and said, 'Son, after I'm gone I want you to keep up the good fight. I never told you, but our life is a war and I have been a traitor all my born days, a spy in the enemy's country ever since I gave up my gun back in the Reconstruction. Live with your head in the Lion's mouth. I want you to overcome 'em with yeses, undermine 'em with grins, agree 'em to death and destruction, let a'em swoller you till they vomit or bust wide open'.[116]

In keeping with Baker's theory, the 'Uncle Tom' mask is used to hide a submerged hatred and desire for revenge. The challenge for African American spokespersons, argues Baker, was to transform 'the mask and its sounds into a negligible discursive currency'.[117] It may be illuminating to consider Emlyn Williams in such terms – as a playwright whose works are characterized by the 'self-conscious adoption of minstrel tones and types to keep his audience tuned in'.[118] If figures such as the comical Squire and philanthropic Miss Moffat suggest that *The Corn is Green* offers an affirmation of Britishness, there is evidence of other motivations at work. While Old Tom is made to seem foolish, he is also described as 'an elderly, distinguished-looking, grey-bearded peasant'.[119] Russell Stephens has noted Williams's extensive use of Welsh, often untranslated, 'which in places gives the play a bilingual quality', thus testifying to the presence and strength of an indigenous culture.[120] While the play's familiar Pygmalion narrative is clearly appealing to an English audience, behind what F. W. Bateson described as the 'peculiar lucidity' of Williams's prose lies a submerged and probably unconscious critique of cultural imperialist assumptions.[121]

That *The Corn is Green* may be more than a work of 'Anglocentric conservatism' is suggested by a fascinating dialogue between Williams and the Monmouthshire anthropologist Lord Raglan.[122] Lord Raglan is a particularly interesting figure in the context of this discussion for, if Ellison's wartime experiences in Wales were one source for *Invisible Man*, he was also 'much concerned with findings such as Lord Raglan's as a literary matter' when composing the novel:[123]

I was reading Lord Raglan's *The Hero*, which has to do with tradition, myth and drama. As you will recall, Lord Raglan was concerned with the manner in which myth became involved with the histories of living persons, became incorporated into their personal legends.[124]

John S. Wright has traced some of the ways in which Raglan's anthropological analyses of heroic myths influenced the structuring of *Invisible Man*, and Ellison's novel may be read as a fictional meditation on the nature of heroic leadership. African American political leaders resurface throughout the novel – Frederick Douglass, Booker T. Washington and Marcus Garvey – offering one model of black heroism, while, perhaps more significantly, there are the nonpolitical, popular, heroes who seem to offer a range of alternative responses to African American invisibility – Jack Johnson, Joe Louis, Paul Robeson and, perhaps most importantly, Louis Armstrong. Jazz, Ellison famously asserted, was 'the art of individual assertion within and against the group'.[125] The jazz musician thus 'loses his identity even as he finds it', a tension embodied in the music of Louis Armstrong who, according to the Invisible Man, 'made poetry out of being invisible'.[126] Armstrong thus offers the most applicable model for the nameless narrator as he deals with his continual 'fretting over my identity'.[127] Such fretting can come to an end only through the resolution of his growing desire for reintegration into the life and traditions of his repressed folk past, on the one hand, and his own leadership ambitions and sense of duty on the other. This is also a tension that one encounters persistently in the life and work of Emlyn Williams and, while his own ambition led him to embrace a wholly English way of life, there were times when a commitment to his own roots would come to the surface. In an article entitled 'I Take My Stand' that appeared in the pages of the journal *Wales* in 1958, the same Lord Raglan who offered a template for Ellison's exploration of black heroism, cast his anthropologist's eye over Wales. His title invokes the highly reactionary manifesto of the Southern Agrarians in the 1930s, and while Allen Tate, John Crowe Ransom and others had vented their dislike of industrialism, urbanization, immigration and the American left in defending the values of the old South, Raglan, defining himself as 'a Monmouthshire man', mounted an attack on the Welsh language:

Most of the speakers of Welsh are, as I have said, illiterate or semi-literate, but there are a few thousand people who have learnt to speak the literary language, and who make a regular cult of it . . . The Welsh language . . . is used for at least three undesirable purposes, to conceal the results of scholarship, to try to lower the standards of official competence, and, worst of all, to create enmity where none existed.[128]

Emlyn Williams responded in the next issue of *Wales* in an ironic mode signalled by his title: 'A Dyma Fi, Druan o Gymro, Yn Sefyll' (And here am I, a poor Welshman, taking my stand).

> My blood has never boiled – perhaps it doesn't belong to the right group – but when I finished reading Lord Raglan's article 'I Take My Stand', in my October 'Wales', I was conscious of a low but steady simmer; I can still hear it. It's getting louder. I am a Welshman who spoke no colloquial English till I was eight; but since I was 21 I have lived mainly in London, working in English, which has naturally, through the years, become for me a sharper instrument than my native and cherished Welsh. I am not a Welsh Nationalist, Oxford and London have been very good to me, I have not even any strong feelings that a Welsh child brought up outside Wales in a completely English social milieu should be made to speak Welsh. So I am presumably fairly impartial. Yet when I see, in print, a dictum that when Welsh ceases to be spoken 'it will be a happy day for Wales', I don't feel impartial at all . . . I must be fair to my mother – she can't have been quite hopeless – nor can my father, for they acquired a smattering of English, and in no time were making sprightly use of it, particularly my father. But I must make a clean breast of Taid and Nain, on both sides: all four grandparents can only have spoken English of the most broken (not to say estropié) kind, and the whole job-lot qualify, straight away as pretty well 100 per cent illiterates. My maternal grandfather could recite most mellifluously from the Song of Solomon, and from poems by Ceiriog as sweetly elegiac as 'Lycidas'; but, alas, he did it in Welsh.[129]

Here we witness a Welsh equivalent of what Houston A. Baker describes as the deliberate adoption of 'minstrel tones'. Behind a veneer of Britishness – 'Oxford and London have been good to me' – lies a robust defence of Welsh-language culture in the face of Raglan's bigotry. It is an example of a dominant society's language being used against itself. Both the tone and content of Williams's response to Raglan is captured in John Goronwy Jones's ironically charged words in *The Corn is Green*:

> It is terrible, isn't it, the people on these green fields and flowery hillsides bein' turned out of Heaven because they cannot answer Saint Peter when he asks them who they are in English? It is wicked, isn't it, the Welsh children not bein' born knowing English, isn't it? (In a crescendo of ironic mimicry) Good heavens, God bless my soul, by Jove, this that and the other![130]

While these words are uttered by a minor character in the play of 1938, the tone is very similar to that adopted by Williams in his exchange with

Lord Raglan twenty years later. To dismiss *The Corn is Green* as a simplistic reflection of a colonial mindset is to ignore the tensions embodied within the play.

To foreground the critique of cultural imperialist assumptions implicit in *The Corn is Green*, is to read the play in a way that Williams would never have condoned. Such a reading may, however, explain why the play should have made an impression on Ralph Ellison, and why it remained of interest to African American writers and actors. James Baldwin's fourth novel, *Tell Me How Long the Train's Been Gone* (1968), includes a lengthy description of the rehearsals and performance of *The Corn is Green*.[131] It is likely that Baldwin would have heard of the play as a result of his acquaintance with the Welsh Hollywood star Richard Burton, with whom he once stayed in Puerto Vallarta, Mexico.[132] Burton's first screen role was in Williams's *The Last Days of Dolwyn*, and he played the role of Morgan Evans in a radio version of *The Corn is Green* in 1946.[133] Baldwin's novel tells the story of bisexual African American actor Leo Proudhammer, who gets his first break playing Morgan Evans in Emlyn Williams's play. Ray Fisher, a friend of the director, persuades Leo to take on the role by noting:

> 'One of the things that's most impressed me in this country is the struggle of black people to get an education. I always think it's one of the great stories, and nobody knows anything about it. If there were a play on that subject, I'd probably do that. But I don't know of any, so I thought I'd try this experiment with this play. I think you'll see what I mean when you read it. I certainly hope you do. Very few of the elements in the play are really alien to American life . . . I thought I'd take this play, this mining town situation, with no comment, so to say, only making the miners and servants, people like that black. It's true that the play takes place in Wales, but I think we can make the audience forget that after the first few minutes, and hell, anyway, there are black people in Wales. And I figured we'd let the Negro kids improvise around the stretches of Welsh dialogue – dialect really – and of course we've got tremendous musical opportunities with this play.'[134]

Baldwin was profoundly aware of the state's power to limit and oppress minorities, noting in an essay on 'Black English' that 'much of the tension in the Basque country and in Wales is due to the Basques and Welsh determination not to allow their languages to be destroyed'.[135] *Tell Me How Long the Train's Been Gone* is similar to Ralph Ellison's *Invisible Man* in that it explores a man's struggle to contain and make sense of the conflicting identities that make up his inherently plural self, within contexts that are rarely of his own making.

Baldwin's fictional account of an African American version of *The Corn is Green* became reality in 1974 when Dorian Harewood – who would later play the lead role in *The Jesse Owens Story* (1984) – began his career playing the role of Morgan Evans in 'Miss Moffat', an acclaimed musical version of *The Corn is Green*.[136] More significantly, *The Corn is Green* was briefly revived on Broadway in 1983 by the Elizabeth Taylor Theatre Group, with the African American actress Cicely Tyson playing the role of Miss Moffat.[137] Elizabeth Taylor (who was famously married twice to Richard Burton) originally hoped to have the play adapted for an all-black cast, and amongst Emlyn Williams's papers at the National Library of Wales there is a 'Black Version' of the play adapted in 1976. Morgan Lewis is now Philip Coleman, and the play is set in 'the small mining town of Affinity, West Virginia', where the submerged linguistic tensions of the original play become overt racial tensions in the adaptation: 'My old friends at the mine ignore me now, because I've been so busy trying to better myself, and talk and act like and think like a white man', states Philip.[138] Tyson agreed to take on the part of Miss Moffat as long as the play was performed as originally written.[139] Emlyn Williams suggested that efforts should be made to revise the play slightly so that Miss Moffat would become the black descendant of a Welsh West Indian plantation owner. 'The play is a realistic one, not a fantasy', stated Williams in a letter to director Vivian Matalon and, therefore, some explanation was needed of where 'a black Miss Moffat has come from'.[140] There is no evidence that the directors incorporated this rather convoluted amendment. Williams was initially 'elated' that Tyson and Matalon were going to revive his play, but the negative reviews that were sent to him from the United States led to some reservations.[141] The *New York Times* review was typical of many:

> The play's old fashioned sentiments are almost entirely dependent on the strength of the actress playing the central role. As Bette Davis and Katherine Hepburn proved in the film and television adaptations, a charismatic Miss Moffat can override the simplistic conventions of the plot and even the questionable conclusion that elevates an Oxford education over all considerations of personal liability and identity. The principal difficulty with Miss Tyson's performance does not pertain to color – although admittedly in real life it would have been a severe shock for the narrow-minded village squire to encounter a black woman in these circumstances. The difficulty is in the actress's stilted characterization.[142]

Williams was further dismayed when he saw the *Washington Post*'s photograph of Cicely Tyson as Miss Moffat. He feared that his beloved schoolteacher had been transformed into 'an embittered black activist glaring at a political audience, fighting not only for education but for the black cause – a fine cause, but not what this particular play is about. The idea of this woman having a sense of humour is inconceivable.'[143] In a letter intended for Tyson, Williams recalled the first production of the play and noted that

> Sybil [Thorndyke] was (like most of us in the theatre, thank God!) intensely liberal, a passionate champion of the under-privileged; and she tended, at first, to emphasise too strongly the philanthropic essence of the character, making her sound too much the preaching 'do gooder' as if she was carrying a play 'with a message', <u>which this play is not</u>. [Underlined in original][144]

While Tyson seemed willing to go along with Williams's reading of the play, telling Leslie Bennetts of the *New York Times* that 'I don't see *The Corn is Green* as an ethnic piece at all', the debates surrounding the production foreground tensions inherent within the play itself.[145] Williams was made uneasy by the fact that having an African American actress playing the role of Miss Moffat politicized his play. This was perhaps especially the case as Tyson's reputation had been built on her performances of powerful African American women such as Kunta Kinte's mother in 'Roots' and the nineteenth-century abolitionist Harriet Tubman, and that she was in 1983 married to the always controversial and incessantly creative and uncompromising jazz trumpeter, Miles Davis.[146] Having Miss Moffat played by an African American actress seemed to emphasize the 'ethnic' dimension of the play for commentators in 1983, with the *New York Times* reviewer noting that 'Mr Williams's semiautobiographical portrait . . . is set in a highly specific milieu, in which ethnicity is of great importance; the uneducated Welsh don't even speak the same language as the haughty English who condescend to them'.[147] The revival of *The Corn is Green* did not prove a success and folded after less than two weeks on Broadway, but the play's reception in 1983 highlights the truth of David Berry's perceptive observation that, while Williams 'was always at pains to profess his apolitical nature, his writing sometimes seems to betray him'.[148]

To profess the apolitical nature of one's work accords with Houston A. Baker's account of the uses made of strategic minstrelsy by African American authors. While the adoption of 'minstrel tones' allows the African American spokesperson to keep the audience tuned in while engaging in 'crafty political analyses', it is crucial that 'there can be no worry that the Negro is getting "out of hand"'.[149] In the context of 1930s and 1940s Wales *The Corn is Green* can certainly be seen to play an essentially placatory role. The radical working-class politics spawned by the depression caused considerable alarm in middle-class circles as did the less widespread but widely observed growth in Welsh national consciousness. The story of Morgan Evans's rise from the mine to Oxford, and from Wales to England, through education, forms a link between classes and nations, and suggests that a common set of values exist which transcend the divisions of class and nationhood – a message that proved particularly congenial for wartime Britain and accounts for the play's remarkable success in early 1940s New York. If, by setting his play in the late nineteenth century, Williams sought to detach his work from the challenge posed by an emergent Welsh nationalism, and from the radicalized politics of 1930s Wales, Ralph Ellison's passing references to *The Corn is Green* and Emlyn Williams in his story 'The Red Cross' draw our attention to the political implications of a play that, like Ellison's stories, is centrally concerned with the question of identity, and the relationship between majority and minority cultures. In representing the tensions and accommodations between 'Welsh' and 'British', and between 'Black' and 'American', Williams and Ellison offer contrapuntal meditations on the position of minorities within the larger nation states to which they also bear an allegiance.


## THE INTERNATIONALE: MAKING CONNECTIONS

In attempting to capture the character of Aneurin Bevan – Labour minister, founder of Britain's National Health Service and 'pure proletarian type' – for readers of *The Nation* in 1947, the Canadian Robert McKenzie compared him to the central figure of *The Corn is Green*, Morgan Evans. McKenzie's comparison testifies to the influence of Williams's play on North American views of the Welsh, and the narrative of the individual's progress from humble beginnings is reinforced as Mackenzie describes Bevan's post-war transformation from a 'permanent dissenter' from the Welsh valleys to 'a brilliant socialist administrator'.[150] The dissenting Bevan had been expelled from the Labour Party in 1939 for 'persisting with public agitation for Popular Front alliances' and, when he introduced Paul Robeson at the Ebbw Vale Eisteddfod in 1958, one representative of anti-fascist internationalism was paying his respects to another. This connection between Welsh and African American radicalisms – given a belated expression in 1958 and discussed in chapter 3 in relation to the 1930s – took on a fictional form during the war in Ralph Ellison's short stories. Having sung the Welsh national anthem 'Hen Wlad fy Nhadau' with gusto, followed by a less stirring rendition of 'God Save the King', the choir vividly described in Ellison's 'In a Strange Country' sweep into the 'Internationale' before concluding with 'The Star Spangled Banner'. The anthem of international communism thus connects the anthems of Wales and Britain with the anthem of the United States.

While Ellison offered a searing critique of the Communist Party in the shape of the 'Brotherhood' in *Invisible Man*, he was closely involved with the cultural and political left during the 1930s and early 1940s. Kevin Gaines has noted that with Garveyite nationalism in eclipse 'the Communist Party would, for a time, challenge the NAACP as the pre-eminent organization advocating the cause of African Americans' in the 1930s, and, in addition to the celebrated example of Paul Robeson, authors such as Richard Wright, Margaret Walker and Ellison himself were all associated with the Communist Party in the 1930s.[151] Alan Wald has argued that, with the notable exception of Richard Wright, few African Americans were willing to appear in public as acknowledged members of the Communist Party, but perhaps more significant than formal membership was the use made by Black writers of 'the publications, clubs, and committees that were at least in part created by Party members, and with Party support'. These outlets and forums 'constituted principal venues in which many Black writers came together to formulate ideas, share writings, make contacts, and develop perspectives that sustained their future creative work'.[152] This range of activities on the cultural left created the context for the emergence of Ralph Ellison as a writer. His first book review was published by Richard Wright in the communist-backed journal, *New Challenge*. The late 1930s saw Ellison gathering folk materials in Harlem as part of the New Deal's Federal Writers Project and his writings drawing on that material began to appear in the leftist *New Masses* and the pro-communist publication associated with the League of American Writers, *Direction*. Ellison was also a 'pivotal organiser' of the Fourth American Writers' Congress that opened on 6 June 1941 – and was designated to develop a national magazine to be sponsored by the League of American Writers.[153] Richard Wright delivered the opening speech of that congress, arguing – a few weeks prior to the German invasion of the Soviet Union – that African Americans had no stake in what was an imperialist war. In offering this account of the war he was following the Communist Party's position, as embodied in an ironic wartime joke:

> We, the governments of Great Britain and the United States, in the name of India, Burma, Malaya, Australia, British East Africa, British Guiana, Hong Kong, Siam, Singapore, Egypt, Palestine, Canada, New Zealand, Northern Ireland, Scotland, Wales, as well as Puerto Rico, Guam, the Philippines, Hawaii, Alaska, and the Virgin Islands, hereby declare most emphatically, that this is not an imperialist war.[154]

Ellison would follow Wright in combining this Communist Party line with an African American perspective in his pre-1941 essay on 'The Negro and the War'. The essay launches a powerful critique of the belief – famously espoused by Du Bois during the First World War and by A. Philip Randolph during the Second World War – that black participation in war would function as a catalyst for racial equality, and, while noting some of the valuable advancements resulting from Roosevelt's New Deal, Ellison concluded that

> Negroes must fight against this country's entry into the current imperialist war. The only war worth their taking part is one that would allow the energies released by a war situation to be used in the interests of a progressive, rather than a reactionary governmental form. Negroes, when asked to join in an imperialist war under the slogan of defending democracy against German fascism should remember that the home grown variety which is now spreading from the South is far more deadly to them than the German variety which now only threatens Britain.[155]

When Germany invaded Soviet Russia the Allied Powers' struggle against the Axis Powers was transformed in the eyes of the American Communist Party from an 'imperialist war' to a 'people's war' against fascism. Ellison also shifted from his anti-war position to embrace the revived Popular Front values advocated by the radical left. In warning critics not to read the anti-communist Ellison of *Invisible Man* back into his wartime short stories, Barbara Foley suggests that 'In a Strange Country' is 'embedded in the discourse of CPUSA politics'.[156] Foley evokes the 'nationalist-internationalist songfest' that concludes the story to support her case, and argues persuasively that

> a presence informing this 1944 tale is that of Paul Robeson, the CPUSA's most prominent antifascist publicist, whose highly popular performance of Othello had broken the Broadway color line and whose 'Ballad for Americans' had become a staple of leftist songfests from the late 1930s onward.[157]

Robeson was a figure of some importance for Ellison in the 1940s. American GIs became aware of Robeson's reputation in Britain, with Roi Ottley noting in 1944 that

What contact the British people had with Negroes before the arrival of the American troops was on the whole very good. Paul Robeson and many other Negro artists and entertainers made quite an impression on the British. In the ten years he resided in England Robeson created a good opinion of the American Negro.[158]

It is, therefore, perhaps not surprising that as the Welsh pub regulars gather around Doc at the end of Ellison's 'The Red Cross' he notes that 'You'd a thought I was a special Negro – like Paul Robeson'.[159] Robeson also features twice in another of Ellison's stories of the 1940s, 'A Hard Time Keeping Up', and most significantly is referred to in the concluding section of Ellison's groundbreaking essay of 1945 'Richard Wright's Blues'.[160] In developing an argument that would continue to reappear in his later writings, Ellison notes that

Wright knows perfectly well that Negro life is a by-product of Western civilization, and that in it, if only one possesses the humanity and humility to see, are to be discovered all those impulses, tendencies, life and cultural forms to be found elsewhere in Western society.[161]

Ellison proceeds to argue that the challenge for critics is to identify this humanity in the work of a people 'under pressure', to 'identify themselves with the human content, whatever its outer form; and even with those Southern Negroes to whom Paul Robeson's name is only a rolling sound in the fear-charged air'.[162] The introduction of Robeson's name at this point in the argument is significant. Robeson here represents the African American artist who has transcended racial classification and whose humanity is registered and respected by the wider public. Ellison is also perhaps suggesting that the acclaim bestowed upon Robeson as the voice of the world's proletariat actually, and ironically, derives from the singer's distance from the grim reality of life for the majority of African Americans. Ellison was hugely critical of Robeson's claims to speak for Africa – chuckling at 'neo-Garveyism from a wealthy singer'.[163] Informing Ellison's argument in 'Richard Wright's Blues' is the belief that while racist practices have been perpetuated in the name of a bogus universalism – the imperial notion that the language, beliefs and customs of a dominant group are universal and, therefore, superior to all others – this should not lead to the fetishizing of difference, for an appeal to universalist beliefs has formed the most powerful and far-reaching challenge to racism. 'The role of the writer', argued Ellison, 'is to structure fiction which will allow a universal identification, while at the same time not violating the specificity of the particular experience and the particular character'.[164]

Robeson, as singer, dramatist and anti-fascist, was certainly an important symbol of universal humanity in the 1930s and 1940s. Despite his
later scepticism and subtle undermining of Robeson's cultural authority,
Ellison's 'In a Strange Country' suggests that Robeson was also a significant and enabling model for African Americans fighting in the Second
World War. Although Robeson is never mentioned in the story, Barbara
Foley argues persuasively that Robeson is a presence in the text.[165]
'Ellison's assumption that his readers also would have Robeson on the
mind', states Foley,

> is indicated by his choice to show scattered lines from Othello running through
> Parker's mind as he contemplates the irony of his situation as a Jim-Crowed
> participant in an antifascist war. In particular, the line 'Do the state some
> service' comes from Othello's closing soliloquy, which was a standard item in
> many of Robeson's concert performances.[166]

This is both perceptive and persuasive. Indeed, Robeson was playing
Othello to widespread acclaim on Broadway in 1943.[167] Foley's argument would have been considerably strengthened, however, had she
referred to Robeson's connections with Wales (discussed in chapter 3).
The final scene of 'In a Strange Country', set in the context of a choir
rehearsal, could have been lifted from Robeson's Welsh-based film of
1940, *Proud Valley*, although Parker's comments on the particular
significance of the individual anthems gives the sentimental scene a
broader political significance. The use of the 'Internationale' as a means
of connecting the Welsh and British anthems with the American anthem
reinforces a connection made earlier in the story between Wales and
Russia.

> And as the men sang in hushed tones [Parker] felt a growing poverty of spirit.
> He should have known more of the Welsh, of their history and art. If we only
> had some of what they have, he thought. They are a much smaller nation than
> ours would be, yet I can remember no song of ours that's of love of the soil or
> of country. Nor any song of battle other than those of biblical times. And in his
> mind's eye he saw a Russian peasant kneeling to kiss the earth and rising
> wet-eyed to enter into battle with cries of fierce exultation.[168]

If Ellison believed that the Welsh were 'like the Russians' in being 'a
mature people while we Americans are in painful adolescence', hearing
the 'Internationale' in the final scene of 'In a Strange Country' reminds
Parker of 'the bands that came to his southern town'.[169] It seems that
Ellison is making connections between folk cultures, and the fact that
Welsh folk songs remind Parker of Russia, and that the 'Internationale'

functions as a link between the Welsh and American anthems, suggests that 'In a Strange Country' is embedded in the internationalism promoted by the revived Popular Front politics of the early 1940s. This is a reading reinforced by the hovering presence of Robeson behind the narrative. As discussed in the previous chapter, the desire to connect folk cultures and to see the African American struggle as one example of a wider global struggle was a characteristic of Robeson's activities as an artist from the mid-1930s onwards. Robeson argued that his chief interest on his first visit to Soviet Russia would be to 'study the Soviet national minority policy as it operates among the people of Central Asia', and during his British tours of 1934 he sought to expand his repertoire by supplementing his performances of spirituals with Russian, Chinese, Yiddish and Welsh songs among others.[170] Robeson was far from unique in admiring Soviet Russia, for significant African American authors such as W. E. B. Du Bois, Claude Mckay and Langston Hughes all visited the Soviet Union during the late 1920s and early 1930s. The 'Internationale' functions as an appropriate link between Wales and African America in this respect for many figures on the Welsh left were also to visit Russia in the same period, including S. O. Davies, Aneurin Bevan and Lewis Jones, and the South Wales Miners' Federation was the only significant British organization to seek affiliation to the Moscow-based Red International of Labour Unions.[171] In the early 1930s Robeson could still be regarded in the United States as 'the symbolic Negro, as proof that the system worked', but from the early 1940s onwards the transnational connections forged on the concert stage were increasingly being linked to a collectivist, international socialism.[172] 'Rejecting his previous location as the representative American Negro', argues Kate Baldwin, 'he embraced an openly political aesthetics'.[173] Such a position was tolerated during the Allied fight against fascism, and Robeson's political internationalism was reflected in the African American periodicals of the 1940s.

Alan Wald has noted that 'from the outset, Black Marxists were compromised by faith placed in . . . an illusion that the Soviet Union was a model for anti-racism and the fair treatment of national minorities'.[174] Black communist leader James Ford argued in Nancy Cunard's famous 1933 anthology, *Negro*, that 'Soviet Russia's insistence upon absolute equality for all people . . . has led to the freedom of the nationalities formerly oppressed by the Tsarist regime in the same way that Negroes are oppressed in the United States', and this view, dominant on the African American left in the 1930s, continued into the war years.[175] In *The Crisis* of November 1942 the Trinidadian communist George

Padmore published one of many lengthy articles advocating a comparative approach to racial issues. His 'Race relations: Soviet and British',
despite the title, is primarily concerned with linguistic minorities.
Padmore argues that, while the British seek linguistic uniformity at home
and offer little education to their imperial subjects abroad, the Soviet
Union has adopted an approach of mass literacy in minority languages,
rooted in Lenin's argument that those communists who believed that 'no
instruction is to be given except through the Russian language' were in
fact 'Pan-Russian chauvinists'.[176] The comparative approach to race
relations was particularly evident in *The Negro Quarterly*, a short-lived
journal described as 'a Negro review of thought and opinion' that Ellison
co-edited with Communist Party member Angelo Herndon from 1942 to
1943.[177] *The Negro Quarterly* was in existence for a year and a half and,
unlike the Communist Party – which emphasized victory against fascism
at the expense of any other struggle – it promoted a 'Double V' agenda in
its four issues, advocating victory against fascism abroad and against
Jim Crow racist practices at home. Lawrence Jackson notes that the
journal espoused an analysis of Black oppression within a broad comparative 'international context of Asian and African anticolonial
movements'.[178] 'To fail to protest the wrongs done Negroes as we fight
the war', argued Ellison and Herndon, 'is to participate in a crime, not
only against Negroes, but against all true anti-Fascists'.[179] The second
edition of *The Negro Quarterly* that names Ellison as the 'Managing
Editor' includes articles on 'Anti-Negroism among Jews' and
'Anti-Semitism among Negroes', 'India and the Peoples' War', 'Some
aspects on the color problem in Cuba' and a review by Charles Humboldt
of Alain Locke's and Bernard J. Stern's collection of studies in 'Race and
culture contacts', *When Peoples Meet*, which begins by noting that 'the
present war has raised, with greater urgency than ever before, the question of the rights of national minorities'.[180] Humboldt goes on to argue
that the volume's most significant chapter is that written by Sidney and
Beatrice Webb on national minorities in the USSR, and he quotes the
following excerpt from their discussion:

> The Soviet Union can claim with a high degree of accuracy that it has solved
> the difficult problem presented by the existence of national minorities within
> a strongly centralized state. It has found this solution by the novel device of
> dissociating statehood from both nationality and race. It has put trust in a
> genuine equality of citizenship as completely irrespective of race or language
> or colour or religion.[181]

The centralization of the British state, and the steadfast opposition to Scottish and Welsh claims for self-determination from influential figures in the post-war Labour Party, owed more than a little to the Webbs' vision. What I wish to emphasize here, however, is that these widespread discussions of minority rights amongst the African American left offered a frame within which Ellison could place and contextualize his experiences in Wales.

Ellison's wartime short stories express a desire to locate the African American experience within an internationalist context. It is notable in this respect that the places in which those stories are set were themselves the sites of significant socialist debate and activity in the first half of the twentieth century. At the heart of a group of socialist writers who met in the village of Glais in the Swansea Valley was T. E. Nicholas (1878–1971). Affectionately known as 'Niclas y Glais', he would pay for his idiosyncratic Christian communist convictions by spending over two months in 1940 in Swansea and Brixton prisons, writing the sonnets of *Cerddi'r Carchar* (Prison Poems) (1942) – characterized by a fervent utopian desire for global 'brawdgarwch' (brotherhood) and 'rhyddid' (freedom) – on pieces of slate and toilet paper.[182] In the town of Swansea itself the 'equivalent of the Socialist culture of the mining valleys' was the circle around the Marxist grocer Bert Trick (1889–1973), whose combination of 'radical Socialism, progressive religious feelings and anti-war sentiment' would have a profound impact on the young Dylan Thomas.[183] Thomas dedicated the notebook version of his poem 'The hand that signed the paper' to his Marxist mentor, and the poet was clearly suspected of leftist sympathies when asked, before eventually being granted a visa to visit the United States in 1950, whether 'he would attend a song-recital of Paul Robeson's'.[184] Ellison's short stories thus embody the meeting of cultural and intellectual traditions that had been profoundly influenced by the impact of international socialism. In Ellison's 'The Red Cross' these connections between American and Welsh cultural and political traditions are explored from the perspective of a female Welsh Red Cross worker:

> She asked me if I was familiar with the Eisteddfods held by the Welsh in the United States – which I wasn't. 'In 1927 quite a few choirs came over to take part in the National Eisteddfod'. She said also that John L. Lewis was Welsh, and that he was born a few miles away at a village called Pontydillys [*sic*]. I told her that Lewis was supposed to have been born in Iowa and she said maybe it was his parents. 'Four of the original signers of the Declaration of Independence were Welshmen,' she said proudly. I asked who they were and

she said that she could not remember, but that if I waited, 'Captain Carrol could tell you.' Captain Carrol, I learned, was a Negro Chaplain who was very popular in Wales. He was very enthusiastic about the country, she said; and had mastered the language to the extent of being able to preach to them in their native tongue.[185]

Ellison thus draws his readers' attention to Welsh-American choirs travelling to take part in the Welsh National Eisteddfod, to the widely held Welsh belief that many of the original signers of the Declaration of Independence were from Wales and to the existence of a Welsh-speaking African American chaplain. The narrator admits that the Eisteddfod means nothing to him, and communicates a warranted scepticism regarding the Welsh signers of the Declaration of Independence. Much of the material relating to Wales in Ellison's stories is broadly accurate, however. Cleveland Orpheus Choir and the Anthracite Male Chorus of Scranton, Pennsylvania, won first and second prizes at the National Eisteddfod in Swansea (1926) and Treorchy (1928) respectively, and there was, indeed, an African American Chaplain named Edward Carroll in the Swansea Valley during the Second World War.[186] The reference to John Llewellyn Lewis, president of the United Mine Workers from 1920 to 1960 and founding president of the Congress of Industrial Organization (CIO) is also significant, especially when locating Ellison's short stories in the context of the American left. In 1937 a number of industrial unions, led by the mine workers, broke away from the traditionally craft-union-based American Federation of Labour (AFL) to form a federation of industrial unions, the CIO. During the war years the differences between the racial policies of the two organizations became pronounced with the AFL rejecting resolutions condemning discrimination, and the CIO not only condemning discrimination but also forming a committee to abolish it within the congress itself.[187] Paul Robeson described the CIO as 'the most progressive section of the labor movement' especially when compared to the 'great discrimination in A.F. of L. unions', and the Trinidadian Marxist C. L. R. James noted that John L. Lewis's 'name is a legend among the Negroes and the millions of poor whites'.[188] Ellison's political allegiances thus explain the reference to Lewis, who was indeed a native of Iowa, but was also the son of Welsh-born parents; Thomas Henry Lewis, a miner from Pontarddulais (the Pontydillys of Ellison's story), and Ann Louisa Watkins, from New Tredegar.[189] In 1943, Lewis led over half a million mine workers on strike, demanding wage increases. The government deemed the strike illegal and in the wartime context Lewis was vilified, with rocks hurled through the windows of his house in Alexandria, Virginia. To the miners, however, Lewis was a hero, with a mine worker quoted in the *New York Times* as saying that 'if John L. Lewis told us to go on strike tomorrow, we would go out, even if it meant going to prison for 20 years'.[190] Due to demand for their labour the miners in both the United Sates and Britain enjoyed a considerable amount of bargaining power during the war years. In Wales there were 524 stoppages in the coal industry between 1939 and 1945, with the biggest strike, involving a hundred thousand Welsh miners, taking place in March 1944.[191] It is likely that Ellison would be aware of the strikes during his period in south Wales, and his reference to the Welsh ancestry of American's leading union leader reflects both his own leftist sympathies and a desire to draw attention to correspondences between the Welsh and American experiences.

The comparativist impulse evident in Ellison's Welsh-based short stories results in his awareness and understanding of the range of identities being embraced simultaneously by a national minority within the British state. The plurality of identities expressed by the Welsh choir – from Welsh distinctiveness, to Britishness to socialist internationalism – creates a space where Parker can ultimately, with 'The Star Spangled Banner' as a soundtrack, identify himself as an American. While this act of identification is significant in itself, it is also important that we note that it is the internationalist, anti-fascist, politics of the war years that provides Parker with the means for connecting with the Welsh, and for embracing America.

## CONCLUSION

The diversity of identities that characterize the Welsh experience spoke directly to Ellison's own experience. It becomes particularly clear in his remarkable essays on jazz and literature that, for Ellison, American identity is something that is always trying to be achieved, an identity that is in a process of continual emergence. Ellison never denies the specificities and distinctiveness of African American culture, but at the heart of his fiction and criticism, as John F. Callahan has noted, lies a belief in a common – not homogenous – democratic culture.[192] In reviewing LeRoi Jones's nationalist history of African American music, *Blues People*, Ellison argued that

> Taken as a theory of American Negro culture it can only contribute to more confusion than clarity. For Jones has stumbled over that ironic obstacle which

lies in the path of any who would fashion a theory of American Negro culture while ignoring the intricate network of connections which binds Negroes to the larger society. To do so is to attempt a delicate brain surgery with a switch-blade. And it is possible that any viable theory of Negro American culture obligates us to fashion a more adequate theory of American culture as a whole. The heel bone is, after all, connected to the head bone.[193]

The need to develop theoretical models that are not limited to national or ethnic boundaries is illustrated in a letter written to Ellison on 24 September 1944. The author is Winifred Kealing who 'was born in the USA – but reared in a (Welsh) Cymric home – I speak, read and write the language'. She is writing to tell the author 'that I wept' upon reading 'In a Strange Country' in *The Negro Digest*.

> It is rare to find men as kind as those old Welshmen were, and it is also touching to find young men appreciative of such fine feeling. I pray God our beautiful country may soon see the utter stupidity of race-discrimination . . . May I tell you something? When we are among ourselves we never call ourselves 'Welsh' – but 'Y Cymry'. 'Welsh' is an English word – it means foreigner. We used to resent it as some Negroes resent 'Nigger.' Now we merely shrug our shoulders – God grant we may always be 'foreign' to English imperialism . . . Near me is a Negro Church (of my own denomination) I attend there. I love it when sometimes an old man calls out 'Amen' – my people do that too and we sing in our churches as your people sing, with our hearts. Thanks again for understanding and appreciating my people. I am doing all I can to help my fellow Americans appreciate your people.[194]

These words are a powerful expression of a Welsh-American identity that continued to base itself, even in 1944, on the language and religion characteristic of late nineteenth-century Welsh Nonconformity. In this respect it connects to the opening chapter of this study. Whatever the sentimentality of the letter, the very existence of a Welsh-speaking, white, anti-imperialist American, who attends an African American chapel and reads *The Negro Digest*, testifies to the truth of Ellison's observation that, if ethnic groups are seen to live in separate jugs, those jugs are 'transparent, not opaque, and one is allowed not only to see outside but to read what is going on out there; to make identifications as to values and human quality'.[195] Ellison deemed the letter valuable enough to keep it amongst his papers. It may function here as a distillation of the connections that I have been tracing in this chapter.

# Conclusion: 1945

Narratives of the making of modern multicultural Britain conventionally begin with the arrival of the *Empire Windrush* at Tilbury on 22 June 1948, carrying 492 passengers from Jamaica.[1] However, the critic Hazel Carby – professor of African American studies at Yale and herself the daughter of a Welsh mother and a Jamaican father – has recently suggested that British multiculturalism 'has its origins in official responses to the presence of black American troops and West Indian civilian and Royal Air Force personnel on British soil during World War II'.[2] Drawing on David Reynolds's detailed research, and adopting a Foucauldian approach to social structures, Carby argues that 'the policies and practices of the British Government during the war manufactured racialized subjects in accord with segregated relations of subjugation'.[3] Although I have indicated in this study that processes of racialization have a longer history in Britain than Carby seems to suggest, her argument is useful for my purposes for it allows this study to end at the point where we witness 'the emergence of the UK as a modern racialized state'.[4] One of the manifestations of that racialization relates to the fear, discussed in the previous chapter, of relationships between white British women and African American GIs. Reynolds has documented the ways in which women and African Americans were 'policed and disciplined' during the war years. The Women's Territorial Auxiliary issued an order 'forbidding its members to speak to coloured soldiers except in the presence of a white', and local constabularies 'routinely reported women soldiers found in the company of black GIs to their superiors'.[5] Women who were alleged to have relationships with African American GIs became associated 'within official discourses with venereal disease, thus becoming a threat to the health of the nation'.[6]

These anxieties are overtly expressed in a remarkable series of reports and letters that appeared in the Welsh national newspaper, the *Western Mail*, during the months of September and October 1945. The war was, of course, over by then, and Cardiff was an embarkation point for American troops. The editorial column of the 12 September 1945, issue of the *Western Mail* expressed its alarm at the 'scenes witnessed by our reporters in the vicinity of Maindy Barracks, Cardiff'. During the war years a 'gang of loose women' had followed American troops 'up and down the country for the purposes of prostitution' and had now arrived in Cardiff. The editorial expressed its astonishment that the military police had 'no power beyond the boundaries of the Barracks' and suggested that the only solution might be 'to round [the women] up as vagrants and send them for institutional work or treatment'. 'Scandals of this character occur in all wars, but never before has vice been so flagrantly rampant in any part of Wales.'[7] The full story appeared on page 3 under the heading 'Women tramps menace social life in Wales'. The report reinforces the editorial column's disgust at the women involved and luridly describes 'a scene of almost indescribable filth . . . between the lane and the barracks boundary divided by a broken hedge' where 'women's dirty torn undergarments, coats, skirts, shoes and other things lie everywhere'. If 'one side of the problem is the terrible disease-carrying potentialities of these women', the other relates to the types of soldiers involved.[8] While the editorial column made little reference to the American soldiers, the report quoted a number of the area's inhabitants who expressed racial fears. One mother reported that her daughter was afraid of going out at night 'because a coloured man recently followed her', and feared that the 'coloured soldiers', having encountered some immoral British women, would 'now think that all girls are alike'. Another resident reported that 'one day a girl was soliciting coloured American soldiers dressed in nothing but a skirt'. To make matters worse, these activities were not only taking place in the 'rat-infested thoroughfare' known as Burma Road, but also in the traditionally tranquil surroundings of the local bowling green which seemed now to have become the site for illicit activities, and the space for residents to project their racial and sexual anxieties. 'The parents of a girl attending Cathays High School' reported that 'we thought a girl was being murdered in the bowling green pavilion but found that she was giving birth to a baby'.[9]

Later editions of the *Western Mail* that week registered the 'shock and shame of disclosures' felt by local religious leaders. The Revd William Davies of Albany Road Baptist Church was quoted at length on Monday

17 September, regretting that a band of 'women tramps' were 'robbing others of their money . . . even though they have to destroy the bodies and souls of their victims to do so', and noting that 'although the victims of these camp followers are in the main coloured soldiers it is clear that our own youths and men are not safe from their threat'.[10] Race and sexuality were also preoccupying the mind of Revd R. M. Rosser, vicar of Eglwys Dewi Sant (Saint David's Church), who thanked the *Western Mail* for bringing this 'jungle behaviour' to the community's attention. Despite the racism of his vocabulary, Revd Rosser noted that 'all the blame must not be attributed to the coloured men' for 'the humiliating fact is that white girls in Christian Britain are so utterly base'.[11] Sonya Rose has documented the moral panic surrounding 'the declining morals of girls and young women in British cities and towns' during the Second World War, and Hazel Carby usefully notes that 'women who openly expressed their sexual selves and sexual desires in encounters with black servicemen were particularly vilified and seen as a particular threat to the nation's future'.[12] The *Western Mail* reports offer considerable evidence that racial and sexual anxieties did not, in Carby's words, 'arise from the recognition of an "external" problem which had been foisted to some extent on English society from the outside'.[13] It was 'home grown' and drew

> upon official responses in the past to the existence of black communities in Britain and racialized bodies in colonial territories, a consciousness that gave English [*sic*] national culture its character, meaning, substance and resonance. Before the war this consciousness had been nurtured, given form and realised in the policing and disciplining of colonial subjects and black residents of Bristol, Cardiff, London and Liverpool.[14]

Indeed, in his *Nature Knows No Color-Line* (first published in 1952), the Jamaican-born author, journalist, and historian J. A. Rogers noted that the 'Negro colony' in Cardiff dated back to 1850.[15] Perhaps best known today for his essay on 'Jazz at home' in Alain Locke's seminal collection *The New Negro* (1925), Rogers, in a 1930 report to H. L. Mencken's *American Mercury*, gave an account of multicultural Cardiff:

> The largest Negro settlement in the United Kingdom, perhaps in Europe, is at Cardiff. It is an evil-looking dump, with ugly two-story cottages and alleys full of refuse, which bears the appropriate name of Tiger Bay. This name, it is said, came from the terrible fights that used to take place there between seamen. The regular Negro population is about 4,000, with a floating one of several thousand more. This figure includes another settlement nearby, named Barry . . . Negroes were living in Cardiff before the coming of the steamship,

and some now there have been there for more than fifty years. Most of the men have white wives; the rest, colored ones who were born there of white mothers. There are apparently no foreign colored women . . .

The white women themselves are vigorous in defense of their black husbands and go waspishly after those who attack them . . .They take great interest in their men's activities, and at the Marcus Garvey hall in the East End of London, they shouted the 'Back to Africa!' battlecry as enthusiastically as the men. Indeed, the London leader of the Garvey movement was himself married to a white woman . . . [In] Tiger Bay there is no segregation. White and colored families live in the same cottages. Children are plentiful, all the colored ones being mulattoes . . . There are about 600 such colored children. In one street of three blocks – Nelson street – there are seventy-two, one man alone having twelve. . . . There is little opportunity for these children, even when they win scholarships and are taught grades. The boys usually end by going to sea, while the girls go into domestic service, marry, or go on the stage. There are three groups among the Negroes and hostilities between them are perhaps sharper than the feelings of prejudiced whites towards them. These classes are, those from the West Indies, who are usually the more educated; the Christian Africans, who come from West Africa, and make up with shrewdness for what they lack in education; and the Mohammedans, who came mostly from East Africa and that part of Asia which lies around the Red Sea . . . Nevertheless, during the Cardiff riots, all of these blacks stood solidly together and defied the white men to come in, with the result that they suffered less than elsewhere. Most of the Negroes killed or wounded were outside the Black Belt at the time.[16]

The sense of an emergent black consciousness in Tiger Bay was reinforced by the Irish-language author and translator Seosamh Mac Grianna, who was on his way to Algeria when the thought struck him in London that instead of going to north Africa he should go instead to a country that was much nearer, but perhaps equally foreign: Wales. An encounter in Cardiff leads him to explore Garveyism and the history of the 'Black races':

Ba sin an chéad aithne a fuair mé ar fhear dubh, agus ní fhuair mé droch-bharamhal de'n dream ar chor ar bith le n-a linn . . . 'Tá ceannphort anois orainn', arsa seisean, 'atá ag iarraidh fir dhubha an domhain a thabhairt ar ghualainn a chéile. Mad Garvey is ainm dá, agus ní feasach do dhuine ar bith cé'r díobh é nó carb as é.' . . . D'imigh sé, agus an lá ar n-a bhárach chuaidh mé féin go dtí an leabharlainn go bhfághainn leabharthaí a bhí ag trácht ar na cinidheacha dubha. Chaith mé coicthís ag léigheamh, agus bhí an sgéal comh gránna agus go raibh náire orm a bheith 'mo fhear bhán, agus gur aidmhigh mé nach rabh i n-éagcóir mo thíre féin acht mar bhas a bhuailfidhe ar pháiste le n-a thaobh.

(This was the first time I'd met a Black person, and it did not give me a bad impression of those people . . . 'We now have a leader,' he said, 'who is trying to get the Black people of the world to stand shoulder to shoulder. Mad Garvey is his name, and no one knows who he is or where he comes from.' . . . He left, and the next day I went to the library to obtain books about the Black races. I spent a fortnight reading them, and the story was so disgraceful that I was ashamed to be a White person, forcing me to admit that the wrongs of my own country were merely like a slap you would give a child in comparison.)[17]

Indeed, it could be claimed that Marcus Garvey's United Negro Improvement Association (UNIA) was the first modern nationalist party to appear in Wales. Created as a response to the race riots of 1919, the UNIA branches at Cardiff and Barry Dock were already established by 1925 when Plaid Genedlaethol Cymru (The National Party of Wales) was formed.[18] The combined fear of black political consciousness and of sexual relations between African American soldiers and the British public led to the policing of Cardiff along segregationist lines during the Second World War. American soldiers stationed in Cardiff, Sully and Barry were generally allowed to roam freely, but Tiger Bay was deemed to be 'off limits'. Alan Llwyd notes that signs were erected to keep American servicemen out of the docks area, and suggests that 'the people of Britain were astounded and appalled that the Americans operated a segregationist policy'.[19] Yet it would surely have been difficult for American forms of segregation to be instituted without regional cooperation, and, as Carby notes, 'without the participation of local police forces and local government officials'.[20] The *Western Mail* reports suggest a large number of Cardiff residents shared the concerns voiced by British home secretary Herbert Morrison when he stated 'that a difficult sex problem might be created . . . if there were a substantial number of cases of sex relations between white women and coloured troops and the procreation of half-caste children'.[21] The Maindy Barracks controversy suggests that, with the end of hostilities, social intolerance was becoming more apparent.

If the racist and sexist attitudes present in immediate post-war Wales are clearly exposed in the reports, comments and sermons reproduced in the *Western Mail*, the paper also gives space to alternative accounts of these events. On 14 September, Edith S. Lester-Jones wrote to propose the 'incorporation of women in the city's police force', and Mary Morgan of Gilfach-Bargoed called for the provision of more youth and community centres, for 'under the right influence during their leisure time the young people would develop along the lines approved by decent society'.[22] Rosina Thomas and Nancy Heaton clearly felt that 'womanhood' itself needed to be defended in the face of the 'passions run awry' at Maindy Barracks:

> These women are the products of a bad home life. It is only in the home and educational life of the nation that we shall cradle and nurture that new spirit needed to save our world from moral degradation. Woman has a great part to play in world reconstruction.[23]

These countervailing female voices appeared alongside correspondents defending the 'American Negro'. Under the headline, 'Coloured girls defend U.S. soldiers', the *Western Mail* of 14 September reported that 'two girls, themselves coloured' visited its offices in order to 'state the other side of the case'. Having been associated with the 'coloured American solders since they first came to Cardiff', they wished to state that 'most of these soldiers treat women and girls as they find them. If a girl respects herself and expects others to respect her then almost without exception she will get it.'[24] They draw attention to the fact that a number of the dance halls in the vicinity of Maindy Barracks 'will not admit coloured American soldiers', and that generally 'they are not really welcomed' in those institutions that allow them entry. Furthermore, 'the Docks, the only area where they would be made welcome and there would be able to mix in decent surroundings without fear of being snubbed on account of their colour, is out of bounds'.[25] While stressing that they in no way defended the reported behaviour, 'the blame for what is described in your paper lies not with the soldiers but is due more to the lack of social amenities'. This is significant in that it reflects the attitudes of the black Welsh community in Cardiff to the presence of African American troops. In 1949, following a period spent in Cardiff on a Julius Rosenwald fellowship 'to study the impact of colored American troops on the British people', the African American anthropologist St Clair Drake reported in the pages of *The Crisis* that the natives 'of the colored settlement in Cardiff, Wales: British Bronzeville . . . would like to know their American counterparts better'. The co-author with Horace Clayton of *Black Metropolis*, which focused on the original 'Bronzeville' in Chicago's South Side, noted that

> I could feel it in the quiet courtesy they extended me, in their nostalgic comments on the American colored troops they had met, and in the avid way they asked for copies of *Ebony* and *Negro Digest* and American Negro newspapers.[26]

African American GIs were clearly remembered fondly in Butetown, even if they had been barred from going there. In addition to the two

'coloured girls', a letter from Miss Mable Jackson of the American Red
Cross in Barry criticizing the *Western Mail* for 'pinning the blame on the
negro troops' was published on 17 September. Having defended the
troops, she also gave some insight into the racism experienced by African
American soldiers in Britain:

> When negro troops first came to England people ran away because they had
> heard stories that we all had tails . . . in other words, that we weren't human
> beings. That sounds fantastic doesn't it? How would you overcome such a
> handicap?[27]

This letter forced the *Western Mail* on the defensive, and Mabel Jackson's
letter was prefaced with the comment: 'At no time have we put the blame
on the Americans. Nor do we now . . . There is not, and never was, any
intention to cast a reflection on coloured soldiers generally.'[28] This was
partly true in that the original editorial of 12 September had made no
reference to race. But the report that followed quoted a wide range of
individuals' blaming the 'coloured' troops. Possibly haunted by the
spectre of the race riots of 1919, the paper proceeded in later editions to
emphasize that 'what we especially deplore is the immorality of our own
girls and women who pester the soldiers and are indifferent alike to
appeal and authority'.[29] The paper's apology was clearly insufficient in
the opinion of 1st Sergeant R. S. Winlock and Private Milton Howard for
on 19 September they wrote:

> I am sure that you realise that the American Negro is just another American
> whose skin is not one colour, but many colours. I refer to this due to the fact
> that your article of September 17th clearly states that the only way to find an
> answer to the problem of these girls is to remove all Negro troops from the
> Cardiff area. As a unit in the U.S. Army we came overseas to liberate Europe
> from Nazi-ism along with other Allied Nations . . . To the young lady who
> stated that she was afraid that we may think all the girls in England similar to
> the ones mentioned who are quite comfortable billeting themselves beneath
> the stars, please let her know that we are far too intelligent for that. In closing,
> I would like to add that we, the undersigned, will gladly co-operate with the
> police around Cardiff and Barry in the drastic effort to stamp out the anti-social
> activities of these wanton girls. And will you please co-operate with our
> Government in getting us home as soon as possible.

The sense of offence communicated by the words and the desire to return
expressed in this letter offer a useful corrective to narratives that would
see racism as an American import to a Wales which would otherwise be
a tolerant haven. Following the commonplace American practice of
referring to the whole of the UK as 'England', Winlock and Howard

noted acerbically that 'the English people shall be no happier than we, when we leave "Merry Ole England"'.[30]

Away from the simmering tensions of Cardiff, and in retreat from the bombed streets of his native Swansea, Dylan Thomas was writing in the coastal town of New Quay, west Wales, in May 1945. He was struck by the jarring discrepancy between the trivial everyday goings on of the natural world and the atrocities recently perpetuated, and now being disclosed, on mainland Europe:

> It is very quiet here; only the hunting noise of the hard-away sea, the throbbing of tractors, the squealing of rats and rabbits in the traps, the surging of seagulls, thrushes, blackbirds, finches, cuckooing of cuckoos, cooing of doves . . . barking of dogs, voices of children playing trumpets on the beach, bugling of sea cadets, naying, chucking, quacking, braying, mooing, rabbit-gunning, horse trotting, scraping of magpies on the roof, mice in the kitchen: an ordinary day, nature serene as Fats Waller in Belsen.[31]

The Harlem stride-pianist Thomas 'Fats' Waller (who died in 1943) represents a natural life-force here, seemingly unaffected and oblivious to the barbarism of war. The tendency manifested in this letter to represent the African American as a source of natural primitivism in a hostile and alienating world has a long and problematic history, of course, and that tradition of thought as applied to the 'Celt' conditioned the reception of Dylan Thomas himself during his American tours of the 1950s.[32] By 1945 Waller's presence in Belsen would not have been quite as incongruous as Thomas suggests, however, for many African Americans were involved in the liberation of concentration camps. Paul Gilroy has drawn attention to several examples of concentration camp inmates being liberated by black American troops, and notes 'that these meetings were memorable precisely because they were the first occasions on which a black person had been beheld'.[33] The testimonies of Jewish survivors recounting their encounter with African American GIs embody 'the unity and sameness of the human species' for Gilroy, and are 'all the more valuable for being offered from the twentieth-century core of radical evil'.[34] In Wales, the moments of cultural contact and exchange were obviously less dramatic. Yet, as Ralph Ellison's short stories testify and as Dylan Thomas's letter suggests, the intellectual, cultural and political range of African America extended out to Europe's western periphery. If African American soldiers were departing from Cardiff on their journey home in 1945, their legacy and example would continue to influence the ways in which the peoples of Europe made and remade themselves in the decades to come.

# Notes

## Introduction

1. John Ellis, *Investiture: Royal Ceremony and National Identity in Wales, 1911–1969* (Cardiff: University of Wales Press, 2008). Jacqueline Jenkinson, *Black 1919: Riots, Racism and Resistance in Imperial Britain* (Liverpool: Liverpool University Press, 2009). Neil Evans, 'Red summers 1917–19', *History Today*, 51, 2 (February 2001), pp. 28–33.
2. Paul Gilroy's widely cited account is misleading in that it gives the impression that Gandhi, Tonnies and others were at the conference. Paul Gilroy, *The Black Atlantic* (Cambridge MA.: Harvard University Press, 1993), p. 144. For detailed accounts see: Michael Biddis, 'The Universal Races Congress of 1911', *Race*, 13, 1 (1971), 37–46; Paul Rich, 'The baptism of a new era: the 1911 Universal Races Congress and the liberal ideology of race', *Ethnic and Racial Studies*, 7, 4 (October 1984), 534–50; Ulysses G. Weatherly, 'The first Universal Races Congress', *The American Journal of Sociology*, 17, 3 (November 1911), 315–28; and Duane J. Corpis and Ian Christopher Fletcher (eds), 'Another world was possible: a century of movements', special issue of *Radical History Review*, 92 (spring 2005).
3. Elliott M. Rudwick, 'W. E. B. Du Bois and the Universal Races Congress of 1911', *The Phylon Quarterly*, 20, 4 (1959), 372–8. W. E. B. Du Bois, 'The first Universal Races Congress' (1911), in Eric J. Sundquist (ed.), *The Oxford W. E. B. Du Bois Reader* (Oxford: Oxford University Press, 1996), pp. 55–9.
4. Quoted in Rudwick, 'W. E. B. Du Bois', 378.
5. Rich, 'Baptism of a new era'.
6. Quoted by Biddis, 'The Universal Races Congress', 45.
7. The papers were all published in a volume edited 'for the Congress Executive' by Gustav Spiller. *Papers on Inter-Racial Problems Communicated to the First Universal Races Congress held at the University of London, July 26–29, 1911* (London: P. S. King, and Boston: The Peace Foundation, 1911). Du Bois's paper is on pp. 348–64, followed by Hoggan's paper on pp. 364–7. While both Du Bois

and Hoggan delivered their papers at the conference many of the contributors to
Spiller's volume were not present at the conference itself.

8   Frances Hoggan, 'The Negro problem in relation to white women', in Gustav
    Spiller (ed.), *Papers on Inter-Racial Problems Communicated to the First
    Universal Races Congress*, p. 366.

9   Hoggan, 'The Negro problem in relation to white women', p. 366.

10  Spiller (ed.), *Papers on Inter-Racial Problems*, p. 35.

11  W. E. B. Du Bois, 'The Negro race in the United States of America', in Spiller
    (ed.), *Papers on Inter-Racial Problems*, p. 364.

12  See Kevin Gaines's discussion of this theme in nineteenth-century African
    American thought in *Uplifting the Race: Black Leadership, Politics, and Culture
    in the Twentieth Century* (Chapel Hill: University of North Carolina Press, 1996),
    pp. 128–9.

13  W. E. B. Du Bois, *Dusk of Dawn* (1940), in *Writings: The Suppression of the
    African Slave Trade, The Souls of Black Folk, Dusk of Dawn*, ed. Nathan I.
    Huggins (New York: Library of America, 1986), p. 717. David Levering Lewis,
    *W. E. B. Du Bois: Biography of a Race 1868–1919* (New York: Henry Holt and
    Co., 1993), pp. 370–1, 452, 454, 456, 524.

14  Du Bois, *Dusk of Dawn*, p. 717. W. E. B. Du Bois, *The Autobiography of W. E. B.
    Du Bois: A Soliloquy on Viewing my Life from the Last Decade of its First Century*
    ([1968] New York: International Publishers, 1980), p. 220.

15  The best introductory account of Hoggan's life is by Neil McIntyre, 'Frances
    Hoggan – doctor of medicine, pioneer physician, patriot and philanthropist',
    *Brycheiniog*, 13 (2007), 127–46. See also Onfel Thomas, *Frances Elizabeth
    Hoggan, 1843–1927* (privately printed, Brecon, 1970).

16  Quoted by W. Gareth Evans, *Education and Female Emancipation: The Welsh
    Experience, 1847–1914* (Cardiff: University of Wales Press, 1990), p. 5.

17  W. Gareth Evans, *Education*. Jane Aaron, *Pur fel y Dur: Y Gymraes yn Llên
    Menywod y Bedwaredd Ganrif ar Bymtheg* (Caerdydd: Gwasg Prifysgol Cymru,
    1998).

18  Quoted by W. Gareth Evans, *Education*, p. 128.

19  Quoted by W. Gareth Evans, in ibid., p. 128.

20  Quoted by W. Gareth Evans, in ibid., p. 129.

21  Ibid.

22  Frances Hoggan, 'American Negro women during their first fifty years of
    freedom', *The Individualist* (September–October 1913), 72– 5. Gaines, *Uplifting
    the Race*, p. 129.

23  Hoggan, 'American Negro women', 74–5.

24  Ibid., 75.

25  Ibid., 73.

26  Ibid., 74.

27  Ibid. For useful contextual material on the gendered dimension of 'uplift' see Kate
    Dossett, *Bridging Race Divides: Black Nationalism, Feminism, and Integration
    in the United States, 1896–1935* (Gainesville: Florida University Press, 2008).

28  Gaines, *Uplifting*, p 141. Evelyn Brooks Higginbotham, *Righteous Discontent:
    The Women's Movement in the Black Baptist Church, 1880–1920* (Cambridge,
    MA: Harvard University Press, 1993), p. 101.

29   Hoggan, 'American Negro women', 75.
30   Quoted in Gaines, *Uplifting*, p. 78.
31   Hoggan, 'American Negro women', 75.
32   Luke Gibbons, 'Peripheral modernities: national and global in a post-colonial frame', *Nineteenth-Century Contexts: An Interdisciplinary Journal*, 29, 2 (2007), 274.
33   Gilroy, *The Black Atlantic*, p. 145.
34   Susan Manning and Andrew Taylor, 'Introduction: what is transatlantic literary studies', in Manning and Taylor (eds), *Transatlantic Literary Studies: A Reader* (Edinburgh: Edinburgh University Press, 2007), p. 1.
35   Lucy Evans, 'The Black Atlantic: exploring Gilroy's legacy', *Atlantic Studies*, 6, 2 (August 2009), 264.
36   Paul Gilroy, 'Nationalism, History and Ethnic Absolutism', *History Workshop Journal*, 30,1 (1990), 116.
37   Ibid.
38   Raymond Williams, 'The culture of nations' (1983), *Who Speaks for Wales? Nation, Culture, Identity*, ed. Daniel Williams (Cardiff: University of Wales Press, 2003), p. 193.
39   See my discussion of this in Daniel G. Wiliams, *Ethnicity and Cultural Authority: From Arnold to Du Bois* (Edinburgh: Edinburgh University Press, 2006), pp. 10–11.
40   Houston A. Baker Jr, *Turning South Again: Re-Thinking Modernism / Re-Reading Booker T.* (Durham, NC: Duke University Press, 2001), p. 85.
41   See for example, Chris Williams, 'Problematizing Wales: an exploration in historiography and postcoloniality' in Jane Aaron and Chris Williams (eds), *Postcolonial Wales* (Cardiff: University of Wales Press, 2005) pp. 3–17.
42   Henry Louis Gates Jr, *Loose Canons: Notes on the Culture Wars* (New York: Oxford University Press, 1992), p. 36.
43   Ibid., pp. 39, 38.
44   Ralph Ellison, 'The world and the jug', in *Shadow and Act* ([1953] New York: Quality Paperback Book Club, 1994), pp. 116, 141.
45   Kate Roberts, *Crefft y Stori Fer* (Llandysul: Cyhoeddiadau'r Clwb Llyfrau Cymraeg, 1949), p. 10. See Tudur Hallam's discussion of this debate in *Canon ein Llên: Saunders Lewis, R. M. Jones ac Alan Llwyd* (Caerdydd: Gwasg Prifysgol Cymru, 2007), p. 150.
46   Ellison, 'The world and the jug', p. 108. Charlotte Williams, *Sugar and Slate* (Aberystwyth: *Planet*, 2002), p. 176. It is worth noting in this connection that the experiences of immigrants and minorities in Wales has been a central concern of the African American anthropologist Glenn Jordan at the University of Glamorgan. Jordan was a student of the African American sociologist St Clair Drake at Stanford University. Drake spent two years from 1947–9 analysing the 'Black Britons' of Cardiff's Butetown and wrote his Ph.D. thesis on that subject. Jordan followed his mentor's example in coming to Cardiff and stayed on to become director of the Butetown History and Arts Centre. See Charlotte Williams, 'The reticent ethnographer: a profile of Glenn Jordan', *Planet: The Welsh Internationalist* (April / May 2006), 41–53.

47  Barbara Foley, *Spectres of 1919: Class and Nation in the Making of the New Negro* (Chicago: University of Illinois Press, 2003), p. 160.

48  Quoted in John Davies, *A History of Wales* ([1990 in Welsh] London: Penguin, 1993), p. 422

49  Ibid., p. 427.

50  On Caradoc Evans, see Hywel Teifi Edwards, '"Y Pentre Gwyn" and "Manteg": from blessed plot to hotspot' in Alyce Von Rothkirch and Daniel Williams (eds), *Beyond the Difference: Welsh Literature in Comparative Contexts* (Cardiff: University of Wales Press, 2004), pp. 15–18. W. E. B. Du Bois, 'Two novels', in Henry Louis Gates Jr. et al. (eds.), *The Norton Anthology of African American Literature* (New York: Norton, 1997), pp. 759–60.

51  W. E. B. Du Bois, 'Books: Van Vechten's *Nigger Heaven*' (1926), in *Writings* (New York: The Library of America, 1986), p. 1216.

52  Gilroy, *Black Atlantic*, p. 145

53  Gates Jr, *Loose Canons*, p. 39. As Jane Aaron notes, drawing on Gates's example, a similar argument could be made in relation to attempts at persuading 'stateless nations' that they should abandon 'national status', for 'if they did so they would but doubly privilege nation-states that happen to be preconstituted'. Aaron, 'Bardic anti-colonialism', in Aaron and Williams (eds), *Postcolonial Wales*, p. 156.

54  Aaron, 'Bardic anti-colonialism', pp. 155–6.

55  Cornel West, 'On black–brown relations', in *The Cornel West Reader* (New York: Basic Books, 1999), p. 503.

56  Gates Jr, *Loose Canons*, p. 39.

57  John Redmond, 'Slanderous tongues', *New Welsh Review*, 89 (autumn 2010), 41.

58  John Goodby and Christopher Wigginton, *Dylan Thomas: New Casebooks* (Basingstoke: Palgrave, 2001), p. 12.

59  Eric Hobsbawm, 'Interview: world distempers', *New Left Review* II, 61 (January/February 2010), 148–9.

60  As I was completing this volume Chris Evans's *Slave Wales: The Welsh and Atlantic Slavery 1660–1850* (Cardiff: University of Wales Press, 2010) appeared which offers a useful prehistory for the analyses in this book.

61  Chris Williams, 'Problematizing Wales', p. 11.

62  Francis Mulhern, *The Present Lasts a Long Time: Essays in Cultural Politics* (Cork: Cork University Press, 1998), p. 15.

63  Declan Kiberd, 'The view from Enniskillen', *New Left Review* II, 3 (May/June 2000), 155.

64  Joe Cleary, *Outrageous Fortune: Capital and Culture in Modern Ireland* (Dublin: Field Day Publications, 2006), p. 45.

65  Ibid., p. 46.

66  Ibid.

67  There is a debate regarding the appropriate use of the term 'subaltern'. I use it here in its original Gramscian sense to designate those persons socially, politically and geographically outside of the hegemonic power structure. Hoggan is, of course, in many ways in a position of power, but her struggles on behalf of women in Britain, India and African America may be traced to her own formation as a woman in

Wales. She embodies some of the tensions and contradictions involved in looking at Wales through a post-colonial lens. For a lucid account of the 'subaltern' in relation to discourses of gender and class see Ania Loomba, *Colonialism/Postcolonialism* (London: Routledge, 1998), pp. 231–45.

68  Luke Gibbons, 'Ireland and the colonization of theory', *Interventions: International Journal of Postcolonial Studies*, 1, 1 (1998), 27.

69  Charlotte Williams, 'The Celtic nations and the African Americas', *Comparative American Studies*, 8, 4 (December 2010), 324. This issue of *Comparative American Studies* contains responses by Werner Sollors, Charlotte Williams and Ishmael Reed to Daniel G. Williams ed., 'Special issue on the Celtic nations and the African Americas', *Comparative American Studies*, 8, 2 (June 2010).

70  James Baldwin, 'If Black English isn't a language tell me what is?' (1979), in *Collected Essays* (New York: Library of America, 1998), p. 780.

71  Michael Hechter, *Internal Colonialism: The Celtic Fringe in British National Development 1536–1966* (London: Routledge, 1975), pp. xv–xvii.

72  Alberto Toscano, 'The spectre of analogy', *New Left Review* II, 66 (November/December 2010),153.

73  Ibid.

74  T. Robin Chapman, 'Adolygiad o Daniel G. Williams, gol., *Canu Caeth: Y Cymry a'r Affro-Americaniad*', *Taliesin*, 141 (gaeaf 2010), 135–6.

75  Ross Posnock, *Color and Culture: Black Writers and the Making of the Modern Intellectual* (Cambridge, MA.: Harvard University Press, 1998), p. 21.

76  Stuart Hall, 'Negotiating Caribbean identities', *New Left Review* I, 209 (January–February 1995), 8.

77  A further topic for potential study, to which I do not give much attention in this volume, would be those cases where the comparison is made (often with racist overtones) by individuals who are neither Welsh nor African American. For example, when the English author Rebecca West was asked in America what the prime minister Lloyd George was like, she answered:

'Oh, you can't describe him – you see he's a Welshman.'

'Oh' said the interlocutor, 'and what are Welshmen like?' to which Miss West replied: 'Well, they are an emotional race noted for their music and their revival meetings.' 'Ah, I see,' said the American; 'They are, as it were, your British Niggers.'

The story is told by Clough Williams-Ellis, 'The teaching of art and architecture in Wales', *The Transactions of the Honourable Society of Cymmrodorion, Session 1923–1924* (1925), p. 69. See Peter Lord, *Y Chwaer-Dduwies: Celf, Crefft a'r Eisteddfod* (Llandysul: Gomer, 1992), p. 82.

## Chapter 1

1  W. D. Howells, *Seven English Cities* (New York: Harper and Brothers, 1909), p. 142.

2  Ibid., pp. 144–5.

[3] Eric Lott, *Love and Theft: Blackface Minstrelsy and the American Working Class* (Oxford: Oxford University Press, 1993). David R. Roediger, *The Wages of Whiteness: Race and the Making of the American Working Class* (London: Verso, 1991), pp. 115–25.

[4] W. T. Lhamon, Jr (ed.), *Jump Jim Crow: Lost Plays, Lyrics, and Street Prose of the First Atlantic Popular Culture* (Cambridge, MA; London : Harvard University Press, 2003). Lott, *Love and Theft*.

[5] In much of the literature on the nineteenth century 'anti-slavery' and 'abolitionism' are used as virtually synonymous terms. The index entry for 'abolitionism' in Robert Levine's *Martin Delany, Frederick Douglass and the Politics of Representative Identity* (Chapel Hill: University of North Caroline Press, 1997), for instance, reads 'see Antislavery'. R. J. M. Blackett's seminal *Building an Antislavery Wall* is subtitled *Black Americans in the Atlantic Abolitionist Movement* (Baton Rouge: Louisiana State University Press, 1983). Historians traditionally distinguish between moderate antislavery reformers or gradualists, who concentrated on stopping the spread of slavery, and radical abolitionists or immediatists, whose demands for unconditional emancipation often merged with a concern for black civil rights. There are further tensions between emphases and philosophies of justice and political action within both movements, some of which will be explored in the course of this chapter. 'Anti-slavery' is generally considered the more capacious term as it can include abolitionists. 'Abolitionist' is a more specific term, for many advocates of anti-slavery were not abolitionists.

[6] Quoted in Douglas A. Lorimer, *Colour, Class and the Victorians* (Leicester: Leicester University Press, 1978), pp. 63–4.

[7] Sarah Meer, 'Competing representations: Douglass, the Ethiopian Serenaders, and Ethnic Exhibition in London', in Martin Crawford and Alan Rice (eds), *Liberating Sojourn: Frederick Douglass and Transatlantic Reform* (Athens: The University of Georgia Press, 1999), p. 162.

[8] Lorimer, *Colour, Class*, pp. 86–7.

[9] Quoted in R. J. M. Blackett, 'Cracks in the antislavery wall: Frederick Douglass's second visit to England and the coming of the Civil War', in Crawford and Rice (eds), *Liberating Sojourn*, p. 200.

[10] Quoted by Blackett, 'Cracks', p. 200.

[11] Frederick Douglass to Francis Jackson, 24 January 1846. Frederick Douglass Papers, Library of Congress, Washington, DC. Douglass is alluding ironically to the way in which his appearance diverged form the 'pure' (but completely inauthentic) 'Negro' of the minstrel stage, and to the fact that he was himself 'half-Negro' – born of a black mother and white father.

[12] Lhamon, *Jump Jim Crow*, pp. 90–1.

[13] See Joy Jordan-Lake, *Whitewashing Uncle Tom's Cabin: Nineteenth-Century Women Novelists Respond to Stowe* (Vanderbilt: Vanderbilt University Press, 2005), and Sarah Meer, *Uncle Tom Mania: Slavery, Minstrelsy, and Transatlantic Culture in the 1850s* (Athens: University of Georgia Press, 2005), for more on the connections between *Uncle Tom's Cabin* and minstrel conventions.

[14] Harriet Beecher Stowe, *Uncle Tom's Cabin* ([1852] London: Everyman's Library, 1995), p. 11.

15  Stowe, *Uncle Tom's Cabin*, pp. 267–8.

16  Gerald Early, *The Culture of Bruising: Essays on Prizefighting, Literature and Modern American Culture* (Hopewell, NJ: The Ecco Press, 1994), p. 158.

17  Ibid., p. 158.

18  Ibid., p. 157.

19  Richard Yarborough's phrase in 'Strategies of black characterization in *Uncle Tom's Cabin* and the early Afro-American novel', in Eric Sundquist (ed.), *New Essays on Uncle Tom's Cabin* (Cambridge: Cambridge University Press, 1986), p. 168.

20  W. D. Howells, 'My favorite novelist and his best book', in E. Cady (ed.), *W. D. Howells as Critic* (London: Routledge, 1973), p. 275.

21  Frederick Douglass, *Autobiographies: Narrative of the Life of Frederick Douglass and American Slave* (1845), *My Bondage and My Freedom* (1855), *Life and Times of Frederick Douglass* (1893), ed. H. L. Gates Jr (New York: The Library of America, 1994), p. 726.

22  Robert S. Levine, 'Uncle Tom's Cabin in the Frederick Douglass' Paper: an analysis of reception', *American Literature*, 64, 1 (March 1992), 75.

23  *Frederick Douglass Paper*, 11 March 1853, 1, and 13 March 1853, 3. Quoted in Levine, 'Uncle Tom', 76.

24  *Frederick Douglass Paper*, 31 December 1852. Quoted in Melinda Gray, 'Uncle Tom's Welsh dress: ethnicity, authority and translation', in Alyce Von Rothkirch and Daniel Williams (eds.), *Beyond the Difference: Welsh Literature in Comparative Contexts* (Cardiff: University of Wales Press, 2004) p. 178.

25  *Y Cyfaill o'r Hen Wlad*, 16, 183 (Mawrth 1853), 123. Quoted by Melinda Gray, 'Uncle Tom's Welsh dress', p. 179.

26  The details of the Welsh translations published as books are as follows: Hugh Williams, *Caban F'Ewyrth Twm* (Llundain: John Cassell, 1853); William Rees ('Gwilym Hiraethog'), *Aelwyd F'Ewyrth Robert: Neu Hanes Caban F'Ewythr Tomos* (Dinbych: Gwasg Gee, 1853); Thomas Levi, *Crynodeb o Gaban 'Newyrth Tom; Neu, Fywyd Negroaidd yn America* (Abertawy: J. Rosser, 1853); Robert Everett, *Caban F'Ewythr Twm; Neu Fywyd ym mhlith yr Iselradd* (Remsen, NY: John R, Everett, 1854). On Everett, see Jerry Hunter, *I Ddeffro Ysbryd y Wlad: Robert Everett a'r Ymgyrch yn erbyn Caethwasanaeth Americanaidd* (Llanrwst: Gwasg Carreg Gwalch, 2007).

27  Welsh translations had appeared of Ukawsaw Gronniosaw (John Albert), *A Narrative of the Most remarkable Particulars in the Life of James Albert Ukawsaw Gronniosaw, an African Prince, As related by himself* (1772) and John Marrant, *A Narrative of the Lord's Wonderful Dealings with John Marrant* (1785). Gronniosaw was translated by Wales's leading hymn writer William Williams, Pantycelyn (1717–91). No translator is mentioned in the case of Marrant. See E. Wyn James, 'Morgan John Rhys a Chaethwasiaeth Americanaidd', in D. G. Williams (ed.), *Canu Caeth: Y Cymry a'r Affro-Americaniaid* (Llandysul: Gomer, 2010), pp. 2–25. And E. Wyn James, 'Welsh Ballads and American Slavery', *The Welsh Journal of Religious History*, 2 (2007) 59–86. For the historical context of these works, and accounts of the period before this study commences, see Chris Evans, *Slave Wales: The Welsh and Atlantic Slavery 1660–1850* (Cardiff: University of Wales Press, 2010).

[28]  A translation of E. G. Millward's phrase in *Cenedl o Bobl Ddewrion: Agweddau ar Lenyddiaeth Oes Victoria* (Llandysul: Gwasg Gomer, 1991), p. 93.

[29]  Early, *Culture of Bruising*, p. 159.

[30]  Quoted by Gareth Elwyn Jones, 'Llyfrau Gleision 1847', in Prys Morgan (ed.), *Brad y Llyfrau Gleision* (Llandysul: Gomer, 1991), p. 26. This historical overview is a synthesis of many sources. Of particular relevance: chapter 8 of John Davies, *A History of Wales* ([1990 in Welsh] London: Penguin, 1993); Ieuan Gwynedd Jones, *Communities* (Llandysul: Gomer, 1987); Hywel Teifi Edwards, *Gŵyl Gwalia: Yr Eisteddfod yn Oes Victoria*, (Llandysul: Gwasg Gomer, 1980) and *Codi'r Hen Wlad yn ei Hôl* (Llandysul: Gwasg Gomer, 1990).

[31]  Quoted in Robert Owen Jones, *Hir Oes i'r Iaith: Agweddau ar Hanes y Gymraeg a'r Gymdeithas* (Llandysul: Gomer, 1997), p. 270.

[32]  See especially the works by Hywel Teifi Edwards above, and Gwyneth Tyson Roberts, *The Language of the Blue Books: The Perfect Instrument of Empire* (Cardiff: University of Wales Press, 1998).

[33]  Dale E. Patterson, *Up from Bondage: The Literatures of Russian and African American Soul* (Durham, NC: Duke University Press, 2000), pp. 36–7.

[34]  Patterson, *Up from Bondage*, p. 37.

[35]  Gwyn A. Williams, *When Was Wales? A History of the Welsh* (London: Black Raven Press, 1985), p. 206.

[36]  Paul O'Leary, *Immigration and Integration: The Irish in Wales, 1798–1922* (Cardiff: University of Wales Press, 2000).

[37]  Gwyn A. Williams, *When Was Wales?*, p. 206.

[38]  Quoted in Edwards, *Gŵyl Gwalia*, p. 236. See, for example, Ieuan Gwyllt, 'Purdeb Chwaeth Mewn Cerddoriaeth', *Y Cerddor Cymraeg*, 2, 25 (1 Mawrth 1867), 4–5.

[39]  Quoted in Edwards, *Gŵyl Gwalia*, p. 238, my translation.

[40]  Quoted by Jen Wilson, 'Doing the plantation walkaround skeedaddle', *Planet* 177 (June/July 2006), 80.

[41]  Stowe, *Uncle Tom's Cabin*, p. 493.

[42]  Douglass, *My Bondage and My Freedom* (1855) in *Autobiographies*, ed. H. L. Gates Jr, p. 376. For example, there is not a single reference to Wales in the excellent collection of essays on Douglass in Britain, Martin Crawford and Alan Rice (eds), *Liberating Sojourn*. There is much work to do on the presence of African American abolitionists in nineteenth-century Wales. See, for example, Geoffrey Evans's account of W. A. Jackson (Jefferson Davis's 'runaway Negro coachman') at Aberdare in 1863 in 'The amusement of the people – popular entertainment in Aberdare before moving pictures', *Old Aberdare*, 7 (1993), 48–77. See also the account by Bill Jones and David Wyatt of an English-language slave narrative published in Cardiff, *Caethwas Ffoedig yng Nghaerdydd: Hanes William A. Hall a Diddymiaeth Gymreig 186–65*, in D. G. Williams (ed.), *Canu Caeth*, pp. 39–62. See also chapter 3 on 'The Welsh abolitionists', in Alan Llwyd, *Cymru Ddu/Black Wales: A History* (Cardiff: Hughes a'i Fab, 2005).

[43]  On Douglass in Ireland, see Lee Jenkins, 'Beyond the pale: Frederick Douglass in Cork', *The Irish Review*, 24 (autumn 1999), 80–95, and, on Scotland, Alisdair Pettinger, 'Send back the money: Douglass and the Free Church of Scotland', in Crawford and Rice (eds), *Liberating Sojourn*, pp. 31–55.

44  Supplement to *The Carnarvon and Denbigh Herald*, 16, 826, Saturday 17 October 1846, 1, column 6.

45  'Gwrth-Gaethwasiaeth – Cyfarfod Mawr Gwrexham', *Yr Amserau*, 22 Hydref 1846, 2, column 1.

46  Douglass recalls these debates in chapter 24, 'Twenty-one months in Great Britain', in *My Bondage and My Freedom*.

47  See Pettinger, 'Send back'.

48  William Lloyd Garrison, *No Union With Slave Holders 1841–1849: The Letters of William Lloyd Garrison*, vol. 3, ed. Walter M. Merrill (Cambridge, MA: Harvard University Press, 1973), p. 439.

49  *Yr Amserau*, 22 Hydref 1846, 2, column 3. Supplement to the *Carnarvon and Denbigh Herald*, 17 October 1846, p2, column 6. William Lloyd Garrison, *William Lloyd Garrison 1805–1879: The Story of His Life Told By His Children*, vol. 3, *1841–1860* ([1889] New York: Negro Universities Press, 1969), p. 176.

50  Garrison, 'To Sarah Hilditch, Nov. 4, 1846', in *No Union With Slave Holders 1841–1849: The Letters of William Lloyd Garrison*, vol. 3, ed. Walter M. Merrill (Cambridge, MA: Harvard University Press, 1973), p. 450.

51  I am grateful to the late Oswald Davies for this information, kindly passed on to me by his son, the author Grahame Davies.

52  Supplement to the *Carnarvon and Denbigh Herald*, Saturday 17 October 1846, 2, columns 5–6.

53  See Frank M. Kirkland, 'Enslavement, moral suasion and struggles for recognition: Frederick Douglass's answer to the question – "What is Enlightenment"', in Bill E. Lawson and Frank M. Kirkland (eds), *Frederick Douglass: A Critical Reader* (Oxford: Blackwell, 1999), pp. 243–310.

54  Frederick Douglass, *The Frederick Douglass Papers. Series One: Speeches, Debates and Interviews*, 5 vols, ed. John Blassingame (New Haven: Yale University Press, 1979). I, p. 108.

55  Another plank of the Garrisonians' position, which I do not have space to explore in detail, was their view that the American Constitution was an inherently pro-slavery document and needed to be abolished. This was a position embraced by Douglass during his visit to Britain. His break with the Garrisonians following his return to America led to a shift in his thought towards a view of the Constitution as anti-slavery. See William S. McFeely, *Frederick Douglass* (New York: Norton, 1991), pp. 168–73.

56  For a nuanced and complicating account of the of the tensions between pacificsm, moral suasionism and direct action within Welsh anti-slavery, see Hunter, *I Ddeffro*, pp. 129–70.

57  'Cyfarfod Liverpool ar Gaethwasanaeth Americanaidd', *Yr Amserau*, 22 Hydref 1846, 2, column 5.

58  Audrey Fisch, *American Slaves in Victorian England: Abolitionist Politics in Popular Literature and Culture* (Cambridge: Cambridge University Press, 2000).

59  Supplement to the *Carnarvon and Denbigh Herald*, 2, column 3.

60  Ibid., 2, column 1.

61  Quoted by Gray, 'Uncle Tom's Welsh dress', p. 178.

62  *Frederick Douglass Paper* (Rochester, New York), 3 November 1854.

[63] 'Literary Notices', *Frederick Douglass Paper*, 12 October 1855.

[64] On Ward, see *http://docsouth.unc.edu/wards/summary.html* (accessed September 2006). Samuel Ringgold Ward, *Autobiography of a Fugitive Negro: His Anti-Slavery Labours in the United States, Canada and England* (London: John Snow, 1855), p. 385.

[65] Ibid., p. 392.

[66] Ibid., pp. 393–5.

[67] Ibid., p. 385.

[68] Ibid., p. 396.

[69] Quoted in Jane Aaron, *Pur fel y Dur: Y Gymraes yn Llên Menywod y Bedwaredd Ganrif ar Bymtheg* (Caerdydd: Gwasg Prifysgol Cymru, 1998), p. 100.

[70] Quoted in ibid., p. 101.

[71] Ward, *Autobiography of a Fugitive Negro*, p. 396.

[72] Ibid., p. 392.

[73] Ibid., pp. 98–9.

[74] See H. Teifi Edwards, *Codi'r Hen Wlad*, and for African Americans, Kevin K. Gaines, *Uplifting the Race: Black Leadership, Politics, and Culture in the Twentieth Century* (Chapel Hill: University of North Carolina Press, 1996).

[75] Leonard Harris, 'Honor and Insurrection: A Short Story about Why John Brown was Right and Frederick Douglass was Wrong', in Lawson and Kirkland (eds), *Frederick Douglass: A Critical Reader*, p. 228.

[76] Supplement to *The Carnarvon and Denbigh Herald*, 16, 826, Saturday 17 October 1846, 2, column 5.

[77] Hilditch to Maria Chapman, 31 October 1846, quoted in Blassingame, 'Introduction' to *Frederick Douglass Papers*, series 1, vol. 1, p. liv.

[78] See Levine, *Martin Delany, Frederick Douglass*.

[79] Douglass, *My Bondage*, in *Autobiographies*, pp. 364–5.

[80] Douglass, *Narrative*, in *Autobiographies*, pp. 12, 7.

[81] Douglass, *My Bondage*, p. 366.

[82] Ibid., p. 367.

[83] *Yr Amserau*, 22 Hydref 1846, 2, column 1.

[84] Supplement to the *Carnarvon and Denbigh Herald*, 16, 826, Saturday 17 October 1846, 2, column 1.

[85] Terry Baxter, *Frederick Douglass's Curious Audiences: Ethos in the Age of the Consumable Subject* (New York: Routledge, 2004), p. 89.

[86] See chapters 13 and 14 of McFeely, *Frederick Douglass*.

[87] Henry Louis Gates Jr, *Figures in Black: Words, Signs and the 'Racial' Self* (Oxford: Oxford University Press, 1987), pp. 105–108.

[88] Douglass, *My Bondage*, p. 367.

[89] *Y Dyngarwr* was one of the many enterprises initiated by the Congregationalist minister, Robert Everett, editor of *Y Cenhadwr Americanaidd* (The American Messenger), which received attention in the *Frederick Douglass Paper*. Everett also adapted Hugh Williams's translation of *Uncle Tom's Cabin* for a specifically American audience. In an MA thesis, completed in 1914, on the Welsh in Oneida County, New York – the 'burned over' district recently analysed by Milton Sernett as a hotbed of abolitionist activity – Paul Evans argued that, while abolitionism

would emerge as a major force in Welsh-American society from the 1850s onwards, there was little interest in the subject in the 1840s. Everett published *Y Dyngarwr* for one year only, sending free copies to the hundreds of Welsh ministers in America, and used the paper to introduce the leading voices of the emergent abolitionist movement to a Welsh-speaking audience. Jerry Hunter complicates this picture by drawing attention to the range of positions held by Welsh Americans in *I Ddeffro* and *Sons of Arthur*. On the broader context see Milton Sernett, *North Star Country: Upstate New York and the Crusade for African American Freedom* (Syracuse: Syracuse University Press, 2002).

90   'Y Gymdeithas Wrthgaethiwol Americanaidd', *Y Dyngarwr*, 1, 6, 15 Mehefin 1843, 43. The speech appears in Blassingame, *Frederick Douglass Papers*, vol. 1, pp. 20–1.

91   Douglass, *Life and Times of Frederick Douglass* (1893), in *Autobiographies*, p. 671.

92   See Blassingame, *Frederick Douglass Papers*, series 1, vol. 1, p. 20.

93   Ibid., vol. 2, p. 50.

94   Maria Diedrich, *Love Across Color Lines: Ottilie Assing and Frederick Douglass* (New York: Hill and Wang, 1999), p. 142.

95   Paul Giles, *Virtual Americas: Transnational Fiction and the Transatlantic Imaginary* (Durham, NC: Duke University Press, 2002), p. 15.

96   Ibid.

97   Daniel. G. Williams, *Ethnicity and Cultural Authority: from Arnold to Du Bois* (Edinburgh: Edinburgh University Press, 2006), pp. 10–11, and 'Introduction: Celticism and the Black Atlantic', *Comparative American Studies: Special Issue on the Celtic Nations and the African Americas*, 8, 2 (June 2010) 81–7. See Werner Sollors (ed.), *Multilingual America: Transnationalism, Ethnicity and the Languages of American Literature* (New York: New York University Press, 1998), and Marc Shell (ed.), *American Babel: Literatures of the United States from Abnaki to Zuni* (Cambridge, MA: Harvard University Press, 2002).

98   A translation of E. G. Millward's phrase in *Cenedl o Bobl Ddewrion*, p. 93.

99   See, for example, Terry Baxter's study, *Frederick Douglass's Curious Audiences*.

100  Eric J. Sundquist, *To Wake the Nations: Race in the Making of American Literature* (Cambridge, MA: Harvard University Press, 1993), p. 89. Robert B. Stepto, 'Narration in Frederick Douglass' narrative of 1845', in W. A. Andrews (ed.), *African American Autobiography: A Collection of Critical Essays* (Englewood Cliffs, NJ: Prentice-Hall, 1993), p. 35.

101  Douglass, *Narrative*, in *Autobiographies*, p. 37.

102  Ibid., pp. 92–3.

103  William A. Andrews (ed.), *North Carolina Slave Narratives* (Chapel Hill: University of North Carolina Press, 2003), p. 7.

104  Moses Roper, *A Narrative of the Adventures and Escape of Moses Roper* (1838), in William A. Andrews et al. (eds), *North Carolina Slave Narratives*, p. 66.

105  Helen Thomas, *Romanticism and Slave Narratives: Transatlantic Testimonies* (Cambridge: Cambridge University Press, 2000), pp. 147–8.

106  Roper, *A Narrative*, p. 66.

107  Henry Louis Gates Jr, *The Signifying Monkey: A Theory of African-American Literary Criticism* (Oxford: Oxford University Press, 1988), p. 131.

[108] Moses Roper, 'To the Committee of the British and Foreign Antislavery Society' (9 May 1844), in C. Ripley (ed.), *The Black Abolitionist Papers*, vol. 1, *The British Isles 1830–1865* (Chapel Hill: The University of North Carolina Press, 1985), p. 134.

[109] See Andrews et al. (eds), *North Carolina Slave Narratives*, p. 7. Andrews refers to 'a translation into Celtic'. There is no language known as 'Celtic'. The translation was into Welsh.

[110] Moses Roper, *Hanes Bywyd a Ffoedigaeth Moses Roper o Gaethiwed Americanaidd* (Llanelli: Rees a Thomas, 1841) (an identical edition was published in Aberystwyth by J. Cox in 1842), p. 2.

[111] See Ripley (ed.), *The Black Abolitionist Papers*, vol. 1, pp. 136–7, n.1.

[112] Moses Roper, *Narrative of the Adventures and Escape of Moses Roper, from American Slavery. With an Appendix, Containing a List of Places Visited by the Author in Great Britain and Ireland and the British Isles; and Other Matter* (Berwick-upon-Tweed: published for the author and printed at the Warder Office, 1848), pp. 63–7.

[113] See Robert Owen Jones, *Hir Oes i'r Iaith: Agweddau ar Hanes y Gymraeg a'r Gymdeithas* (Llandysul: Gomer, 1997), pp. 240–1.

[114] Ward, *Autobiography of a Fugitive Negro*, p. 385.

[115] Ibid., p. 395.

[116] Quoted in G. Tyson Roberts, *The Language of the Blue Books*, pp. 23–4.

[117] Quoted in ibid., p .23.

[118] Quoted in ibid., p .24.

[119] Quoted in ibid., p .203.

[120] Gates Jr, *Signifying*, p. 131.

[121] See Tyson Roberts, *The Language of the Blue Books*, p. 203. R. O. Jones, *Hir Oes i'r Iaith*, pp. 270, 272. 'Under the hatches' in the quotation above may also be a saying deriving from the slave ships.

[122] One of the particular ironies of the Blue Books report was that it was published during a golden age for Welsh publishing. Translations and religious texts abounded. See the diverse essays in Geraint Jenkins (ed.), *The Welsh Language and its Social Domains 1801–1911* (Cardiff: University of Wales Press, 2000).

[123] Roper, *Hanes*, p. 2.

[124] At the end of the eighteenth century, thanks to Griffith Jones's circulating schools and the Sunday schools, the majority of the Welsh people were literate in Welsh. According to Brinley Thomas, 'this was on the most remarkable literacy programmes in history', perhaps comparable to the literacy acquired by African Americans in the last twenty-five years of the nineteenth-century. Brinley Thomas, 'A cauldron of rebirth: population and the Welsh language in the nineteenth century', in G. Jenkins (ed.), *The Welsh Language and its Social Domains*, pp. 81–99.

[125] The details of the Welsh translations are listed in n. 26.

[126] Florine Thayer McCray, *The Life-Work of the Author of Uncle Tom's Cabin* (New York: Funk and Wagnalls, 1889), p. 114. See Gray, 'Uncle Tom's Welsh dress', p. 174.

[127] The chapter 'Marwolaeth' (Death) contains good examples of Levi's use of dialect.

[128]  Gray, 'Uncle Tom's Welsh dress', p. 185.

[129]  Millward, *Cenedl o Bobl Ddewrion*, p. 43.

[130]  See Prys Morgan, 'The gwerin of Wales: myth and reality', in Ian Hume and W. T. R. Pryce (eds), *The Welsh and their Country* (Llandysul: Gomer, 1986), p. 138. H. Teifi Edwards, 'Y Prifeirdd wedi'r Brad', in P. Morgan (ed.), *Brad y Llyfrau Gleision*, pp. 194–6.

[131]  Everett had changed the title to *Caban F'Ewythr Twm* by the time he published it as a book in 1854. It seems that Hugh Williams's title had become the accepted form by that point. Everett's initial choice of 'Bwthyn' remains intriguing. See Hunter, *I Ddeffro*, pp. 178–82.

[132]  Millward, *Cenedl*, p. 123.

[133]  Ioan Williams, 'Gwilym Hiraethog (William Rees, 1802–83), in H. Teifi Edwards (ed.), *A Guide to Welsh Literature 1800–1900* (Cardiff: Univeresity of Wales Press, 2000), pp. 62–3. See also Ioan Williams, *Capel A Chomin: Astudiaeth o Ffugchwedlau Pedwar Llenor Fictoraidd* (Caerdydd: Gwasg Prifysgol Cymru, 1989).

[134]  Francis Mulhern, 'Conrad's disavowals', *New Left Review*, 2, 38 (March/April 2006), 60.

[135]  The irony in this respect is that the success of Hiraethog's version of *Uncle Tom's Cabin* relied on a literate peasantry. The Welsh, as Jerry Hunter has noted, were more 'logo-centric' than the Irish peasantry during the same period. This was partly due to the different emphasis that Roman Catholics and Nonconformists placed on local vernaculars. The divisions between oral and print cultures are, therefore, more complex than Hiraethog's hearthside scene suggests, for writing and print had co-existed with oral transmission for some time in Welsh culture. For the historical and theoretical implications of this for Welsh literary studies, see Jerry Hunter and Richard Wyn Jones, 'O'r Chwith: Pa Mor Feirniadol yw Beirniadaeth Ôl-Fodern?, *Taliesin*, 92 (1995), 19.

[136]  Quoted in Aaron, *Pur fel y Dur*, p. 10.

[137]  Wilson J. Moses, *Afrotopia: The Roots of African American Popular History* (Cambridge: Cambridge University Press, 1998), p. 122.

[138]  Stowe, *Uncle Tom's Cabin*, p. 328.

[139]  Ibid., p. 321.

[140]  Rees, *Aelwyd F'Ewythr Robert*, p. 476.

[141]  In the language of literary theory, the reader 'interpellated' in Stowe's text is made flesh and blood in Hiraethog's rewriting of it. On 'interpellation', see Louis Althusser, 'Ideology and ideological state apparatuses: notes toward an investigation', in Slavoj Žižek (ed.), *Mapping Ideology* (London: Verso, 1994), pp. 100–40.

[142]  Ward, *Autobiography*, pp. 390–1.

[143]  Stowe, *Uncle Tom's Cabin*, p. 230.

[144]  Ioan Williams, *Capel a Chomin*, pp. 31–2.

[145]  Ward, *Autobiography*, pp. 98–9.

[146]  Yuval Taylor (ed.), *I Was Born A Slave: An Anthology of Classic Slave Narratives* (Edinburgh: Pauback Press, 1999), pp. 720–2.

[147]  Ibid., p. xx.

[148]  Ibid., p. xvi.
[149]  Josiah Henson, *Uncle Tom's Story of His Life: An Autobiography of the Rev. Josiah Henson. From 1789 to 1877*, ed. John Lobb (London: Christian Age Office, 1877), pp. 70–1.
[150]  Quoted in H. Teifi Edwards, *Codi'r Hen Wlad*, p. 4.
[151]  Quoted in H. Teifi Edwards, *Guide to Welsh Literature*, p. 45. H. Teifi Edwards, *Gŵyl Gwalia*, p. 55.
[152]  Josiah Henson, *Hanes Bywyd 'Uncle Tom' o 1789 hyd 1877 Ganddo Ef Ei Hun sef Bywgraffiad Y Parch. Josiah Henson*, cyfieithiedig gan Y Parch D. Griffith (Dolgellau: Swyddfa *Y Dysgedydd*, 1877), p. 232. Henson, *Uncle Tom's Story*, p. 224.
[153]  Henry Louis Gates Jr, 'The trope of a new Negro and the reconstruction of the image of the Black', *Representations*, 24 (1988), 129–55.
[154]  Gaines, *Uplifting the Race*, p. 76.
[155]  Hywel Teifi Edwards, 'Victorian Wales seeks reinstatement', *Planet*, 52 (August/September 1985), 13.
[156]  Henson, *Uncle Tom's Story*, p. 215. This account appears at the end of the book in a 'Summary of Uncle Tom's public services'. It does not appear in the Welsh version.
[157]  The best book I know on these issues is Michael Cronin, *Translating Ireland: Translation, Languages, Cultures* (Cork: Cork University Press, 1996).
[158]  See John Davies, *A History of Wales*, pp. 415–16.
[159]  See H. Teifi Edwards, *Codi'r Hen Wlad*, and J. Davies, *A History of Wales*, p. 419.
[160]  See Richard Wyn Jones, 'The colonial legacy in Welsh politics', in Jane Aaron and Chris Williams (eds), *Postcolonial Wales* (Cardiff: University of Wales Press, 2005), p. 28.
[161]  See my account in Willams, *Ethnicity and Cultural Authority*, pp. 16–20.
[162]  I discuss this at length in *Ethnicity and Cultural Authority*, pp. 12–20.
[163]  Influential examples are Harold Cruse, *The Crisis of the Negro Intellectual* ([1967] London: W. H. Allen, 1969), and R. M. Jones, *Ysbryd y Cwlwm: Delwedd y Genedl yn ein Llenyddiaeth* (Caerdydd: Gwasg Prifysgol Cymru, 1998).
[164]  Quoted by H. Teifi Edwards in *Gŵyl Gwalia*, p. 335.
[165]  See Edwards, *Gŵyl Gwalia*, and D. Tecwyn Lloyd, *Drych o Genedl* (Abertawe: Gwasg John Penry, 1987).
[166]  Matthew Arnold, *On the Study of Celtic Literature*, in *The Complete Prose Works of Matthew Arnold*, vol. 3, ed. R. H. Super (Ann Arbor: University of Michigan Press, 1962), pp. 296–7.
[167]  See my chapter on Arnold in *Ethnicity and Cultural Authority*.
[168]  Samuel Roberts, 'Cymysgiad Achau', in *Pregethau a Darlithiau* (Utica, NY: T. J. Griffiths, 1865), p. 225.
[169]  Moses, *Afrotopia*, p. 122.
[170]  Ward, *Autobiography*, p. 395. Douglass, 'Our composite nationality', in *The Frederick Douglass Papers*, series 1, vol. 4, pp. 254–5.
[171]  Douglass, 'The United States cannot remain half-slave and half-free' (1883), in Philip Foner (ed.), *The Life and Writings of Fredrick Douglass*, vol. 4, *Reconstruction and After* (New York: International Publishers, 1975), p. 370.

[172]  Douglass, 'The claims of the Negro ethnologically considered' (1854), *The Frederick Douglass Papers*, series 1, vol. 2, p. 522.

[173]  Douglass, *My Bondage*, in *Autobiographies*, p. 137.

[174]  Henry Louis Gates Jr, 'The trope of a new Negro', *Representations*, 24 (1988), 129. Levine, *Martin Delany, Frederick Douglass*, p. 228.

[175]  Douglass, 'Santo Domingo' (1873), in *The Frederick Douglass Papers*, series 1, vol., pp. 344, 354, 355.

[176]  Douglass, 'Santo Domingo', p. 355.

[177]  Houston A. Baker, writing of the contemporary United States, notes that states' rights have now been redubbed 'devolution', which seems 'far less a beneficent compromise to ensure a more perfect union', than a crutch for 'white supremacy and profit'. *Turning South Again: Re-Thinking Modernism / Re-Reading Booker T.* (Durham, NC: Duke University Press, 2001), p. 26. This makes sobering reading for Welsh devolutionists and underlines the dangers of transposing political terms across the Atlantic divide.

[178]  Wilson J. Moses, *The Golden Age of Black Nationalism 1850–1925* (Oxford: Oxford University Press, 1978), pp. 84–5.

[179]  Martin Delany, *The Condition, Elevation, Emigration and Destiny of the Colored People of the United States Politically Considered* (Philadelphia: published by the Author, 1852), pp. 12–13.

[180]  *Y Cenhadwr Americananidd*, Rhagfyr 1848. The whole letter is quoted in R. M. Jones, *Ysbryd y Cwlwm*, pp. 282–3.

[181]  R. M. Jones, *Ysbryd y Cwlwm*, pp. 280–2.

[182]  On Jones's political thought, see Glyn Williams, 'Nationalism in nineteenth-century Wales: the discourse of Michael D. Jones', in Glyn Williams ed., *Crisis of Economy and Ideology: Essays on Welsh Society, 1840–1980* (Bangor: Sociology of Wales Study Group, 1983), pp. 180–200. On Delany, see Levine, *Martin Delany, Frederick Douglass*.

[183]  Moses, *The Golden Age*, p. 33.

[184]  Roberts, 'Cymysgiad', p. 207.

[185]  See Glanmor Williams, *Samuel Roberts* (Cardiff: University of Wales Press, 1950). Wilbur S. Shepperson, *Samuel Roberts: A Welsh Colonizer in Civil War Tennessee* (Knoxville: University of Tennessee Press, 1961).

[186]  *The North Star*, 3 December 1847, quoted in Moses, *The Golden Age*, p. 84.

[187]  Gaines, *Uplifting the Race*, p. 76. Patterson, *Up from Bondage*, pp. 36–7.

[188]  Patterson, *Up from Bondage*, pp. 36–7.

[189]  For a wide-ranging debate on the question of universality see Judith Butler, Ernesto Laclau and Slavoj Žižek, *Contingency, Hegemony, Universality: Contemporary Dialogues on the Left* (London: Verso, 2000).

[190]  Frederick Douglass, 'The future of the colored race' (1886), in Philip Foner (ed.), *The Life and Writings of Fredrick Douglass*, vol. 4, p. 195.

[191]  Ibid., p. 195.

[192]  Frederick Douglass, 'The question of amalgamation' (1860), *Douglass Monthly*, 3, 7 (December 1860), 371–2, quoted in Werner Sollors, *Neither Black Nor White Yet Both: Thematic Explorations in Interracial Literature* (Cambridge, MA: Harvard University Press, 1997), p. 465. *Miscegenation* (New York, 1863)

was published anonymously, but was written by David Goodman Croly and George Wakeman. The key sections are included in Werner Sollors, *An Anthology of Interracial Literature: Black–White Contacts in the Old World and the New* (New York: New York University Press, 2004), pp. 350–80.

[193]  Quoted in Sidney Kaplan, 'The miscegenation issue in the election of 1864' (1949), in Sollors ed., *Interracialism: Black–White Intermarriage in American History, Literature and Law* (New York: Oxford University Press, 2000), p. 223.

[194]  Quoted in ibid.

[195]  Ibid.

[196]  Quoted in English only in Diedrich, *Love Across Color Lines*, pp. 256–7.

[197]  Roberts, 'Cymysgiad', pp. 206–7.

[198]  Elise Lemire, *'Miscegenation': Making Race in America* (Philadelphia: University of Pennsylvania Press, 2002).

[199]  Samuel Roberts, *Hunan-Amddiffyniad S. R. Yng Ngwyneb y Camddarlunio Fu Arno Drwy Adeg Cynddaredd y Rhyfel Cartrefol yn America* (Conwy: R. E. Jones, 1882), pp. 12, 15.

[200]  Werner Sollors, *Beyond Ethnicity: Consent and Descent in American Culture* (New York: Oxford University Press, 1986), p. 84.

[201]  Roberts, 'Cymysgiad', p. 209.

[202]  For a wide ranging discussion on this linkage see Sollors, *Neither Black*, pp. 285–335.

[203]  Quoted in Kaplan, p.309. Mississippi law referred to in Sollors, *Neither Black*, p. 299.

[204]  Marc Shell, 'The Want of Incest in the Human Family, Or, Kin and Kind in Christian Thought', *Journal of the American Academy of Religion* LXII/3 (1995), 625–50.

[205]  Roberts, 'Cymysgiad', pp. 209, 210, 211.

[206]  Sollors, *Beyond Ethnicity*, p. 81.

[207]  On the use of Paul's letters see Sollors, *Beyond Ethnicity*, pp. 81–6.

[208]  Roberts, 'Cymysgiad', pp. 221–2.

[209]  Patterson, *Up From Bondage*, pp. 36–7.

[210]  On the 'inferiority complex', and its application to Wales in the works of Freud's colleague Ernest Jones, see R. M. Jones, *Ysbryd y Cwlwm*, pp. 184–5.

[211]  Roberts, 'Cymysgiad', p. 223.

[212]  Douglass, 'Our composite nationality' (1869), *The Frederick Douglass Papers*, series 1, vol. 4, p. 259.

[213]  Douglass, *My Bondage*, p. 146.

[214]  Ibid., p. 160.

[215]  Ibid.

[216]  Paul Gilroy, *The Black Atlantic* (Cambridge, MA: Harvard University Press, 1993), p. 59.

[217]  Douglass, 'The nation's problem' (1885), in *The Frederick Douglass Papers*, series 1, vol. 5, p. 415.

[218]  Michael Cronin, 'Global questions and local visions: a microcosmopolitan perspective', in Alyce von Rothkirch and Daniel Williams (eds), *Beyond the Difference: Welsh Literature in Comparative Contexts* (Cardiff: University of

Wales Press, 2004), p. 197. W. E. B Du Bois, *The Souls of Black Folk* (1903), in *Writings* (New York: The Library of America, 1986), p. 397.
219  Julia Griffiths Croft to Douglass 25 November 1865, Frederick Douglass Papers, Library of Congress.
220  Douglass, *Narrative*, in *Autobiographies*, p. 59.
221  Quoted in Martin Crawford and Alan J. Rice, 'Triumphant exile: Frederick Douglass in Britain 1845–1847', in Crawford and Rice (eds), *Liberating Sojourn: Frederick Douglass and Transatlantic Reform* (Athens: The University of Georgia Press, 1999), p. 1.
222  R. J. M. Blackett, *Building an Antislavery Wall*, p. 208.

## Chapter 2

1  David Margolick, *Beyond Glory: Max Schmeling vs. Joe Louis and a World on the Brink* (London: Bloosbury, 2005), p. 235.
2  See ibid., pp. 234–8. Dai Smith, 'Call me Tommy: Tommy Farr the Tonypandy Kid', in Peter Stead and Gareth Williams (eds), *Wales and its Boxers: The Fighting Tradition* (Cardiff: University of Wales Press, 2008), pp. 87–100.
3  In Lowri Roberts (ed.), *Canu Clod y Campau: Detholiad o Farddonaieth y Maes Chwarae* (Llanrwst: Gwasg Carreg Gwalch, 2009), p. 33. Thanks to Cyril Jones for drawing my attention to this poem.
4  Miles Davis (with Quincy Troupe), *The Autobiography* (London: Macmillan, 1989), pp. 8–9.
5  Lawrence W. Levine, *Black Culture and Black Consciousness: Afro-American Folk Thought from Slavery to Freedom* (Oxford: Oxford University Press, 1977), p. 436. Also Randy Roberts, *Joe Louis: Hard Times Man* (New Haven: Yale University Press, 2010), pp. 86–120. Kasia Boddy, *Boxing: A Cultural History* (London: Reaktion Books, 2008), pp. 280–315.
6  Malcolm X, *The Autobiography of Malcolm X* (as told to Alex Haley) (New York: Ballantine Books, 1964), pp. 23–4.
7  See Mike Marqusee, *Redemption Song: Muhammad Ali and the Spirit of the Sixties* (London: Verso, 1999), p. 24. Levine, *Black Culture*, p. 432. See also Geoffrey Ward, *Unforgivable Blackness: The Rise and Fall of Jack Johnson* (London: Pimlico, 2006).
8  Paul Robeson, with the Count Basie Orchestra, 'King Joe' (1941), on *The Essential Paul Robeson* (ASV Ltd., 2000).
9  Gerald Early, 'Introduction' to Countee Cullen, *My Soul's High Song: The Collected Writings of Countee Cullen*, ed. Gerald Early (New York: Anchor Books, 1991), p. 54.
10  Dai Smith, *Aneurin Bevan and the World of South Wales* (Cardiff: University of Wales Press, 1993), pp. 321–2.
11  'Sport: Louis v. Farr', *Time Magazine*, 6 September 1937.
12  Tommy Farr, *Thus Farr* (London: Optomen Press, 1989), pp. 69, 81.
13  Margolick, *Beyond Glory*, p. 38. Dai Smith, *Aneurin Bevan*, p. 323.
14  Andrew Gallimore, *Occupation Prizefighter: The Freddie Welsh Story* (Bridgend: Seren, 2006), pp. 56–7.

15  'Sport: Louis v. Farr', *Time Magazine*, 6 September 1937.

16  Ralph Ellison, *Invisible Man* ([1952] New York: Vintage, 1995), p. 8.

17  Gerald Early, *The Culture of Bruising: Essays on Prizefighting, Literature and Modern American Culture* (Hopewell, NJ: The Ecco Press, 1994), pp. 11–12.

18  Quoted in Dai Smith, *Aneurin Bevan*, p. 321.

19  W. J. Gruffydd, 'Hen Atgofion', *Y Llenor*, 17 (1938), 8–9; translated by D. Myrddin Lloyd as W. J. Gruffydd, *The Years of the Locust* (Llandysul: Gomer, 1976), p. 175.

20  Quoted in Early, *The Culture of Bruising*, p. 41.

21  Kevin K. Gaines, *Uplifting the Race: Black Leadership, Politics, and Culture in the Twentieth Century* (Chapel Hill: University of North Carolina Press, 1996), p. 93.

22  Gaines, *Uplifting*, p. 223.

23  Marshall Berman, *All That Is Solid Melts into Air: The Experience of Modernity* ([1982] London: Verso, 1983), p. 15.

24  Gwyn A. Williams, *When Was Wales? A History of the Welsh* (London: Black Raven Press, 1985), pp. 173–81. Gwyn A. Williams, *The Welsh in Their History* (London: Croom Helm, 1982), p. 177. Dai Smith, *Wales! Wales?* (London: Allen and Unwin, 1984), pp. 20–7.

25  Quoted in Gilbert Osofsky, *Harlem: The Making of a Ghetto* ([1963] 2nd edn, London: Harper and Row, 1971), p. 128. See also Mary White Ovington, *Half a Man: The Status of the Negro in New York* (New York: Longmans, Green & Co., 1911), p. 48.

26  Osofsky, *Harlem*, p. 128.

27  Alain Locke, 'The new Negro' (1925), in Henry Louis Gates Jr (ed.), *The Norton Anthology of African American Literature* (New York: Norton, 1997), p. 964. Johnson quoted in Osofsky, *Half a Man*, p. 128.

28  Quoted in Osofsky, *Half a Man*, p. 128.

29  Henry Louis Gates Jr, 'Harlem on our minds', in *Rhapsodies on Black: Art of the Harlem Renaissance* (London: South Bank Centre, 1997), p. 166.

30  Ibid.

31  Hywel Francis and Dai Smith, *The Fed: A History of the South Wales Miners in the Twentieth Century* ([1980] Cardiff: University of Wales Press, 1998), pp. 33–6. John Davies, *A History of Wales* ([1990 in Welsh] London: Penguin, 1993), pp. 549, 582–3.

32  Gwyn A. Williams, 'Mother Wales get off me back', *Marxism Today* (December 1981), 16.

33  Idris Davies, *Gwalia Deserta*, in *The Complete Poems of Idris Davies*, ed. Dafydd Johnston (Cardiff: University of Wales Press, 1994), p. 6.

34  On affirmative art, see Herbert Marcuse, 'The affirmative character of culture', in *Negations: Essays in Critical Theory*, trans. Jeremy J. Shapiro (Boston: Beacon Press, 1968), pp. 88–133.

35  Theodor Adorno, 'On the fetish character in music and the regression in listening', in Theodor Adorno, *Essays on Music*, introduced by Richard Leppert, trans. Susan Gillespie (Berkeley: University of California Press, 2002), p. 303.

36  Andreas Huyssen, *After the Great Divide: Modernism, Mass Culture and Postmodernism* ([1986] London: Macmillan, 1988), p. vii.

37  Ibid., pp. 44–62.
38  Houston A. Baker Jr, *Modernism and the Harlem Renaissance* (Chicago: University of Chicago Press, 1987). George Hutchinson, *The Harlem Renaissance in Black and White* (Cambridge, MA: Harvard University Press, 1995). Ann Douglas, *Terrible Honesty: Mongrel Manhattan in the 1920s* (New York: Noonday Press, 1995).
39  See Alex Davis and Lee Jenkins, *Locations of Literary Modernism: Region and Nation in American Modernist Poetry* (Cambridge: Cambridge University Press, 2000).
40  Baker Jr, *Modernism*.
41  See, for instance, Alan Filreis, *Wallace Stevens and the Actual World* (Princeton, NJ: Princeton University Press, 1991).
42  See Raymond Williams, *The Politics of Modernism: Against the New Conformists*, ed. Tony Pinkney (London: Verso, 1989).
43  See Richard Begam and Michale Valdez Moses (eds), *Modernism and Colonialism: British and Irish Literature 1899 – 1939* (Durham, NC: Duke University Press, 2007). Werner Sollors, *Ethnic Modernism* (Cambridge, MA: Harvard University Press, 2008).
44  See Marianne Dekoven, 'Modernism and gender', in Michael Levenson (ed.), *The Cambridge Companion to Modernism* (Cambridge: Cambridge University Press, 1999), pp.174–93.
45  Nicholas Daly, 'Colonialism and popular literature in the fin de siècle', in Begam and Valdez Moses (eds), *Modernism and Colonialism*, pp. 19–20.
46  R. Williams, *Politics of Modernism*, p. 33.
47  Ibid., p. 66.
48  Ibid., pp. 67, 77. See John Higgins, *Raymond Williams: Literature, Marxism and Cultural Materialism* (London: Routledge, 1999), pp. 160–8.
49  R. Williams, *Politics of Modernism*, p. 79.
50  Ibid., pp. 44, 47
51  Ibid., p. 44.
52  Ibid., pp. 79, 183.
53  Ibid., p. 79.
54  Marcus Klein, *Foreigners: The Making of American Literature 1900–1940* (Chicago: University of Chicago Press, 1981), p. 37.
55  Ibid., p. 38.
56  Baker Jr, *Modernism and the Harlem Renaissance*. This quotation is Baker's lucid synopsis of his thesis in *Afro-American Poetics: Revisions of Harlem and the Black Aesthetic* (Madison: University of Wisconsin Press, 1988), p. 4.
57  Huyssen, *After the Great Divide*, p. 6.
58  Quoted in Judith Stein, 'Defining the race 1890–1930', in Werner Sollors (ed.), *The Invention of Ethnicity* (Oxford: Oxford University Press, 1989), p. 86.
59  Du Bois, 'The talented tenth' (1903), in *Writings: The Suppression of the African Slave Trade, The Souls of Black Folk, Dusk of Dawn*, ed. Nathan I. Huggins (New York: The Library of America, 1986), pp. 846–7.
60  Stein, 'Defining the race', p. 85. Saunder Lewis, 'Cyflwyniad' i Molière, *Doctor Er Ei Waethaf* (Wrecsam: Cyfres y Werin, 1924), p. 7.

61  Saunders Lewis, 'Safonau Beirniadaeth Lenyddol', *Y Llenor*,1, 4 (gaeaf 1922), 254.

62  Saunders Lewis, 'Cyflwyniad', p. 7.

63  Saunders Lewis a Kate Roberts, *Annwyl Kate, Annwyl Saunders*, gol. Dafydd Ifans (Aberystwyth: Llyfrgell Genedlaethol Cymru, 1992), p. 4.

64  Dafydd Glyn Jones, 'His politics', in Alun R. Jones and Gwyn Thomas (eds.), *Presenting Saunders Lewis* (Cardiff: University of Wales Press, 1973), p. 47. Ezra Pound, *Selected Poems* ([1975] London: Faber, 1977), p. 101.

65  Gareth Miles, 'A personal view', in Jones and Thomas (eds), *Presenting Saunders Lewis*, p. 18.

66  Henry Louis Gates Jr and Cornel West, *The Future of the Race* (New York: Alfred A. Knopf, 1996), p. 126.

67  Du Bois, *Dusk of Dawn*, in *Writings*, p. 565.

68  Du Bois, *Souls*, in *Writings*, p. 364. See Keith E. Byerman's discussion in *Seizing the Word: History, Art and Self in the Work of W. E. B. Du Bois* (Athens: University of Georgia Press, 1994), pp. 13–14.

69  For an account of the significance of this scene in terms of gender, see Hazel Carby, *Race Men* (Cambridge, MA: Harvard University Press, 1998), p. 31.

70  Du Bois, *Souls*, p. 440.

71  Ibid., p. 444.

72  David Levering Lewis, *W. E. B. Du Bois: Biography of a Race 1868–1919* (New York: Henry Holt and Co., 1993), p. 72.

73  Quoted by Gareth Miles, 'A personal view', pp. 16–17. See Saunders Lewis, 'Dylanwadau: Saunders Lewis mewn ymgom ag Aneirin Talfan Davies', *Taliesin*, 2 (Nadolig 1961), pp. 5–18.

74  Miles, 'A personal view', p. 17.

75  See Ioan Williams on Lewis and Barrès, *A Straitened Stage: A Study of the Theatre of J. Saunders Lewis* (Bridgend: Seren, 1991), pp. 22–7.

76  See my discussion of Arnold and Du Bois in Daniel G. Willams, *Ethnicity and Cultural Authority: From Arnold to Du Bois* (Edinburgh: Edinburgh University Press, 2006), pp. 1–7, 189–98. Also Ben Knights, *The Idea of the Clerisy in the Nineteenth Century*, (Cambridge: Cambridge University Press, 1978).

77  Saunders Lewis, *Ceiriog: Yr Artist yn Philistia I* (Aberystwyth: Gwasg Aberystwyth, 1929). Saunders Lewis, *Daniel Owen: Yr Artist yn Philistia II* (Aberystwyth: Gwasg Aberystwyth, 1936). Saunders Lewis, 'Swyddogaeth Celfyddyd', *Y Traethodydd*, 89, 3 (1934), 390–3.

78  Matthew Arnold, 'The bishop and the philosopher' (1863), in *The Complete Prose Works of Matthew Arnold*, vol. 3, ed. R. H. Super (Ann Arbor: University of Michigan Press, 1962), pp. 43–4.

79  W. E. B. Du Bois, 'Two novels' (1928), in Gates Jr (ed.), *The Norton Anthology of African American Literature*, p. 760.

80  Ibid., p. 759.

81  Du Bois, 'Van Vechten's *Nigger Heaven*', in *Writings*, p. 1216.

82  W. E. B. Du Bois, *The Autobiography of W. E. B. Du Bois: A Soliloquy on Viewing my Life from the Last Decade of its First Century* ([1968] New York: International Publishers, 1980), p. 416.

83 Saunders Lewis, 'Y Dilyw 1939', yn R. Geraint Gruffydd (gol.), *Cerddi* (Caerdydd: Gwasg Prifydgol Cymru, 1992), p. 12; translated by Gwyn Thomas in Jones and Thomas (eds), *Presenting Saunders Lewis*, p. 179.

84 Saunders Lewis, 'Welsh writers of today', in Jones and Thomas (eds), *Presenting Saunders Lewis*, p. 166.

85 Saunders Lewis, *Is There an Anglo-Welsh Literature?* (Cardiff: Guild of Graduates of the University of Wales, 1939), p. 9.

86 Saunders Lewis, 'Deg pwynt polisi Plaid Cymru', *Y Ddraig Goch* (Mawrth 1934), 1; quoted in translation by Dafydd Glyn Jones, 'His politics', in Jones and Thomas (eds), *Presenting Saunders Lewis*, p. 37.

87 Saunders Lewis, *Letters to Margaret Gilcriest*, ed. Mair Saunders Jones, Ned Thomas and Harri Pritchard Jones (Cardiff: University of Wales Press, 1993), p. 516. See Grahame Davies's discussion, *Sefyll yn y Bwlch: R. S. Thomas, Saunders Lewis, T. S. Eliot, a Simone Weil* (Caerdydd: Gwasg Prifysgol Cymru, 1999), pp. 62–7.

88 Lewis, *Is there an Anglo-Welsh Literature?*, pp. 6–9. Lewis, 'Anglo Welsh theatre: the problem of language' (1919), quoted by Ioan Williams in his introduction to *Dramâu Saunders Lewis: Y Casglaid Cyflawn*, Cyfrol 1, gol. Ioan M. Williams (Caerdydd: Gwasg Prifysgol Cymru, 1996), p. 7.

89 Lewis, 'Anglo Welsh theatre: the problem of language', p. 7.

90 Saunders Lewis, 'Tueddiadau Cymru Rhwng 1919 a 1923', *Baner ac Amserau Cymru*, 6 Medi (1923), 5; quoted in D. Tecwyn Lloyd, *John Saunders Lewis: Y Gyfrol Gyntaf* (Dinbych: Gwasg Gee, 1988), p. 228.

91 See also his comments on the 'barbarism' of Blaendulais (Seven Sisters) in a letter to Kate Roberts in *Annwyl Kate, Annwyl Saunders*, p. 16.

92 Du Bois, 'The talented tenth' (1903), in *Writings*, pp. 851–2.

93 W. E. B. Du Bois, *The Philadelphia Negro: A Social Study* (1899. New York: Schocken Books, 1967), p. 389.

94 Ibid., p. 389.

95 Ibid., p. 311.

96 Du Bois, *Souls*, pp. 435–6.

97 West compares this element in the thought of Arnold and Du Bois in 'Black strivings in a twilight civilization', in Henry Louis Gates Jr and Cornel West, *The Future of the Race* (New York: Alfred Knopf, 1996), p. 67.

98 Arnold, *On the Study of Celtic Literature* in *The Complete Prose Works of Matthew Arnold*, vol. 3, ed. R. H. Super (Ann Arbor: University of Michigan Press, 1962), p. 390. W. D. Howells, *An Imperative Duty*, in Martha Bunta (ed.), *The Shadow of a Dream* and *An Imperative Duty* ([1891] Bloomington: Indiana University Press, 1970), p. 5. See my *Ethnicity and Cultural Authority*, pp. 110–14.

99 W. B. Yeats, *Uncollected Prose*, vol. 2, ed. John P. Frayne and Colton Johnson (London: Macmillan, 1975), p. 70. Lewis, *Is There an Anglo-Welsh Literature?*, p. 9.

100 Saunders Lewis, 'Foreword' to *The Eve of Saint John*, in Ioan Williams (ed.), *Dramâu Saunders Lewis*, cyfrol 1, p. 14.

101 Lewis, *Is There an Anglo-Welsh Literature?*, p. 9.

[102]   Du Bois, *Souls*, p. 370.
[103]   Ibid., p. 499.
[104]   Ibid., pp. 529–30.
[105]   Ibid., p. 530.
[106]   Ibid., p. 493.
[107]   Ibid.., p. 494. I am drawing here on Shamoon Zamir's '"The Sorrow Songs"/ "Song of Myself": Du Bois, the crisis of leadership and prophetic imagination', in Maria Diedrich and Werner Sollors (eds), *The Black Columbiad: Defining Moments in African American Literature and Culture* (Cambridge, MA: Harvard University Press, 1994), pp. 158–9.
[108]   Du Bois, *Souls*, p. 494.
[109]   Lewis, *Letters to Margaret Gilcriest*, p. 442. See Grahame Davies's discussion in *Sefyll yn y Bwlch*, pp. 74–9.
[110]   Saunders Lewis, *Letters to Margaret Gilcriest*, p. 471. Saunders Lewis, 'The literary man's life in Wales', *Welsh Outlook*, 16 (October 1929), 295; quoted by T. Robin Chapman, 'Theism's last hurrah: Saunders Lewis's Caernarfon court speech of 1936', in Chapman (ed.), *The Idiom of Dissent: Protest and Propaganda in Wales* (Llandysul: Gomer, 2006), p. 33.
[111]   See Hywel Teifi Edwards, '"Y Pentre Gwyn" and "Manteg": from blessed plot to hotspot', in Alyce Von Rothkirch and Daniel Williams (eds), *Beyond the Difference: Welsh Literature in Comparative Contexts* (Cardiff: University of Wales Press, 2004), pp. 9–12.
[112]   Richard Wyn Jones, *Rhoi Cymru'n Gyntaf: Syniadaeth Plaid Cymru* (Caerdydd: Gwasg Prifysgol Cymru, 2007), pp.70–9.
[113]   Lewis, 'Pwy Yw y Werin', *Y Darian* (Aberdar), 10 Chwefror 1921; quoted by D. Tecwyn Lloyd, *John Saunders Lewis*, pp. 128–9.
[114]   Karl Marx and Frederick Engels, *The Communist Manifesto: A Modern Edition* ([1848] London: Verso, 1988), p. 40.
[115]   Tom Nairn, *The Break-Up of Britain* (London: New Left Books, 1977), pp. 100–1.
[116]   Du Bois, *Souls*, p. 364.
[117]   On Du Bois and Emerson, see Brian A. Bremen, 'Du Bois, Emerson and the "fate" of black folk', *American Literary Realism* 24 (spring 1992), pp. 80–8. For a general discussion of the uses of 'double consciousness' see, Dickson D. Bruce, 'W. E. B. Du Bois and the idea of double consciousness', *American Literature*, 64 (June 1992), 299–309.
[118]   Shamoon Zamir, *W. E. B. Du Bois and American Thought 1888–1903* (Chicago: University of Chicago Press, 1995), p.154. Kenneth Warren, *Black and White Strangers: Race and American Literary Realism* (Chicago: University of Chicago Press, 1993), p. 12.
[119]   Saunders Lewis, *Letters to Margaret Gilcriest*, p. 21.
[120]   Saunders Lewis, 'Welsh literature and nationalism' (1965), in A. R. Jones and G Thomas (eds), *Presenting Saunders Lewis* (Cardiff: University of Wales Press, 1973), p. 144.
[121]   I am drawing here on a suggestion made by Dafydd Glyn Jones, 'Dwy olwg ar Saunders Lewis', *Taliesin*, 66 (Mawrth 1989), 22.

[122]  M. Wynn Thomas has suggested that 'Blodeuwedd' is, in part, a portrayal of the American 'New Woman' whom Lewis saw as embodying the anarchic individualism of modernity. See M. Wynn Thomas, 'Gwlad o bosibiliadau: golwg ar lên Cymru ac America', *Y Traethodydd*, 157 (2002), 38–52. The similarities with Du Bois are again striking and worthy of study. See Susan Gillman and Alys Eve Weinbaum (eds), *Next to the Color Line: Gender, Sexuality and W. E. B. Du Bois* (Minneapolis: University of Minnesota Press, 2007).

[123]  Lewis, 1923/1925 version of Blodeuwedd, in *Dramâu Saunders Lewis*, cyfrol 1, p. 300; translated by Gwyn Thomas in Jones and Thomas (eds), *Presenting Saunders Lewis*, p. 213.

[124]  Saunders Lewis, *Blodeuwedd*, in *Dramâu Saunders Lewis*, cyfrol 1, p. 295. I have amended the translation by Gwyn Thomas that appears in *Presenting Saunders Lewis*, p. 208.

[125]  Terry Eagleton's phrase in *Heathcliff and the Great Hunger: Studies in Irish Culture* (London: Verso, 1995), p. 237.

[126]  Lewis, *Blodeuwedd*, p. 313.

[127]  Samuel Beckett, *Wrth Aros Godot / En Attendant Godot*, trans. Saunders Lewis (Cardiff: University of Wales Press, 1970).

[128]  Quoted in Dale E. Patterson, *Up from Bondage: The Literatures of Russian and African American Soul* (Durham, NC: Duke University Press, 2000), p. 58.

[129]  Lewis, 'Cwrs y Byd', *Baner ac Amserau Cymru*, 13 Ionawr 1943; quoted in T. Robin Chapman, *Un Bywyd o Blith Nifer: Cofiant Saunders Lewis* (Llandysul: Gomer, 2006), pp. 259–60.

[130]  Langston Hughes, 'The Negro artist and the racial mountain' (1926), in H. L. Gates Jr (ed.), *The Norton Anthology of African American Literature*, p. 1267.

[131]  Ibid., pp. 1268, 1270.

[132]  Quoted in Arnold Rampersad, *The Life of Langston Hughes*, vol. 1, *I, Too, Sing America* (Oxford: Oxford University Press, 1986), p. 146. Hughes's debate with Cullen and George Schuyler has been widely discussed. Ann Douglas defends Cullen in *Terrible Honesty*, pp. 340–4.

[133]  Idris Davies, 'Response to Geoffrey Grigson', in *The Complete Poems of Idris Davies*, ed. Dafydd Johnston (Cardiff: University of Wales Press, 1994), p. 328.

[134]  Hughes, 'The Negro artist', p. 1271.

[135]  Davies, Diary, 5 November 1939; quoted in Dafydd Johnston, 'The development of Idris Davies's poetry', in *The Complete Poems of Idris Davies*, ed. Dafydd Johnston (Cardiff: University of Wales Press, 1994), p. lvi.

[136]  M. Wynn Thomas, *In the Shadow of the Pulpit: Literature and Nonconformist Wales* (Cardiff: University of Wales Press, 2010), p. 173.

[137]  James Edward Smethurst, *The New Red Negro: The Literary Left and African American Poetry, 1930–1946* (Oxford: Oxford University Press, 1999), p. 108.

[138]  Malcolm X, *The Autobiography*, pp. 23–4.

[139]  Langston Hughes, *The Collected Poems of Langston Hughes*, ed. Arnold Rampersad (New York: Vintage, 1994), p. 113; from now on, Hughes, *CP*. Idris Davies, *The Complete Poems of Idris Davies*, ed. Dafydd Johnston (Cardiff: University of Wales Press, 1994), p. 143; from now on, Davies, *CP*.

[140]  Anthony Conran offers a reading of this aspect of Davies's work in *The Cost of*

*Strangeness: Essays on the English Poets of Wales* (Llandysul: Gomer Press, 1982), p. 123.

[141]  Davies, *CP*, pp. 26, 36, 37, 41. Hughes, *CP*, pp. 82, 112, 113, 88, 35, 68, 60.

[142]  Davies, *CP*, pp. 177, 173, 207–8. Hughes, *CP*, pp. 217, 195, 185.

[143]  Davies, *CP*, p. 35. Hughes, *CP*, p. 88.

[144]  Douglas, *Terrible Honesty*, p. 376.

[145]  Seamus Deane, *Celtic Revivals: Essays in Modern Irish Literature, 1880–1980* (London: Faber, 1985), p. 13. John Aitchison and Harold Carter, *A Geography of the Welsh Language 1961–1991* (Cardiff: University of Wales Press, 1994).

[146]  Douglas, *Terrible Honesty*, p. 375.

[147]  Ibid.

[148]  Ibid., p. 374.

[149]  Hughes, *CP*, p. 50.

[150]  Ibid., p. 50.

[151]  On the idea of a 'hierarchy of discourse', see Colin McCabe, *James Joyce and the Revolution of the Word* (London: Macmillan, 1978), p. 16.

[152]  Hughes, *CP*, p. 72.

[153]  Douglas, *Terrible Honesty*, p. 404. See also Brent Hayes Edwards's discussions of Hughes in *The Practice of Diaspora: Literature, Translation and the Rise of Black Internationalism* (Cambridge, MA: Harvard University Press, 2003).

[154]  Davies, *CP*, p. 78.

[155]  Johnston, 'Idris Davies's life', *CP*, pp. xii–xiii.

[156]  Davies, *CP*, p. 97.

[157]  This is Ralph Ellison's apt phrase in *Shadow and Act* ([1953] New York: Quality Paperback Book Club, 1994), p. 26.

[158]  On Gwenallt and Idris Davies see Dafydd Johnston, 'Dwy Lenyddiaeth Cymru yn y Tridegau', yn John Rowlands (gol.), *Sglefrio ar Eiriau* (Llandysul: Gomer, 1992), pp. 42–62.

[159]  Hughes, *CP*, pp. 192–3.

[160]  Davies, *CP*, p. 48.

[161]  Ibid., p. 30.

[162]  Ibid., pp. 9–10.

[163]  Ibid., p. 150.

[164]  Ibid., p. 37.

[165]  Ibid., p. 6.

[166]  William Shakespeare, *Much Ado About Nothing* (1600), *The Norton Shakespeare*, ed. Stephen Greenblatt et al. (New York: Norton, 1997), p. 1440.

[167]  W. B. Yeats, *The Collected Poems*, ed. R. Finneran (New York: Collier, 1989), p. 59.

[168]  Robin Young quoted by Dafydd Johnston in 'Introduction' to Davies, *CP*, p. lxxx.

[169]  Smethurst, *The New Red Negro*, p 97.

[170]  Raymond Williams, *Marxism and Literature* (Oxford: Oxford University Press, 1977), pp. 121–7.

[171]  Davies, 'Bugle in Cardigan', *CP*, p. 186. Hughes, 'Goodbye Christ', *CP*, p. 166.

[172]  Davies, 'Cwrdd Mawr', *CP*, p. 217.

173  Davies, *CP*, p. 11. See M. Wynn Thomas's discussion of Davies's religious values in *In the Shadow*, pp. 171–9.

174  Davies, *CP*, p. 13.

175  Hughes, 'Christ in Alabama', *CP*, p. 143.

176  Cary Nelson, *Revolutionary Memory: Recovering the Poetry of the American Left* (New York: Routledge, 2001), p. 72.

177  The Scottsboro Boys were nine black teenage boys accused of raping two white women in Alabama in 1931. The case became a renowned miscarriage of justice that led to the end of all-white juries in the South.

178  Davies, *CP*, p. 14.

179  Smethurst, *The New Red Negro*, p. 109.

180  Davies, *CP*, pp. 225, 275.

181  Hughes, *CP*, p. 175. This largely neglected poem is discussed in detail by Seth Moglen in 'Modernism and the Black diaspora: Langston Hughes and the broken cubes of Picasso', *Callaloo*, 25, 4 (autumn 2002), pp. 1188–1205. Thanks to Rachel Farebrother for drawing my attention to this.

182  'Culture is ordinary' is the title of an article written by Raymond Williams in the 1950s. Collected in *Resources of Hope* (London: Verso, 1989).

183  David Levering Lewis, *When Harlem Was in Vogue* ([1981] Oxford: Oxford University Press, 1989), p. 98.

184  Quoted in Robert E. Hemenway, *Zora Neale Hurston: A Literary Biography* ([1977] London: Camden Press, 1986), p. 206.

185  Quoted in ibid.

186  Quoted in ibid.

187  Werner Sollors, *Ethnic Modernism* (Cambridge, MA: Harvard University Press, 2008), p. 167.

188  Zora Neale Hurston, 'What white publishers won't print' (1950), in *I Love Myself When I am Laughing*, ed. Alice Walker (New York: The Feminist Press, 1979), pp. 169, 170.

189  H. E. Bates, 'Review of Kate Roberts' *A Summer Day*', *Welsh Review*, 5 (1946), 217–18. See Tony Brown, '"Stories from foreign countries": the short stories of Kate Roberts and Margiad Evans', in Alyce Von Rothkirch and Daniel Williams (eds), *Beyond the Difference: Welsh Literature in Comparative Contexts* (Cardiff: University of Wales Press, 2004), pp. 21–3.

190  Margiad Evans, 'Review of Kate Roberts, *A Summer Day*', *Life and Letters To-Day*, 51 (November 1946), 54; quoted in Tony Brown, 'Stories from foreign countries', p. 37.

191  Evans, 'Review of Kate Roberts', 57.

192  Raymond Williams, *The Politics of Modernism*, p. 58.

193  However, see Mark Christian Thompson's discussion of Hurston's thought in *Black Fascisms* (Charlottesville: University of Virginia Press, 2007), pp. 117–42.

194  Susan Hegeman, *Patterns for America: Modernism and the Concept of Culture* (Princeton: Princeton University Press, 1999), p. 36. See also Adam Kuper, *Culture: The Anthropologists' Account* (Cambridge, MA: Harvard University Press, 1999), and Marc Manganaro, *Culture, 1922: The Emergence of a Concept* (Princeton, NJ: Princeton University Press, 2002).

[195] Hegeman, *Patterns for America*, p. 37.

[196] Ibid.

[197] W. E. B. Du Bois, *Black Folk Then and Now* (1939; Milwood, NY: Kraus-Thomson Organization, 1975), p. vii. See also Hutchinson, *The Harlem Renaissance in Black and White*, p. 63.

[198] George Stocking, *The Ethnographer's Magic and other Essays in the History of Anthropology* (Madison: University of Wisconsin Press, 1992), p. 117.

[199] Franz Boas, 'Instability of human types', in Gustav Spiller (ed.), *Papers on Inter-Racial Problems Communicated to the First Universal Races Congress held at the University of London, July 26–29, 1911* (London: P. S. King, and Boston: The Peace Foundation, 1911), p. 103. On the social and intellectual consequences of these views, see Elazar Barkan, *The Retreat of Scientific Racism* (Cambridge: Cambridge University Press, 1992), p. 84.

[200] Between 1908 and 1910 Fleure was in charge of the Zoology Department at University College of Wales, Aberystwyth. In 1910 he was appointed professor of zoology; and then in 1918 he took up the chair of geography and anthropology. See E. L. Ellis, *The University College of Wales, Aberystwyth 1872–1972* (Cardiff: University of Wales Press, 1972).

[201] David N. Livingstone, *The Geographical Tradition* (Oxford: Blackwells, 1992), p. 287. For accounts of Fleure in a Welsh context, see Pyrs Gruffudd, 'Back to the land: historiography, rurality and the nation in interwar Wales', *Transactions of the Institute of British Geographers*, 19 (1994), 61–77. Also, Pyrs Gruffudd, 'Yr Iaith Gymraeg a'r Dychymyg Daearyddol 1918–1950', in Geraint Jenkins and Mari Williams (eds), *'Eu Hiaith a Gadwant'? Y Gymraeg yn yr Ugeinfed Ganrif* (Caerdydd: Gwasg Prifysgol Cymru, 2000), pp. 107–32.

[202] Quoted in Livingstone, *Geographical*, p. 287. See also Nancy Stepan, *The Idea of Race in Science: Great Britain 1800–1960* (London: Macmillan, 1982), p. 106.

[203] Quoted in Livingstone, *Geographical*, p. 288.

[204] Quoted in Barkan, *Retreat*, p. 64.

[205] See ibid, p. 60. Livingstone, *Geographical*, p. 285.

[206] H. J. Fleure (ed.), *Gyda'r Wawr: Braslun o Hanes Cymru'r Oesoedd Cyntefig* (Wrecsam: Hughes a'i Fab, 1923), p. i.

[207] H. J. Fleure, 'The racial history of the British people', *Geographical Review*, 5 (1918), 230–1.

[208] H. J. Fleure, 'Wales', in Alan G. Ogilvie (ed.), *Great Britain: Essays in Regional Geography* (Cambridge: Cambridge University Press, 1928), p. 230.

[209] Livingstone, *Geographical*, p. 284.

[210] George Hutchinson, *The Harlem Renaissance*, p. 66. Also Susan Hegeman, *Patterns for America*, p. 36.

[211] Hutchinson, *The Harlem Renaissance*, p. 66.

[212] Hutchinson, *The Harlem Renaissance*, pp. 66–7.

[213] Langston Hughes, *The Big Sea* (New York: Knopf, 1940), p. 239; see also p. 236.

[214] Ibid., p. 239.

[215] Zora Neale Hurston, *Mules and Men* (1935) in *Zora Neale Hurston: Folklore,*

*Memoirs, and Other Writings: Mules and Men, Tell My Horse, Dust Tracks on a Road, Selected Articles* (New York: The Library of America, 1995), p. 9.

216   Ibid., p. 9.
217   Franz Boas, 'Preface' to Hurston, *Mules*, p. iii.
218   H. J. Fleure, 'The Welsh people', *Wales*, 10 (October 1939), reprinted in *Wales 1–11* (London: Frank Cass, 1969), pp. 265–6.
219   Margiad Evans, 'Book reviews', *Wales*, 10 (October 1939), 285–6.
220   Ibid.
221   Ibid., p. 285.
222   Hurston, *Mules*, p. 9.
223   Barbara Johnson, 'Thresholds of difference: structures of address in Zora Neale Hurston', in Henry Louis Gates Jr (ed.), *'Race', Writing and Difference* (Chicago: University of Chicago Press, 1986), pp. 317–28.
224   Ceridwen Lloyd-Morgan, *Margiad Evans* (Bridgend: Seren, 1998). Harri Roberts, *Embodying Identity: Representations of the Body in Welsh Literature* (Cardiff: University of Wales Press, 2009), p. 76.
225   Stephen Knight, *A Hundred Years of Fiction: Writing Wales in English* (Cardiff: University of Wales Press, 2004), p. 47.
226   Knight, *A Hundred Years*, p. 49. Evans, 'Letter to Gwyn Jones', quoted in Lloyd-Morgan, *Margiad Evans*, p. 32.
227   Tony Brown, 'Stories from foreign countries', p. 24.
228   Rhys Davies, *My Wales* (London: Jarrolds, 1937), pp. 214–15. Stephen Knight, *A Hundred Years*, p. 49.
229   Zora Neale Hurston, *Color Struck*, in Kathy A. Perkins (ed.), *Black Female Playwrights: An Anthology of Plays Before 1950* (Bloomington: Indiana University Press, 1990), p. 97. Margiad Evans, *Country Dance* ([1932] Cardigan: Parthian, 2006), p. 20. Zora Neale Hurston, *Their Eyes Were Watching God* ([1937] London: Virago, 1992), p. 196.
230   Michael Fischer and George E. Marcus, *Anthropology as Cultural Critique: An Experimental Moment in the Human Sciences* ([1986] Chicago: University of Chicago Press, 1999), p. 24.
231   Ibid., p. 129.
232   See Clare Morgan, 'Exile and the kingdom: Margiad Evans and the mythic landscape of Wales', in *Welsh Writing in English*, vol. 6 (2000), pp. 89–118.
233   Hazel Carby, 'The politics of fiction, anthropology and the folk: Zora Neale Hurston', in Michael Awkward (ed.), *New Essays on 'Their Eyes Were Watching God'* (Cambridge: Cambridge University Press, 1990), p. 80.
234   Quoted in Pyrs Gruffudd, 'Back to the land', 69.
235   Sollors, *Ethnic Modernism*, p. 168.
236   Evans, *Country Dance*, p. 53.
237   Ibid., p. 54.
238   Ibid., p. 3.
239   Zora Neale Hurston, 'The Gilded Six-Bits' (1933), in Henry Louis Gates Jr, (ed.), *The Norton Anthology of African American Literature* (New York: Norton, 1997), pp. 1011–19.
240   Carby, 'The politics of fiction', pp. 77, 78.

[241] See, for instance, Tony Brown, 'Stories from foreign countries', p. 23.

[242] For an extended analysis, see Pyrs Gruffudd, 'Back to the land'.

[243] Dale Patterson, *Up From Bondage*, p. 81.

[244] Doris Sommer, *Proceed with Caution when Engaged by Minority Writing in the Americas* (Cambridge, MA: Harvard University Press, 1999), p. ix.

[245] Hurston, *Mules and Men*, p. 10.

[246] Barbara Johnson, 'Thresholds of difference', p. 325.

[247] Evans, *Country Dance*, pp. 103–4.

[248] Sommer, *Proceed with Caution*, p. 17.

[249] Evans, *Country Dance*, p. 1.

[250] Evans, *Country Dance* (London: Arthur Barker, 1932), p. 90. References to *Country Dance* in this book are generally to the widely available Library of Wales edition. There are some cases where this version differs from the 1932 original with translations omitted. Compare with p. 96 of the Library of Wales edition.

[251] Evans, *Country Dance* ([1932] Cardigan: Parthian, 2006), p. 18.

[252] Ibid., p. 29.

[253] Patterson, *Up from Bondage*, p. 101.

[254] Kirsti Bohata, *Postcolonialism Revisited* (Cardiff: University of Wales Press, 2004), pp. 119–21.

[255] Delmore Schwartz, 'The fiction of Ernest Hemingway', in *Selected Essays of Delmore Schwartz*, ed. Donald Dike and David Zucker (Chicago: University of Chicago Press, 1970), p. 259. See Sollors's discussion in *Ethnic Modernism*, p. 128.

[256] Quoted by Tony Brown, 'Stories from foreign countries', p. 22.

[257] Henry Louis Gates Jr, *The Signifying Monkey: A Theory of African-American Literary Criticism* (Oxford: Oxford University Press, 1988), pp. 170–216.

[258] Hurston, *Their Eyes*, pp. 188–9.

[259] Gates Jr, *The Signifying Monkey*, p. 208.

[260] Ibid., pp. 192–3. See also Patterson, *Up from Bondage*, p. 194.

[261] Zora Neale Hurston, *Moses, Man of the Mountain* ([1939] New York: Harper Collins, 1991), p. 204.

[262] Hurston, *Mules and Men*, pp. 43–4.

[263] Alice Gambrell, *Women Intellectuals, Modernism and Difference: Transatlantic Culture 1919–1945* (Cambridge: Cambridge University Press, 1997), p. 137.

[264] Zora Neale Hurston, *Dust Tracks on a Road* ([1942] New York: Harper Collins, 1991), pp. 63–4.

[265] Evans, *Country Dance*, pp. 41–3.

[266] Ceridwen Lloyd-Morgan's phrase in *Margiad Evans*, p. 28.

[267] Margiad Evans, *Country Dance*, p. 9.

[268] Ibid., p. 23.

[269] Ibid., p. 24.

[270] Ibid., p. 4.

[271] Gates Jr, *The Signifying Monkey*, p. 189.

[272] Hurston, *Their Eyes*, pp. 110–11.

[273] Ibid., p. 112.

274   Ibid., pp. 112–13.
275   Carby, 'The politics', p. 77.
276   Quoted in Gambrell, *Women Intellectuals*, p. 141.
277   Sommer, *Proceed with Caution*, p. 19.
278   R. Williams, *The Politics of Modernism*, p. 35.
279   Ibid., p. 47.
280   Raymond Williams, 'The importance of community', in *Who Speaks for Wales? Nation, Culture, Identity*, ed. Daniel Williams (Cardiff: University of Wales Press, 2003), p. 180.
281   Raymond Williams, *Culture* (London: Fontana, 1981), p. 85.
282   Raymond Williams, 'The social significance of 1926', in *Who Speaks for Wales?*, p. 40.
283   R. Williams, *The Politics of Modernism*, p. 139.
284   Harry Williams Diary, Raymond Williams Papers, Swansea University. The diaries also inform us that on 4 September the family went to London on holiday, and father and son attended a cinema on the 9th to see a film of the Farr vs. Louis fight.

## Chapter 3

1   Information supplied by Michael Harper in a brief discussion with him at a conference entitled 'Criss Cross: Confluence and Influence in 20th Century African American Music, Visual Art and Literature', Nottingham University, 19 June 2004.
2   Michael S. Harper, 'Visit to Abercanaid', *The Anglo-Welsh Review*, 26, 58 (spring 1977), pp. 18–19.
3   Joan Miller quoted in Hywel Francis and Dai Smith, *The Fed: A History of the South Wales Miners in the Twentieth Century* ([1980] Cardiff: University of Wales Press, 1998), p. 460. Joan Miller, *Aberfan: A Disaster and its Aftermath* (London: Constable, 1974).
4   Barbara Johnson, *A World of Difference* (Baltimore: Johns Hopkins University Press, 1987), p. 185.
5   Kimberly W. Benston, *Performing Blackness: Enactments of African-American Modernism* (London: Routlegde, 2000), pp. 173–4.
6   Ibid., p. 180.
7   Denise Levertov, 'Denise Levertov Writes', in Jeni Couzyn (ed.), *The Bloodaxe Book of Contemporary Women Poets* (Newcastle: Bloodaxe, 1985), p. 75. On the role of Wales in Levertov's 'construction of origins' see Barbara Prys-Williams, 'Web of connection: Denise Levertov's construction of origins', in Alyce von Rothkirch and Daniel Williams (eds), *Beyond the Difference: Welsh Literature in Comparative Contexts* (Cardiff: University of Wales Press, 2004), pp. 116–31.
8   Quoted in Benston, *Performing Blackness*, p. 178.
9   *Let Robeson Sing! A celebration of the life of Paul Robeson and his relationship with Wales* (Cardiff: Paul Robeson Cymru Committee/Bevan Foundation, 2001), p. 8.

[10]  The Caernarfon Pavilion (demolished in 1961) was filled to capacity four times
      during the 1930s. In 1934 for the Robeson concert, in 1935 for the National
      Eisteddfod, in 1937 for a meeting to welcome Saunders Lewis, Lewis Valentine
      and D. J. Williams back from their period of incarceration for setting light to an
      RAF bombing school in Penyberth, and for a Labour Day Festival in 1938. The
      title of the memorial meeting appears on the programme held at the South Wales
      Miners' Library, Swansea.
[11]  See Alan Llwyd, *Cymru Ddu/Black Wales: A History* (Cardiff: Hughes a'i Fab,
      2005), pp. 119–20. Neil Sinclair, *The Tiger Bay Story* (Cardiff: Dragon and Tiger
      Enterprises, 1997), p. 42.
[12]  Hywel Francis has produced a useful list of Robeson's connections with Wales,
      'Paul Robeson and Wales', held in the 'Paul Robeson File' at the South Wales
      Miners' Library, Swansea.
[13]  Neil Evans, 'Immigrants and minorities in Wales, 1840–1990: a comparative
      perspective', in Neil Evans, Paul O'Leary and Charlotte Williams (eds), *A
      Tolerant Nation? Exploring Ethnic Diversity in Wales* (Cardiff: University of
      Wales Press, 2003), p. 14.
[14]  Dai Smith, *Aneurin Bevan and the World of South Wales* (Cardiff: University of
      Wales Press, 1993), p. 10.
[15]  Dai Smith, *Wales: A Question for History* (Bridgend: Seren, 1999), p. 203. Francis
      quoted in *Let Robeson Sing!*, p. 60.
[16]  *Let Robeson Sing!*, p. 4.
[17]  Manic Street Preachers, *Let Robeson Sing*, Sony Music, 2001.
[18]  Such phrases appear in *The Let Robeson Sing* book published to coincide with the
      exhibition, and in Martha Edwards's touching pamphlet *Paul Robeson: Honorary
      Welshman* (Treorchy: Paul Robeson Exhibition, 1998).
[19]  M. Wynn Thomas, *James Kitchener Davies* (Cardiff: University of Wales Press,
      2002), p. x.
[20]  Josef Škvorecký, 'Red Music', Foreword to the English edition of *The Bass
      Saxophone* ([1977] London: Vintage, 1994), p. 10.
[21]  Ibid., p. 23.
[22]  Feffer was shot three years later. See Martin Duberman, *Paul Robeson: A
      Biography* (1988. New York: New Press, 1989), p. 353.
[23]  Quoted in Jonathan Karp, 'Performing Black-Jewish symbiosis: the 'Hassidic
      Chant' of Paul Robeson', *American Jewish History*, 91, 1 (March 2003), 77.
[24]  Duberman, *Paul Robeson*, p. 353. David Levering Lewis, 'Paul Robeson and the
      USSR', in Jeffrey C. Stewart (ed.), *Paul Robeson: Artist and Citizen* (New
      Brunswick: Rutgers University Press, 1998), p. 226.
[25]  Lewis, 'Paul Robeson and the USSR', p. 226.
[26]  Duberman, *Paul Robeson*, p. 506. Lewis, 'Paul Robeson and the USSR', p. 229.
[27]  Duberman, *Paul Robeson*, p. 499. Lewis, 'Paul Robeson and the USSR', p. 230.
      Paul Robeson Jr is convinced that his father was drugged. Paul Robeson Jr, 'The
      Paul Robeson files', *The Nation*, 20 December 1999, 30–5.
[28]  Robert Stradling, *Wales and the Spanish Civil War: The Dragon's Dearest Cause?*
      (Cardiff: University of Wales Press, 2004).

29  Hywel Francis, *Miners Against Fascism: Wales and the Spanish Civil War* ([1984]
    Abersychan: Warren and Pell, 2004), p. 108. Stradling, *Wales and the Spanish
    Civil War*, pp. 177, 158–9.

30  Stradling, *Wales and the Spanish Civil War*, p. 102.

31  Stefan Collini, 'On Variousness', *New Left Review*, 2, 27 (May/June 2004), 94–5.

32  Kate A. Baldwin, *Beyond the Color Line and the Iron Curtain: Reading
    Encounters Between Black and Red, 1922–1963* (Durham: Duke University
    Press, 2002), p. 8.

33  Hywel Francis, 'Paul Robeson: His Legacy for Wales', a lecture to the Friends of
    the National Library of Wales, Aberystwyth, 12 July 2003; reproduced and
    expanded in Welsh in Daniel G. Williams (ed.), *Canu Caeth: Y Cymry a'r
    Affro-Americaniaid* (Llandysul: Gomer, 2010), pp. 64–73.

34  Quoted from the *Western Mail*, 24 February 1949, in *Let Robeson Sing*, p. 38.
    Quoted in Sheila Tully Boyle and Andrew Bunie, *Paul Robeson: The Years of
    Promise and Achievement* (Amherst: University of Massachusetts Press, 2001),
    p. 416.

35  Karp, 'Performing Black-Jewish symbiosis', 69.

36  Paul Robeson, *Here I Stand* ([1958] Boston, Beacon Press, 1988), p. 58; abbrevi-
    ated from now on as *HIS*. Paul Robeson, 'I Know the Irish People', *The Irish
    Democrat* (August 1949), 8.

37  Robeson, *HIS*, p. 58. Quoted in Duberman, *Paul Robeson*, p. 424.

38  Quoted in Karp, 'Performing Black-Jewish symbiosis', 69.

39  Quoted in ibid. 'Robeson spurns music he "doesn't understand"' (1933), in Paul
    Robeson, *Paul Robeson Speaks: Writings, Speeches, Interviews 1918–1974*, ed.
    Philip S. Foner (London: Quartet Books, 1978), p. 85; abbreviated from now on
    as *PRS*.

40  Robeson, *HIS*, pp. 48–9.

41  See Robeson, *HIS*, pp. 48–62

42  Robeson, 'I, too, am American' (1949), in *PRS*, p. 191. 'The UAW should set the
    pace' (1953), *PRS*, p. 340.

43  See Robeson, *HIS*, pp. 67–70.

44  Robeson, 'Speech at the Peace Bridge Arch' (1953), *PRS*, p. 364.

45  Robeson, 'Pacifica Radio interview' (1958), *PRS*, p. 453.

46  W. E. B. Du Bois, 'Paul LeRoy Robeson' (1918), in Du Bois, *Writings* (New York:
    The Library of America, 1986), p. 1176.

47  Du Bois, 'Criteria of Negro art' (1926), in *Writings*, p. 1002.

48  For a discussion of this in the works of Arnold and Howells, see Daniel G.
    Williams, *Ethnicity and Cultural Authority* (Edinburgh: Edinburgh University
    Press, 2006).

49  Quoted in Michael North, *The Dialect of Modernism: Race, Language and
    Twentieth-Century Literature* (Oxford: Oxford University Press, 1994), p. 137.

50  Elizabeth Shepley Sergeant, 'The man with his home in a rock: Paul Robeson',
    *New Republic*, March 3 1926, 40.

51  Quoted in Hazel Carby, *Race Men* (Cambridge, MA: Harvard University Press,
    1998), pp. 92, 98.

52 'Paul Robeson speaks about art and the Negro' (1930), *PRS*, p. 79. 'Robeson spurns music he "doesn't understand"' (1933), *PRS*, p. 85. Quoted in Sterling Stuckey, *Slave Culture: Nationalist Theory and the Foundations of Black America* (Oxford: Oxford University Press, 1987), pp. 324, 336.

53 Stuckey, *Slave Culture*, p. 336.

54 Du Bois, *The Souls of Black Folk* (1903), in *Writings*, p. 370. Robeson, 'The culture of the Negro' (1934), *PRS*, p. 86.

55 Robeson, 'Negroes – don't ape the whites' (1935), *PRS*, p. 91.

56 Robeson, 'Primitives' (1936), *PRS*, p. 111.

57 Robeson, 'I want to be African' (1934), *PRS*, p. 90.

58 Ibid., p. 88.

59 Ibid., p. 91.

60 Eslanda Robeson, *African Journey* (London: Victor Gollancz, 1946), p. 9.

61 Paul Robeson, *HIS*, p. 33.

62 Edward Said, *Culture and Imperialism* ([1993] London, Vintage, 1994), pp. 294–5.

63 See Robert J. C. Young, *Postcolonialism: An Historical Introduction* (Oxford: Blackwell, 2001), p. 225.

64 Raymond Williams, *Culture* (London: Fontana, 1981), p. 83.

65 Ibid., p. 84.

66 Ibid.

67 Robeson, 'The culture of the Negro' (1934), *PRS*, p. 86.

68 Robeson, *HIS*, p. 34.

69 Lewis quoted in John Davies, *A History of Wales* ([1990 in Welsh] London: Penguin, 1993), p. 591. Du Bois, 'Conservation of races' (1897), in *Writings*, p. 822. Robeson, 'The culture of the Negro' (1934), *PRS*, p. 87. Quoted in Duberman, *Paul Robeson*, p. 176.

70 Gertrude Stein, *The Autobiography of Alice B. Toklas* (New York: Random House, 1933), pp. 237–8.

71 George S. Schuyler, 'The Negro art hokum', in David Levering Lewis (ed.), *The Portable Harlem Renaissance Reader* (London: Penguin, 1994), p. 97.

72 Quoted in Lawrence Jackson, *Ralph Ellison: The Emergence of Genius* (New York: John Wiley and Sons, 2002), p. 318.

73 Robeson, *HIS*, p. 36.

74 Robeson, 'How I discovered Africa' (1953), *PRS*, p. 352; also *HIS*, p. 36.

75 Quoted in Duberman, *Paul Robeson*, p. 190.

76 Quoted in ibid.

77 Quoted in ibid.

78 See Alan M. Wald, *Exiles from a Future Time: The Forging of the Mid-Twentieth-Century Left* (Chapel Hill: University of North Carolina Press, 2002), p. 267.

79 Locke and Thompson, quoted in William J. Maxwell, *New Negro, Old Left: African-American Writing and Communism Between the Wars* (New York: Columbia University Press, 1999), p. 164. Langston Hughes, *I Wonder as I Wander* (New York: Hill and Wang, 1956), pp. 101–89.

80 Richard Wright, *American Hunger* ([1977] New York: Harper and Row 1983), pp. 81–2.

81  Joseph Stalin, 'Marxism and the national question' (1913), in *Marxism and the National Question: Selected Writings and Speeches* (New York: International Publishers, 1942), p. 12. On Soviet attitudes towards African Americans and the emergence of the 'Black belt nation thesis', see Baldwin, *Beyond the Color Line*, pp. 36–47.

82  Maxwell, *New Negro, Old Left*, p. 7.

83  Ibid., p. 164.

84  Zora Neale Hurston, 'Why the Negro won't buy communism', *American Legion* 50 (June 1951), 15. The Welsh modernist poet Lynette Roberts argued somewhat similarly that 'Communism and Socialism' were examples of 'the imposition of bourgeois and shallow town culture forced' on the 'wholesome ways' of rural folk. Lynette Roberts, *Diaries, Letters, Recollections*, ed. Patrick McGuinness (Manchester: Carcanet Press, 2008) p. 17. Thanks to Gareth Evans for drawing my attention to this.

85  Kenneth Mostern, *Autobiography and Black Identity Politics: Racialization in Twentieth-Century America* (Cambridge: Cambridge University Press, 1999), p. 120.

86  Robeson, *HIS*, p. 54.

87  Chris Williams, *Democratic Rhondda: Politics and Society, 1855–1951* (Cardiff: University of Wales Press, 1996), p. 212.

88  Mostern, *Autobiography*, p. 120.

89  Gareth Williams, *George Ewart Evans* (Cardiff: University of Wales Press, 1991), p. 12.

90  Ibid., pp. 70–1.

91  Idris Cox, *The People Can Save South Wales* (London: Communist Party of Great Britain, 1937), p. 5. Thanks to Chris Williams for sharing material related to Cox.

92  Gwyn A. Williams, *When Was Wales? A History of the Welsh* (London: Black Raven Press, 1985), p. 274.

93  Quoted in Francis, *Miners Against Fascism*, p. 108. Duberman, *Paul Robeson*, p. 228.

94  T. J. Davies, *Paul Robeson* (Abertawe: Gwasg Christopher Davies, 1981), pp. 194–5; my translation.

95  Robeson, 'The People of America are the Power' (1951), *PRS*, p. 271.

96  *Western Mail*, 24 August 1939; quoted in Mark A. Exton, 'Paul Robeson and south Wales: a partial guide to a man's beliefs', MA thesis, University of Exeter, 1984, 59; copy held at the South Wales Miners' Library, Swansea University.

97  'Robeson and Bevan get big welcome', *Western Mail*, 4 August 1958. See my discussion of this event in Daniel G. Williams, *Aneurin Bevan and Paul Robeson: Socialism, Class and Identity* (Cardiff: Institute of Welsh Affairs, 2010).

98  Charles L. Blockson, 'Paul Robeson: a bibliophile in spite of himself', in Jeffrey C. Stewart (ed.), *Paul Robeson: Artist and Citizen* (New Brunswick: Rutgers University Press, 1998), p. 243. 'Mr Bevan and Paul Robeson at Eisteddfod opening', *Merthyr Express*, 9 August 1958, 6.

99  Interview with Professor J. Beverley Smith, 5 August 2005.

100 Quoted in the *Merthyr Express*, 9 August 1958, 6.

[101]   Programme for concert held at the Majestic Cinema, Wrexham, Sunday 25
        March 1934; copy in the Paul Robeson Collection at the Miners Library,
        University of Wales Swansea. See also the programme for a concert held at the
        Empire Cinema, Neath, in the Schomburg Library, Lawrence Brown Collection
        (Microfilm Reel 5). Duberman, *Paul Robeson*, p. 178.

[102]   Robeson, *HIS*, p. 54.

[103]   Mostern, *Autobiography*, p. 132.

[104]   Robeson, 'Robeson spurns music he doesn't understand' (1933), *PRS*, p. 85.

[105]   Robeson, 'I want to be African' (1934), *PRS*, p. 90.

[106]   Robeson, 'Pacifica Radio interview' (1958), *PRS*, p. 453.

[107]   Suny, quoted by Baldwin, *Beyond the Color Line and the Iron Curtain*, p. 211.

[108]   Ibid.

[109]   Duberman, *Paul Robeson*, pp. 172–3.

[110]   Eric J. Sundquist, *To Wake the Nations: Race in the Making of American
        Literature* (Cambridge, MA: Harvard University Press, 1993), p. 450.

[111]   Hazel Carby, *Race Men*, p. 79.

[112]   Quoted in Daniel J. Leab, *From Sambo to Superspade: The Black Experience in
        Motion Pictures* (Boston: Houghton Mifflin, 1976), p. 114.

[113]   See Carby, *Race Men*, p. 81. Duberman, *Paul Robeson*, pp. 224–5.

[114]   David Berry, *Wales and the Cinema: The First Hundred Years* (Cardiff:
        University of Wales Press, 1994), p. 166. The foregoing analysis relies consider-
        ably on Berry's fine analysis, which has been supplemented in Welsh by Gwenno
        Ffrancon, *Cyfaredd y Cysgodion; Delweddu Cymru a'i Phobl ar Ffilm, 1935–
        1951* (Caerdydd: Gwasg Prifysgol Cymru, 2003).

[115]   See Laura Marcus, 'Cinema and visual culture: Close Up (1927–33)', in Peter
        Brooker and Andrew Thacker (eds), *The Oxford Critical and Cultural History of
        Modernism Magazines*, vol. 1, *Britain and Ireland 1880–1955* (Oxford: Oxford
        University Press, 2009), pp. 505–29.

[116]   Essie Robeson quoted in Duberman, *Paul Robeson*, p. 131. Bryher (1894–1983)
        was the pen name of the novelist, poet, memoirist and magazine editor Annie
        Winifred Ellerman. H.D. (born Hilda Doolittle) (1886–1961) was an American
        poet and novelist. Bryher, H.D. and Macpherson formed the film magazine
        *Close Up*.

[117]   Kenneth Macpherson, 'As Is', *Close Up*, 7, 5 (November 1930), 293–4.

[118]   H.D., '*Borderline*', in James Donald, Anne Friedberg and Laura Marcus (eds),
        *Close Up 1927–1933: Cinema and Modernism* (London: Cassell, 1998), p. 233.

[119]   Carby, *Race Men*, p. 81.

[120]   See Gwenno Ffrancon, 'Affro-Americaniaid a'r Cymry ar y Sgrin Fawr', in D.
        G. Williams (ed.), *Canu Caeth: Y Cymry a'r Affro-Americaniaid*, p. 13,. n. 14.

[121]   Stephen Bourne, *Black in the British Frame: The Black Experience in British
        Film and Television* (London: Continuum, 2001), p. 27.

[122]   Pwyllgor y Llyfr Emynau Cydenwadol, *Caneuon Ffydd: Hen Nodiant*
        (Llandysul: Gomer, 2001), p. 896.

[123]   Jack Jones, *Me and Mine: Further Chapters in the Autobiography* (London:
        Hamish Hamilton, 1946), p. 112. The hymn is sung to the tune 'Ebenezer', also
        known as 'Tôn Y Botel'.

124  Jeffrey C. Stewart, 'The black body: Robeson as a work of art and politics', in
     Stewart (ed.), *Paul Robeson: Artist and Citizen*, p. 157.
125  See Charles Musser, 'Troubled relations: Robeson, O'Neill and Micheaux', in
     Stewart (ed.), *Paul Robeson: Artist and Citizen*, pp. 82–8.
126  Eugene O'Neill, *The Emperor Jones* (1921) in O'Neill, *Anna Christie and Other
     Plays* (London: Penguin, 1960), pp. 122–3.
127  Carby, *Race Men*, p. 79.
128  Ibid., p. 68.
129  Quoted in David Levering Lewis, *When Harlem Was in Vogue* ([1981] Oxford:
     Oxford University Press, 1989), p. 92.
130  See George Hutchinson, *The Harlem Renaissance in Black and White*
     (Cambridge, MA: Harvard University Press, 1995), pp. 193–4.
131  Robeson, 'Reflections on O'Neill's plays' (1924), *PRS*, p. 70.
132  Quoted by Musser, 'Troubled relations', p. 94. *The Pittsburgh Courier*, 7
     November 1925, 10.
133  Quoted by Musser, 'Troubled relations', p. 94. *The Pittsburgh Courier*, 7
     November 1925, p.10.
134  Fredric Jameson, *Fables of Aggression: Wyndham Lewis, the Modernist as
     Fascist* (Berkeley; University of California Press, 1979), p. 2. See Carby's
     discussion in *Race Men*, p. 66.
135  Francis, *Miners Against Fascism*, p. 108.
136  Stewart, 'The black body', pp. 157–8.
137  Ibid., p. 157.
138  Quoted in Duberman, *Paul Robeson*, p. 239.
139  Grahame Greene, *The Spectator*, 15 March 1940, in *The Pleasure Dome: The
     Collected Film Criticism 1935–40*, ed. John Russell Taylor (London: Secker and
     Warburg, 1972), p. 275. Quoted by Berry, *Wales and Cinema*, p. 159.
140  Berry, *Wales and Cinema*, p. 169.
141  Ibid.
142  Quoted in ibid.
143  See Stephen Bourne, *Black in the British Frame*, pp. 28–9.
144  Both Peter Stead and Gwenno Ffrancon draw attention to the film's perpetuation
     of outmoded music-hall stereotypes. Stead, 'Wales in the movies', in Tony Curtis
     (ed.), *Wales: The Imagined Nation* (Bridgend: Poetry Wales Press, 1986), p. 171.
     Ffrancon, *Cyfaredd y Cysgodion*, p. 89.
145  Hywel Teifi Edwards, *Arwr Glew Erwau'r Glo: Delwedd y Glowr yn
     Llenyddiaeth y Gymraeg 1850–1950* (Llandysul: Gomer, 1994); in English, 'The
     Welsh collier as hero: 1850–1950', in Tony Brown (ed.), *Welsh Writing in
     English: A Yearbook of Critical Essays*, vol. 2 (Cardiff: University of Wales
     Press, 1996), pp. 22–48.
146  Edwards, 'The Welsh collier', p. 25.
147  Ibid., p. 27.
148  Ibid., p. 37. For a full account see Edwards, *Arwr Glew*, pp. 114–38.
149  See Gareth Williams, *Valleys of Song: Music and Society in Wales 1840–1914*
     (Cardiff: University of Wales Press, 1998), pp. 46–53.
150  See Edwards, 'The Welsh collier', pp. 37–9.

[151]   See ibid., p. 38.

[152]   'Defnyddiwyd yr ymadrodd "mam yn Israel" dro ar ôl tro yn ysgrifau cofiannol
        y bedwaredd ganrif ar bymtheg i ddisgrifio'r Gymraes ddelfrydol, ac y mae
        ysbryd ymosodol Debora yn rhan o ddelwedd y Fam Gymreig. Ei phrif nodwed-
        dion yw diwydrwydd egniol a dygnwch milriawthus yn wyneb caledi bywyd.'
        ('The expression "mother in Israel" was used repeatedly in the memoirs of the
        nineteenth century to describe the ideal Welsh woman, and the aggressive spirit
        of Debora is part of the image of the Welsh Mother. Her main features are ener-
        getic diligence and a soldierly endurance in the face of the hardships of life.' My
        translation.) Jane Aaron, *Pur fel y Dur: Y Gymraes yn Llên Menywod y
        Bedwaredd Ganrif ar Bymtheg* (Caerdydd: Gwasg Prifysgol Cymru, 1998),
        p. 20. Also Jane Aaron, *Nineteenth-Century Women's Writing in Wales: Nation,
        Gender and Identity* (Cardiff: University of Wales Press, 2007).

[153]   Deirdre Beddoe, *Out of the Shadows: A History of Women in Twentieth-Century
        Wales* (Cardiff: University of Wales Press, 2000), p. 13.

[154]   Quoted in Ffrancon, *Cyfaredd*, p. 89.

[155]   See ibid., p. 89.

[156]   James A. Snead, 'Spectatorship and capture in King Kong', in V. Smith (ed.),
        *Representing Blackness: Issues in Film and Video* (London: The Athlone Press,
        1997), pp. 26–7.

[157]   Ibid., p. 27.

[158]   Matthew Arnold, *On the Study of Celtic Literature* (1867), in *The Complete
        Prose Works of Matthew Arnold*, vol. 3, ed. R. H. Super (Ann Arbor, University
        of Michigan Press, 1962), p. 311.

[159]   Ibid., pp. 344, 345, 347.

[160]   Ibid., 346.

[161]   Gerald Early, *The Culture of Bruising: Essays on Prizefighting, Literature and
        Modern American Culture* (Hopewell, NJ: The Ecco Press, 1994), pp. 159–60.

[162]   Henry Louis Gates Jr, 'The trope of a new Negro and the reconstruction of the
        image of the Black', *Representations*, 24 (1988), 129–55.

[163]   Booker T. Washington, *Up From Slavery* ([1901] Harmondsworth: Penguin,
        1986), p. 221.

[164]   Edwards, 'The Welsh collier', p. 35.

[165]   Ibid.

[166]   I am drawing here on Berry's fine analysis in *Wales and Cinema*, p. 171.

[167]   Berry, *Wales and Cinema*, p. 171. See also Ffrancon, *Cyfaredd*, p. 83.

[168]   Stead, 'Wales in the movies', p. 171.

[169]   See Duberman, *Paul Robeson*, p. 233.

[170]   Ibid., pp. 233–5.

[171]   Quoted in Carby, *Race Men*, p. 80.

[172]   Quoted in Kevin K. Gaines, *Uplifting the Race: Black Leadership, Politics, and
        Culture in the Twentieth Century* (Chapel Hill: University of North Carolina
        Press, 1996), p. 250.

[173]   B. L. Coombes, *These Poor Hands: The Autobiography of a Miner in South
        Wales* ([1939] Cardiff: University of Wales Press, 2002), p. 180.

[174]   See T. J. Davies, *Paul Robeson*, p. 89.

175  Jack Jones, 'Nofelau'r Cymry Seisnig', *Tir Newydd*, 8 (Mai 1937), 9.
176  See Berry, *Wales and Cinema*, p. 168. Jack Jones, *Me and Mine*, p. 118.
177  Berry, *Wales and Cinema*, p. 168.
178  Raymond Williams, 'The Welsh industrial novel' (1979), in *Who Speaks for Wales? Nation, Culture, Identity*, ed. Daniel Williams (Cardiff: University of Wales Press, 2003), p. 100.
179  Ibid., p. 105.
180  Ibid.
181  Ibid., p. 98.
182  David R. Roediger, *The Wages of Whiteness: Race and the Making of the American Working Class* (London: Verso, 1991), p. 9.
183  Quoted in Dai Smith, *Wales! Wales?* (London: Allen and Unwin, 1984), p. 100.
184  Dai Smith, *Aneurin Bevan and the World of South Wales* (Cardiff: University of Wales Press, 1993), p. 5.
185  Smith, *Aneurin Bevan*, p. 190.
186  Glenn Jordan, '"We never really noticed you were coloured": postcolonialist reflections on immigrants and minorities in Wales', in Jane Aaron and Chris Williams (eds), *Postcolonial Wales* (Cardiff: University of Wales Press, 2005), pp. 70–1.
187  Roediger, *The Wages*, p. 3.
188  Gwyn Jones, *Times Like These* ([1936] London: Victor Gollancz, 1979), p. 303.
189  Donald Bogle, *Toms, Coons, Mulattoes, Mammies and Bucks: An Interpretive History of Blacks in American Films* ([1973] London: Continuum, 2001), pp. 7, 10.
190  See Melvyn Stokes, 'The endless re-birth of the birth of a nation', *Interdisciplinary Journal of German Linguistics and Semiotic Analysis*, 5, 2 (fall 2000), 199–212.
191  See Bogle, *Toms, Coons, Mulattoes*, pp.10–18.
192  Jones, *Times Like These*, p. 88.
193  H. V. Morton, *In Search of Wales* (New York: Dodd, Mead, 1932), p. 318.
194  Jack Jones, *Black Parade* (London: Faber, 1935), p. 1.
195  Stephen Knight, *A Hundred Years of Fiction: Writing Wales in English* (Cardiff: University of Wales Press, 2004), p. 78.
196  See Susan Gubar's discussion of the film in *Racechanges: White Skin, Black Face in American Culture* (Oxford: Oxford University Press, 1997), pp. 57–66.
197  Jack Jones, *Black Parade*, pp. 72–3, 96, 280.
198  See Melinda Gray, 'Uncle Tom's Welsh dress: ethnicity, authority and translation', in Rothkirch and Williams (eds), *Beyond the Difference*, pp. 173–85.
199  See Werner Sollors, *Beyond Ethnicity: Consent and Descent in American Culture* (New York: Oxford University Press, 1986), p. 225.
200  See Berry, *Wales and Cinema*, p. 122.
201  Eric Lott, *Love and Theft: Blackface Minstrelsy and the American Working Class* (Oxford: Oxford University Press, 1993), is a brilliant analysis of both the history and meaning of blackface minstrelsy.
202  David (Dai) Smith, 'Myth and meaning in the literature of the south Wales coalfield – the 1930s', *The Anglo-Welsh Review*, 25, 56 (1976), 24.
203  Jack Jones, *Bidden to the Feast* ([1938] London: Corgi Books, 1968), p. 381.

[204]  See Roediger, *The Wages*, p. 115. Gareth Williams, *Valleys of Song*, p. 222, n. 31.

[205]  Quoted in Hywel Teifi Edwards, *Gŵyl Gwalia: Yr Eisteddfod yn Oes Victoria*, (Llandysul: Gwasg Gomer, 1980), p. 236. Ieuan Gwyllt, 'Purdeb Chwaeth Mewn Cerddoriaeth', *Y Cerddor Cymraeg*, 2, 25 (1 Mawrth 1867), 4–5.

[206]  Francis and Smith, *The Fed*, p. 58.

[207]  Lewis Jones, *Cwmardy: The Story of a Welsh Mining Valley* ([1937] London: Lawrence and Wishart, 1979), p. 134.

[208]  Lott, *Love and Theft*, p. 29.

[209]  See Dai Smith, *Aneurin Bevan*, p. 46. Gwyn A. Williams, *When Was Wales?*, pp. 177–8.

[210]  On population changes in Wales, see John Davies, *A History of Wales*, p. 398. Dai Smith, *Wales: A Question*, p. 64. Gwyn A. Williams, *When Was Wales?*, pp. 173–81.

[211]  Gubar, *Racechanges*, p. 65.

[212]  Gaines, *Uplifting*, p. 70. Gubar, p. 48.

[213]  Dai Smith, 'Myth and meaning', 21.

[214]  Richard Llewellyn, *How Green Was My Valley* ([1939] London: Penguin, 1991), pp.188–9.

[215]  John Harris, 'A Hallelujah of a Book': *How Green Was My Valley* as Bestseller', in Tony Brown (ed.), *Welsh Writing in English: A Yearbook of Critical Essays*, vol. 3 (Cardiff: University of Wales Press, 1997), pp. 47–8.

[216]  Gubar, p. 63. On the film see Berry, *Wales and the Cinema*, pp. 161–6.

[217]  Ian Bell, 'How Green *Was* My Valley', *Planet: The Welsh Internationalist*, 73 (February/March 1989), 3–9. Edwards, *Arwr Glew*, p. xxxiv. Smith, 'Myth and meaning', 33–4. Harris, 'A Hallelujah', p. 47.

[218]  Ibid., p. 56.

[219]  George Ewart Evans, 'The Valleys', *Wales*, 3 (autumn 1937), 128.

[220]  Rhys Davies, *My Wales* (London: Jarrolds, 1937), pp. 49, 50, 70.

[221]  Jack Jones, *Unfinished Journey* (London: Hamish Hamilton, 1937), p. 22.

[222]  Ibid., p. 100.

[223]  Jack Jones, *Rhondda Roundabout* ([1934] London: Hamish Hamilton, 1949), p. 123.

[224]  Jack Jones, *Bidden to the Feast*, p. 142.

[225]  The phrase is Lewis Jones's, from the 'Foreword' to *Cwmardy*.

[226]  Lewis Jones, *We Live: The Story of a Welsh Mining Valley* ([1939] London: Lawrence and Wishart, 1978), pp. 190, 255.

[227]  L. Jones, *Cwmardy*, p. 239.

[228]  Rhys Davies, 'Blodwen', in *Collected Stories*, vol. 1, ed. Meic Stephens (Llandysul: Gomer, 1996), p. 81. Rhys Davies, *The Withered Root* (London: Robert Holden and Company, 1927), p. 27.

[229]  L. Jones, *Cwmardy*, p. 11. Glyn Jones, 'Porth-Y-Rhyd' in *The Collected Short Stores*, ed. Tony Brown (Cardiff: University of Wales Press, 1999), p. 85.

[230]  'Mulciber', 'The future of the industrial novel in Great Britain', *The Welsh Review*, 2, 3 (1939), quoted by David (Dai) Smith in, 'Myth and meaning' 23.

[231]  H. J. Fleure, 'The Welsh people', *Wales*, 10 (October 1939), reprinted in *Wales 1–11* (London: Frank Cass, 1969), pp. 265–9.

[232]  Gareth Williams, 'Compulsory sterilisation of Welsh miners, 1936', *Llafur*, 3, 3 (1982), 67–73.

[233]  E. W. MacBride, 'Cultivation of the unfit' (1936), reprinted by Gareth Williams at the end of his article on 'Compulsory sterilisation',70.

[234]  Alan Llwyd, *Cymru Ddu/Black Wales*, pp. 105–22.

[235]  Quoted in ibid., p. 117.

[236]  Ibid., p. 118.

[237]  Idris Davies, 'Tiger Bay', in *The Complete Poems*, ed. Dafydd Johnston (Cardiff: University of Wales Press, 1994), p. 73.

[238]  Gwyn Jones, *Times Like These*, p. 101.

[239]  On the 1919 riots, see Llwyd, *Cymru Ddu*, pp. 92–103. Neil Evans, 'Immigrants and minorities in Wales', pp. 20–1.

[240]  Jack Jones, *Black Parade*, p. 47.

[241]  Ibid., pp. 145–6.

[242]  Randy Roberts, *Jack Dempsey: The Manassa Mauler* (London: Robson Books, 1987), pp. 213–15. I am grateful to Gareth Williams for this reference.

[243]  Paul O'Leary, *Immigration and Integration: The Irish in Wales, 1798–1922* (Cardiff: University of Wales Press, 2000), pp. 144–51, 302–4.

[244]  Homi Bhabha, *The Location of Culture* (London: Routledge, 1994), pp. 93–101. Applied to Wales, see Stephen Knight, 'The voices of Glamorgan: Gwyn Thomas's colonial fiction', in Tony Brown (ed.), *Welsh Writing in English: A Yearbook of Critical Essays*, vol. 7 (Cardiff: University of Wales Press, 2001–2), pp. 16–34. The concept is discussed in relation to Emlyn Williams and Ralph Ellison in chapter 4.

[245]  Lott, *Love and Theft*, p. 52.

[246]  Duberman, *Paul Robeson*, p. 52.

[247]  Quoted by Maxwell, *New Negro, Old Left*, pp. 83–4. See also David Roediger, *Towards the Abolition of Whiteness: Essays on Race, Politics and Working Class History* (London: Verso, 1994), p. 64.

[248]  Quoted by Maxwell, *New Negro, Old Left*, p. 84.

[249]  Rhys Davies, *The Black Venus* (London: William Heineman, 1944), pp. 1, 65. For a detailed analysis of the novel, see Kirsti Bohata, *Postcolonialism Revisited* (Cardiff: University of Wales Press, 2004), pp. 40–50. On strategies of surveillance in industrial Wales, see Andy Croll, *Civilizing the Urban: Popular Culture and Public Space in Merthyr, c.1870–1914* (Cardiff: University of Wales Press, 2000), pp. 62–103.

[250]  Davies, *The Black Venus*, p. 65.

[251]  Lott, *Love and Theft*, p. 149.

[252]  M. Wynn Thomas, *James Kitchener Davies*, p. 29.

[253]  Coombes, *These Poor Hands*, p 24. Also the tale of a Frenchman believed to be a Welsh speaker, p. 54.

[254]  See, for example, the description of miners' leader Mabon in Jack Jones, *Black Parade*, p. 147.

[255]  Llewellyn, *How Green Was My Valley*, p. 165.

256   L. Jones, *Cwmardy*, p. 2.
257   L. Jones, *Cwmardy*, p. 99.
258   Coombes, p. 59.
259   Nathaniel Mackey, 'Other: from verb to noun', in Robert G. O'Meally (ed.), *The Jazz Cadence of American Culture* (New York: Columbia University Press, 1998), p. 526.
260   Lott, *Love and Theft*, p. 92.
261   'Fluellyn', *Reply to the Perfidious Welshman* (Wrexham: Hughes and Son, 1911), p. 76. For an account of this controversy, see the entry in Meic Stephens (ed.), *The New Companion to the Literature of Wales* (Cardiff: University of Wales Pres, 1998), pp. 581–2.
262   Jack Jones, 'The Black Welshman', manuscript in the Jack Jones Papers, National Library of Wales, Aberystwyth, 1. The novel was serialized in *The Empire News*, beginning on 23 June 1957, 6.
263   I discuss 'The Black Welshman' in 'Black and white: writing about fighting in Wales', in Peter Stead and Gareth Williams (eds), *Wales and its Boxers: The Fighting Tradition* (Cardiff: University of Wales Press, 2008), pp. 132–3.
264   Quoted in Berry, *Wales and Cinema*, p. 169.
265   See Doris Evans McGinty and Wayne Shirley, 'Paul Robeson, musician', in J. C. Stewart (ed.), *Paul Robeson: Artist and Citizen*, (New Brunswick: Rutgers University Press, 1998), p. 115.
266   *Merthyr Express*, Saturday 9 August 1958, 6.
267   Lewis Jones, *We Live*, p. 322. This scene may have been written by Mavis Llewellyn who completed the last chapter and a half of the novel following Jones's early death in 1939. I am concerned with the resonances of the scene here, not its authorship.
268   Lewis Jones (or Mavis Llewellyn) is probably thinking of the popular song 'Y Bwthyn Bach Tô Gwellt'. See Huw Williams, *Canu'r Bobl* (Dinbych: Gee, 1978), pp. 183–5.
269   Charlotte Williams, *Sugar and Slate* (Aberystwyth: Planet, 2002), p. 176.

## Chapter 4

1    Ralph Ellison, 'Introduction' to *Invisible Man* ([1981] New York: Vintage, 1995), p. xiv.
2    Ibid., p. vii.
3    F. W. Dupee, 'On *Invisible Man*', *The Washington Post*, 26 September 1965, 4. On the short stories as prefigurations of *Invisible Man*, see John F. Callahan, 'Introduction' to Ralph Ellison, *Flying Home and Other Stories*, ed. John F. Callahan ([1996] London: Penguin, 1998), pp. ix–xxxviii, and Shelby Steele, 'The content of his character', *The New Republic*, 1 March 1999, 27–34.
4    On Ellison's wartime experience in Wales, see Lawrence Jackson, *Ralph Ellison: The Emergence of Genius* (New York: John Wiley and Sons, 2002), pp. 297–8. Arnold Rampersad, *Ralph Ellison: A Biography* ([2007] New York: Vintage,

2008), pp. 170–1. Ralph Ellison, 'Letter to G. A. Smith, March 20,1977', *The New Republic*, 1 March 1999, 44–5.

5  The comment appears on an unpaginated page of typescript beginning, 'He sat now in the Red Cross Club and gazed into the glowing coals . . .' Ralph Ellison, 'A Storm of Blizzard Proportions', several drafts, The Ralph Ellison Papers, Library of Congress, Washington DC, box 165, file 7.

6  Quoted in Callahan, 'Introduction', p. xvii.

7  Ellison, 'A Storm'.

8  Ibid.

9  James Joyce, 'The Dead', in *Dubliners* ([1914] London: Penguin, 1992), p. 225.

10  Benedict Anderson, *Imagined Communities* (London: Verso, 1983).

11  T. S. Eliot, 'The Journey of the Magi', in *Collected Poems* ([1936] London: Faber, 1974), p. 109.

12  See W. E. B. Du Bois, *The Souls of Black Folk* (1903), in *Writings* (New York: The Library of America, 1986), p. 364.

13  Ralph Ellison, 'In a Strange Country', in *Flying Home and Other Stories* ([1996] London: Penguin, 1998), p. 139.

14  Ibid., pp. 145–6.

15  Dai Smith, *Aneurin Bevan and the World of South Wales* (Cardiff: University of Wales Press, 1993), p. 10. Smith quotes selectively to give the impression that 'The Star Spangled Banner' is the only anthem sung in the story.

16  Callahan, 'Introduction', p. xxxvi.

17  Ellison, 'A Storm', no page numbers. On Ellison and boxing see Kasia Boddy, *Boxing: A Cultural History* (London: Reakton Books, 2008), pp. 309–15.

18  Gerald Early, 'Introduction' to Countee Cullen, *My Soul's High Song: The Collected Writings of Countee Cullen*, ed. Gerald Early (New York: Anchor Books, 1991), p. 54.

19  Harvard Sitkoff, 'African American militancy in the World War II South: another perspective', in Neil R. McMillen (ed.), *Remaking Dixie: The Impact of World War II on the American South* (Jackson: University Press of Mississippi, 1997), p. 72. On Louis in Bangor, see John Cowell, *Bangor at War 1939–45* (Menai Bridge: John Cowell, 2000), p. 68. On Louis as GI, see Neil A. Wynn, *The Afro-American and the Second World War* ([1975] New York: Holmes and Meier, 1993), p. 31.

20  James Baldwin, *The Fire Next Time* (New York: Dial Press, 1963), pp. 68–9.

21  Richard Dalfiume, 'The forgotten years of the Negro revolution', *Journal of American History* 55 (June 1968), 90–106.

22  Langston Hughes, 'How About it Dixie', in *Jim Crow's Last Stand* (1943), in Arnold Rampersad (ed.), *The Collected Poems*, vol. 2, *The Poems: 1941–1950* (Columbia: University of Missouri Press, 2001), pp. 79–80. The origin of the phrase 'Jim Crow' has often been attributed to 'Jump Jim Crow', the song-and-dance caricature of Negroes performed by white actor Thomas D. Rice in blackface, which first surfaced in 1832. As a result of the popularity of black-face minstrelsy, the name had become a pejorative expression meaning 'Negro' by the mid-nineteenth century. When, following the period of reconstruction (1865–77), laws of racial segregation were enacted they became known as 'Jim Crow' laws. See C. Van Woodward, *The Strange Career of Jim Crow* (New York: Oxford University Press, 1955).

23  Quoted in Sitkoff, 'African American militancy', p. 75, and Wynn, *The Afro-American*, p. 100.
24  Wynn, *The Afro-American*, pp. 36–7. James Clyde Sellman, 'Blacks in the American military', in K. Appiah and H. L. Gates Jr (eds), *Africana: The Encyclopaedia of the African and African American Experience* (New York: Basic Books, 1999), p. 1308.
25  Wynn, *The Afro-American*, pp. 42–5.
26  Sitkoff, 'African American militancy', pp. 75, 85.
27  Ibid., p. 92.
28  See Eric Lott, 'Double V, double-time: bebop's politics of style', in Robert G. O'Meally (ed.), *The Jazz Cadence of American Culture* (New York: Columbia University Press, 1998), pp. 458–9.
29  Leroi Jones, *Blues People: Negro Music in White America* (New York: William Morrow, 1963), p. 179.
30  On the transformation of Ali's reputation see Mike Marqusee, *Redemption Song: Muhammad Ali and the Spirit of the Sixties* (London: Verso, 1999), pp. 3–6.
31  David Reynolds, *Rich Relations: The American Occupation of Britain 1942–1945* (London: Harper Collins, 1995), pp. 174–5.
32  St Clair Drake, 'A Report on the Brown Britishers', *The Crisis*, 56 (June 1949), 174. Graham A. Smith, *When Jim Crow Met John Bull: Black American soldiers in World War II Britain* (London: Tauris, 1987), p. 118. See also Reynolds, *Rich Relations*, pp. 304–5.
33  Ellison, 'In a Strange Country', pp. 138–9.
34  Ibid., p. 140.
35  Ralph Waldo Emerson, 'Nature' (1836), in *Nature and Selected Essays* (New York: Penguin, 2003) p. 39.
36  Ralph Ellison, *Invisible Man* ([1952] New York: Vintage, 1995), pp. 3–4.
37  Henry Louis Gates Jr, *The Signifying Monkey: A Theory of African-American Literary Criticism* (Oxford: Oxford University Press, 1988), p. 106.
38  Ellison, 'In a Strange Country', pp. 139, 146.
39  Reynolds, *Rich Relations*, p. 442.
40  Maggi M. Moorehouse, *Fighting in the Jim Crow Army: Black Men and Women Remember World War II* (New York: Rowman and Littlefield Publishers, 2000), p. 201. Reynolds, *Rich Relations*, p. 443.
41  Ellison, Introduction to *Invisible Man*, p. xii.
42  Ellison, 'Letter to Mr. G. A. Smith'.
43  Roi Ottley, 'Ottley reports on Negro–White troop relations', *PM*, Thursday 21 September 1944, 10. Copy in Ralph Ellison Papers, Library of Congress, box 203, file 12. Florence Murray (ed.), *The Negro Handbook 1944: A Manual of Current Facts, Statistics and General Information Concerning Negroes in the United States* (New York: Current Reference Publications, 1944), pp. 98–9.
44  *Monthly Summary of Events and Trends in Race Relations*, 2, 8 (March 1945), 229. Copy held in the Ralph Ellison Papers, Library of Congress, box 204 file 8.
45  Ottley, 'Ottley reports', 10.
46  Quoted in Phillip McGuire, *Taps for a Jim Crow Army: Letters from Black Soldiers in World War II* (Oxford: ABC-Clio, 1983), p. 229. Neil R. McMillen,

'Fighting for what we didn't have: how Mississippi's black veterans remember World War II', in Neil R. McMillen (ed.), *Remaking Dixie: The Impact of World War II on the American South* (Jackson: University Press of Mississippi, 1997), p. 97.

47  Ralph Ellison, 'The Red Cross in Morriston, Swansea, S.W.', several drafts, The Ralph Ellison Papers, Library of Congress, Washington DC. box 165, files 3 and 7. This version is to be found in the Ralph Ellison Papers, box 165, file 7.

48  Graham A. Smith, *When Jim Crow Met John Bull*, p. 202. Reynolds, *Rich Relations*, p. 307.

49  In Wales it came to a head with widespread complaints about sexual liaisons between white girls and African American troops around Maindy Barracks in Cardiff in September and October 1945. This will be discussed in the Conclusion to this volume.

50  Reynolds, *Rich Relations*, p. 303.

51  Ottley, 'Ottley reports',10. A Foreign Office official's view in 1942 that 'the recruitment to the United Kingdom of coloured British subjects, whose remaining in the United Kingdom after the war might create a social problem, was not considered desirable', was also reflected in attitudes towards black GIs. In May 1942 there were only about 800 black GIs in Britain but, given the Pentagon's quota of 10 per cent African American in the army and the Marshall Plan target of one million American soldiers in Britain by April 1943, British policymakers were forecasting around 100,000 African American GIs stationed in Britain by the following spring. By the end of 1943 there were around 65,000 black GIs in Britain, increasing to 130,000 by the time of D-Day. See Reynolds, *Rich Relations*, pp. 217, 227.

52  Quoted in Reynolds, *Rich Relations*, p. 217.

53  Quoted in ibid., p. 218.

54  *A Monthly Summary of Events and Trends in Race Relations*, pp. 229–30. See also *Daily Telegraph*, 11 May 1944.

55  James Grigg and Walter White quoted in Reynolds, *Rich Relations*, p. 232.

56  Quoted in ibid., p. 229.

57  Ibid., p. 229.

58  'This American Red Cross Centre is strictly Jim Crow', *The Crisis*, 50, 3 (March 1943), 76–7.

59  Quoted in Reynolds, *Rich Relations*, p. 155.

60  Quoted in ibid., pp. 160–1.

61  Ellison, 'Letter to Mr. G. A. Smith'.

62  Ellison, 'The Red Cross', no page numbers.

63  Quoted in Reynolds, *Rich Relations*, p. 223. Mr Ken Jeffreys of Morriston/ Treforys told me that his Welsh-speaking mother worked at the Red Cross club in Libanus Chapel during the war years. Jeffreys, who as a child would help his mother at the club, recalled that it was run by a 'mixed-race woman called Trent'. This was before I mentioned the names in Ellison's story. Interview with Ken Jeffreys, Abertawe Sectional Buildings Ltd, Kemys Way, Morriston, Swansea, 15 May 2006. For further evidence of the historical accuracy, and autobiographical basis, of Ellison's stories, see n. 186 below.

[64]  The words of Lieutenant Colonel Douglass B. Kendricks of the Medical Corps, quoted in Murray (ed.), *The Negro Handbook 1944*, p. 127.

[65]  Langston Hughes, 'Red Cross', in *Jim Crow's Last Stand*, p. 78.

[66]  Ross Russell suggests that the song was named after Billy Eckstine's valet, but gives no sources for this assumption. Ross Russell, *Bird Lives: The High Life and Hard Times of Charlie 'Yardbird' Parker* ([1973] New York: Da Capo, 1996), p. 169.

[67]  Werner Sollors, 'Anthropological and sociological tendencies in American literature of the 1930s and 1940s: Richard Wright, Zora Neale Hurston and American culture', in Steve Ickringill (ed.), *Looking Inward, Looking Outward: From the 1930s through the 1940s* (Amsterdam: VU University Press, 1990), p. 23.

[68]  'Our National Anthem' is the Welsh anthem 'Hen Wlad fy Nhadau' (Land of My Fathers).

[69]  Ellison's phrase in his 'Introduction' to *Invisible Man*, p. xiv.

[70]  Ellison, 'In a Strange Country', p. 145.

[71]  Ellison, 'The Red Cross'.

[72]  Ralph Ellison, 'Letter to Senora Babb', 18 August 1944, Ralph Ellison Papers, Library of Congress; quoted in Rampersad, *Ralph Ellison*, pp. 170–1.

[73]  Sitkoff, 'African American militancy', p. 71. Kenneth O. Morgan, 'Power and glory: war and reconstruction, 1939–1951', in Deian Hopkin, Duncan Tanner and Chris Williams (eds), *The Labour Party in Wales 1900–2000* (Cardiff: University of Wales Press, 2000), p. 166.

[74]  See Hywel Francis and Dai Smith, *The Fed: A History of the South Wales Miners in the Twentieth Century* ([1980] Cardiff: University of Wales Press, 1998), pp. 400–3.

[75]  On those who resisted the war see, in the Welsh context, D. Hywel Davies, *The Welsh Nationalist Party 1925–1945: A Call to Arms* (Cardiff: University of Wales Press, 1983), pp. 223–59. There were more Welshmen, in proportional terms, than Scotsmen or Englishmen unwilling to fight. See John Davies, *A History of Wales* ([1990 in Welsh] London: Penguin, 1993), p. 599. For African American resistance to war, and the growth of a youth subculture during the war years, see Robin D. G. Kelley, 'The riddle of the zoot: Malcolm Little and black cultural politics during World War II', in Joe Wood (ed.) *Malcolm X: In Our Own Image* (New York: St Martin's Press, 1992), pp. 155–82. Malcolm X describes his tactic for avoiding the draft in his autobiography, confiding to the army psychiatrist that 'Daddy-o, now you and me, we're from up North here, so don't you tell nobody . . . I want to get sent down South. Organize them Nigger soldiers, you dig? Steal us some guns and kill up crackers!'; quoted in Kelley, 'The riddle of the zoot', p. 165. He was voicing feelings widespread amongst the zoot-suited, hep-talking counterculture of the be-boppers in the war years. A small (if not zoot-suited) group of Welsh nationalists argued that a small nation such as Wales should have the right not to take part in a conflict between great imperial powers. Saunders Lewis, the architect of the Plaid Cymru (Welsh Nationalist Party) policy was disappointed by the response to his call on Welshmen to refuse to fight on the grounds of nationality, but considered the stand made by about two dozen members of the party proof that 'assimilation of Wales by England was being

withstood, even under the most extreme pressures'; Quoted in John Davies, *A History of Wales*, p. 599.

76  Reynolds, *Rich Relations*, p. 444. McMillen, 'Fighting for what we didn't have', pp. 95–6.

77  On the war context and the rise of Labour, see Morgan, 'Power and glory'.

78  Quoted in Francis and Smith, *The Fed*, p. 435.

79  Davies, *A History of Wales*, p. 602.

80  Ibid..

81  Idris Cox, *The People Can Save South Wales* (London: Communist Party of Great Britian, 1937), p. 5. Lewis Jones, *Cwmardy: The Story of a Welsh Mining Valley* ([1937] London: Lawrence and Wishart, 1979), pp. 2–3. On Lewis and Bebb in the 1930s, see Davies, *The Welsh Nationalist Party*, pp. 61–219. Thanks to Chris Williams for kindly sharing materials related to Cox.

82  On the emergence of these journals, see M. Wynn. Thomas, *Corresponding Cultures: The Two Literatures of Wales* (Cardiff: University of Wales Press, 1999), pp. 82–94.

83  Davies, *A History of Wales*, pp. 590, 603. The 'Welsh Region' was re-established in 1945.

84  Quoted in Davies, *A History of Wales*, p.602. Gruffydd was primarily concerned about evacuees.

85  Ellison, 'The Red Cross'. This introductory material is omitted from later drafts of the story, but offers a fascinating account of Ellison's first encounters with Wales.

86  Phil Carradice, *Wales at War* (Llandysul: Gomer, 2003), p. 47.

87  Davies, *A History of Wales*, p. 597.

88  Davies, *A History of Wales*, pp. 597, 601. Deirdre Beddoe, *Out of the Shadows: A History of Women in Twentieth-Century Wales* (Cardiff: University of Wales Press, 2000), p. 126.

89  On Zimmern, see Dai Smith, *Aneurin Bevan and the World of South Wales*, p. i.

90  Ellison, 'The Red Cross'.

91  See Dai Smith, *Wales! Wales?* (London: Allen and Unwin, 1984), and *Aneurin Bevan*.

92  The names of Dylan Thomas and Alun Lewis are included in earlier drafts of this story, but presumably omitted as they were not dramatists. While I have not the space to do so here, it would be worth comparing the wartime stories of Alun Lewis (in India) and Ralph Ellison (in Wales).

93  See David Berry, *Wales and the Cinema: The First Hundred Years* (Cardiff: University of Wales Press, 1994), pp. 166–72.

94  Russell Stephens, *Emlyn Williams: the Making of a Dramatist* (Bridgend: Seren, 2000), p. 191. Also David Berry, *Wales and the Cinema*, pp. 199–212.

95  On 'contrapuntal readings' see Edward Said, *Culture and Imperialism* ([1993] London, Vintage, 1994), p. 134. Also Dai Smith, *Aneurin Bevan*, p. 12.

96  Ellison, *Invisible Man*, p. 581.

97  Emlyn Williams, *The Corn is Green with Two Other Plays* (London: Pan Books, 1950), p. 37.

98   M. Wynn Thomas, *Internal Difference: Literature in 20th Century Wales* (Cardiff: University of Wales Press, 1992), p. 71.
99   Ibid.
100  Ibid., p. 72.
101  Williams, *The Corn is Green*, p. 44.
102  Stephens, *Emlyn Williams*, p. 191. Stephen Knight, '"A new enormous music": industrial fictions in Wales', in M. Wynn Thomas (ed.), *Welsh Writing in English: A Guide To Welsh Literature* (Cardiff: University of Wales Press, 2003), p. 48.
103  Emlyn Williams, 'The corn was green in England: in which Mr Williams, as in another world, writes the story of one of Times Square's current hits', *New York Times*, 16 February 1941, 11.
104  Emlyn Williams, 'The corn was green in England', 11, 13.
105  Stephen Knight, *A Hundred Years of Fiction: Writing Wales in English* (Cardiff: University of Wales Press, 2004), pp. xii–xiv. On 'sly civility', see Homi K. Bhabha, *The Location of Culture* (London: Routledge, 1994), pp. 93–101. The quotation is by Robert Young who offers a useful account of Bhabha's argument in *Colonial Desire: Hybridity in Theory Culture and Race* (London: Routledge, 1995), p. 22.
106  Young, *Colonial Desire*, p. 51.
107  Williams, *The Corn is Green*, p. 94. Ellison, *Invisible Man*, p. 18.
108  Williams, *The Corn is Green*, p. 42. Ellison, *Invisible Man*, p. 47.
109  Ellison, *Invisible Man*, p. 47.
110  Ibid., p. 36.
111  Williams, *The Corn is Green,* p. 62.
112  Ibid., p. 96.
113  Thomas, *Internal Difference*, p. 73.
114  John O. Killens quoted in Harold Cruse, *The Crisis of the Negro Intellectual* ([1967] London: W. H. Allen, 1969), p. 235. On the black nationalist attacks on Ralph Ellison, see Adam Bradley, *Ralph Ellison in Progress* (New Haven: Yale University Press, 2010), pp. 57–88.
115  Houston A. Baker Jr, *Modernism and the Harlem Renaissance* (Chicago: University of Chicago Press, 1987).
116  Ellison, *Invisible Man*, p. 17.
117  Baker, *Modernism*, p. 24.
118  Ibid., p. 30.
119  Williams, *The Corn is Green*, p. 42.
120  Stephens, *Emlyn Williams*, p. 182.
121  F. W. Bateson, *English Poetry: A Critical Introduction* (London: Longmans, Green and Co., 1950), p. 93.
122  Knight's description in 'A new enormous music', p. 48. M. Wynn Thomas discusses the Williams–Raglan debate in *Internal Difference*, pp. 73–5.
123  Ralph Ellison, 'On initiation rites and power: Ralph Ellison speaks at West Point', *Going to the Territory* (New York: Vintage, 1987), p. 44.
124  Ellison, 'On initiation rites', p. 43.
125  Ralph Ellison, *Shadow and Act* ([1953] New York: Quality Paperback Book Club, 1994), p. 36.

126   Ellison, *Shadow*, p. 36. *Invisible Man*, p. 8.

127   Ellison, *Invisible Man*, p. 242.

128   Lord Raglan, 'I take my stand', *Wales*, October 1958, 17.

129   Emlyn Williams, 'A dyma fi druan o Gymro yn sefyll (I take my stand)', *Wales*, November 1958, 16, 18.

130   Williams, *The Corn is Green*, p. 13.

131   James Baldwin, *Tell Me How Long the Train's Been Gone* ([1968] London Corgi, 1970), pp. 348–71.

132   In his diaries Burton suspects Baldwin of having stolen money. See Melvyn Bragg, *Rich: The Life of Richard Burton* (London: Coronet, 1988), pp. 294–5. Also discussed in James Campbell, *Talking at the Gates: A Life of James Baldwin* (London: Faber, 1991), pp. 230–2. Thanks to Chris Williams for drawing my attention to this.

133   See Gwenno Ffrancon, *Cyfaredd y Cysgodion: Delweddu Cymru a'i Phobl ar Ffilm, 1935–1951* (Caerdydd: Gwasg Prifysgol Cymru, 2003), pp. 153, 141. Peter Stead, *Acting Wales: Stars of Stage and Screen* (Cardiff: University of Wales Press, 2002), pp. 38–41.

134   Baldwin, *Tell Me How Long*, p. 352.

135   James Baldwin, 'If Black English isn't a language tell me what is?' (1979), in *Collected Essays* (New York: Library of America, 1998), p. 780.

136   See any dedicated web page on Harewood; for instance *http://www.hollywood. com/celebs/detail/celeb/191623*, accessed May 2005.

137   It is likely that Elizabeth Taylor would have instigated the revival as Richard Burton, to whom she was married twice, had close contacts with Emlyn Williams, as noted.

138   Emlyn Williams Papers, National Library of Wales, box 8, file 1.

139   See Leslie Bennetts, 'How Cicely Tyson got to teach in Wales', *New York Times*, 22 August 1983, C14.

140   Emlyn Williams, 'Letter to Vivian Matalon', 21 July 1983, Emlyn Williams Papers, National Library of Wales, box 8, file 1.

141   Emlyn Williams, 'Undated Letter to Vivian Matalon'. Emlyn Williams Papers, National Library of Wales, box 8, file 1.

142   Mel Gussow, 'Theater: "The Corn is Green"', *New York Times*, 23 August 1983, C13.

143   Emlyn Williams, 'Letter to Vivian Matalon', 21 July 1983.

144   Emlyn Williams, 'Letter to Cicely Tyson care of Vivian Matalon', 7 August 1983, Emlyn Williams Papers, National Library of Wales, box 8, file 1.

145   Quoted in Bennetts, 'How Cicely Tyson got to teach in Wales', C14.

146   See Daniel G. Williams, 'Green in Black', *New Welsh Review*, 86 (winter 2009), 42–51.

147   Bennetts, 'How Cicely Tyson got to teach in Wales', C14.

148   The production ended in acrimony. Tyson was fired for taking a night off to attend an award ceremony with her husband Miles Davis. Tyson sued, maintaining that she was entitled to the full $750,000, even though the show closed and the planned TV video of the Broadway show was scrapped. She eventually

won her case. 'Cicley Tyson awarded $607,000', *Jet Magazine*, 29 April 1985, 53. David Berry, *Wales and the Cinema*, p. 201.

149   Baker, *Modernism and the Harlem Renaissance*, p. 30.

150   Quoted in Dai Smith, *Aneurin Bevan*, pp. 253–4.

151   Kevin K. Gaines, *Uplifting the Race: Black Leadership, Politics, and Culture in the Twentieth Century* (Chapel Hill: University of North Carolina Press, 1996), p. 251. In her book *Divided Minds: American Intellectuals and the Civil Rights Movement* (New York: W. W. Norton, 2001), Carol Posgrove argues that Ellison was a member of the Communist Party (pp. 66–72), a view reinforced by Rampersad in *Ralph Ellison* (p. 93). Lawrence Jackson describes Ellison as a close fellow-traveller, but never committed to joining the party (*Ralph Ellison*, pp. 184–6). Alan Wald notes that, while A. B. Magil and Howard Johnson (a Harlem Party leader in the 1940s) believe that Ellison held party membership, Richard Wright's widow Ellen denies this. Alan M. Wald, *Exiles from a Future Time: The Forging of the Mid-Twentieth-Century Left* (Chapel Hill: University of North Carolina Press, 2002), p. 287.

152   Wald, *Exiles*, p. 267.

153   Ibid., p. 266.

154   Quoted in Howard Zinn, *A People's History of the United States 1492–Present* ([1980] New York: Harper Collins, 1995), p. 398.

155   Ralph Ellison, 'The Negro and the war', undated typescript, MS AM 2238, Houghton Library, Harvard University.

156   Barbara Foley, 'Reading redness: politics and audience in Ralph Ellison's early short fiction', *Journal of Narrative Theory*, 29, 3 (fall 1999), 332.

157   Ibid., pp. 333, 334.

158   Ottley, 'Ottley reports', 10.

159   Ellison, 'The Red Cross'.

160   Ralph Ellison, 'A Hard Time Keeping Up', in *Flying Home and Other Stories* ([1996] London: Penguin, 1998), pp. 101, 106.

161   Ralph Ellison, 'Richard Wright's Blues', *Shadow and Act* ([1953] New York: Quality Paperback Book Club, 1994), p. 93.

162   Ellison, 'Richard Wright's Blues', p. 94.

163   Jackson, *Ralph Ellison*, p. 318.

164   Ellison, 'On initiation rites', p. 56.

165   Foley, 'Reading redness', pp. 332, 334.

166   Ibid., p. 334.

167   See Martin Duberman, *Paul Robeson: A Biography* ([1988] New York: New Press, 1989), pp. 263–79.

168   Ellison, 'In a Strange Country', p. 142.

169   Ralph Ellison, 'Letter to Senora Babb', quoted in Rampersad, *Ralph Ellison*, p. 171.

170   Duberman, *Paul Robeson*, pp. 186, 178.

171   On African Americans in the Soviet Union, see Kate A. Baldwin, *Beyond the Color Line and the Iron Curtain: Reading Encounters Between Black and Red, 1922–1963* (Durham: Duke University Press, 2002), and William J. Maxwell, *New Negro, Old Left: African-American Writing and Communism Between the*

*Wars* (New York: Columbia University Press, 1999). On Welsh connections, see Robert Griffiths, *S. O. Davies: A Socialist Faith* (Llandysul: Gomer Press, 1983), Francis and Smith, *The Fed*, and Merfyn Jones, 'Beyond identity? The reconstruction of the Welsh', *Journal of British Studies*, 31, 4 (October 1992), 341.

172  Martin Duberman quoted in Baldwin, *Beyond the Color Line*, p. 208.

173  Baldwin, *Beyond the Color Line*, p. 209.

174  Wald, *Exiles*, p. 294.

175  Quoted in ibid.

176  George Padmore, 'Race relations: Soviet and British', *The Crisis*, 50, 11 (November 1942), 346–7.

177  Herndon had been arrested in Atlanta in 1932 for leading a bi-racial demonstration of the unemployed and had been sentenced to eighteen to twenty years on a chain gang. In 1935 the Communist Party led a widely supported petition drive that led in 1937 to the court's narrowly overturning Herndon's conviction. See Duberman, *Paul Robeson*, p. 230.

178  Jackson, *Ralph Ellison*, pp. 265–6.

179  Quoted in Wald, *Exiles*, p. 284.

180  Charles Humboldt, 'When peoples meet', *The Negro Quarterly*, 1, 2 (summer 1942), 184–6.

181  Quoted in ibid., 185. Beatrice Webb and Sidney Webb, 'National minorities in the Soviet Union', in Alain Locke and Bernhard J. Stern (eds), *When Peoples Meet: A Study in Race and Culture Contacts* (New York: Progressive Educations Association, 1942), pp. 672–83.

182  Gerwyn Wiliams, *Tir Newydd: Agweddau ar Lenyddiaeth Gymraeg a'r Ail Ryfel Byd* (Caerdydd: Gwasg Prifysgol Cymru), pp. 114–28. For a discussion of T. E. Nicholas in English, see M. Wynn Thomas, *Transatlantic Connections: Whitman U.S., Whitman U.K.* (Iowa City: University of Iowa Press, 2005), pp. 243–6.

183  Victor Golightly, '"Writing with dreams and blood": Dylan Thomas, Marxism and 1930s Swansea', Tony Brown (ed.), *Welsh Writing in English: A Yearbook*, vol. 8 (Cardiff: University of Wales Press, 2003), p. 69.

184  John Malcolm Brinnin, *Dylan Thomas in America* (Boston: Little Brown, 1955), p. 33. While in the company of the American Michael Gold and others at the 1949 writers' Peace Congress in Prague, Thomas described himself as 'A Communist, but . . . also a bloody fool'. See Victor A. Paananen, 'The social vision of Dylan Thomas', *Welsh Writing in English: A Yearbook*, 8, p. 51.

185  Ellison, 'The Red Cross'.

186  Thanks to Gareth Williams for the information on American choirs. On Reverend Edward Carroll (1910–2000), see the touching letter from Gwilym L. G. Thomas of Ystalyfera in the *Western Mail*, Saturday 6 December 2008, 10. Gwilym Thomas recalls that after the war 'my family and the Carrolls had kept in close contact and I was fortunate in having access to the generous hospitality of Eddie and Philomena's Harlem home. By this time he was minister of the First Methodist Church in Washington Heights, New York . . . [D]uring one visit to the Carrolls I shared the company of two young gentlemen who happened to be staying there going by the surname King, sons of an Alabama minister. The older of the two brothers was himself an ordained Christian minister of an Alabama church, who had come up to NY for his younger brother's graduation from

university. It was only years later that I realised that through this family friend-ship I had met one of the world's greatest leaders, sadly to be assassinated – the victim of rampant racialism. The Christian and middle names of that young Alabama minister were Martin Luther.'

187   On the AFL and CIO see Neil A. Wynn, *The Afro-American and the Second World War*, p. 53.

188   Robeson quoted in Duberman, *Paul Robeson*, p. 281. C. L. R. James, *American Civilization* (Oxford: Blackwell, 1993), p. 270.

189   See Jack Jones, 'American industry listens when the Welsh lion roars', *Western Mail*, Wednesday 30 July 1958, 4, B–H. Gwynfor Evans, president of Plaid Cymru (The Welsh Nationalist Party), met Lewis during his visit to America in 1958. 'If I were your age and in Wales', said the 78-year-old union leader, described as 'the greatest Welshman in America' by Evans, 'I would be with you in this job'. Gwynfor Evans, *Bywyd Cymro* (Caernarfon: Gwasg Gwynedd, 1982), p. 220.

190   Quoted in 'Coal miner's hero', on PBS website, January 2005, *http://www.pbs. org/greatspeeches/timeline/j_lewis_b.html*.

191   John Davies, *A History of Wales*, p. 606. Francis and Smith, *The Fed*, pp. 406–19.

192   Callahan, 'Introduction' to Ralph Ellison, *Flying Home and Other Stories*, p. xxxviii.

193   Ralph Ellison, 'Blues people', in *Shadow and Act*, p. 253.

194   Winifred Kealing, 'Letter to Ralph Ellison', 24 September 1944, The Ralph Ellison Papers, Library of Congress, box 165, file 7. The first letter of Winifred's surname is unclear; it could also be 'Reading' or 'Tealing'.

195   Ralph Ellison, 'The world and the jug', in *Shadow and Act*, p. 116.

## *Conclusion*

1   See, for example, Mike Phillips and Trevor Phillips, *Windrush: The Irresistible Rise of Multi-racial Britain* (London: Harper Collins, 2000).

2   Hazel Carby, 'Becoming modern racialized subjects: detours through our pasts to produce ourselves anew', *Cultural Studies*, 23, 4 (July 2009), 624.

3   Carby, 'Becoming modern', 642. David Reynolds, *Rich Relations: The American Occupation of Britain 1942–1945* (London: Harper Collins, 1995).

4   Carby, 'Becoming modern', 641.

5   Reynolds, *Rich Relations*, p. 229. Carby, 'Becoming modern', 648.

6   Carby, 'Becoming modern', 649.

7   'Cardiff's Burma Road', *Western Mail*, 12 September 1945, 2, column 3.

8   'Women tramps menace social life in Wales', *Western Mail*, 12 September 1945, 3, columns 2 and 3.

9   Ibid.

10   'Shock and shame of disclosures', *Western Mail*, Monday 17 September 1945, 3, columns 4 and 5.

11   Ibid.

[12] S. O. Rose, 'Sex, citizenship and the nation in WWII Britain', *The American Historical Review*, 3, 4 (1998), 1147–76; quoted by Carby, 'Becoming modern', 649.

[13] Carby, 'Becoming modern', 646.

[14] Ibid., 647.

[15] J. A. Rogers, *Nature Knows No Color-Line: Research into the Negro Ancestry in the White Race* ([c.1952] St Petersburg, FL: Helga M. Rogers, 3rd edn, repr., 1980), p. 183.

[16] J. A. Rogers, 'The American Negro in Europe', *American Mercury* (May 1930), 8–9. I am grateful to Werner Sollors for these references by Rogers; see Werner Sollors, 'The Celtic nations and the African Americas', *Comparative American Studies*, 8, 4 (2010), 316–22.

[17] From Seosamh Mac Grianna, *Mo Bhealach Féin* (Baile Átha Cliath: Oifig an tSoláthair, 1940). Translation amended from *http://www.fortunecity.com/victorian/harris/953/irish10.htm* (last accessed 20 March 2011). Mac Grianna also wrote a volume on Wales, *An Bhreatain Bheag* (Baile Átha Cliath: Oifig an tSoláthair, 1937). Michael Cronin, 'Global questions and local visions: a micro-cosmopolitan perspective', in Alyce von Rothkirch and Daniel Williams (eds), *Beyond the Difference: Welsh Literature in Comparative Contexts* (Cardiff: University of Wales Press, 2004), p. 186.

[18] See the Appendix to Tony Martin, *Race First: The Ideological and Organizational Struggles of Marcus Garvey and the United Negro Improvement Association* (Westport, CT: Greenwood Press, 1976), p. 373. Wales had as many UNIA branches as England (London and Manchester) in 1926.

[19] Alan Llwyd, *Cymru Ddu/Black Wales: A History* (Cardiff: Hughes a'i Fab, 2005), p. 127.

[20] Carby, 'Becoming modern', 644.

[21] Paul Rich, *Race and Empire in British Politics* (Cambridge: Cambridge University Press, 1990), p. 152.

[22] *Western Mail*, 14 September 1945, 3, columns 2 and 3.

[23] 'Womanhood', *Western Mail*, 19 September 1945, 3, column 5.

[24] 'Coloured girls defend U.S. soldiers', *Western Mail*, 14 September 1945, 3, column 2.

[25] Ibid.

[26] St Clair Drake, 'A report on the brown Britishers', *The Crisis*, 56 (June 1949), 189.

[27] 'Shock and shame of disclosures', *Western Mail*, 17 September 1945, 3, column 5.

[28] Ibid.

[29] 'The American Negro', *Western Mail*, 19 September 1945, 3, column 6.

[30] Ibid.

[31] Dylan Thomas, *The Collected Letters*, ed. Paul Ferris (New York: Macmillan, 1985), p. 617.

[32] See, for example, the comparison made between the African American bebop saxophonist Charlie Parker and Dylan Thomas by the poet Kenneth Rexroth in 'Disengagement: the art of the Beat Generation' (1959), in *The Alternative Society*

(New York: Herder and Herder, 1970), pp. 1–16. For a discussion of Thomas's reception in the United States see M. Wynn Thomas and Daniel Williams, '"A Sweet Union"?: Dylan Thomas and post-war American poetry', in Gilbert Bennett et al. (eds.), *I Sang in My Chains: Essays and Poems in Tribute to Dylan Thomas* (Swansea: The Dylan Thomas Society of Great Britain, 2003), pp. 68–79.

33  Paul Gilroy, *Between Camps: Race, Identity and Nationalism at the End of the Colour Line* (London: Penguin, 2000), p. 305.

34  Ibid.

# Bibliography

**Audio recordings**
Manic Street Preachers, *Let Robeson Sing*, Sony Music, 2001.
Parker, Charlie, 'Red Cross' (1944), *The Complete Savoy Recordings*.
Robeson, Paul, *Freedom Train and the Welsh Transatlantic Concert*, Folk Era Records, 1998.
——, with the Count Basie Orchestra, 'King Joe' (1941), on *The Essential Paul Robeson* (ASV Ltd, 2000).

**Manuscript collections**
Lawrence Brown Collection, Schomburg Centre for Research in Black Culture, New York.
Frederick Douglass Collection, Library of Congress, Washington DC.
St Clair Drake Collection, Schomburg Centre for Research in Black Culture, New York.
W. E. B. Du Bois Collection, University of Massachusetts, Amherst.
Ralph Ellison Collection, The Library Of Congress, Washington DC.
Jack Jones Collection, National Library of Wales, Aberystwyth.
Paul Robeson Collection, Howard University, Washington DC.
Paul Robeson Collection, Schomburg Centre for Research in Black Culture, New York.
Paul Robeson File, South Wales Miners' Library, Swansea University.
Emlyn Williams Collection, National Library of Wales, Aberystwyth.
Raymond Williams Collection, Richard Burton Archives, Swansea University.

**Newspapers and magazines**
*Aberdare Leader*
*Yr Amserau*
*The Carnarvon and Denbigh Herald*
*Y Cenhadwr Americanaidd*

*Y Cerddor Cymraeg*
*Close Up*
*The Crisis*
*Y Cyfaill o'r Hen Wlad*
*Y Dyngarwr*
*Frederick Douglass' Paper*
*Merthyr Express*
*The North Star*
*Opportunity*
*PM*
*South Wales Argus*
*Time Magazine*
*Western Mail*

## Published sources

Aaron, Jane, *Pur fel y Dur: Y Gymraes yn Llên Menywod y Bedwaredd Ganrif ar Bymtheg* (Caerdydd: Gwasg Prifysgol Cymru, 1998).

——, 'Bardic anti-colonialism', in Jane Aaron and Chris Williams (eds), *Postcolonial Wales* (Cardiff: University of Wales Press, 2005), pp. 137–58.

——, *Nineteenth-Century Women's Writing in Wales: Nation, Gender and Identity* (Cardiff: University of Wales Press, 2007).

—— and Chris Williams (eds), *Postcolonial Wales* (Cardiff: University of Wales Press, 2005).

Adorno, Theodor, *Essays on Music*, introduced by Richard Leppert, trans. Susan Gillespie (Berkeley: University of California Press, 2002).

——, 'On the fetish character in music and the regression in listening', in Theodor Adorno, *Essays on Music*, introduced by Richard Leppert, trans. Susan Gillespie (Berkeley: University of California Press, 2002), pp. 288–317.

Aitchison, John and Harold Carter, *A Geography of the Welsh Language 1961–1991* (Cardiff: University of Wales Press, 1994).

Althusser, Louis, 'Ideology and ideological state apparatuses: notes toward an investigation', in Slavoj Žižek (ed.), *Mapping Ideology* (London: Verso, 1994), pp. 100–40.

Anderson, Benedict, *Imagined Communities* (London: Verso, 1983).

Andrews, William A. (ed), *African American Autobiography: A Collection of Critical Essays* (Englewood Cliffs, NJ: Prentice-Hall, 1993).

—— (ed.), *North Carolina Slave Narratives* (Chapel Hill: University of North Carolina Press, 2003).

Anonymous, 'Sport: Louis v. Farr', *Time Magazine*, 6 September 1937.

Appiah, Kwame Anthony and Henry Louis Gates Jr, (eds), *Africana: The Encyclopaedia of the African and African American Experience* (New York: Basic Books, 1999).

Arac Jonathan and Ronald A. T. Judy (eds), *Ralph Ellison: The Next Fifty Years. A Special Issue of Boundary 2*, 30, 2 (summer 2003).

Arnold, Matthew, *The Complete Prose Works of Matthew Arnold*, ed. R. H. Super, 11 volumes (Ann Arbor: University of Michigan Press, 1960–77)

——, *On the Study of Celtic Literature*, in *The Complete Prose Works of Matthew Arnold*, vol. 3, ed. R. H. Super (Ann Arbor, University of Michigan Press, 1962).

Baker Jr, Houston A., *Long Black Song: Essays in Black American Literature and Culture* (Charlottesville: University of Virginia Press, 1972).

——, *Modernism and the Harlem Renaissance* (Chicago: University of Chicago Press, 1987).

——, *Afro-American Poetics: Revisions of Harlem and the Black Aesthetic* (Madison: University of Wisconsin Press, 1988).

——, *Turning South Again: Re-Thinking Modernism / Re-Reading Booker T.* (Durham, NC: Duke University Press, 2001).

Baldwin, James, *The Fire Next Time* (New York: Dial Press, 1963).

——, *Tell Me How Long the Train's Been Gone* ([1968] London Corgi, 1970).

——, 'If Black English isn't a language, what is?', in *Collected Essays* (New York: Library of America, 1998), pp. 780–3.

Baldwin, Kate A., *Beyond the Color Line and the Iron Curtain: Reading Encounters Between Black and Red, 1922–1963* (Durham, NC: Duke University Press, 2002).

Barkan, Elazar, *The Retreat of Scientific Racism* (Cambridge: Cambridge University Press, 1992).

Bates, H. E., 'Review of Kate Roberts, *A Summer Day*', *Welsh Review*, 5 (1946), 217–20.

Bateson, F. W., *English Poetry: A Critical Introduction* (London: Longmans, Green and Co., 1950).

Baxter, Terry, *Frederick Douglass's Curious Audiences: Ethos in the Age of the Consumable Subject* (New York: Routledge, 2004).

Beckett, Samuel, *Wrth Aros Godot / En Attendant Godot*, trans. Saunders Lewis (Cardiff: University of Wales Press, 1970).

Beddoe, Deirdre, *Out of the Shadows: A History of Women in Twentieth-Century Wales* (Cardiff: University of Wales Press, 2000).

Begam, Richard and Michael Valdez Moses (eds), *Modernism and Colonialism: British and Irish Literature 1899–1939* (Durham, NC: Duke University Press, 2007).

Bell, Ian, 'How Green *Was* My Valley', *Planet: The Welsh Internationalist*, 73 (February/March 1989), 3–9.

Bennett, Gilbert, Eryl Jenkins and Eurwen Price (eds), *I Sang in My Chains: Essays and Poems in Tribute to Dylan Thomas* (Swansea: The Dylan Thomas Society of Great Britain, 2003).

Bennetts, Leslie, 'How Cicely Tyson got to teach in Wales', *New York Times*, 22 August 1983, C14.

Benston, Kimberly W., *Performing Blackness: Enactments of African-American Modernism* (London: Routledge, 2000).

Berman, Marshall, *All That Is Solid Melts into Air: The Experience of Modernity* ([1982] London: Verso, 1983).

Bernier, Celeste-Marie, 'From Fugitive Slave to Fugitive Abolitionist: The Oratory of Frederick Douglass and the Emerging Heroic Slave Tradition', *Atlantic Studies*, 3(2) (October 2006), 201–24.

Berry, David, *Wales and Cinema: The First Hundred Years* (Cardiff: University of Wales Press, 1994).

Bhabha, Homi, *The Location of Culture* (London: Routledge, 1994).

Biddis, Michael, 'The Universal Races Congress of 1911', *Race*, 13, 1 (1971), 37–46.

Blackett, R. J. M., *Building an Antislavery Wall: Black Americans in the Atlantic Abolitionist Movement* (Baton Rouge, LA: Louisiana State University Press, 1983).

——, 'Cracks in the antislavery wall: Frederick Douglass's second visit to England and the coming of the Civil War', in Martin Crawford and Alan J. Rice (eds), *Liberating Sojourn: Frederick Douglass and Transatlantic Reform* (Athens, GA: The University of Georgia Press, 1999), pp. 187–206.

Blassingame, John W. (ed.), *Slave Testimony: Two Centuries of Letters, Speeches, Interviews and Autobiographies* (Baton Rouge, LA: Louisiana State University Press, 1977).

Blockson, Charles L., 'Paul Robeson: a bibliophile in spite of himself', in J. C. Stewart (ed.), *Paul Robeson: Artist and Citizen* (New Brunswick: Rutgers University Press, 1998), pp. 235–250.

Boas, Franz, 'Instability of human types', in Gustav Spiller (ed.), *Papers on Inter-Racial Problems Communicated to the First Universal Races Congress held at the University of London, July 26–29, 1911* (London: P. S. King, and Boston: The Peace Foundation, 1911), pp. 99–103.

——, 'Preface' to Zora Neale Hurston, *Mules and Men* (1935), in *Zora Neale Hurston: Folklore, Memoirs, and Other Writings: Mules and Men, Tell My Horse, Dust Tracks on a Road, Selected Articles* (New York: The Library of America, 1995), p. iii.

Boddy, Kasia, *Boxing: A Cultural History* (London: Reaktion Books, 2008).

Bogle, Donald, *Toms, Coons, Mulattoes, Mammies and Bucks: An Interpretive History of Blacks in American Films* ([1973] London: Continuum, 2001).

Bohata, Kirsti, *Postcolonialism Revisited* (Cardiff: University of Wales Press, 2004).

Bourne, Stephen, *Black in the British Frame: The Black Experience in British Film and Television* (London: Continuum, 2001).

Boyd, Valerie, *Wrapped in Rainbows: The Life of Zora Neale Hurston* (New York: Simon & Schuster, 2004).

Boyle, Sheila Tully and Andrew Bunie, *Paul Robeson: The Years of Promise and Achievement* (Amherst: University of Massachusetts Press, 2001).

Bradley, Adam, *Ralph Ellison in Progress* (New Haven: Yale University Press, 2010).

Bragg, Melvyn, *Rich: The Life of Richard Burton* (London: Coronet, 1988).

Bremen, Brian A., 'Du Bois, Emerson and the "fate" of black folk', *American Literary Realism*, 24 (spring 1992), 80–8.

Brinnin, John Malcolm, *Dylan Thomas in America* (Boston: Little Brown, 1955).

Brown, Tony, 'Stories from foreign countries': the short stories of Kate Roberts and Margiad Evans', in Alyce Von Rothkirch and Daniel Williams (eds), *Beyond the Difference: Welsh Literature in Comparative Contexts* (Cardiff: University of Wales Press, 2004), pp. 21–37.

Bruce, Dickson D., 'W. E. B. Du Bois and the idea of double consciousness', *American Literature*, 64 (June 1992), 299–309.

Butler, Judith, Ernesto Laclau and Slavoj Žižek, *Contingency, Hegemony, Universality: Contemporary Dialogues on the Left* (London: Verso, 2000).

Byerman, Keith E., *Seizing the Word: History, Art and Self in the Work of W. E. B. Du Bois* (Athens, GA: University of Georgia Press, 1994).

Callahan, John F., 'Introduction' to Ralph Ellison, *Flying Home and Other Stories*, ed. John F. Callahan ([1996] London: Penguin, 1998), pp. ix–xxxviii.

—— (ed.), *Ralph Ellison's Invisible Man: A Casebook* (Oxford: Oxford University Press, 2004).

Campbell, James, *Talking at the Gates: A Life of James Baldwin* (London: Faber, 1991).

Carby, Hazel, 'The politics of fiction, anthropology and the folk: Zora Neale Hurston', in Michael Awkward (ed.), *New Essays on Their Eyes Were Watching God* (Cambridge: Cambridge University Press, 1990), pp. 71–90.

——, *Race Men* (Cambridge, MA: Harvard University Press, 1998).

——, 'Becoming modern racialized subjects', *Cultural Studies*, 23, 4 (July 2009), 624–57.

Carradice, Phil, *Wales at War* (Llandysul: Gomer, 2003).

Chapman, T. Robin, 'Theism's last hurrah: Saunders Lewis's Caernarfon Court speech of 1936' in Chapman (ed.), *The Idiom of Dissent: Protest and Propaganda in Wales* (Llandysul: Gomer, 2006), pp. 24–42.

——, *Un Bywyd o Blith Nifer: Cofiant Saunders Lewis* (Llandysul: Gomer, 2006).

——, 'Adolygiad o Daniel G. Williams, gol., *Canu Caeth: Y Cymry a'r Affro-Americaniaid*', *Taliesin*, 141 (gaeaf 2010), 133–6.

—— (ed.), *The Idiom of Dissent : Protest and Propaganda in Wales* (Llandysul: Gomer, 2006).

Cleary, Joe, *Outrageous Fortune: Capital and Culture in Modern Ireland* (Dublin: Field Day Publications, 2006).

Collini, Stefan, 'On variousness', *New Left Review* II, 27 (May/June 2004), 65–97.

Conran, Anthony, *The Cost of Strangeness: Essays on the English Poets of Wales* (Llandysul: Gomer Press, 1982).

Coombes, B. L., *These Poor Hands: The Autobiography of a Miner in South Wales* ([1939] Cardiff: University of Wales Press, 2002).

Corpis, Duane J. and Ian Christopher Fletcher (eds), 'Another world was possible: a century of movements', special issue of *Radical History Review*, 92 (spring 2005).

Cowell, John, *Bangor at War 1939–45* (Menai Bridge: John Cowell, 2000).

Cox, Idris, *The People Can Save South Wales* (London: Communist Party of Great Britian, 1937).

Crawford, Martin and Alan J. Rice, 'Triumphant exile: Frederick Douglass in Britain 1845–1847', in Crawford and Rice (eds.), *Liberating Sojourn: Frederick Douglass and Transatlantic Reform* (Athens: The University of Georgia Press, 1999), pp. 1–12.

—— (eds), *Liberating Sojourn: Frederick Douglass and Transatlantic Reform* (Athens, GA: The University of Georgia Press, 1999).

Croll, Andy, *Civilizing the Urban: Popular Culture and Public Space in Merthyr, c.1870–1914* (Cardiff: University of Wales Press, 2000).

Cronin, Michael, *Translating Ireland: Translation, Languages, Cultures* (Cork: Cork University Press, 1996).

——, 'Global questions and local visions: a microcosmopolitan perspective', in Alyce von Rothkirch and Daniel Williams (eds), *Beyond the Difference: Welsh Literature in Comparative Contexts* (Cardiff: University of Wales Press, 2004), pp. 186–202.

Cruse, Harold, *The Crisis of the Negro Intellectual* ([1967] London: W. H. Allen, 1969).

Cullen, Greg, *Paul Robeson Knew My Father*, in Val Hill (ed.), *Hijinx Theatre* (Cardigan: Parthian, 2006), pp. 8–95.

Dalfiume, Richard, *Fighting on Two Fronts: Desegregation of the Armed Forces, 1939–1953* (Columbia, MO: University of Missouri Press, 1969).

——, 'The forgotten years of the Negro revolution', *Journal of American History*, 55 (June 1968), 90–106.

Daly, Nicholas, 'Colonialism and popular literature in the fin de siècle', in Richard Begam and Michale Valdez Moses (eds.), *Modernism and Colonialism: British and Irish Literature 1899–1939* (Durham, NC: Duke University Press, 2007), pp. 19–40.

Davies, D. Hywel, *The Welsh Nationalist Party 1925–1945: A Call to Arms* (Cardiff: University of Wales Press, 1983).

Davies, Grahame, *Sefyll yn y Bwlch: R. S. Thomas, Saunders Lewis, T. S. Eliot, a Simone Weil* (Caerdydd: Gwasg Prifysgol Cymru, 1999).

Davies, Idris, 'Response to Geoffrey Grigson', in *The Complete Poems of Idris Davies*, ed. Dafydd Johnston (Cardiff: University of Wales Press, 1994), pp. 328–9.

——, *The Complete Poems of Idris Davies*, ed. Dafydd Johnston (Cardiff: University of Wales Press, 1994).

Davies, John, *A History of Wales* ([1990 in Welsh] London: Penguin, 1993).

Davies, Rhys, *The Withered Root* (London: Robert Holden and Company, 1927).

——, *My Wales* (London: Jarrolds, 1937).

——, *The Black Venus* (London: William Heineman, 1944).

——, *Collected Stories 1*, ed. Meic Stephens (Llandysul: Gomer, 1996).

Davies, T. J., *Paul Robeson* (Abertawe: Gwasg Christopher Davies, 1981).

Davis, Alex and Lee Jenkins, *Locations of Literary Modernism: Region and Nation in American Modernist Poetry* (Cambridge: Cambridge University Press, 2000).

Davis, Charles T. and Henry Louis Gates Jr (eds), *The Slave's Narrative* (Oxford: Oxford University Press, 1985).

Davis, Miles (with Quincy Troupe), *The Autobiography* (London: Macmillan, 1989).

Deane, Seamus, *Celtic Revivals: Essays in Modern Irish Literature, 1880–1980* (London: Faber, 1985).

Dekoven, Marianne, 'Modernism and gender', in Michael Levenson (ed.), *The Cambridge Companion to Modernism* (Cambridge: Cambridge University Press, 1999), pp.174–93.

Delany, Martin, *The Condition, Elevation, Emigration and Destiny of the Colored People of the United States Politically Considered* (Philadelphia: published by the author, 1852).

Denning, Michael, *The Cultural Front: The Laboring of American Culture in the Twentieth Century* (London: Verso, 1996).

DeVeaux, Scott, *The Birth of BeBop: A Social and Musical History* ([1997] London: Picador, 1999).

Diedrich, Maria, *Love Across Color Lines: Ottilie Assing and Frederick Douglass* (New York: Hill and Wang, 1999).

Donald, James, Anne Friedberg and Laura Marcus (eds), *Close Up 1927–1933: Cinema and Modernism* (London: Cassell, 1998).

Dossett, Kate, *Bridging Race Divides: Black Nationalism, Feminism, and Integration in the United States, 1896–1935* (Gainesville: Florida University Press, 2008).

Douglas, Ann, *Terrible Honesty: Mongrel Manhattan in the 1920s* (New York: Noonday Press, 1995).

Douglas, Christopher, *A Genealogy of Literary Multiculturalism* (Ithaca: Cornell University Press, 2009).

Douglass, Frederick, 'The United States cannot remain half-slave and half-free' (1883), in Philip Foner (ed.), *The Life and Writings of Fredrick Douglass*, vol. 4, *Reconstruction and After* (New York: International Publishers, 1975), pp. 368–74.

——, 'The future of the colored race' (1886), in Philip Foner (ed.), *The Life and Writings of Fredrick Douglass*, vol. 4, pp. 191–6.

——, *The Frederick Douglass Papers. Series One: Speeches, Debates and Interviews*, ed. John Blassingame, 5 vols. (New Haven: Yale University Press, 1979).

——, *Autobiographies*: *Narrative of the Life of Frederick Douglass and American Slave* (1845); *My Bondage and My Freedom* (1855); *Life and Times of Frederick Douglass* (1893), ed. H. L. Gates Jr (New York: The Library of America, 1994).

Drake, St Clair, 'A report on the brown Britishers', *The Crisis*, 56 (June 1949), 174, 188–9.

Duberman, Martin, *Paul Robeson: A Biography* ([1988] New York: New Press, 1989).

Du Bois, W. E. B., 'The Negro race in the United States of America', in Gustav Spiller (ed.), *Papers on Inter-Racial Problems Communicated to the First Universal Races Congress* held at the University of London, July 26–29, 1911 (London: P. S. King, and Boston: The Peace Foundation, 1911), pp. 348–64.

——, *The Philadelphia Negro: A Social Study* ([1899] New York: Schocken Books, 1967).

——, *Black Folk Then and Now* ([1939] Milwood. N.Y.: Kraus-Thomson Organization, 1975).

——, *The Autobiography of W. E. B. Du Bois: A Soliloquy on Viewing my Life from the Last Decade of its First Century* ([1968] New York: International Publishers, 1980).

——, *Writings: The Suppression of the African Slave Trade, The Souls of Black Folk, Dusk of Dawn*, ed. Nathan I. Huggins (New York: The Library of America, 1986).

——, 'Books: Van Vechten's *Nigger Heaven*' (1926), in *Writings* (New York: The Library of America, 1986), pp. 1216–18.

——, 'The conservation of races' (1897), in *Writings* (New York: The Library of America, 1986), pp. 815–26.

——, 'Criteria of Negro art' (1926), in *Writings* (New York: The Library of America, 1986), pp. 993–1002.

——, *Dusk of Dawn* (1940) in *Writings* (New York: Library of America, 1986).

——, 'Paul LeRoy Robeson' (1918), in *Writings* (New York: The Library of America, 1986), pp. 1175–6.

——, *The Souls of Black Folk* (1903), in *Writings* (New York: The Library of America, 1986) 357–547.

——, 'The talented tenth' (1903), in *Writings*, pp. 846–7.

——, 'The first Universal Races Congress' (1911), in Eric J. Sundquist (ed.), *The Oxford W. E. B. Du Bois Reader* (Oxford: Oxford University Press, 1996), pp. 55–9.

——, 'Two novels', in Henry Louis Gates Jr et al. (eds.), *The Norton Anthology of African American Literature* (New York: Norton, 1997), pp. 759–60.

Dupee, F. W., 'On *Invisible Man*', *The Washington Post* (26 September 1965), 4.

Eagleton, Terry, *Heathcliff and the Great Hunger: Studies in Irish Culture* (London: Verso, 1995).

Early, Gerald, 'Introduction' to Countee Cullen, *My Soul's High Song: The Collected Writings of Countee Cullen*, ed. Gerald Early (New York: Anchor Books, 1991), pp. 3–73.

——, *The Culture of Bruising: Essays on Prizefighting, Literature and Modern American Culture* (Hopewell, NJ: The Ecco Press, 1994).

Edwards, Brent Hayes, *The Practice of Diaspora: Literature, Translation and the Rise of Black Internationalism* (Cambridge, MA: Harvard University Press, 2003).

Edwards, Hywel Teifi, *Gŵyl Gwalia: Yr Eisteddfod yn Oes Victoria*, (Llandysul: Gwasg Gomer, 1980).

——, 'Victorian Wales seeks reinstatement', *Planet*, 52 (August/September 1985), 12–24.

——, *Codi'r Hen Wlad yn ei Hôl* (Llandysul: Gwasg Gomer, 1990).

——, 'Y Prifeirdd wedi'r Brad', in Prys Morgan (ed.), *Brad y Llyfrau Gleision* (Llandysul: Gomer, 1991), pp. 166–200.

——, *Arwr Glew Erwau'r Glo: Delwedd y Glowr yn Llenyddiaeth y Gymraeg 1850–1950* (Llandysul: Gomer, 1994).

——, 'The Welsh collier as hero: 1850–1950', in Tony Brown (ed.), *Welsh Writing in English: A Yearbook of Critical Essays*, vol. 2 (Cardiff: University of Wales Press, 1996), pp. 22–48.

——, *O'r Pentre Gwyn i Gwmderi: Delwedd y Pentref yn Llenyddiaeth Cymru* (Llandysul: Gomer, 2004).

——, '"Y Pentre Gwyn" and "Manteg": from blessed plot to hotspot', in A. Von Rothkirch and D. Williams (eds.) *Beyond the Difference: Welsh Literature in Comparative Contexts* (Cardiff: University of Wales Press, 2004), pp. 8–20.

—— (ed.), *A Guide to Welsh Literature 1800–1900* (Cardiff: University of Wales Press, 2000).

Edwards, Martha, *Paul Robeson: Honorary Welshman* (Treorchy: Paul Robeson Exhibition, 1998).

Eliot, T. S., *Collected Poems* ([1936] London: Faber, 1974).

Ellis, E. L., *The University College of Wales, Aberystwyth 1872–1972* (Cardiff: University of Wales Press, 1972).

Ellis, John, *Investiture: Royal Ceremony and National Identity in Wales, 1911–1969* (Cardiff: University of Wales Press, 2008).

Ellison, Ralph, 'A Storm of Blizzard Proportions', several drafts, The Ralph Ellison Papers, Library of Congress, Washington DC, box 165, file 7.

——, 'The Negro and the war', undated typescript, MS AM 2238, Houghton Library, Harvard University.

——, 'The Red Cross in Morriston, Swansea, S.W.', several drafts, The Ralph Ellison Papers, Library of Congress, Washington DC, box 165, files 3 and 7.

——, 'On initiation rites and power: Ralph Ellison speaks at West Point', *Going to the Territory* (New York: Vintage, 1987), pp. 39–63.

——, 'Blues people', *Shadow and Act* ([1953] New York: Quality Paperback, 1994), pp. 247–58.

——, 'Richard Wright's blues', *Shadow and Act* ([1953] New York: Quality Paperback Book Club, 1994), pp. 77–94.

——, *Shadow and Act* ([1953] New York: Quality Paperback Book Club, 1994).

——, 'The world and the jug', *Shadow and Act* ([1953] New York: Quality Paperback Book Club, 1994), pp.107–43.

——, 'Introduction' to *Invisible Man* ([1981] New York: Vintage, 1995), vii–xxiii.

——, *Invisible Man* ([1952] New York: Vintage, 1995).

——, 'A Hard Time Keeping Up', in *Flying Home and Other Stories* ([1996] London: Penguin, 1998), pp. 97–109.

——, 'In a Strange Country', in *Flying Home and Other Stories* ([1996] London: Penguin, 1998), pp. 137–46.

——, 'Letter to G. A. Smith' [20 March 1977], *The New Republic* (1 March 1999), pp. 44–5.

—— and Albert Murray, *Trading Twelves: The Selected Letters of Ralph Ellison and Albert Murray* (New York: Vintage Books, 2000).

Emerson, Ralph Waldo, *Nature and Selected Essays* (New York: Penguin, 2003).

Evans, Chris, *Slave Wales: The Welsh and Atlantic Slavery 1660–1850* (Cardiff: University of Wales Press, 2010).

Evans, Geoffrey, 'The amusement of the people – popular entertainment in Aberdare before moving pictures', *Old Aberdare*, 7 (1993), 48–77.

Evans, George Ewart, 'The Valleys', *Wales*, 3 (autumn 1937), 128 9.

Evans, Gwynfor, *Bywyd Cymro* (Caernarfon: Gwasg Gwynedd, 1982).

Evans, Lucy, 'The Black Atlantic: exploring Gilroy's legacy', *Atlantic Studies*, 6 2 (August 2009), 225–68.

Evans, Margiad, 'Review of Kate Roberts, *A Summer Day*', *Life and Letters To-Day*, 51 (November 1946), 54–8.

——, *Country Dance* ([1932] Cardigan: Parthian, 2006).

Evans, Neil, 'Red summers 1917–19', *History Today*, 51, 2 (February 2001), 28–33.

——, 'Immigrants and minorities in Wales, 1840–1990: a comparative perspective', in Evans, O'Leary and Williams (eds), *A Tolerant Nation? Exploring Ethnic Diversity in Wales* (Cardiff: University of Wales Press, 2003), pp. 14–34.

——, Paul O'Leary and Charlotte Williams, *A Tolerant Nation? Exploring Ethnic Diversity in Wales* (Cardiff: University of Wales Press, 2003).

Evans, W. Gareth, *Education and Female Emancipation: The Welsh Experience, 1847–1914* (Cardiff: University of Wales Press, 1990).

Everett, Robert, *Caban F'Ewythr Twm; Neu Fywyd ym mhlith yr Iselradd* (Remsen, NY: John R, Everett, 1854) (amended version of Hugh Williams's Welsh translation of Stowe's *Uncle Tom's Cabin*).

Fanon, Frantz, *Black Skin, White Masks*, trans. Charles Markmann ([1952 in French] London: Pluto, 1986).

Farebrother, Rachel, *The Collage Aesthetic in the Harlem Renaissance* (Farnham: Ashgate, 2009).

Farr, Tommy, *Thus Farr* (London: Optomen Press, 1989).

Ffrancon, Gwenno, *Cyfaredd y Cysgodion; Delweddu Cymru a'i Phobl ar Ffilm, 193 1951* (Caerdydd: Gwasg Prifysgol Cymru, 2003).

——, 'Affro-Americaniaid a'r Cymry ar y Sgrin Fawr', in D. G. Williams (ed.), *Canu Caeth: Y Cymry a'r Affro-Americaniaid* (Llandysul: Gomer, 2010), pp. 117–33.

Filreis, Alan, *Wallace Stevens and the Actual World* (Princeton, NJ: Princeton University Press, 1991).

Fisch, Audrey, *American Slaves in Victorian England: Abolitionist Politics in Popular Literature and Culture* (Cambridge: Cambridge University Press, 2000).

Fischer, Michael M. J., and George E. Marcus, *Anthropology as Cultural Critique: An Experimental Moment in the Human Sciences* ([1986] Chicago: University of Chicago Press, 1999).

Fleure, H. J., 'The racial history of the British people', *Geographical Review*, 5 (1918), 216–31.

——, 'Wales', in Alan G. Ogilvie (ed.), *Great Britain: Essays in Regional Geography* (Cambridge: Cambridge University Press, 1928), pp. 237–63.

——, 'The Welsh people', *Wales*, 10 (October 1939), reprinted in *Wales 1–11* (London: Frank Cass, 1969), pp. 265–9.

—— (ed.), *Gyda'r Wawr: Braslun o Hanes Cymru'r Oesoedd Cynteffig* (Gwrecsam: Hughes a'i Fab, 1923).

'Fluellyn', *Reply to the Perfidious Welshman* (Wrexham: Hughes and Son, 1911).

Foley, Barbara, 'Ralph Ellison as proletarian journalist', *Science and Society*, 62, 4 (winter 1998–9), pp. 537–56.

——, 'Reading redness: politics and audience in Ralph Ellison's early short fiction', *Journal of Narrative Theory*, 29, 3 (fall 1999), 323–39.

——, 'From communism to brotherhood: the drafts of *Invisible Man*', in Bill V. Mullen and James Smethurst (eds.), *Left of the Color Line: Race, Radicalism and the Twentieth-Century Literature of the United States* (Chapel Hill: University of North Carolina Press, 2003), pp. 163–82.

——, *Spectres of 1919: Class and Nation in the Making of the New Negro* (Chicago: University of Illinois Press, 2003).

Francis, Hywel, 'Paul Robeson: his legacy For Wales', a lecture to the Friends of the National Library of Wales, Aberystwyth, 12 July 2003, *http://www.epolitix.com/EN/MPWebsites/Hywel+Francis/b8a07531-f84c-4862-92db-b59a4790da4f.htm*, consulted 15 August 2005.

——, *Miners Against Fascism: Wales and the Spanish Civil War* ([1984] Abersychan: Warren and Pell, 2004).

——, 'Paul Robeson: Ei Etifeddiaeth i Gymru', in Daniel G. Williams (ed.), *Canu Caeth: Y Cymry a'r Affro-Americaniaid* (Llandysul: Gomer, 2010), pp. 64–73.

—— and Dai Smith, *The Fed: A History of the South Wales Miners in the Twentieth Century* ([1980] Cardiff: University of Wales Press, 1998).

Freud, Sigmund, *Totem and Taboo* ([1913] London; Routledge, 1999).

Gaines, Kevin K., *Uplifting the Race: Black Leadership, Politics, and Culture in the Twentieth Century* (Chapel Hill: University of North Carolina Press, 1996).

Gallimore, Andrew, *Occupation Prizefighter: The Freddie Welsh Story* (Bridgend: Seren, 2006).

Gambrell, Alice, *Women Intellectuals, Modernism and Difference: Transatlantic Culture 1919–1945* (Cambridge: Cambridge University Press, 1997).

Garrison, Wendell Phillips and Francis Jackson Garrison, *William Lloyd Garrison 1805–1879: The Story of His Life Told By His Children*, vol. 3, *1841–1860* ([1889] New York: Negro Universities Press, 1969).

Garrison, William Lloyd, *No Union With Slave Holders 1841–1849: The Letters of William Lloyd Garrison*, vol. 3, ed. Walter M. Merrill (Cambridge, MA: Harvard University Press, 1973).

Gates Jr., Henry Louis, *Tradition and the Black Atlantic: Critical Theory in the African Diaspora* (New York: Basic Civitas Books, 2010).

——, *Figures in Black: Words, Signs and the 'Racial' Self* (Oxford: Oxford University Press, 1987).

——, *The Signifying Monkey: A Theory of African-American Literary Criticism* (Oxford: Oxford University Press, 1988).

——, 'The trope of a new Negro and the reconstruction of the image of the Black', *Representations*, 24 (1988), 129–55.

——, *Loose Canons: Notes on the Culture Wars* (New York: Oxford University Press, 1992).

——, 'Harlem on our minds', in Richard J. Powell and David A. Bailey (eds), *Rhapsodies in Black: Art of the Harlem Renaissance* (London: South Bank Centre, 1997), pp. 162–7.

—— (ed.), *'Race', Writing and Difference* (Chicago: University of Chicago Press, 1986).

—— (general ed.), *The Norton Anthology of African American Literature* (New York: Norton, 1997).

—— and Cornel West, *The Future of the Race* (New York: Alfred A. Knopf, 1996).

Gerzina, Gretchen H. (ed.), *Black Victorians, Black Victoriana* (New Brunswick: Rutgers University Press, 2003).

Gibbons, Luke, 'Ireland and the colonization of theory', *Interventions: International Journal of Postcolonial Studies*, 1, 1 (1998), 27.

——, 'Peripheral modernities: national and global in a post-colonial frame', *Nineteenth-Century Contexts: An Interdisciplinary Journal*, 29, 2 (2007), 271–81.

Giles, Paul. *Virtual Americas: Transnational Fiction and the Transatlantic Imaginary* (Durham, NC: Duke University Press, 2002).

Gillman, Susan and Alys Eve Weinbaum (eds.), *Next to the Color Line: Gender, Sexuality and W. E. B. Du Bois* (Minneapolis: University of Minnesota Press, 2007).

Gilroy, Paul. 'Nationalism, history and ethnic absolutism', *History Workshop Journal*, 30, 1 (1990), 114–20.

——, *The Black Atlantic: Modernity and Double Consciousness* (Cambridge MA: Harvard University Press, 1993).

——, *Between Camps: Race, Identity and Nationalism at the End of the Colour Line* (London: Penguin, 2000).

Golightly, Victor, '"Writing with dreams and blood": Dylan Thomas, Marxism and 1930s Swansea', in Tony Brown (ed.), *Welsh Writing in English: A Yearbook*, vol. 8 (Cardiff: University of Wales Press, 2003), pp. 67–91.

Goodby, John and Christopher Wigginton, *Dylan Thomas: New Casebooks* (Basingstoke: Palgrave, 2001).

Gray, Melinda, 'Uncle Tom's Welsh dress: ethnicity, authority and translation', in Alyce Von Rothkirch and Daniel Williams (eds), *Beyond the Difference: Welsh Literature in Comparative Contexts* (Cardiff: University of Wales Press, 2004), pp. 173–85.

Greene, Graham, *The Pleasure Dome: The Collected Film Criticism 1935–40*, ed. John Russell Taylor (London: Secker and Warburg, 1972).

Griffith, Selwyn, 'Arwyr' in Lowri Roberts (ed.), *Canu Clod y Campau: Detholiad o Farddonaieth y Maes Chwarae* (Llanrwst: Gwasg Carreg Gwalch, 2009), pp. 31–3.

Griffiths, Robert, *S. O. Davies: A Socialist Faith* (Llandysul: Gomer Press, 1983).

Gruffudd, Pyrs, 'Back to the land: historiography, rurality and the nation in interwar Wales', *Transactions of the Institute of British Geographers*, 19 (1994), 61–77.

——, 'Yr Iaith Gymraeg a'r Dychymyg Daearyddol 1918–1950', in Geraint Jenkins and Mari Williams (eds), *'Eu Hiaith a Gadwant'? Y Gymraeg yn yr Ugeinfed Ganrif* (Caerdydd: Gwasg Prifysgol Cymru, 2000), pp. 107–32.

Gruffydd, W. J., 'Hen Atgofion', *Y Llenor*, 17 (1938), 8–9.

—— *The Years of the Locust*, trans. D. Myrddin Lloyd (Llandysul: Gomer, 1976).

Gubar, Susan, *Racechanges: White Skin, Black Face in American Culture* (Oxford: Oxford University Press, 1997).

Gussow, Mel, 'Theater: "The Corn is Green"', *New York Times*, 23 August 1983, C13.

Gwyllt, Ieuan, 'Purdeb Chwaeth Mewn Cerddoriaeth', *Y Cerddor Cymraeg*, 2, 25 (1 Mawrth 1867), 4–5.

Hall, Stuart, 'Negotiating Caribbean identities', *New Left Review*, 1, 209 (January–February 1995), 3–14.

Hallam, Tudur, *Canon ein Llên: Saunder Lewis, R. M. Jones ac Alan Llwyd* (Caerdydd: Gwasg Prifysgol Cymru, 2007).

Harper, Michael S., 'Visit to Abercanaid', *The Anglo-Welsh Review*, 26, 58 (spring 1977), 18–19.

Harris, John, 'A Hallelujah of a book': *How Green Was My Valley* as bestseller', in Tony Brown (ed.), *Welsh Writing in English: A Yearbook of Critical Essays*, vol. 3 (Cardiff: University of Wales Press, 1997), pp. 42–62.

Harris, Leonard, 'Honor and insurrection: a short story about why John Brown was right and Frederick Douglass was wrong', in Bill Lawson and Frank Kirkland (eds.), *Frederick Douglass: A Critical Reader* (Oxford: Blackwell, 1999), pp. 227–42.

Hechter, Michael, *Internal Colonialism: The Celtic Fringe in British National Development 153 1966* (London: Routledge, 1975).

Hegeman, Susan, *Patterns for America: Modernism and the Concept of Culture* (Princeton: Princeton University Press, 1999).

Hemenway, Robert E., *Zora Neale Hurston: A Literary Biography* ([1977] London: Camden Press, 1986).

Henson, Josiah, *Uncle Tom's Story of His Life: An Autobiography of the Rev. Josiah Henson. From 1789 to 1877*, ed. John Lobb (London: *Christian Age* Office, 1877).

——, *Hanes Bywyd 'Uncle Tom' o 1789 hyd 1877 Ganddo Ef Ei Hun sef Bywgraffiad Y Parch. Josiah Henson*, cyfieithiedig gan Y Parch D. Griffith (Dolgellau: Swyddfa *Y Dysgedydd*, 1877).

Higginbotham, Evelyn Brooks, *Righteous Discontent: The Women's Movement in the Black Baptist Church, 1880–1920* (Cambridge, MA: Harvard University Press, 1993).

Higgins, John, *Raymond Williams: Literature, Marxism and Cultural Materialism* (London: Routledge, 1999).

Hobsbawm, Eric, 'Interview: world distempers', *New Left Review II*, 61 (January/February 2010), 133–50.

Hoggan, Frances. 'The Negro problem in relation to white women', in Gustav Spiller (ed.), *Papers on Inter-Racial Problems Communicated to the First Universal Races Congress held at the University of London, July 26–29, 1911* (London: P. S. King, and Boston: The Peace Foundation, 1911), pp. 364–7.

——, 'American Negro women during their first fifty years of freedom', *The Individualist* (September–October 1913), 72–5.

Hopkin, Deian, Duncan Tanner and Chris Williams (eds), *The Labour Party in Wales 1900–2000* (Cardiff: University of Wales Press, 2000).

Howells, W. D., *Seven English Cities* (New York: Harper and Brothers, 1909).

——, *An Imperative Duty* in Martha Bunta (ed.), *The Shadow of a Dream* and *An Imperative Duty* ([1891] Bloomington: Indiana University Press, 1970).

——, 'My favorite novelist and his best book', in Howells, *W. D. Howells as Critic* (London: Routledge, 1973), pp. 268–80.

——, *W. D. Howells as Critic*, ed. Edwin H. Cady (London: Routledge, 1973).

Hughes, Langston, *The Big Sea* (New York: Knopf, 1940).

——, *I Wonder as I Wander* (New York: Hill and Wang, 1956).

——, *The Collected Poems of Langston Hughes*, ed. Arnold Rampersad (New York: Vintage, 1994).

——, 'The Negro artist and the racial mountain' (1926), in Gates Jr (ed), *The Norton Anthology of African American Literature* (New York: Norton, 1997), pp. 1267–71.

——, *Jim Crow's Last Stand* (1943), in Arnold Rampersad (ed.), *The Collected Poems*. vol. 2 (Columbia: University of Missouri Press, 2001), pp. 73–100.

Humboldt, Charles, 'When peoples meet', *The Negro Quarterly*, 1, 2 (summer 1942), 184–86.

Hunter, Jerry, *Llwch Cenhedloedd: Y Cymry a Rhyfel Cartref America* (Llanrwst: Gwasg Carreg Gwalch, 2003).

——, *I Ddeffro Ysbryd y Wlad: Robert Everett a'r Ymgyrch yn erbyn Caethwasanaeth Americanaidd* (Llanrwst: Gwasg Carreg Gwalch, 2007).

——, *Sons of Arthur, Children of Lincoln: Welsh Writing from the American Civil War* (Cardiff: University of Wales Press, 2007).

—— a Richard Wyn Jones, 'O'r Chwith: Pa Mor Feirniadol yw Beirniadaeth Ôl-Fodern?', *Taliesin*, 92 (1995), 9–32.

Hurston, Zora Neale, 'Why the Negro won't buy communism', *American Legion,* 50 (June 1951), 14–15, 55–60.

——, 'What white publishers won't print' (1950), in *I Love Myself When I am Laughing*, ed. Alice Walker (New York: The Feminist Press, 1979), pp. 169–73.

——, *I Love Myself When I am Laughing*, ed. Alice Walker (New York: The Feminist Press, 1979).

——, *Color Struck*, in Kathy A. Perkins (ed.), *Black Female Playwrights: An Anthology of Plays Before 1950* (Bloomington: Indiana University Press, 1990), pp. 89–102.

——, *Moses, Man of the Mountain* ([1939] New York: Harper Collins, 1991).

——, *Dust Tracks on a Road* ([1942] New York: Harper Collins, 1991).

——, *Their Eyes Were Watching God* ([1937] London: Virago, 1992).

——, *Mules and Men* (1935), in *Zora Neale Hurston: Folklore, Memoirs, and Other Writings: Mules and Men, Tell My Horse, Dust Tracks on a Road, Selected Articles* (New York: The Library of America, 1995), pp. 1–268.

——, 'The Gilded Six-Bits' (1933), in Henry Louis Gates Jr (ed.), *The Norton Anthology of African American Literature* (New York: Norton, 1997), pp. 1011–19.

Hutchinson, George, *The Harlem Renaissance in Black and White* (Cambridge, MA: Harvard University Press, 1995).

Huyssen, Andreas, *After the Great Divide: Modernism, Mass Culture and Postmodernism* ([1986] London: Macmillan, 1988).

Jackson, Lawrence, *Ralph Ellison: The Emergence of Genius* (New York: John Wiley and Sons, 2002).

James, C. L. R., *American Civilization* (Oxford: Blackwell, 1993).

James, E. Wyn, 'Welsh ballads and American slavery', *The Welsh Journal of Religious History*, 2 (2007), 59–86.

——, 'Morgan John Rhys a Chaethwasiaeth Americanaidd', in D. G. Williams (ed.), *Canu Caeth: Y Cymry a'r Affro-Americaniaid* (Llandysul: Gomer, 2010), pp. 2–25.

Jameson, Fredric, *Fables of Aggression: Wyndham Lewis, the Modernist as Fascist* (Berkeley: University of California Press, 1979).

Jenkins, Geraint (ed.), *Iaith Carreg fy Aelwyd: Iaith a Chymuned yn y Bedwaredd Ganrif ar Bymtheg* (Caedydd: Gwasg Prifysgol Cymru, 1998).

—— (ed.), *The Welsh Language and its Social Domains 1801–1911* (Cardiff: University of Wales Press, 2000).

—— and Mari Williams (eds), *'Eu Hiaith a Gadwant'? Y Gymraeg yn yr Ugeinfed Ganrif* (Caerdydd: Gwasg Prifysgol Cymru, 2000).

Jenkins, Lee, 'Beyond the pale: Frederick Douglass in Cork', *The Irish Review*, 24 (autumn 1999), 80–95.

Jenkinson, Jacqueline, *Black 1919: Riots, Racism and Resistance in Imperial Britain* (Liverpool: Liverpool University Press, 2009).

Johnson, Barbara, 'Thresholds of difference: structures of address in Zora Neale Hurston', in H. L. Gates Jr (ed.), *'Race', Writing and Difference* (Chicago: University of Chicago Press, 1986), pp. 317–28.

——, *A World of Difference* (Baltimore: Johns Hopkins University Press, 1987).

Johnston, Dafydd, 'Dwy Lenyddiaeth Cymru yn y Tridegau' yn John Rowlands, ed., *Sglefrio ar Eiriau* (Llandysul: Gomer, 1992), pp. 42–62.

——, 'The development of Idris Davies's poetry', in *The Complete Poems of Idris Davies*, ed. Dafydd Johnston (Cardiff: University of Wales Press, 1994), pp. xxxvi–lxxx.

Jones Alun R. and Gwyn Thomas (eds), *Presenting Saunders Lewis* (Cardiff: University of Wales Press, 1973).

Jones, Bill and David Wyatt, 'Caethwas Ffoedig yng Nghaerdydd: Hanes William A. Hall a Diddymiaeth Gymreig 1861–65', in D. G. Williams (ed.), *Canu Caeth: Y Cymry a'r Affro-Americaniaid* (Llandysul: Gomer, 2010), pp. 39–62.

Jones, Dafydd Glyn, 'His politics', in Alun R. Jones and Gwyn Thomas (eds), *Presenting Saunders Lewis* (Cardiff: University of Wales Press, 1973), pp. 23–78.

——, 'Dwy Olwg ar Saunders Lewis', *Taliesin*, 66 (Mawrth 1989), 16–26.

Jones, Gareth Elwyn, 'Llyfrau Gleision 1847', in Prys Morgan (ed.), *Brad y Llyfrau Gleision* (Llandysul: Gomer, 1991), pp. 22–48.

Jones, Glyn, 'Porth-Y-Rhyd', in Tony Brown (ed.), *The Collected Stories of Glyn Jones* (Cardiff: University of Wales Press, 1999), pp. 85–90.

Jones, Gwyn, *Times Like These* (1936. London: Victor Gollancz, 1979).

Jones, Jack, *Black Parade* (London: Faber, 1935).

——, 'Nofelau'r Cymry Seisnig', *Tir Newydd*, 8 (Mai 1937), 5–9.

——, *Unfinished Journey* (London: Hamish Hamilton, 1937).

——, *Me and Mine: Further Chapters in the Autobiography* (London: Hamish Hamilton, 1946).

——, *Rhondda Roundabout* ([1934] London: Hamish Hamilton, 1949).

——, 'American industry listens when the Welsh lion roars', *Western Mail*, Wednesday 30 July 1958, 4:B–H.

——, *Bidden to the Feast* ([1938] London: Corgi Books, 1968).

Jones, Leroi, *Blues People: Negro Music in White America* (New York: William Morrow, 1963).

Jones, Lewis, *We Live: The Story of a Welsh Mining Valley* ([1939] London: Lawrence and Wishart, 1978).

——, *Cwmardy: The Story of a Welsh Mining Valley* ([1937] London: Lawrence and Wishart, 1979).

Jones, Mervyn, 'Beyond identity? The reconstruction of the Welsh', *Journal of British Studies*, 31, 4 (October 1992), 330–57.

Jones, Richard Wyn, 'The colonial legacy in Welsh politics', in Jane Aaron and Chris Williams (eds), *Postcolonial Wales* (Cardiff: University of Wales Press, 2005) pp. 23–38.

——, *Rhoi Cymru'n Gyntaf: Syniadaeth Plaid Cymru* (Caerdydd: Gwasg Prifysgol Cymru, 2007).

Jones, R. M., *Ysbryd y Cwlwm: Delwedd y Genedl yn ein Llenyddiaeth* (Caerdydd: Gwasg Prifysgol Cymru, 1998).

Jones, Robert Owen, *Hir Oes i'r Iaith: Agweddau ar Hanes y Gymraeg a'r Gymdeithas* (Llandysul: Gomer, 1997).

Jordan, Glenn, '"We never really noticed you were coloured": postcolonialist reflections on immigrants and minorities in Wales', in Jane Aaron and Chris Williams (eds), *Postcolonial Wales* (Cardiff: University of Wales Press, 2005), pp. 55–81.

Jordan-Lake, Joy, *Whitewashing Uncle Tom's Cabin: Nineteenth-Century Women Novelists Respond to Stowe* (Vanderbilt: Vanderbilt University Press, 2005).

Joyce, James, 'The Dead', in *Dubliners* ([1914] London: Penguin, 1992), pp. 175–225.

Kaplan, Sidney, 'The miscegenation issue in the election of 1864' (1949), in Werner Sollors (ed.), *Interracialism: Black–White Intermarriage in American History, Literature and Law* (New York: Oxford University Press, 2000), pp. 219–65.

Karp, Jonathan, 'Performing Black-Jewish symbiosis: the "Hassidic chant" of Paul Robeson', *American Jewish History*, 91, 1 (March 2003), 53–81.

Kealing, Winifred, 'Letter to Ralph Ellison', 24 September 1944, The Ralph Ellison Papers, Library of Congress, box 165, file 7.

Kelley, Robin D. G., 'The riddle of the zoot: Malcolm Little and Black cultural politics during World War II', in Joe Wood (ed.), *Malcolm X: In Our Own Image* (New York: St Martin's Press, 1992), pp. 155–82.

Kent, Graeme, *A Welshman in the Bronx: Tommy Farr vs. Joe Louis* (Llandysul: Gomer, 2009).

Kiberd, Declan, 'The view from Enniskillen', *New Left Review* II, 3 (May/June 2000), 153–7.

Kirkland, Frank M., 'Enslavement, moral suasion and struggles for recognition: Frederick Douglass's answer to the question – "What is enlightenment"', in Bill E. Lawson and Frank M. Kirkland (eds.), *Frederick Douglass: A Critical Reader* (Oxford: Blackwell, 1999), pp. 243–310.

Klein, Marcus, *Foreigners: The Making of American Literature 1900–1940* (Chicago: University of Chicago Press, 1981).

Knight, Stephen, 'The voices of Glamorgan: Gwyn Thomas's colonial fiction', in Tony Brown (ed.), *Welsh Writing in English: A Yearbook of Critical Essays*, vol. 7 (Cardiff: University of Wales Press, 2001–2), pp. 16–34.

——, '"A new enormous music": industrial fictions in Wales', in M. Wynn Thomas (ed.), *Welsh Writing in English: A Guide To Welsh Literature* (Cardiff: University of Wales Press, 2003), pp. 47–90.

——, *A Hundred Years of Fiction: Writing Wales in English* (Cardiff: University of Wales Press, 2004).

Knights, Ben, *The Idea of the Clerisy in the Nineteenth Century* (Cambridge: Cambridge University Press, 1978).

Kronfeld, Barbara, *On the Margins of Modernism: Decentering Literary Dynamics* (Los Angeles: University of California Press, 1993).

Lawson, Bill E. and Frank M. Kirkland (eds.), *Frederick Douglass: A Critical Reader* (Oxford: Blackwell, 1999).

Leab, Daniel J., *From Sambo to Superspade: The Black Experience in Motion Pictures* (Boston: Houghton Mifflin, 1976).

Lee, A. Robert, *Designs of Blackness: Mappings in the Literature and Culture of Afro-America* (London: Pluto Press, 1998).

Lemire, Elise, *'Miscegenation': Making Race in America* (Philadelphia: University of Pennsylvania Press, 2002).

*Let Robeson Sing! A Celebration of the Life of Paul Robeson and his Relationship with Wales* (Cardiff: Paul Robeson Cymru Committee/Bevan Foundation, 2001).

Levertov, Denise, 'Denise Levertov writes', in Jeni Couzyn (ed.), *The Bloodaxe Book of Contemporary Women Poets* (Newcastle: Bloodaxe, 1985), pp. 75–9.

Levi, Thomas, *Crynodeb o Gaban 'Newyrth Tom; Neu, Fywyd Negroaidd yn America*, translation of Stowe, *Uncle Tom's Cabin* (Abertawy: J. Rosser, 1853).

Levine, Lawrence W., *Black Culture and Black Consciousness: Afro-American Folk Thought from Slavery to Freedom* (Oxford: Oxford University Press, 1977).

Levine, Robert S., 'Uncle Tom's Cabin in the Frederick Douglass' Paper: an analysis of reception', *American Literature*, 64, 1 (March 1992), 71–93.

——, *Martin Delany, Frederick Douglass and the Politics of Representative Identity* (Chapel Hill: University of North Caroline Press, 1997).

Lewis, David Levering, *When Harlem Was in Vogue* ([1981] Oxford: Oxford University Press, 1989).

——, *W. E. B. Du Bois: Biography of a Race 1868–1919* (New York: Henry Holt and Co. 1993).

——, 'Paul Robeson and the U.S.S.R', in J. C. Stewart (ed.), *Paul Robeson: Artist and Citizen* (New Brunswick: Rutgers University Press, 1998), pp. 217–33.

——, *W. E. B. Du Bois: The Fight for Equality and the American Century, 1919–1963* (New York: Henry Holt and Co., 2000).

—— (ed.), *The Portable Harlem Renaissance Reader* (London: Penguin, 1994).

Lewis, Saunders, 'Safonau Beirniadaeth Lenyddol', *Y Llenor*, 1, 4 (gaeaf 1922), 245.

——, 'Tueddiadau Cymru Rhwng 1919 a 1923', *Baner ac Amserau Cymru*, 6 (Medi 1923), 5.

——, 'Cyflwyniad' i Molière, *Doctor Er Ei Waethaf* (Wrecsam: Cyfres y Werin, 1924), pp. 5–7.

——, *Ceiriog: Yr Artist yn Philistia I* (Aberystwyth: Gwasg Aberystwyth, 1929).

——, 'The literary man's life in Wales', *Welsh Outlook*, 16 (October 1929), 295.

——, 'Deg pwynt polisi Plaid Cymru', *Y Ddraig Goch* (Mawrth 1934), 1.

——, 'Swyddogaeth Celfyddyd', *Y Traethodydd*, 89, 3 (1934), 390–3.

——, *Daniel Owen: Yr Artist yn Philistia II* (Aberystwyth: Gwasg Aberystwyth, 1936).

——, *Is There an Anglo-Welsh Literature?* (Cardiff: Guild of Graduates of the University of Wales, 1939), pamphlet.

——, 'Dylanwadau: Saunders Lewis mewn ymgom ag Aneirin Talfan Davies', *Taliesin*, 2 (Nadolig 1961), 5–18.

——, 'Welsh literature and nationalism' (1965), in Alun R. Jones and Gwyn Thomas (eds), *Presenting Saunders Lewis* (Cardiff: University of Wales Press, 1973), pp. 142–4.

——, 'Welsh writers of today', in Alun R. Jones and Gwyn Thomas (eds.), *Presenting Saunders Lewis* (Cardiff: University of Wales Press, 1973), pp. 164–70.

——, *Canlyn Arthur: Ysgrifau Gwleidyddol* ([1938] Llandysul: Gomer, 1985).

——, 'Y Dilyw 1939', yn R. Geraint Gruffydd (gol.), *Cerddi* (Caerdydd: Gwasg Prifysgol Cymru, 1992), pp. 10–12; trans. by Gwyn Thomas in Alun R. Jones and Gwyn Thomas (eds.), *Presenting Saunders Lewis* (Cardiff: University of Wales Press, 1973), pp. 177–9.

——, *Letters to Margaret Gilcriest*, ed. Mair Saunders Jones, Ned Thomas and Harri Pritchard Jones (Cardiff: University of Wales Press, 1993).

——, 'Blodeuwedd (*Y Llenor* 1923)', yn *Dramâu Saunders Lewis: Y Casgliad Cyflawn*, Cyfrol 1, gol. Ioan M. Williams (Caerdydd: Gwasg Prifysgol Cymru, 1996).

——, *Dramâu Saunders Lewis: Y Casglaid Cyflawn*, Cyfrol 1, gol. Ioan M. Williams (Caerdydd: Gwasg Prifysgol Cymru, 1996).

—— a Kate Roberts, *Annwyl Kate, Annwyl Saunders*, gol., Dafydd Ifans (Aberystwyth: Llyfrgell Genedlaethol Cymru, 1992).

Lhamon, Jr, W. T. (ed.), *Jump Jim Crow: Lost Plays, Lyrics, and Street Prose of the First Atlantic Popular Culture* (Cambridge, MA, and London : Harvard University Press, 2003).

Livingstone, David N., *The Geographical Tradition* (Oxford: Blackwell, 1992).

Llewellyn, Richard, *How Green Was My Valley* ([1939] London: Penguin, 1991).

Lloyd, D. Tecwyn, *Drych o Genedl* (Abertawe: Gwasg John Penry, 1987).

——, *John Saunders Lewis: Y Gyfrol Gyntaf* (Dinbych: Gwasg Gee, 1988).

Lloyd-Morgan, Ceridwen, *Margiad Evans* (Bridgend: Seren, 1998).

Llwyd, Alan, *Cymru Ddu/Black Wales: A History* (Cardiff: Hughes a'i Fab, 2005).

Locke, Alain, 'The new Negro' (1925), in Henry Louis Gates Jr (ed.), *The Norton Anthology of African American Literature* (New York: Norton, 1997), pp. 961–70.

—— and Bernhard J. Stern (eds), *When Peoples Meet: A Study in Race and Culture Contacts* (New York: Progressive Educations Association, 1942).

Loomba, Ania, *Colonialism/Postcolonialism* (London: Routledge, 1998).

Lord, Peter, *Y Chwaer-Dduwies: Celf, Crefft a'r Eisteddfod* (Llandysul: Gomer, 1992).

Lorimer, Douglas A., *Colour, Class and the Victorians: English Attitudes to the Negro in the Mid-Nineteenth Century* (Leicester: Leicester University Press, 1978).

Lott, Eric, *Love and Theft: Blackface Minstrelsy and the American Working Class* (Oxford: Oxford University Press, 1993).

——, 'Double V, double-time: be-bop's politics of style', in Robert G. O'Meally (ed.), *The Jazz Cadence of American Culture* (New York: Columbia University Press, 1998), pp. 457–68.

MacCabe, Colin, *James Joyce and the Revolution of the Word* (London: Macmillan, 1978).

McCray, Florine Thayer, *The Life-Work of the Author of Uncle Tom's Cabin* (New York: Funk and Wagnalls, 1889).

McFeely, William S., *Frederick Douglass* (New York: Norton, 1991).

McGinty, Doris Evans and Wayne Shirley, 'Paul Robeson, musician', in J. C. Stewart (ed.), *Paul Robeson: Artist and Citizen* (New Brunswick: Rutgers University Press, 1998), pp. 105–20.

McGuire, Phillip, *Taps for a Jim Crow Army: Letters from Black Soldiers in World War II* (Oxford: ABC-Clio, 1983).

McIntyre, Neil, 'Frances Hoggan – doctor of medicine, pioneer physician, patriot and philanthropist', *Brycheiniog*, 39 (2007), 127–46.

McMillen, Neil R., 'Fighting for what we didn't have: how Mississippi's black veterans remember World War II', in Neil R. McMillen (ed.), *Remaking*

*Dixie: The Impact of World War II on the American South* (Jackson: University Press of Mississippi, 1997), pp. 93–110.

—— (ed.), *Remaking Dixie: The Impact of World War II on the American South* (Jackson: University Press of Mississippi, 1997).

Mac Grianna, Seosamh, *An Bhreatain Bheag* (Baile Átha Cliath: Oifig an tSoláthair, 1937).

——, *Mo Bhealach Féin* (Baile Átha Cliath: Oifig an tSoláthair, 1940).

Mackey, Nathaniel, 'Other: from verb to noun', in Robert G. O'Meally (ed.), *The Jazz Cadence of American Culture* (New York: Columbia University Press, 1998), pp. 513–32.

Manning, Susan and Andrew Taylor, 'Introduction: what is transatlantic literary studies', *Transatlantic Literary Studies: A Reader* (Edinburgh: Edinburgh University Press, 2007), pp. 1–13.

Marcus, Laura, 'Cinema and visual culture: Close Up (1927–33)', in Peter Brooker and Andrew Thacker (eds), *The Oxford Critical and Cultural History of Modernist Magazines*, vol. 1, *Britain and Ireland 1880–1955* (Oxford: Oxford University Press, 2009), pp. 505–29.

Marcuse, Herbert, 'The affirmative character of culture', in *Negations: Essays in Critical Theory*, trans. Jeremy J. Shapiro (Boston: Beacon Press, 1968), pp. 88–133.

Margolick, David, *Beyond Glory: Max Schmeling vs. Joe Louis and a World on the Brink* (London: Bloosbury, 2005).

Marqusee, Mike, *Redemption Song: Muhammad Ali and the Spirit of the Sixties* (London: Verso, 1999).

Martin, Tony, *Race First: The Ideological and Organizational Struggles of Marcus Garvey and the United Negro Improvement Association* (Westport, CT: Greenwood Press, 1976).

Martin Jr, Waldo E., *The Mind of Frederick Douglass* (Chapel Hill: The University of North Carolina Press, 1984).

Marx, Karl and Frederick Engels, *The Communist Manifesto: A Modern Edition* ([1848] London: Verso, 1988).

Maxwell, William J., *New Negro, Old Left: African-American Writing and Communism Between the Wars* (New York: Columbia University Press, 1999).

Mazurek, Raymond A., 'Writer on the Left: class and race in Ellison's early fiction', *College Literature*, 29, 4 (fall 2002), pp. 109–35.

Meer, Sarah, 'Competing representations: Douglass, the Ethiopian Serenaders, and Ethnic Exhibition in London', in Martin Crawford and Alan J. Rice (eds), *Liberating Sojourn: Frederick Douglass and Transatlantic Reform* (Athens, GA: The University of Georgia Press, 1999), pp. 141–65.

——, *Uncle Tom Mania: Slavery, Minstrelsy, and Transatlantic Culture in the 1850s* (Athens, GA: University of Georgia Press, 2005).

Miles, Gareth, 'A personal view', in Alun R. Jones and Gwyn Thomas (eds), *Presenting Saunders Lewis* (Cardiff: University of Wales Press, 1973), pp. 14–19.

Miller, Joan, *Aberfan: A Disaster and its Aftermath* (London: Constable, 1974).

Millward, E. G., *Cenedl o Bobl Ddewrion: Agweddau ar Lenyddiaeth Oes Victoria* (Llandysul: Gwasg Gomer, 1991).

Moglen, Seth, 'Modernism and the Black diaspora: Langston Hughes and the broken cubes of Picasso', *Callaloo*, 25, 4 (autumn 2002), pp. 1188–205.

*Monthly Summary of Events and Trends in Race Relations*, 2, 8 (March 1945), copy held in the Ralph Ellison Papers, Library of Congress, box 204, file 8.

Moorehouse, Maggi M., *Fighting in the Jim Crow Army: Black Men and Women Remember World War II* (New York: Rowman and Littlefield Publishers, 2000).

Morgan, Clare, 'Exile and the kingdom: Margiad Evans and the mythic landscape of Wales', in Tony Brown (ed.), *Welsh Writing in English: A Yearbook of Critical Essays*, vol. 6 (Cardiff: University of Wales Press, 2000), pp. 89–118.

Morgan, Kenneth, 'Power and glory: war and reconstruction, 1939–1951', in Deian Hopkin, Duncan Tanner and Chris Williams (eds), *The Labour Party in Wales 1900–2000* (Cardiff: University of Wales Press, 2000), pp. 166–88.

Morgan, Prys, 'The gwerin of Wales: myth and reality', in Ian Hume and W. T. R. Pryce (eds), *The Welsh and their Country* (Llandysul: Gomer, 1986), pp. 134–52.

—— (ed.), *Brad y Llyfrau Gleision* (Llandysul: Gomer, 1991).

Morton, H. V., *In Search of Wales* (New York: Dodd, Mead, 1932).

Moses, Wilson J., *The Golden Age of Black Nationalism 1850–1925* (Oxford: Oxford University Press, 1978).

——, *Alexander Crummell: A Study of Civilisation and Discontent* (New York: Oxford University Press, 1989).

——, *Afrotopia: The Roots of African American Popular History* (Cambridge: Cambridge University Press, 1998).

Mostern, Kenneth, *Autobiography and Black Identity Politics: Racialization in Twentieth-Century America* (Cambridge: Cambridge University Press, 1999).

Mulhern, Francis, *The Present Lasts a Long Time: Essays in Cultural Politics* (Cork: Cork University Press, 1998).

——, 'Conrad's disavowals', *New Left Review* II, 38 (March/April 2006), 59–93.

Mullen, Bill V. and James Smethurst, *Left of the Color Line: Race, Radicalism and the Twentieth-Century Literature of the United States* (Chapel Hill: University of North Carolina Press, 2003).

Murray, Florence (ed.), *The Negro Handbook 1944: A Manual of Current Facts, Statistics and General Information Concerning Negroes in the United States* (New York: Current Reference Publications, 1944).

Musser, Charles, 'Troubled relations: Robeson, O'Neill and Micheaux', in J. C. Stewart (ed.), *Paul Robeson: Artist and Citizen* (New Brunswick: Rutgers University Press, 1998), pp. 81–102.

Nairn, Tom, *The Break-Up of Britain* (London: New Left Books, 1977).

Nelson, Cary, *Revolutionary Memory: Recovering the Poetry of the American Left* (New York: Routledge, 2001).

North, Michael, *The Dialect of Modernism: Race, Language and Twentieth-Century Literature* (Oxford: Oxford University Press, 1994).

Ogilvie, Alan G. (ed.), *Great Britain: Essays in Regional Geography* (Cambridge: Cambridge University Press, 1928).

O'Leary, Paul, *Immigration and Integration: The Irish in Wales, 1798–1922* (Cardiff: University of Wales Press, 2000).

O'Meally, Robert G., *The Craft of Ralph Ellison* (Cambridge, MA: Harvard University Press, 1980).

O'Neill, Eugene, *The Emperor Jones* (1921), in O'Neill, *Anna Christie and Other Plays* (London: Penguin, 1960).

Osofsky, Gilbert, *Harlem: The Making of a Ghetto* ([1963] 2nd edn, London: Harper and Row, 1971).

Ottley, Roi. 'Ottley reports on Negro–white troop relations', *PM*, Thursday September 21, 1944, 10, copy in Ralph Ellison Papers, Library of Congress, box 203, file 12.

Ovington, Mary White, *Half a Man: The Status of the Negro in New York* (New York: Longmans, Green & Co., 1911).

Paananen, Victor A., 'The social vision of Dylan Thomas', in Tony Brown (ed.), *Welsh Writing in English: A Yearbook*, vol. 8 (Cardiff: University of Wales Press, 2003), pp. 46–66.

Padmore, George, 'Race relations: Soviet and British', *The Crisis*, 50, 11, whole number, 383 (November 1942), 345–48.

Patterson, Dale E., *Up from Bondage: The Literatures of Russian and African American Soul* (Durham, NC: Duke University Press, 2000).

Pennybacker, Susan D., *From Scottsboro to Munich: Race and Political Culture in 1930s Britain* (Princeton: Princeton University Press, 2009).

Pettinger, Alasdair, 'Send back the money: Douglass and the Free Church of Scotland', in Martin Crawford and Alan J. Rice (eds.), *Liberating Sojourn: Frederick Douglass and Transatlantic Reform* (Athens, GA: The University of Georgia Press, 1999), pp. 31–55.

Phillips, Mike and Trevor Phillips, *Windrush: The Irresistible Rise of Multi-racial Britain* (London: Harper Collins, 2000).

Posgrove, Carol, *Divided Minds: American Intellectuals and the Civil Rights Movement* (New York: W. W. Norton, 2001).

Posnock, Ross, *Color and Culture: Black Writers and the Making of the Modern Intellectual* (Cambridge, MA: Harvard University Press, 1998).

Pound, Ezra, *Selected Poems* ([1975] London: Faber, 1977).

Prys-Williams, Barbara, 'Web of connection: Denise Levertov's construction of origins', in Alyce von Rothkirch and Daniel Williams (eds), *Beyond the Difference: Welsh Literature in Comparative Contexts* (Cardiff: University of Wales Press, 2004), pp. 116–31.

Pwyllgor y Llyfr Emynau Cydenwadol, *Caneuon Ffydd: Hen Nodiant* (Llandysul: Gomer, 2001).

Raglan, Lord. 'I take my stand', *Wales* (October 1958), 17.

Rampersad, Arnold, *The Art and Imagination of W. E. B. Du Bois* (Cambridge MA: Harvard University Press, 1976).

——, *The Life of Langston Hughes*, vol. 1, *I, Too, Sing America* (Oxford: Oxford University Press, 1986).

——, *The Life of Langston Hughes*, vol. 2, *I Dream a World* (Oxford: Oxford University Press, 1988).

——, *Ralph Ellison: A Biography* ([2007] New York: Vintage, 2008)

Redmond, John, 'Slanderous tongues', *New Welsh Review*, 89 (autumn 2010), 41–7.

Rees, William ('Gwilym Hiraethog'), *Aelwyd F'Ewyrth Robert: Neu Hanes Caban F'Ewythr Tomos*, version of Stowe, *Uncle Tom's Cabin* (Dinbych: Gwasg Gee, 1853).

Rexroth, Kenneth, 'Disengagement: the art of the Beat generation' (1959), in *The Alternative Society* (New York: Herder and Herder, 1970), pp. 1–16.

Reynolds, David, *Rich Relations: The American Occupation of Britain 1942–1945* (London: Harper Collins, 1995).

Rice, Alan, *Radical Narratives of the Black Atlantic* (London: Continuum, 2003).

Rich, Paul, 'The baptism of a new era: the 1911 Universal Races Congress and the liberal ideology of race', *Ethnic and Racial Studies*, 7, 4 (October 1984), 534–50.

——, *Race and Empire in British Politics* (Cambridge: Cambridge University Press, 1990).

Ripley, C. Peter (ed.), *The Black Abolitionist Papers*, vol. 1, *The British Isles 1830–1865* (Chapel Hill: The University of North Carolina Press, 1985).

Roberts, Gwyneth Tyson, *The Language of the Blue Books: The Perfect Instrument of Empire* (Cardiff: University of Wales Press, 1998).

Roberts, Harri, *Embodying Identity: Representations of the Body in Welsh Literature* (Cardiff: University of Wales Press, 2009).

Roberts, Kate, *Crefft y Stori Fer* (Llandysul: Cyhoeddiadau'r Clwb Llyfrau Cymraeg, 1949).

Roberts, Lowri (ed.), *Canu Clod y Campau: Detholiad o Farddonaieth y Maes Chwarae* (Llanrwst: Gwasg Carreg Gwalch, 2009).

Roberts, Lynette, *Diaries, Letters, Recollections*, ed. Patrick McGuinness (Manchester: Carcanet Press, 2008).

Roberts, Randy, *Jack Dempsey: The Manassa Mauler* (London: Robson Books, 1987).

——, *Joe Louis: Hard Times Man* (New Haven: Yale University Press, 2010).

Roberts, Samuel, 'Cymysgiad Achau', in *Pregethau a Darlithiau* (Utica, NY: T. J. Griffiths, 1865), pp. 206–40.

——, *Pregethau a Darlithiau* (Utica, NY: T. J. Griffiths, 1865).

——, *Hunan-Amddiffyniad S. R. Yng Ngwyneb y Camddarlunio Fu Arno Drwy Adeg Cynddaredd y Rhyfel Cartrefol yn America* (Conwy: R. E. Jones, 1882).

Robeson, Eslanda, *African Journey* (London: Victor Gollancz, 1946).

Robeson, Paul, 'I know the Irish people', *The Irish Democrat*, August 1949, 3.

——, *Paul Robeson Speaks: Writings, Speeches, Interviews 1918–1974*, ed. Philip S. Foner (London: Quartet Books, 1978).

——, *Here I Stand* ([1958] Boston, Beacon Press, 1988).

Robeson Jr, Paul, 'The Paul Robeson files', *The Nation*, 20 December 1999, 30–5.

——, *The Undiscovered Paul Robeson: An Artist's Journey, 1898–1939* (New York: John Wiley, 2001).

Roediger, David, *The Wages of Whiteness: Race and the Making of the American Working Class* (London: Verso, 1991).

——, *Towards the Abolition of Whiteness: Essays on Race, Politics and Working Class History* (London: Verso, 1994).

Rogers, J. A., 'The American Negro in Europe', *American Mercury*, May 1930, 8–9.

——, *Nature Knows No Color-Line: Research into the Negro Ancestry in the White Race* ([c.1952] 3rd edn, repr., St Petersburg, FL: Helga M. Rogers, 1980).

Rohrbach, Augusta, *Truth Stranger than Fiction: Race, Realism and the US Literary Marketplace* (New York: Plagrave, 2002).

Roper, Moses, *Hanes Bywyd a Ffoedigaeth Moses Roper o Gaethiwed Americanaidd* (Llanelli: Rees a Thomas, 1841) (an identical edition was published in Aberystwyth by J. Cox in 1842).

——, *Narrative of the Adventures and Escape of Moses Roper, from American Slavery. With an Appendix, Containing a List of Places Visited by the Author in Great Britain and Ireland and the British Isles; and Other Matter* (Berwick-upon-Tweed: published for the author and printed at the Warder Office, 1848).

——, 'To the Committee of the British and Foreign Antislavery Society', 9 May 1844, in C. Ripley (ed.), *The Black Abolitionist Papers*, vol. 1, *The British Isles 1830–1865* (Chapel Hill: The University of North Carolina Press, 1985), pp. 134–7.

——, *A Narrative of the Adventures and Escape of Moses Roper* (1838), in William A. Andrews et al. (eds), *North Carolina Slave Narratives* (Chapel Hill: University of North Carolina Press, 2003), pp. 35–76.

Rose, S. O., 'Sex, citizenship and the nation in WWII Britain', *The American Historical Review*, 3, 4 (1998), 1147–76.

Rothkirch, Alyce Von and Daniel Williams (eds), *Beyond the Difference: Welsh Literature in Comparative Contexts* (Cardiff: University of Wales Press, 2004).

Rudwick, Elliott M., 'W. E. B. Du Bois and the Universal Races Congress of 1911', *The Phylon Quarterly*, 20, 4 (1959), 372–8.

Russell, Ross, *Bird Lives: The High Life and Hard Times of Charlie 'Yardbird' Parker* ([1973] New York: Da Capo, 1996).

Said, Edward, *Culture and Imperialism* ([1993] London, Vintage, 1994).

Schor, Edith, *Visible Ellison: A Study of Ralph Ellison's Fiction* (Westport, CT: Greenwood Press, 1993).

Schuyler, George S., 'The Negro art hokum', in David Levering Lewis (ed.), *The Portable Harlem Renaissance Reader* (London: Pengiun, 1994), pp. 96–9.

Schwartz, Delmore, *Selected Essays of Delmore Schwartz*, ed. Donald Dike and David Zucker (Chicago: University of Chicago Press, 1970).

Sellman, James Clyde, 'Blacks in the American military', in K. Appiah and H. L. Gates Jr (eds), *Africana: The Encyclopaedia of the African and African American Experience* (New York: Basic Books, 1999), pp. 1304–10.

Sergeant, Elizabeth Shepley, 'The man with his home in a rock: Paul Robeson', *New Republic*, 3 March 1926, 40–4.

Sernett, Milton, *North Star Country: Upstate New York and the Crusade for African American Freedom* (Syracuse: Syracuse University Press, 2002).

Shakespeare, William, *Much Ado About Nothing*, in *The Norton Shakespeare*, ed. Stephen Greenblatt et al. (New York: Norton, 1997) pp. 1381–444.

Shell, Marc, 'The want of incest in the human family, or, kin and kind in Christian thought', *Journal of the American Academy of Religion*, 62, 3 (1995), 625–50.

—— (ed.), *American Babel: Literatures of the United States from Abnaki to Zuni* (Cambridge, MA: Harvard University Press, 2002).

Shepperson, Wilbur S., *Samuel Roberts: A Welsh Colonizer in Civil War Tennessee* (Knoxville: University of Tennessee Press, 1961).

Sinclair, Neil, *The Tiger Bay Story* (Cardiff: Dragon and Tiger Enterprises, 1997).

Sitkoff, Harvard, 'African American militancy in the World War II South: another perspective', in Neil R. McMillen (ed.), *Remaking Dixie: The Impact of World War II on the American South* (Jackson: University Press of Mississippi, 1997), pp. 70–92.

Škvorecký, Josef, 'Red music', Foreword to the English edition of *The Bass Saxophone* ([1977] London: Vintage, 1994), pp. 9–31.

Smethurst, James Edward, *The New Red Negro: The Literary Left and African American Poetry, 1930–1946* (Oxford: Oxford University Press, 1999).

Smith, David (Dai), 'Myth and meaning in the literature of the south Wales coalfield – the 1930s', *The Anglo-Welsh Review*, 25, 56 (1976), 21–42.

——, *Lewis Jones* (Cardiff: University of Wales Press, 1982).

——, *Wales! Wales?* (London: Allen and Unwin, 1984).

——, *Aneurin Bevan and the World of South Wales* (Cardiff: University of Wales Press, 1993).

——, *Wales: A Question for History* (Bridgend: Seren, 1999).

——, 'Call me Tommy: Tommy Farr the Tonypandy Kidd', in Peter Stead and Gareth Williams (eds), *Wales and its Boxers: The Fighting Tradition* (Cardiff: University of Wales Press, 2008), pp. 87–100.

Smith, Graham A., *When Jim Crow Met John Bull: Black American soldiers in World War II Britain* (London: Tauris, 1987).

Snead, James A., 'Spectatorship and capture in King Kong', in V. Smith (ed.), *Representing Blackness: Issues in Film and Video* (London: The Atholne Press, 1997), pp. 25–45.

——, *White Screens, Black Images: Hollywood from the Dark Side* (New York: Routledge, 1994).

Sollors, Werner, 'A critique of pure pluralism', in Sacvan Bercovitch (ed.), *Reconstructing American Literary History*, Harvard English Studies, 13 (Cambridge, MA: Harvard University Press, 1986), pp. 250–79.

——, *Beyond Ethnicity: Consent and Descent in American Culture* (New York: Oxford University Press, 1986).

——, 'Anthropological and sociological tendencies in American literature of the 1930s and 1940s: Richard Wright, Zora Neale Hurston and American culture', in Steve Ickringill (ed.), *Looking Inward, Looking Outward: From the 1930s through the 1940s* (Amsterdam: VU University Press, 1990), pp. 22–75.

——, *Neither Black Nor White Yet Both: Thematic Explorations in Interracial Literature* (Cambridge, MA: Harvard University Press, 1997).

——, *Ethnic Modernism* (Cambridge, MA: Harvard University Press, 2008).

——, 'The Celtic nations and the African Americas', *Comparative American Studies*, 8, 4 (2010), 316–22.

—— (ed.), *The Invention of Ethnicity* (Oxford: Oxford University Press, 1989).

—— (ed.), *Theories of Ethnicity: A Classical Reader* (New York: New York University Press, 1996).

—— (ed.), *Multilingual America: Transnationalism, Ethnicity and the Languages of American Literature* (New York: New York University Press, 1998).

—— (ed.), *Interracialism: Black–White Intermarriage in American History, Literature and Law* (New York: Oxford University Press, 2000).

—— (ed.), *An Anthology of Interracial Literature: Black–White Contacts in the Old World and the New* (New York: New York University Press, 2004).

Sommer, Doris, *Proceed with Caution when Engaged by Minority Writing in the Americas* (Cambridge, MA: Harvard University Press, 1999).

Spiller, Gustav, *Papers on Inter-Racial Problems Communicated to the First Universal Races Congress held at the University of London, July 26–29, 1911* (London: P. S. King, and Boston: The Peace Foundation, 1911).

Stalin, Joseph. 'Marxism and the national question' (1913), in *Marxism and the National Question: Selected Writings and Speeches* (New York: International Publishers, 1942), pp. 7–68.

Starling, Marion Wilson, *The Slave Narrative: Its Place in American History* (Boston, MA: G. K. Hall, 1981).

Stauffer, John, *The Black Hearts of Men: Radical Abolitionists and the Transformation of Race* (Cambridge, MA: Harvard University Press, 2002).

Stead, Peter, 'Wales in the movies', in Tony Curtis (ed.), *Wales: The Imagined Nation* (Bridgend: Poetry Wales Press, 1986), pp. 159–79.

——, *Acting Wales: Stars of Stage and Screen* (Cardiff: University of Wales Press, 2002).

—— and Gareth Williams (eds), *Wales and its Boxers: The Fighting Tradition* (Cardiff: University of Wales Press, 2008).

Steele, Shelby, 'The content of his character', *The New Republic*, 1 March 1999, 27–34.

Stein, Gertrude, *The Autobiography of Alice B. Toklas* (New York: Random House, 1933).

Stein, Judith, 'Defining the race 1890–1930', in Werner Sollors (ed.), *The Invention of Ethnicity* (Oxford: Oxford University Press, 1989).

Stephens, Russell, *Emlyn Williams: The Making of a Dramatist* (Bridgend: Seren, 2000).

Stepan, Nancy, *The Idea of Race in Science: Great Britain 1800–1960* (London: Macmillan, 1982).

Stepto, Robert B., 'Michael S. Harper, poet as kinsman: the family sequences', *Massachusetts Review*, 17, 3 (fall 1976), 477–502.

——, 'Narration in Frederick Douglass' narrative of 1845', in W. A. Andrews (ed.), *African American Autobiography: A Collection of Critical Essays* (Englewood Cliffs, NJ: Prentice-Hall, 1993), pp. 26–35.

Stewart, Jeffrey C., 'The black body: Robeson as a work of art and politics', in J. C. Stewart (ed.), *Paul Robeson: Artist and Citizen* (New Brunswick: Rutgers University Press, 1998), pp. 135–163.

—— (ed.), *Paul Robeson: Artist and Citizen* (New Brunswick: Rutgers University Press, 1998).

Stocking, George, *The Ethnographer's Magic and other Essays in the History of Anthropology* (Madison: University of Wisconsin Press, 1992).

Stokes, Melvyn, 'The endless re-birth of the birth of a nation', *Interdisciplinary Journal of German Linguistics and Semiotic Analysis*, 5, 2 (fall 2000), 199–212.

Stowe, Harriet Beecher, *Uncle Tom's Cabin* ([1852] London: Everyman's Library, 1995).

Stradling, Robert, *Wales and the Spanish Civil War: The Dragon's Dearest Cause?* (Cardiff: University of Wales Press, 2004).

Stuckey, Sterling, *Slave Culture: Nationalist Theory and the Foundations of Black America* (Oxford: Oxford University Press, 1987).

Sundquist, Eric J., *To Wake the Nations: Race in the Making of American Literature* (Cambridge, MA: Harvard University Press, 1993).

Taylor, Yuval (ed.), *I Was Born A Slave: An Anthology of Classic Slave Narratives* (Edinburgh: Pauback Press, 1999).

'This American Red Cross Centre is strictly Jim Crow', *The Crisis*, 50, 3 (March 1943), whole number 387, 76–7.

Thomas, Brinley, 'A cauldron of rebirth: population and the Welsh language in the nineteenth century', in Geraint Jenkins (ed.), *The Welsh Language and its Social Domains* (Cardiff: University of Wales Press, 2000), pp. 81–99.

Thomas, Dylan, *The Collected Letters*, ed. Paul Ferris (New York: Macmillan, 1985).

Thomas, Helen, *Romanticism and Slave Narratives: Transatlantic Testimonies* (Cambridge: Cambridge University Press, 2000).

Thomas, M. Wynn, *Internal Difference: Literature in 20th Century Wales* (Cardiff: University of Wales Press, 1992).

——, *Corresponding Cultures: The Two Literatures of Wales* (Cardiff: University of Wales Press, 1999).

——, 'Gwlad o Bosibiliadau: Golwg ar Lên Cymru ac America', *Y Traethodydd*, 157 (2002), 38–52.

——, *James Kitchener Davies* (Cardiff: University of Wales Press, 2002).

——, *Transatlantic Connections: Whitman U.S., Whitman U.K.* (Iowa City: University of Iowa Press, 2005).

——, *In the Shadow of the Pulpit: Literature and Nonconformist Wales* (Cardiff: University of Wales Press, 2010).

—— (ed.), *Welsh Writing in English: A Guide To Welsh Literature* (Cardiff: University of Wales Press, 2003).

—— and Daniel Williams, '"A sweet union"?: Dylan Thomas and post-war American poetry', in Gilbert Bennett, Eryl Jenkins and Eurwen Price (eds.), *I Sang in My Chains: Essays and Poems in Tribute to Dylan Thomas* (Swansea: The Dylan Thomas Society of Great Britain, 2003), pp. 68–79.

Thomas, Onfel, *Frances Elizabeth Hoggan, 1843–1927* (privately printed, Brecon, 1970).

Thompson, Mark Christian, *Black Fascisms* (Charlottesville: University of Virginia Press, 2007).

Toscano, Alberto, 'The spectre of anaolgy', *New Left Review II*, 66 (November/December 2010), 152–60.

Wald, Alan M., *Exiles from a Future Time: The Forging of the Mid-Twentieth-Century Left* (Chapel Hill: University of North Carolina Press, 2002).

Ward, Geoffrey C., *Unforgivable Blackness: The Rise and Fall of Jack Johnson* (London: Pimlico, 2006).

Ward, Samuel Ringgold, *Autobiography of a Fugitive Negro: His Anti-Slavery Labours in the United States, Canada and England* (London: John Snow, 1855).

Warren, Kenneth, *Black and White Strangers: Race and American Literary Realism* (Chicago: University of Chicago Press, 1993).

Washington, Booker T., *Up From Slavery* ([1901] Harmondsworth: Penguin, 1986).

Weatherly, Ulysses G., 'The first Universal Races Congress', *The American Journal of Sociology*, 17, 3 (November 1911), 315–28.

Webb, Beatrice and Sidney Webb, 'National minorities in the Soviet Union', in Alain Locke and Bernhard J. Stern (eds), *When Peoples Meet: A Study in Race and Culture Contacts* (New York: Progressive Educations Association, 1942), pp. 672–83.

West, Cornel, 'Black strivings in a twilight civilization', in Henry Louis Gates Jr and Cornel West, *The Future of the Race* (New York: Alfred Knopf, 1996), pp. 53–112.

——, 'On black–brown relations', *The Cornel West Reader* (New York: Basic Books, 1999), pp. 499–513.

Wiliams, Gerwyn, *Tir Newydd: Agweddau ar Lenyddiaeth Gymraeg a'r Ail Ryfel Byd* (Caerdydd: Gwasg Prifysgol Cymru, 2005).

Williams, Charlotte, *Sugar and Slate* (Aberystwyth: Planet, 2002).

——, 'The reticent ethnographer: a profile of Glenn Jordan', *Planet*, 176 (April/ May 2006), 41–53.

——, 'The Celtic nations and the African Americas', *Comparative American Studies*, 8, 4 (December 2010), 323–6.

Williams, Chris, *Democratic Rhondda: Politics and Society, 1855–1951* (Cardiff: University of Wales Press, 1996).

——, 'Problematizing Wales: an exploration in historiography and postcoloniality', in Jane Aaron and Chris Williams (eds.), *Postcolonial Wales* (Cardiff: University of Wales Press, 2005), pp. 3–17.

Williams, Daniel G., *Ethnicity and Cultural Authority: From Arnold to Du Bois* (Edinburgh: Edinburgh University Press, 2006).

——, 'Black and white: writing about fighting in Wales', in Peter Stead and Gareth Williams (eds), *Wales and its Boxers: The Fighting Tradition* (Cardiff: University of Wales Press, 2008), pp. 132–3.

——, 'Green in black', *New Welsh Review*, 86 (winter 2009), 42–51.

——, *Aneurin Bevan and Paul Robeson: Socialism, Class and Identity* (Cardiff: Institute of Welsh Affairs, 2010).

——, 'Introduction: Celticism and the Black Atlantic', *Comparative American Studies: Special Issue on the Celtic Nations and the African Americas*, 8, 2 (June 2010), 81–7.

—— (ed.), *Canu Caeth: Y Cymry a'r Affro-Americaniaid* (Llandysul: Gomer, 2010).

—— (ed.), 'Special issue on the Celtic nations and the African Americas', *Comparative American Studies*, 8, 2 (June 2010).

Williams, Emlyn, 'The corn was green in England: in which Mr. Williams, as in another world, writes the story of one of Times Square's current hits', *New York Times*, 16 February 1941, X1, X3.

——, *The Corn is Green* (1938), *with Two Other Plays* (London: Pan Books, 1950).

——, 'A Dyma Fi Druan o Gymro yn Sefyll (I take my Stand)' *Wales*, November 1958, 16–20.

——, 'Letter to Vivian Matalon', 21 July 1983, Emlyn Williams Papers, National Library of Wales, box 8, file 1.

——, 'Letter to Cicely Tyson care of Vivian Matalon', 7 August 1983, Emlyn Williams Papers, National Library of Wales, box 8, file 1.

——, 'Letter to Vivian Matalon', undated, Emlyn Williams Papers, National Library of Wales, box 8, file 1.

Williams, Gareth, 'Compulsory sterilisation of Welsh miners, 1936', *Llafur*, 3, 3 (1982), 67–73.

——, *George Ewart Evans* (Cardiff: University of Wales Press, 1991).

——, *Valleys of Song: Music and Society in Wales 1840–1914* (Cardiff: University of Wales Press, 1998).

Williams, Glanmor, *Samuel Roberts* (Cardiff: University of Wales Press, 1950).

Williams, Glyn, 'Nationalism in nineteenth century Wales: the discourse of Michael D. Jones', in Glyn Williams (ed.), *Crisis of Economy and Ideology: Essays on Welsh Society, 1840–1980* (Bangor: Sociology of Wales Study Group, 1983), pp. 180–200.

—— (ed.), *Crisis of Economy and Ideology: Essays on Welsh Society, 1840–1980* (Bangor: Sociology of Wales Study Group, 1983).

Williams, Gwyn A., 'Mother Wales get off me back', *Marxism Today* (December 1981), 14–20.

——, *The Welsh in Their History* (London: Croom Helm, 1982).

——, *When Was Wales? A History of the Welsh* (London: Black Raven Press, 1985).

Williams, Hugh, *Caban F'Ewyrth Twm*, translation of Stowe, *Uncle Tom's Cabin* (Llundain: John Cassell, 1853).

Williams, Huw, *Canu'r Bobl* (Dinbych: Gee, 1978).

Williams, Ioan, *Capel A Chomin: Astudiaeth o Ffugchwedlau Pedwar Llenor Fictoraidd* (Caerdydd: Gwasg Prifysgol Cymru, 1989).

——, *A Straitened Stage: A Study of the Theatre of J. Saunders Lewis* (Bridgend: Seren, 1991).

——, 'Gwilym Hiraethog (William Rees, 1802–83), in Hywel Teifi Edwards (ed.), *A Guide to Welsh Literature 1800–1900* (Cardiff: University of Wales Press, 2000), pp. 48–68.

Williams, Raymond, *Marxism and Literature* (Oxford: Oxford University Press, 1977).

——, *Culture* (London: Fontana, 1981).

——, *The Politics of Modernism: Against the New Conformists*, ed. Tony Pinkney (London: Verso, 1989).

——, 'The culture of nations' (1983), in *Who Speaks for Wales? Nation, Culture, Identity*, ed. Daniel Williams (Cardiff: University of Wales Press, 2003), pp. 191–203.

——, 'The Welsh Industrial Novel' (1979), in *Who Speaks for Wales? Nation, Culture, Identity*, ed. Daniel Williams (Cardiff: University of Wales Press, 2003), pp. 95–111.

Williams-Ellis, Clough, 'The teaching of art and architecture in Wales', *The Transactions of the Honourable Society of Cymmrodorion, Session 192–1924* (1925), 63–70.

Wilson, Jen, 'Doing the plantation walkaround skeedaddle', *Planet*, 177 (June/ July 2006), 75–83.

Woodward, C. Van, *The Strange Career of Jim Crow* (New York: Oxford University Press, 1955).

Wright, Richard, *American Hunger* ([1977] New York: Harper and Row, 1983).

Wynn, Neil A., *The Afro-American and the Second World War* ([1975] New York: Holmes and Meier, 1993).

X, Malcolm, *The Autobiography of Malcolm X: as told to Alex Haley* (New York: Ballantine Books, 1964).

Yarborough, Richard, 'Strategies of black characterization in *Uncle Tom's Cabin* and the early Afro-American novel', in Eric J. Sundquist (ed.), *New Essays on Uncle Tom's Cabin* (Cambridge: Cambridge University Press, 1986), pp. 166–87.

Yeats, W. B., *Uncollected Prose*, vol. 1, ed. John P. Frayne (London: Macmillan, 1970).

——, *Uncollected Prose*, vol. 2, ed. John P. Frayne and Colton Johnson (London: Macmillan, 1975).

——, *The Collected Poems*, ed. R. Finneran (New York: Collier, 1989).

Young, Robert J. C., *White Mythologies: Writing History and the West* (London: Routledge, 1990).

——, *Colonial Desire: Hybridity in Theory Culture and Race* (London: Routledge, 1995).

——, *Postcolonialism: An Historical Introduction* (Oxford: Blackwell, 2001).

Zamir, Shamoon, '"The Sorrow Songs"/ "Song of Myself": Du Bois, the crisis of leadership and prophetic imagination', in Maria Diedrich and Werner Sollors (eds), *The Black Columbiad: Defining Moments in African American Literature and Culture* (Cambridge, MA: Harvard University Press, 1994), pp. 145–66.

——, *W. E. B. Du Bois and American Thought 1888–1903* (Chicago: University of Chicago Press, 1995).

Zieger, Robert H., *John L. Lewis: Labour Leader* (New York: Twayne Publishers, 1988).

Ziff, Larzer, *Literary Democracy: The Declaration of Cultural Independence in America* (New York: Penguin Books, 1981).

Zinn, Howard, *A People's History of the United States 1492–Present* (1980. New York: Harper Collins, 1995).

**Unpublished sources**

Exton, Mark A., 'Paul Robeson and south Wales: a partial guide to a man's beliefs', MA thesis, University of Exeter, 1984.

# Index